International Education at Community Colleges

Rosalind Latiner Raby • Edward J. Valeau
Editors

International
Education at
Community Colleges

Themes, Practices, and Case Studies

Editors
Rosalind Latiner Raby
California State University
Northridge, Chatsworth
California, USA

Edward J. Valeau
Superintendent/President Emeritus
Hartnell Community College District
President Emeritus, CCIE

ISBN 978-1-137-53335-7   ISBN 978-1-137-53336-4   (eBook)
DOI 10.1057/978-1-137-53336-4

Library of Congress Control Number: 2016937715

Printed on acid-free paper

This Palgrave Macmillan imprint is published by Springer Nature
The registered company is Nature America Inc. New York

PREFACE

The worldwide preoccupation with the internationalization of higher education is intensifying—both in terms of the rhetoric of policymakers and institutional leaders about the importance of internationalization and in terms of the action agendas of governments and institutions.[1] Much of the energy around internationalization in the United States and abroad, alas, is centered on recruiting international students, as institutions and countries seek to heighten their prestige and generate revenue. But as the chapters in this volume indicate, such a narrow lens on internationalization does higher education a disservice, ignoring the much wider impact that internationalization can have on the overall quality of an institution and especially on student learning.

The current conversation about internationalization among scholars frames internationalization not as a goal unto itself, but as a means of advancing the multiple larger goals of an institution, be they improving institutional quality, enhancing teaching and learning, ensuring that research is on the cutting edge, creating meaningful ties between the global and local through global engagement, and yes, enhancing revenue and prestige. This conceptualization of internationalization helps policymakers and the public (as well as faculty and students) see it not as a frill or simply as a moneymaker, but as an integral part of what a quality education should be in the twenty-first century.

Unfortunately, US higher education is not alone in needing to close the gap between rhetoric and reality; it is a worldwide challenge. And even more unfortunately, the US narrative about its higher education system that it is "the best in the world," does not apply to internationalization. A

2013 survey conducted by the International Association of Universities, which included 209 US institutions in its respondent population of 1336 showed that the USA lagged behind other countries in several important indicators of internationalization.[2] US institutions are less likely than others around the world to have a strategic plan for internationalization in place or under development, and their leaders are perceived as assigning less importance than others to internationalization. In all measures of infrastructural supports, US institutions lag behind, including the likelihood of having a dedicated office, dedicated budget, monitoring and evaluation system, or explicit targets or benchmarks.[3]

Nor are the US data on internationalization particularly encouraging. According to the 2012 study of the American Council on Education, the overall level of internationalization at community colleges is lower than that of four-year institutions.[4] This finding is not surprising, given the history and culture of community colleges and the challenges addressed in this volume. The good news in the study is that some progress has been made by community colleges since 2006, such as starting up international partnerships for the first time. The conclusion of the ACE report emphatically notes the importance of internationalization at community colleges which serve some 40% of US undergraduates. It underscores the need to use models that work for non-traditional student populations.

Internationalizing community colleges requires a shift in mindset of policymakers and other stakeholders toward a recognition that international and global learning is an integral part of preparation for work and for citizenship. Citizenship is not tied simply to one's local community; the families, businesses, and culture of those local communities are inextricably linked with the rest of the world. The second shift required will be the recognition "that internationalization at home"—global learning opportunities that occur in the classroom, on the campus, or in the community—will be the key strategy for providing community college students with a global outlook and global competencies. Education abroad is without doubt a peerless learning opportunity (properly designed), but even if we greatly improve the participation rate in education abroad, the vast majority of all students will be non-mobile. Our focus should be on them.

This volume addresses a wide array of themes and includes many different perspectives. The editors and authors are among a growing group of educators seeking to stimulate reflection, dialogue, and action concerning the vital role that internationalization plays in defining quality in higher education.

Madeleine F. Green

Notes

1. For a useful list of national policies on internationalization, see the website of the International Association of Universities http://www.iau-aiu.net/content/national-policies.
2. The survey population included only four-year institutions in the USA, and their equivalents in other countries. See Egron-Polak, Eva and Ross Hudson. (2013). *The 4th Global Survey of Internationalization in Higher Education* http://www.iau-aiu.net/content/iau-global-surveys.
3. For details on these comparisons, see Madeline Green. (2014). "The Best in the World? Not in Internationalization." http://www.nafsa.org/Content.aspx?id=49170.
4. See American Council on Education (2012). Mapping Internationalization on U.S. Campuses: A 2012 Edition. http://www.acenet.edu/news-room/Pages/2012-Mapping-Internationalization-on-U-S-Campuses.aspx.

ACKNOWLEDGMENTS AND DEDICATION

We thank our community college colleagues and contributing authors, without whose voices this book would not have been possible. We would like to especially thank our special reviewers who helped with the blind review of the chapters: Marion Froehlich, Shahrzad Kamyab, Wendy Patriguin, and Michael Roggow. We would also like to thank the staff at Palgrave Macmillan for their support to which the editorship offers deep appreciation. Finally, we want to thank our spouses, Vera C. Valeau and Ronald S. Raby for their patience and their loving support.

We write this book for community college leaders whose decisions will impact learning across generations. We also want to dedicate this book to a pioneer in the field of US community college internationalization, Dr. Donald R. Culton. His inspiration and vision is seen throughout all the examples of community college internationalization shared in this book.

The original version of this book was revised.
An Erratum to this book can be found at
(DOI 10.1057/978-1-137-53336-4)

CONTENTS

Abbreviations and Acronyms

AACC	American Association of Community Colleges
AACJC	American Association of Community and Junior Colleges
ACE	American Council on Education
CCCSE	Center for Community College Student Engagement
CCID	Community Colleges for International Development
CCIE	California Colleges for International Education
GLAI	Global Learning Across Indiana
GLC	Global Learning Certificate
HEIs	Higher Education Institutions
IAE	Community College Initiative Instructors and Administrators of Egypt program
ICAB	Internationalization Collaboration Across Bloomington
IIE	Institute for International Education
ISO	International Students' Office
NACADA	National Academic Advising Association
NAFSA	Association of International Educators
SCI	System of Comprehensive Internationalization
SEVIS	Student and Exchange Visitor Information System
URM	Under-Represented Minority

Community College Acronyms

ACC	Austin Community College
BCC	Bannockburn Community College (Pseudonym)
BCC	Berkeley City College
CCC	Coastline College

CCCD	Coast Community College District
CCSF	City College of San Francisco
COA	College of Alameda
COC	College of the Canyons
FVTC	Fox Valley Technical College
GWC	Golden West College
Harper College	William Rainey Harper College
IU	Indiana University
LC	Laney College
MC	Merritt College
MCCD	Mesa Community College District
MDC	Miami-Dade College
OCC	Orange County College
PCC	Pima Community College District
PCCCD	Pima County Community College District
PCCD	Peralta Community College District
RCCD	Riverside Community College District
SCCCD	Santa Clarita Community College District
VC	Valencia Campus

LIST OF FIGURES

LIST OF TABLES

CHAPTER 1

Introduction

Rosalind Latiner Raby and Edward J. Valeau

We approach this book with 30 years of experience and continuing commitment to the field of community college internationalization. Our first effort resulted in the 2007 *New Directions in Community College* publication that asked national leaders to define advocacy for community college internationalization, which includes internationalizing curricula, faculty/staff exchanges, international students, study-abroad programs, and partnerships with institutions in other countries. This book allows well-known scholars, community college practitioners, and emerging leaders an opportunity to expand and reflect on existing practices that demonstrate the dynamic nature of community college internationalization.

About 13 million students attend US community colleges. Students enroll for multiple reasons, including to earn their first credential, cer-

R.L. Raby (✉)
Educational Leadership and Policy Studies Department, Michael D. Eisner College of Education, California State University, Northridge

California Colleges for International Education

College of Humanities and Sciences, Southern California Campus, University of Phoenix

E.J. Valeau
Superintendent/President Emeritus, Hartnell Community College District Salinas, California, Co-Founder, the ELS Group, LLC

© The Editor(s) (if applicable) and The Author(s) 2016
R.L. Raby, E.J. Valeau (eds.), *International Education at Community Colleges*, DOI 10.1057/978-1-137-53336-4_1

1

tificate or degree, to gain multiple credentials to advance their career pathway, to enhance remedial skills, to engage in lifelong education, or prepare to transfer to a four-year college/university. In meeting these diverse student needs, international education varies considerably within and between colleges. Grounding the various international programs is a belief that "it is important that college graduates, whatever their location, be not just *globally competitive* but also *globally competent*, understanding their roles as citizens and workers in an international context" (AACC 2012, p. 20).

Unfortunately, of the 1200 US community colleges, too few are internationalized and there is inconsistent benchmarking of which colleges are involved in internationalization efforts. In 2011, the American Council on Education surveyed 239 community colleges and found that less than 25 % had an internationalization plan (ACE 2012). In 2014, Institute for International Education (IIE) *Open Doors* showed that community colleges served 76,586 international students based on responses from 309 colleges and 4843 study-abroad students based on responses from 85 colleges (IIE 2014). There is no national benchmark for any other kind of international program.

This book assesses prior advancements in the field, current challenges, and where new emphasis needs to be placed to produce viable and sustained results that impact programming across all spectrums. In doing so, the book explores the trajectory of a changing construct that is moving international education from optional to integral (King and Fersh 1983).

Book Themes

This book is divided into two parts. The first explores theoretical constructs to help the reader understand the change process. The second part describes academic and case studies that identify how specific changes inform practice.

Part One: Exploring the Field

In *Exploring the Field*, authors delineate two theoretical constructs. The first uses theory for advocacy and to ground best practices. Raby and Valeau explore the historical and current applications of why an emphasis on global is not in opposition to the US community college local mission and how to avoid elements that contribute to keeping internationalization sidelined. Bista examines the profiles of community college faculty who are foreign-born, US-born with prior international experiences, and US-born without prior international experiences to show how personal profiles can enhance campus internationalization. Treat defines elements for effective mentoring that enhance mentee learning outcomes. Woodin defines categorical metrics of leadership and policy, organizational resources, curricular, co-curricular, professional development, and international student services to track internationalization progress in a college. Finally, Valeau and Raby build a comprehensive profile of those mid-level managers currently leading international programs to understand their role and importance in the college leadership pipeline.

The second set of theoretical chapters focus on changing practices that, when purposefully directed, can enhance overall student learning. Hagedorn, Pei, and Yan explore how some international students who study at four-year colleges/universities need the extra assistance that they find at the community colleges. They theorize how those elements that serve this population can be expanded to serve other student populations. Hollis and Davis reveal how and why knowledge of Title IX regulations prohibiting sexual assault is needed by international students. They define how to add this knowledge to current advising policies. Zhang depicts how academic advising in general, and appreciative advising specifically can meet international student needs and affect non-traditional learning experiences. Willis explores how purposeful advising in terms of racial, class, and gender dynamics influences peer interactions, student comfort, and ultimately, engagement with faculty. Zamani-Gallaher, Lang, and Leon share how the process of student self-authorship, the internal capacity to define one's beliefs, identity, and social relations, when added to the study-abroad experience, can enhance student career readiness and advancement.

Part Two: Research and Case Studies

In *Research and Case Studies*, examples of internationalization are shared from programs in colleges of various sizes in Arizona, California, Florida, Illinois, Indiana, Iowa, Mid-Atlantic, Mid-West, Michigan, New Jersey, Oregon, Texas, Washington, and Wisconsin. These studies are grouped into categories that focus on (a) systemic college change, (b) CEO-directed change, (c) specific programmatic change, and (d) learning from student stories.

Comprehensive internationalization is a term currently used to illustrate how internationalization influences systemic change. Castro-Salazar, Perez, and Merriam examine how a single program established new college procedures and routes of communication that resulted in a comprehensive college-wide plan. Sipe uses regression analysis to represent how three environmental factors, namely setting, student demographics in terms of ethnic diversity, and primary industry in the college's service area help to promote or discourage institutionalization. These studies reveal how colleges do not operate independently and are affected by internal and external variants.

Leadership theories define the importance of executive officers in charting reforms at community colleges. Vargas uses frames of organizational decision-making to demonstrate how a president transformed and institutionalized a reciprocal faculty and student exchange program. Budd, Serban, VanHook, and Raby use content analysis, informal observations, and seat analysis to clearly show that the chief executive officer's opinion not only guides reform efforts but can also counter traditional myths about the role of international students in the community college. Rodriguez focuses on content analysis to show how the leadership of the provost and the president can facilitate development of a global learning certificate program whose e-portfolio activity is enhancing overall student learning.

Changes to specific international programs illustrate not only application but also a process through which staff, administrators, and faculty are involved in reform efforts. Bartzis, Kirkwood, and Mulvihill use faculty interviews to compare how faculty-driven efforts at two community colleges impact overall college reform efforts. Cierniak and Ruddy employ faculty/staff survey and policy content analysis to explain the process involved in developing a first-year global learning certificate and the role of collaboration between a university and a community college system. Quezada and Coreiro analyze study-abroad director interviews and webpage analysis to compare how five community colleges provide innovative pedagogies and practices for students of color to participate in study-abroad programs. Rhodes, Raby, Thomas, Codding, and Lynch examine statistics at California and New Jersey community colleges to reveal how the programmatic change of studying abroad influences student success measures.

Finally, the importance of the student voice shows how student reflection can chart student learning and career preparation. Brenner employs ethnography to illustrate the broad spectrum of learning that results from participating in short-term education-abroad programs designed to capitalize on transformative experiences. Miller uses interviews to define elements needed to be adopted by international student advisors to help international students manage cultural and social stress. Thomas uses interviews to explore how education-abroad can be a vehicle for building student global competencies that are attractive to future employers. Combined, these studies show that community colleges are integrally involved in transformative learning based on lived student experiences which are integral to understanding the impact of internationalization and its importance to the mission of the community college.

MOVING FORWARD

There is a special challenge for US community colleges to move from celebration of singular programs that make internationalization available to only a few students to sustainable change that influences the entire college community. This book shows a transformation is occurring in which commitment from all stakeholders is setting the pace for future endeavors. However, without sustained and systemic support for internationalization by all stakeholders, this book and all that has been said will serve only as a footnote and a contribution to the literature on internationalization. The danger is that if we continue to remain insular on internationalization, we further seal our fate and lose our opportunity to lead, thus relegating us to the role of being followers in the global economic competitive arena and race to the top. A key awakening is realization that reform is not based on chance, but on intentional designs created to guide comprehensive reform efforts. As editors, we found the experiences of the authors and their research to be both inspiring and critical in the quest to bring international education to the diverse populations served by US community colleges. We hope that the theoretical and practical commonalities found in this book will be acted upon in future publications of revised Board policies in community colleges and associations across the USA and in innovative programming dedicated to curricula and training our future international education leaders. Such a sustained and ingrained focus will prove the efficacy of this book.

REFERENCES

American Association of Community Colleges (AACC). (2012). *Reclaiming the American dream: A report from the 21st-Century commission on the future of community colleges.* April. Washington, DC: American Association of Community Colleges Press. http://www.aacc.nche.edu/21stCenturyReport

American Council on Education. (2012). *Mapping internationalization on U.S. campuses: 2012 edition.* http://www.acenet.edu/news-room/Documents/MappingInternationalizationUS Campuses2012-full.pdf

Institute of International Education. (2014). Community college data resource. *2013/2014 Open Doors Report on International Educational Exchange.* http://www.iie.org/opendoors

King, Maxwell, & Fersh, Seymour (1983). International education and the U.S. community college: From optional to integral. *ERIC Junior College Resource Review*, Spring, ERIC Number: ED233780.

PART I

Exploring the Field

Global Is Not the Opposite of Local: Advocacy for Community College International Education

Rosalind Latiner Raby and Edward J. Valeau

INTERNATIONAL EDUCATION

The vast majority of US community college students enroll in educational programs to advance a career pathway that often has labor market value. Most of these programs are terminal and hence, the only opportunity that a student has to gain international knowledge is during studies at the community college. International education is not new to US community colleges. For 60 years, faculty and leaders have understood the benefits of learning beyond borders, be it between local neighborhoods, inter-state, or cross-national. Internationalization is included in curriculum and pedagogy as community colleges define educational programs

R.L. Raby (✉)
Educational Leadership and Policy Studies Department, Michael D. Eisner College of Education, California State University, Northridge, CA, USA

California Colleges for International Education, Los Angeles, CA, USA

College of Humanities and Sciences, Southern California Campus, University of Phoenix, Costa Mesa, CA, USA

E.J. Valeau
Superintendent/President Emeritus, Hartnell Community College District, Salinas, California, Co-Founder, the ELS Group, LLC

© The Editor(s) (if applicable) and The Author(s) 2016
R.L. Raby, E.J. Valeau (eds.), *International Education at Community Colleges*, DOI 10.1057/978-1-137-53336-4_2

and student services to serve changing multicultural communities (Raby and Tarrow 1996) and to create new credential and degree requirements to serve changing global employment needs (Treat and Hagedorn 2013). There are now multiple generations of community college leaders who argue that internationalization is an inherent component of community colleges that advances student knowledge and serves the needs of local communities (Gleazer 1975; Hess 1982; Eddy 2014; Ardalan and Sevanthinathan 2015).

Despite exemplary practices and empirical evidence that proves the importance of internationalization, the King and Fersh (1983) prophecy that "international education programs are no longer optional for community colleges, they have become integral" (p. 2) has not come true. Although there is no national community college policy that opposes internationalization, there remains a belief that serving the local community is the opposite of a global connection. As a result, internationalization is not included in community college leadership training programs (Opp and Gosetti 2014), is not a component of budget and finance discussions (Sutin et al. 2011), and is not institutionalized in strategic planning or college level action items (American Council on Education 2012).

In this chapter, we respectfully question why internationalization remains on the periphery and why global initiatives are not widely embraced. We look at the historic policies and voices of community college leaders and then unpack elements that contribute to keeping internationalization on the sidelines.

HISTORIC ROOTS OF COMMUNITY COLLEGES INTERNATIONALIZATION

The most frequently mentioned reason why community colleges do not embrace internationalization is that in some locations local funding sources must serve students within specific local geographic boundaries. This supposes that enhanced global knowledge would not serve local students. As authors, we are part of the literature that defined economic globalization as something that forced changes to the core community college mission (serving the local community). In this context, local and global are viewed as separate entities (Green and Siaya 2005; Levin 2010). Green (2007) explains that "given the local roots and focus of community colleges, it is not surprising that institutional leaders, board members, and community members may not value global learning as much as the more immediate tasks of workforce development and teaching basic skills" (p. 19). In preparing this chapter, we conclude that internationalization does not simply broaden the mission, but rather it is a vital and integral component that specifically serves the mission of student success.

Throughout the history of community colleges, there has been a discussion on what it means to *fulfill local needs* and how these needs relate to the multiple missions of the institution (Fields 1962; Cohen 1974; Dougherty and Towsend 2006). The Carnegie Commission report, "The Open Door College" (1970), mandated that the community college be "flexible and geared to the changing requirements of society" (p. 1). With those requirements, community colleges have been "wrestling with distinctions we have created between liberal and technical education, between campus and community, between egalitarianism and meritocracy, between system and self" (Birenbaum 1974, p. viii). Application of this flexibility includes questioning who has the control to design curriculum, who oversees funding and governance, and how local emphasis can, in actuality, perpetuate inequalities and deny open access (Karabel 1972; Cohen 1974). Today, leaders in the field are questioning "if old rules can promote the causes that they were intended to, or if they are barriers to implementation of new initiatives" (AACC 2015).

Internationalization is an example of this flexibility. Community colleges adopted internationalization to support the needs of the local community, as the original dictates of the community college were to produce an international citizenry (Zook 1947)[1], to respond to global economic flows (Cohen and Brawer 1996), to support first-generation and immigrant populations (Karabel 1972), and to respond to "world dependencies [we] are receiving and which in turn are calling for innovative ways of dealing with them" (Gleazer 1975, p. 1). Gleazer, the first American Association of Community and Junior Colleges (AACJC) president, said that "while the Association [AACJC] has many high program priorities ... we believe that a fair share of time and attention should be given to the international dimension ... without neglect to the domestic scene" (Gleazer 1976, p. 5). In the 1974 issue of *New Directions in Community Colleges*, that charted noted changes in the field, Eskow and Caffrey (1974) claimed that local was never intended to be the opposite of global as there was a perceived need to "balance between local roots and a sense of world community" (p. 71). Hess (1982) echoes this as he questions why should serving local "imply an emphasis on regionalism and the immediate area to the exclusion of internationalism and a concern for global awareness"

(p. 34). Today, the drive for internationalization at the community college remains an internal choice that is linked to serve local communities as opposed to an external strategy adopted by universities that positions the institution in world-class competition (Shields 2013).

ELEMENTS THAT KEEP INTERNATIONAL AS OPTIONAL

Systemic issues maintain community college international education efforts as optional to the general educational reform movement.

Differential Rationales

Four rationales have historically explained why internationalization is important to higher education (Raby and Tarrow 1996; De Wit 2002; Altbach and Knight 2007; Raby and Valeau 2007; Green 2012; Lee 2014). These rationales guide institutional and national policies that place internationalization as a key component in higher education. While the rationales have not changed over time, their application is time stamped (Treat and Hagedorn 2013). As such, while these rationales guide community college advocacy, they also are a contributing factor that keeps internationalization as optional.

The political rationale indicates a need to understand others as part of national security and foreign relations and of people-to-people diplomacy by creating opportunities for social, business, and political networking (Schulman 2011). *The economic rationale* links education as a producer of human capital through supplying workforce skills to support a global economy and, with money-producing programs, leverages higher education as a global economic industry (Violino 2011; NAFSA 2014). *The humanistic rationale* focuses on lived experiences that result from the impact of cross-cultural learning that challenge how a student approaches gender relations and ethnic social networks (Green 2012). *The academic rationale* links international content to student comprehension, persistence, and measures of success (Mamiseishvili 2012; Raby et al. 2014, b).

The roots of these four rationales are linked to time-specific events that influence community college policy. The *Council on Learning* (1981) was influenced by changing multicultural relationships, the AACJC *Building New Communities* (1998) was influenced by changing global economies, and the *Commission on the Abraham Lincoln* (2006) was influenced by changing political climate. In each context, the rationale for an event-specific response was lessened over time as that event held less relevance or was no longer supported through budgeting. In turn, the momentum garnered to support internationalization is curtailed which then is often in need of a serious event to jettison it to the front of the national agenda.

Culture of Individualism

Internationalization centers on the individual. For example, without staff/faculty advocates, there is no one to teach an internationalized curriculum, serve on an international committee, or lead an internationalized program. Faculty has always studied the world. They have created links in their courses, no matter if the subject was biology, modern language, music, or business (O'Connor et al. 2013; Raby et al. 2014a, b). Faculty builds special bonds with students that are instrumental in getting them involved in internationalization efforts (Robertson 2015). Community college presidents make contacts with leaders at global counterparts and lead internationalization efforts (King and Breuder 1979; Manns 2014). The role of the individual is so pronounced that an industry of faculty and staff development programming through online webinars and in-person conferences supports internationalization efforts (Diversity Abroad 2015; CCID 2015; Forum 2015; NAFSA 2015). Often, it remains the role of the chief executive officer and trustee members whose personal interests extend to controlling monetary as well as non-monetary incentives (Brennan and Dellow 2013; Opp and Gosetti 2014) to shape, support, and define how international education is integrated into the campus. Executive officer's approach to internationalization is the first line of advocacy and sets the tone for programmatic changes.

While change is grounded in the individual, three systemic problems tend to emerge from such a focus. First, personal values are not always enough to enact transformational leadership patterns and singular efforts limit impact on systemic change (Frost et al. 2011). When an individual retires, changes positions or colleges, or gives up due to lack of support, another equally passionate champion is needed to offer their services to fill the void. Second, academia, government, business, foundations, and associations target specific stakeholders and then negotiate support accordingly. Such behavior bypasses comprehensive outreach and good governance. Thus, each time a new circumstance arises, learning must begin again with a new set of stakeholders. Finally, powerful opposing interests, from any corner of the organization, are committed to block internationalization efforts. These anti-internationalists claim that international students take seats away from domestic students, that sending students away to study is counter to the community college mission, and that local is the opposite of global. However, no evidence exists to show that any of these positions are valid. Nonetheless, post-2008 recession, it remains that these individuals have the power to make choices to decrease overall support and, in some instances, eliminate international programs (Raby 2012).

Programmatic Insularity

Marginalization of community college international education is directly linked to a conceptual and developmental pattern that supports singular programming rather than holistic integration. Despite advocacy for holistic change (King and Breuder 1979; Green and Siaya 2005; Treat and Hagedorn 2013), all too frequently, the first mode of behavior and decision-making is to develop a singular form of international education. A consequence is that as some programs gain a profit margin, the need to remain separate takes on a matter of rivalry in political and budget power struggles. An insularity of programs creates an insularity of offices. Today, few campuses support multiple international education programs under a common frame with a strategic plan for growth (Bissonette and Woodin 2013).

Exclusion in National Community College Reform Efforts

National, state, and some accreditation agency policies that define retention, success, and completion objectives ignore the intersection of internationalization to these objectives (Green 2015). For example, while the AACC "Reclaiming the American Dream" (2012) states how local communities are linked between and beyond borders and that "it is important that college graduates, whatever their location, be not just *globally competitive* but also *globally competent*, understand their roles as citizens and workers in an international context" (p. 10), it still does not explicitly mention internationalization as a course of action. International education is not visible in the Center for Community College Student Engagement (CCCSE) best practices report (2013) or in the Lumina Foundation 2025 Goals (2015). While the Aspen Institute (2014) has been widely received throughout the nation and details tools needed by leaders to advance student access and success, it also mentions nothing about international programming to ensure student success. Based on exclusionary policies, it is no wonder that revised community college mission and vision statements are eliminating "global" or "international" verbiage that once marked a pivotal reform strategy for internationalization. At best, some revisions still mention "global economy" but not as an academic support integral to student learning. The loss of these concepts to mission statements will have long-reaching consequences.

INTERNATIONALIZATION AS INTEGRAL TO THE COMMUNITY COLLEGE

For six decades, governmental, association, and academic publications have defined internationalization as being central to community colleges. Community college internationalization is celebrated in national awards, such as Senator Paul Simon Award for Campus Internationalization (NAFSA) and the Andrew Heiskell Award (IIE). Beacons of excellence showcase unique contributions that can only be made by community colleges. Contemporary research evidences that community college students who are involved in any form of international education have an intensified learning experience (Malkan and Pisani 2011). This is seen for international students (Hagedorn and Lee 2005; Brennan and Dellow 2013), for students who study abroad (Drexler and Campbell 2011; Raby et al. 2014a, b) and for students who study with an internationalized curriculum (Guerin 2009; Raby et al. 2012). New studies as shown throughout this book continue to add to the research in the field.

Internationalization continues not necessarily as a result of planned change but as a result of default connections. In the late-1980s, faculty were forced to address internationalized components because of changes in their professional fields. The random chapter on international business or international health concerns forced faculty to reconsider parochial views (Raby and Valeau 2007). During the 2008 economic crisis, colleges were forced to accept internationalization as a way to increase a profit margin and, for some, to expand enrollment opportunities through studying abroad (Raby 2012). In the process, a default creation of an internationalized student body, curriculum, and college community was redefined. A final default connection results from a cycle in which research and practice are validated in peer-review journals. These articles then inspire a new cohort of doctoral students who are preparing to be the next generation of community college leaders (Brennan and Dellow 2013).

CONCLUSION

Regardless of intent, rationale, or application, international education has always been part of the US community college because there has always been a need for students to deal with cross-border and global agendas. Yet, despite increasing public attention, the number of international programs has not grown appreciably in the last few decades and the field has not advanced beyond a negligible level (Green and Siaya 2005; Harder 2011; Zhang 2011; ACE 2012; Treat and Hagedorn 2013; Eddy 2014). Consistently, research finds that the predominant issue preventing community college students from gaining international literacy skills is *not* a lack of student interest but lack of institutionalization that truncates access to programmatic options. We suggest that at the core lies the incorrect belief that there is a diametrical connection between local and global.

The global economy has always made an imprint on community colleges. In 1996, Raby and Tarrow discussed how "with the current recession, however, the fate of IMEP are in jeopardy" (p. 20). In 2013, another recession became the backdrop against choices in severe budget cuts that severely impacted "periphery programs" (Raby 2012). In each period, economics affected the number of students and faculty who can afford to travel and how much institutional support would be given to offices, full-time positions, and consortia membership. Yet, in those time periods, when the global economy stabilized, so did internationalization efforts. Even more important is that after each crisis period, a new generation of individuals emerges as international advocates, who continually seek to implement changes in the college. Herein lays the promise of the future.

Internationalization speaks to the generations. In a satirical article Eskow and Caffrey (1974) note that by 2020, "these thousand American colleges see themselves as a network for bringing intercultural and international education to their campuses and their host communities; they continue to experiment in bringing the world to the campus" (p. 81). While the number of community colleges has not occurred, the actions have. Then, and now, local is not the opposite of global. At a few community colleges, there is an acceptance that international education is not just an optional activity that exists on the periphery of the college needs. Yet, for most of the country, an academic shift still needs to occur in order for long-term change that promotes international literacy as an integral component of the college and that celebrates the needs of the changing local community to occur. Change is a choice needed to be made by visionary leaders who must prioritize and then lead these reform efforts that are sustainable and not impacted by the shifting of time and institutional circumstances.

This chapter has outlined why there is no reason for internationalization to not be systematically embraced at community colleges. Since there is no national community college policy that opposes internationalization and there is no policy that defines serving the local community as the opposite of a global connection, we want to encourage the debate that will result in changing the status quo. We hope that moving forward, the topic of internationalization becomes part of the national agenda for reform.

NOTE

1. The 1947 President's Commission on Higher Education, (Truman Commission Report), subheading, "Preparation for World Citizenship" noted that "for effective international understanding and cooperation we need to acquire knowledge of, and respect for, other peoples and their cultures—their traditions, their customs, and attitudes, their social institutions, their needs and aspirations for the future. We must learn to admit the possible worth of human values and ways of living we ourselves do not accept." (pp. 14–15) cited in Frost and Raby, 2009.

REFERENCES

Altbach, Phill, & Knight, Jane (2007). The internationalization of higher education: Motivations and realities. *Journal of Studies in International Education, 11*(3–4), 290–306.

American Association of Community and Junior Colleges. (1998). *Building communities: A vision for a new century.* A report of the Commission on the Future of Community Colleges. Washington, DC: AACJC Press.

American Association of Community Colleges (AACC). (2012). *Reclaiming the American Dream: A report from the 21st-Century Commission on the Future of Community Colleges.* April. Washington, DC: American Association of community Colleges Press. http://www.aacc.nche.edu/21stCenturyReport

American Association of Community Colleges (AACC). (2015). *Community college completion: Progress towards goal of 50%.* Washington, DC: American

Association of community Colleges Press. http://www.aacc.nche.edu/AboutCC/Trends/Documents/completion_report_05212015.pdf

American Council on Education. (2012). *Mapping internationalization on U.S. Campuses: 2012 edition.* http://www.acenet.edu/news-room/Documents/MappingInternationalizationonUSCampuses2012-full.pdf

Ardalan, Shah, & Sevanthinathan, Nithy (2015). Community colleges: The perfect enterprise for the 21st Century. In P. Bradley (Ed.), *A collection of community college week's POVs: Opinions, issues, solutions* (pp. 28–30). Fairfax, VA: Autumn Publishing Enterprises, Inc.

Aspen Institute. (2014). *Tools for hiring leaders who advance student access and success.* AspenInstitute.http://www.aspeninstitute.org/publications/hiring-exceptional-community-college-presidents-tools-hiring-leaders-who-advance.pdf

Birenbaum, William (1974). Editor notes. *New Directions in Community Colleges,* 7(Autumn (Fall)), v–viii. doi:10.1002/cc.36819740709.

Bissonette, Bonnie, & Woodin, Shawn (2013). Building support for internationalization through institutional assessment and leadership engagement. In Tod Treat & Linda Serra Hagedorn (Eds.), *The community college in a global context* (pp. 11–26). New Directions for Community Colleges. No. 161. San Francisco: Jossey-Bass Publications. doi:10.1002/cc.

Brennan, Michael, & Dellow, Donald A. (2013). International students as a resource for achieving comprehensive internationalization. In Tod Treat & Linda S. Hagedorn (Eds.), *The community college in a global context* (pp. 27–37). *New* Directions for Community Colleges: No. 161. San Francisco: Jossey-Bass. doi:10.1002/cc.

Carnegie Commission on Higher Education (1970). *The open-door college.* New York: McGraw-Hill.

Center for Community College Student Engagement (CCCSE) (2013). *A matter of degrees: Engaging practices, engaging students (high-impact practices for community college student engagement).* Austin, TX: The University of Texas at Austin, Community College Leadership Program.

Cohen, Arthur (1974). Political influences and curriculum and instruction. *New Directions in Community Colleges,* 7(Autumn (Fall), 39–53, San Francisco: Jossey-Bass. doi:10.1002/cc.36819740706.

Cohen, Arthur M., & Brawer, Florence B. (1996). *The American community college* (3rd ed.). Higher and Adults Education Series. San Francisco: Jossey-Bass Publishers.

Commission on the Abraham Lincoln Study Abroad Fellowship Program. (2006). *Global competence and national needs.* Washington, DC: 2005. http://www.lincolncommission.org/LincolnReport.pdf

Community Colleges for International Development. (2015). http://www.ccidinc.org/

Council on Learning. (1981). Statement and recommendations on American responsibilities as a global power and appropriate educational directions.

National Task Force Statement on Education and the World View. New Rochelle, NY: Change Magazine Press.

De Wit, Hans (2002). *Internationalization of higher education in the United States of America and Europe: A historical, comparative and conceptual analysis.* Westport, CT: Greenwood.

Diversity Abroad. (2015). Events. http://www.diversitynetwork.org/

Dougherty, Kevin, & Towsend, Barbara (2006). Community college missions: A theoretical and historical perspective. *New Directions for Community Colleges, 136*(winter), King and Fersh: ERIC Number: ED233780, Dougherty and Towsend: p. 5–13.

Drexler, Devi S., & Campbell, Dale F. (2011). Student development among community college participants in study abroad programs. *Community College Journal of Research & Practice, 35*(8), 608–619.

Eddy, Pamela (Ed.). (2014). Special issue: Community colleges and their internationalization efforts. *Community College Journal of Research and Practice, 38*(8). doi:10.1080/10668926.2014.897077.

Eskow, Seymour, & Caffrey, John (1974). *World community college: A 20:20 vision. New Directions in Community Colleges* (pp. 71–83). *7*(Autumn (Fall)). San Francisco: Jossey-Bass. doi:10.1002/cc.36819740709.

Fields, R. R. (1962). *The community college movement.* New York: McGraw-Hill.

Forum on Education Abroad. (2015). *Training and events.* http://www.forumea.org/training-events

Frost, Robert, & Raby, Rosalind Latiner (2009). Creating global citizens: The democratization of community college open access. In Ross Lewin (Ed.), *The handbook of practice and research in study abroad: Higher education and the quest for global citizenship.* New York: Routledge Publishers.

Frost, Robert, & "Ted" Raspiller, Edward, & "Ski" Sygielski, John J. (2011). The role of leadership: Leaders' practice in financing transformation. In Stewart E. Sutin, Dan Derrico, Edward J. Valeau, & Rosalind Latiner Raby (Eds.), *Increasing effectiveness of the community college financial model: A global perspective for the global economy* (pp. 49–65). New York: Palgrave Publishers.

Gleazer, Edmund J. Jr. (1975). *Memorandum to community college presidents.* American Association of Community and Junior Colleges, March 24, 1975.

Gleazer Jr., Edmund J. (1976). Editorial. *Community and Junior College Journal, 46*(7), 5.

Green, Madeline F. (2007). Internationalization of community colleges: Barriers and strategies. In Edward J. Valeau & Rosalind Latiner Raby (Eds.), *International reform efforts and challenges in community colleges* (pp. 15–25). New Directors for Community Colleges (138, Summer). San Francisco: Jossey-Bass.

Green, Madeline F. (2012). *Measuring and assessing internationalization.* Washington, DC: NAFSA: Association of International Educators. http://www.nafsa.org/resourcelibrary/Default.aspx?id=32455

Green, Madeleine F. (2015). *Mapping the landscape: Accreditation and the international dimensions of U.S. higher education.* Washington, DC: NAFSA: Association of International Educators. www.nafsa.org/epubs

Green, Madeleine, & Siaya, Laura (2005). *Measuring internationalization at community colleges.* Washington, DC: American Council on Education.

Guerin, Stephen H. (2009). Internationalizing the curriculum: Improving learning through international Education: Preparing students for success in a global society. *Community College Journal of Research and Practice, 33*(4), 611–614.

Hagedorn, Linda S. & Lee, Mi-Chung. (2005). *International community college students: The neglected minority? Online submission to ERIC.* http://www.eric.ed.gov/PDFS/ED490516.pdf

Harder, Natalie J. (2011). Internationalization efforts in United States community colleges: A comparative analysis of urban, suburban, and rural institutions. *Community College Journal of Research and Practice, 35*(1–2), 152–164.

Hess, Gerhard (1982). *Freshmen and sophomores abroad: Community colleges and overseas academic programs.* New York: Teachers College Press.

Karabel, Jerome (1972). Community colleges and social stratification. *Harvard Educational Review, 42,* 521–562.

King, Maxwell C., & Breuder, Robert L. (Eds.). (1979). *Advancing international education.* New directions for community colleges. No. 26. San Francisco: Jossey-Bass Publishers.

King, Maxwell & Fersh, Seymour (1983). International education and the U.S. community college: From optional to integral. *ERIC Junior College Resource Review*, Spring, ERIC Number: ED233780.

Lee, Jack T. (2014). *Education hubs in the making: Policy rationales and international relations.* Dissertation, Department of Leadership, Higher and Adult Education. Ontario Institute for Studies in Education. University of Toronto.

Levin, John (2010). Global culture and the community college. *Community College Journal of Research and Practice, 26*(2), 121–145. doi:10.1080/10668920202753385474.

Lumina Foundation. (2015). *Goals 2025.* http://www.luminafoundation.org/goal_2025

Malkan, Rajiv, & Pisani, Michael J. (2011). Internationalizing the community college experience. *Community College Journal of Research & Practice, 35*(11), 825–841.

Mamiseishvili, Ketevan (2012). Academic and social integration and persistence of international students at U.S. two-year institutions. *Community College Journal of Research and Practice, 36*(1), 15–27. doi:10.1080/10668926.2012.619093.

Manns, Derrick. (2014). Redefining the role, scope, and mission of community colleges in an international context. In P. Eddy (Ed.), *Special issue: Community colleges and their internationalization efforts. Community College. Journal of Research and Practice, 38*(8), 705–709.

NAFSA. (2014). *The International Student Value Economic Tool.* Powered by Indiana University, Office of International Services. http://www.nafsa.org/Explore_International_Education/Impact/Data_And_Statistics/The_International_Student_Economic_Value_Tool/

NAFSA. (2015). *Online professional learning and training.* www.nafsa.org/Attend_Events/Online/Online_Professional_LearningTraining/

O'Connor, Gavin C., Farnsworth, Kent A., & Utley, Mary E. (2013). Internationalization of general education curricula in community colleges: A faculty perspective. *Community College Journal of Research & Practice, 37,* 966–978. doi:10.1080/10668926.2010.515512.

Opp, Ronald D., & Gosetti, Penny Poplin (2014). The role of key administrators in internationalizing the community college student experience. In Michael J. Roggow (Ed.), *Strengthening community colleges through institutional collaborations* (pp. 67–75). New Directions for Community Colleges: No. 165. San Francisco: Jossey-Bass.

Raby, Rosalind Latiner (2012). Re-imagining international education at community colleges. *Audem: International Journal of Higher Education and Democracy, 3,* 81–99.

Raby, Rosalind Latiner, Kaufman, Joyce P., & Rebb, Greg (2012). The international negotiation modules project: Using simulation to enhance teaching and learning strategies in the community college. In Rebecca Clothey, S. Austin-Li, & John Weidman (Eds.), *Post-secondary education and technology. A global perspective on opportunities and obstacles to development.* New York: Palgrave Macmillan.

Raby, Rosalind Latiner, & Tarrow, Norma (Eds.) (1996). *Dimensions of the community college: International and inter/multicultural perspectives.* Garland Studies in Higher Education Volume 6, Vol. 1075. New York: Garland Publishing, Inc.

Raby, Rosalind Latiner, & Valeau, Edward J. (2007). Community college international education: Looking back to forecast the future. In Edward J. Valeau, & Rosalind Latiner Raby (Eds.), *International reform efforts and challenges in community colleges* (pp. 5–14). New Directors for Community Colleges (138, Summer). San Francisco: Jossey-Bass.

Raby, Rosalind Latiner, Culton, Donald R., & Valeau, Edward J. (2014a). Collaboration: Use of consortium to promote international education. In Michael J. Roggow (Ed.), *Strengthening community colleges through institutional collaborations* (pp. 77–87). New Directions for Community Colleges: No. 165. San Francisco: Jossey-Bass.

Raby, Rosalind Latiner, Rhodes, Gary M., & Biscarra, Albert (2014b). Community college study abroad: Implications for student success. *Community College Journal of Research and Practice, 38*(2–3), 174–183.

Robertson, Jennifer J. (2015). Student interest in international education at the community college. *Community College Journal of Research and Practice*, *39*(5), 473–484. doi:10.1080/10668926.2013.879377.

Schulman, Kori (2011). *White House Blog*. http://www.whitehouse.gov/blog/2011/01/19/first-lady-michelle-obama-when-you-study-abroad-you-re-helping-make-america-stronger

Shields, Robin (2013). Globalization and international student mobility: A network analysis. *Comparative Education Review*, *57*(4), 609–636.

Sutin, Robin, Derrico, Daniel, Valeau, Edward, & Raby, Rosalind Latiner (Eds.) (2011). *Increasing effectiveness of the community college financial model: A global perspective for the global economy*. New York: Palgrave Macmillan Publishers.

Treat, Tod, & Hagedorn, Linda Serra (Eds.). (2013). Resituating the community college in a global context in The community college in a global context. *New Directions for Community Colleges*. San Francisco: Jossey-Bass Publications.

Violino, Bob (2011). Community abroad: International partnerships generate revenue. Opportunity for colleges in tough fiscal times. *Community College Journal*, *82*(1), 14–16.

Zhang, Yi (Leaf). (2011). Education abroad in the U.S. Community Colleges. *Community College Review*, *39*(2), 181–200.

Zook, G. (1947). *The President's commission on higher education: Higher education for American democracy* (Vol. 1, Establishing Goals). New York: Harper & Brothers.

CHAPTER 3

Faculty International Experience and Internationalization Efforts at Community Colleges in the United States

Krishna Bista

INTRODUCTION

In recent years, internationalization has been a strategy for colleges and universities to recruit overseas students, as well as to raise institutional and national revenue (Raby 2007; de Wit et al. 2013; Raby and Valeau 2013). Internationalization at colleges helps to "educate their students for global citizenship, to keep pace with their peers, to better serve the national and international community, and to remain great universities" (Biddle 2002, p. 7). Faculty can enhance their international experiences by teaching in another country or by traveling and participating in programs such as study-abroad, exchange program, Fulbright fellowship, and international seminars. In addition to such out-bound opportunities (in which US-born faculty get educated), faculty who were born abroad bring linguistic and cultural diversity, different worldviews, and international skills to American colleges (in-bound). When faculty exchange ideas, innovative curricula with colleagues, and participate in international development program, the college gets involved in the process

K. Bista (✉)
School of Education, University of Louisiana at Monroe, Monroe, LA, USA

© The Editor(s) (if applicable) and The Author(s) 2016   23
R.L. Raby, E.J. Valeau (eds.), *International Education at Community Colleges*, DOI 10.1057/978-1-137-53336-4_3

of internationalization (Raby 1995). Such occasions develop faculty's awareness of and appreciation for the rich diversity of human experience found in the customs, traditions, and cultural contributions outside of their frame of reference. Along with globally emerging technology, cross-cultural communications, and shifting political alignment, institutions of American higher education have reshaped the strategies for "global consciousness and a critical understanding of how national and international issues intersect" (Biddle 2002, p. 5).

Although some community colleges have made a commitment to internationalization, there are no significant changes in promoting international experiences of faculty when compared to four-year institutions in the last few decades (Green and Siaya 2005; O'Hara 2009; Raby 2012; Siaya and Hayward 2012). There are limited opportunities for the faculty members in the community colleges that focus on international experiences. In this line of inquiry, the purpose of this chapter is to examine the demographic and career-profile characteristics, the perceptions of community college faculty's international experience and resulting internationalization at their campuses. The author examines whether two groups of faculty, that is, (a) with and without a prior international experience; and (b) foreign-born faculty and the US-born faculty, report the perceptions of internationalization differently at community colleges.

REVIEW OF RELATED LITERATURE

Faculty International Experience

In universities and community colleges, faculty international experience builds an international perspective into "courses and research agendas where it did not currently exist" (Biddle 2002, p. 8). It is one of the least expensive and most effective ways to globalize the campus resources (Czarra 2002; Bales 2008). Internationalization plays an important role in creating a global curriculum, expanding study-abroad, and developing cross-border education (Raby 1995; Sandgren et al. 1999).

However, there are limited empirical studies that focus on community college faculty's international experience and their perceptions toward internationalization of college resources in particular. Some studies suggest that community college faculty seem to have positive attitudes about infusing an international and intercultural perspective into their teaching, research, and service (Bissonette and Woodin 2013; Bradshaw 2013; O'Connor et al. 2013; Watson 2014). A few empirical studies related to community colleges show a positive relationship between international experiences of faculty and satisfaction with instruction, workplace perceptions, and tenure process (Wells 2007; Mamiseishvili 2011; Siaya and Hayward 2012).

For instance, Watson (2014) interviewed 23 community college faculty to examine how they understand, describe, and practice internationalization. Her study suggested that early life experiences of faculty influenced their global practice. Similarly, teaching was "the most prevalent way faculty globalized their work, followed by research and service" (Watson 2014, p. 10). Burdzinski's (2014) study conducted in Florida community colleges suggested that an extensive international travel experiences is correlated with support for internalization activities, and those who possess more international experience are more likely to have higher perceptions in internationalizing community colleges.

Despite positive attitude for internationalization, faculty also have reported organizational barriers in implementing internationalization into their practice at their colleges (Harder 2010; O'Connor et al. 2013; Watson 2014). For instance, lack of resources, lack of curriculum infusion, heavy workload/lack of time, and lack of faculty inclusion were the major barriers to further internationalization (Watson 2014).

In another quantitative study, O'Connor et al. (2013) surveyed 243 general education faculty at 18 Missouri community colleges. They found that administrative support, geographical location (urban vs. rural), and faculty with international awareness were the key indicators of successful internationalization efforts. Blair et al.'s (2000) study found that 82 % of college faculty had international components in their courses. Also, 44 % of the colleges recruited international faculty and staff on their campuses, and 50 % of the colleges offered faculty development and training (Blair et al. 2000). Similarly, Iuspa's (2010) study found both students and faculty had positive attitudes and perceptions regarding international experience and internationalization of education.

The role of college faculty is significant when educating students about world views and making curriculum and instruction competitive and creative. Childress (2010) mentioned the positive role of faculty in promoting international and global experience in order to internationalize curriculum, skills, and technology. Childress (2010) also reported that colleges should have intention, investment, infrastructure, networking, and individual support to promote international education and global knowledge. Bradshaw (2013) presents an example of faculty-led study-abroad programs at Madison Area Technical College as a case study to present the breadth and depth of internationalization in community college education. Reports

related to award-winning community colleges for "internationalization" indicate that faculty are engaged in a variety of activities related to teaching, research, and services (NAFSA 2014). For instance, faculty at Albion College developed exchange programs for both faculty and students in Costa Rica, Cameroon, and France. Kapi'oani Community College faculty created Project Shine, a service learning project infused into some of the courses at the college. Similarly, faculty at the Community College of Philadelphia developed international studies courses (NAFSA 2014).

Foreign-Born and US-Born Faculty

According to National Science Foundation report (2014), foreign-born faculty increased from 12 % in 1973 to 26 % in 2010 with particularly high proportions in engineering (49 %) and computer sciences (51 %). The benefit of international faculty is associated with better global literacy or transnational competence (Biddle 2002). Previous research indicates the importance of services and experiences of foreign-born faculty in the US higher education system, particularly at four-year institutions (Wells 2007; Lin et al. 2009; Mamiseishvili 2012; US Census Bureau, 2013). Their international experience promotes campus diversity, helps students develop worldviews, and offers an array of perspectives and experiences to the institution (Pascarella 2001; Wells 2007; Mamiseishvili 2011).

There is limited literature on the work and scholarship of foreign-born faculty at community colleges. Wells (2007) noted that foreign-born faculty were more satisfied with their jobs than US-born faculty in community colleges. On the contrary, Mamiseishvili's (2011) study indicated that foreign-born faculty reported lower scores on job satisfaction and workplaces than the US-born professoriate at two-year colleges. Some foreign-born faculty's dissatisfaction with employment and workplace might be attributed to their cultural differences such as country of origin, language, and religious background (Mamiseishvili 2011).

RESEARCH METHOD

This is a cross-sectional study—that is, descriptive in nature (neither longitudinal nor experimental). Cross-sectional research is based on observations that take place in different groups at one time on several variables such as gender, income, and education (Johnson and Christensen 2014). This means there is no experimental procedure; no variables are manipulated by the researcher.

As a convenience sampling technique, two community colleges were selected in this study. As Johnson and Christensen (2014, p. 263) describes, a convenience sampling includes participants "who are available or volunteer or can be easily recruited and are willing to participate in the research study." An online survey was used to collect data. In addition to descriptive data, chi-square and independent t-tests were used to analyze the data.

Data and Participants

Based on the Institute for International Education (IIE) list of top five hosting institutions for international students (Open Doors 2014), two US public community colleges were randomly chosen to be part of the study. Both colleges, Santa Monica Community College located in California and Lone Star Montgomery Community College located in Texas, offer a wide range of associate degree programs (more than 75 fields of study), and campus communities are diverse and vibrant. Both colleges offer programs that prepare students for careers of the twenty-first century, host study-abroad programs, enroll international students, and conduct cross-cultural activities on campuses.

A staff contact was made at each institution to be the liaison in getting an online survey to all full-time faculty members. The online survey was distributed to this staff contact after the approval of my university's Institutional Review Board (IRB). I did not have direct access to faculty and as such, could not verify the total number of faculty who received the survey nor how many faculty from each campus received the survey. Of the 400 potential full-time faculty from both institutions, (300 from the first site and 100 from the second site), only 263 ($N = 263$) usable samples (i.e., completely filled out sample; no outlier) was included in the final analysis after data screening. Female faculty participants doubled (70 %) male faculty (30 %). Over half of the total faculty were 50 and older. Similarly, 51.3 % of total faculty were tenured; 36.1 % of faculty had 20 or more years teaching; 74.1 % of faculty identified themselves as White. Nearly half of the total participants represented humanities (49.4 %), education (12.5 %), and business and management programs (5.3 %). Also, 13.3 % of professoriates were international faculty (foreign-born) compared to 86.3 % US-born peers. Faculty members with international experiences (50.2 %) were almost equal with faculty without international experience (49.4 %). Likewise, 82.5 % faculty expressed interest to participate in study-abroad programs.

Instrument and Measures

Data was collected using the *Faculty International Experience* question-naire. Developed by Adebay and Paracka (2010), this instrument includes 35 items (eight items on faculty attitudes about international experience, five on faculty support for internationalization, seven on international learning interest, six on the effects of internationalization, and seven demographic items). Previous studies indicated a strong validity and reli-ability of this instrument (Iuspa 2010; Bacalis-Ariman 2012). The fol-lowing reliability was measured in the current study: Attitudes about International Experience (α = .74), Support for Internationalization (α = .78), International Learning Interest (α = .81), and Effects of Internationalization (α = .89).

Demographic Characteristics. Three demographic variables were exam-ined in the current study: gender, age, and ethnicity. Male and female status was coded as 1 = male, and 2 = female. Age was merged into five categories: under 35, 35–40, 41–45, 46–50, and 51 and above. Faculty ethnicity was coded as 1 = African-American, 2 = Latino/a, 3 = Asian, 4 = White, 5 = other. Six career-related variables were included in the analysis: primary teaching field/discipline, years of teaching, tenure sta-tus, types of institutional affiliation, prior international experience, and interest in international experience. The primary teaching field of fac-ulty was grouped into eight broad areas: 1 = humanities, 2 = education, 3 = business and management studies, 4 = social sciences, 5 = health professions, 6 = physical/natural sciences and engineering, 7 = math and computer sciences, 8 = other. The number of years of teaching was listed into five groups: 1 = less than 5, 2 = 5–10, 3 = 11–15, 4 = 16–20, and 5 = 21 and more. Academic tenure status indicated as 1 = tenured, 2 = non-tenured/tenure-track, 3 = non-tenure track, and 4 = other. Other variables such as (faculty prior international experience, inter-est in study-abroad program, birth status–foreign born) were coded as 1 = yes, no = 0.

International Experience and Internationalization Perceptions. Twenty-six items were included to measure faculty international experiences and campus internationalization perceptions: attitudes, support, interest, and effects of internationalization. The responses were coded as follows: 1 = *strongly agree*, 2 = *agree*, 3 = *neutral*, 4 = *disagree*, and 5 = *strongly disagree*.

DATA ANALYSIS AND RESULTS

Descriptive statistics were used to report the demographic and career related characteristics of community college faculty, the international experience ratings, and the campus internationalization perceptions. Chi-square tests were conducted to observe whether the differences in the demographic and career-profile characteristics between the two faculty groups (a) foreign-born faculty vs. US-born faculty, and (b) faculty with a prior international experience vs. faculty without an international experience were statistically significant. Means, standard deviations, and independent t-test scores were used to examine faculty international experience ratings and campus internationalization perceptions.

Chi-square tests revealed that 9.5 % of foreign-born faculty participants were female compared to 60.3 % of the US-born professoriate. Similarly, 67.9 % of the US-born faculty participants were White compared to 6.1 % of foreign-born faculty. A chi-square test indicated that there was a significant difference in the racial make-up of the two groups, χ^2 (4) = 20.37, $p < .001$. Cramer's statistic was .28 (out of a possible value of 1) which suggests a small and a positive significant relationship ($p < .001$). Cramer's value provides a test of statistical significance and also provides information about the strength of the association between two categorical variables (Morgan et al. 2014). Other demographic and career profile variables such as gender, tenure status, years of teaching, discipline/department, faculty prior international experience, and interest in study-abroad were not statistically significant between the US-born faculty and foreign-born faculty.

Similarly, faculty with prior international experience were similar to faculty without international experience in terms of their ethnicity, gender, age group, years of teaching, and tenure status. The majority of faculty with international experience were female (34.4 %), were White (37 %), were in the age group of 51 and above (25.6 %), were tenured (30.5 %), were interested in a study-abroad program (45 %), and were US-born faculty (42.5 %) ; this was very consistent with the characteristics of the faculty without international experience (35.5 %, 28.3 %, 20.6 %, 15.3 %, 22.1 %, 38.1 %, and 44.1 % respectively). There were more tenured faculty with international experience (30.5 %) or in tenure-track (5.7 %) than faculty without international experience (20.6 % and 5.3 % respectively).

There were more faculty with international experience in humanities (27.1 %) and social sciences (5 %) than faculty without experiences (22.1 % and 3.1 % respectively). Also, the majority of community college faculty members without international experience were in education (7.6 %), business and management studies (3.4 %), health professions (4.6 %), and math and computer sciences (2.7 %). Interestingly, faculty with international experience indicated an interest in a study-abroad program (45 %) than faculty without an international experience (11.5 %).

Chi-squared tests also revealed that whether faculty were interested in study-abroad or not was statistically significant between faculty with international experience and faculty without international experience, χ^2 (1) = 7.303, N = 263, p < .05 with a Phi's value of .17 (p < .05). Foreign-born faculty members reported lower values (i.e., positive scores on a Likert scale 1–5) on their perceptions related to international experiences, campus support for internationalization, international learning interest and effects of internationalization than US-born faculty members (Table 3.1). Further analysis showed that foreign-born college faculty were significantly different from US-born college faculty on attitudes regarding international experience (p < .05), international learning interest (p < .001), and effects of internationalization (p < .001). These two groups of faculty were not significantly different on faculty support for internationalization on campuses (p > .5).

Community college faculty with international experience were significantly different from faculty without international experience on attitudes (p < .001), learning interest, and effects of internationalization (both p < .05). Inspection of the two group means indicates that the average mean scores for faculty with international experience were significantly

Table 3.1 Comparison of the foreign-born and the US-born faculty on international experience, support for internationalization, international learning interest, and effects of internationalization, N = 263

Variables	Community college faculty members		
	Foreign born, M (SD)	US born, M (SD)	p
Attitudes on international experience	1.44 (.40)	1.69 (.47)	.004*
Support for internationalization	2.61 (.92)	2.71 (.83)	.593
International learning interest	1.47 (.42)	1.81 (.57)	.000**
Effects of internationalization	1.15 (.30)	1.45 (.53)	.000**

Note. M Mean, SD Standard deviation. Mean ratings on a scale of 1–5 where 1 = *strongly agree* and 5 = *strongly disagree*

* p < .05; ** p < .001

Table 3.2 Comparison between faculty with an international experience and faculty without an international experience, $N = 263$

Variables	Faculty members		
	Faculty with an international experience, M (SD)	Faculty without an international experience, M (SD)	P
Attitudes on international experience	1.53 (.37)	1.78 (.52)	.000**
Support for internationalization	2.61 (.92)	2.77 (.74)	.119
International learning interest	1.67 (.54)	1.84 (.56)	.011*
Effects of internationalization	1.32 (.43)	1.51 (.57)	.002*

Note. M Mean, *SD* Standard deviation. Mean ratings on a scale of 1–5 where 1 = *strongly agree* and 5 = *strongly disagree*

* $p < .05$; ** $p < .001$

lower than the scores for faculty without international experiences in perceptions related to attitudes, support, learning interest, and effects of internalization (Table 3.2).

LIMITATION OF THE STUDY

This study has several limitations worth mentioning. First, the results of this study are based on a small sample drawn from two public community colleges, located in California and Texas. Findings presented in this study (based on 263 retuned sample) are pertinent for full-time (regular) faculty in two community colleges and do not generalize to part-time faculty, nor those in four-year institutions.

International experience of foreign-born faculty may depend on the country of origin, duration of stay in the USA, and institutions attended or affiliated with during their college career. Some of these variables were not collected in the current study. Finally, this study relied on self-reported data. It is important to note that self-reported data may not have "real" responses to questions and the answers may be biased (Fowler 2014). Thus, faculty who participated in this study may be biased, or have little or high interests on internationalization. The researcher has made an attempt to check multiple measures of international experience. The researcher, however, would like to suggest future research with a larger sample size including faculty from multiple community colleges. Future researchers may choose a different research design such as a mixed-method to uncover international experiences and internationalization perceptions of diverse college faculty.

DISCUSSION

This study examined the demographic characteristics, the perceptions of faculty international experiences, and support for internationalization at their campuses. Results from this study show some distinct differences in international experiences and internationalization perceptions between foreign-born faculty and US-born peers as well as between faculty with a prior international experience and without an experience. This difference may be attributed in part due to faculty's individual and institutional characteristics such as sociocultural backgrounds, international education/study-abroad expectations, institutional available resources, and academic workloads.

As results indicated, there is a growing number of foreign-born faculty, mostly White (non-US-born 6.1 % vs. US-born 67.9 %) and females (non-US-born 9.5 % vs. US-born 60.3 %) at community colleges. This finding reflects the national trends pointed out in previous research that foreign-born faculty proportion is present (8.4 % foreign-born faculty and 91.6 % US-born community college faculty in a sample of 5220 faculties) at community colleges (Mamiseishvili 2011). This indicates that faculty composition in the US community colleges are diverse and contribute in fostering global and international perspectives in academic discourse and teaching. However, these statistics may need a caution because foreign-born faculty in the current study was affiliated largely in humanities, education, physical/natural science, and engineering disciplines.

The findings that foreign-born faculty were significantly different on attitudes on international experience, international learning interests, and effects of internationalization might be because of the sociocultural differences between US-born faculty and foreign-born faculty. It may also be because of various disciplinary affiliations, years of services, tenure status, and age within the study sample. However, the findings indicated that both groups of faculty were not different in terms of faculty support for internationalization (engagement, encouragement, community resources, and teaching content related to international experience).

Where differences in faculty international experience occurred, faculty with prior international experience reported lower score on attitudes, support, learning interest, and effects of internationalization. As seen in the results, this finding does not seem surprising because the majority of faculty with international experience were tenured faculty with aged 51 and over. A possible explanation for this finding could be a combination of individual and cultural characteristics of faculty and/or other opportunities and resources available to senior and tenured faculty (Mamiseishvili 2011).

Previous researches (Green and Olson 2003; Bacalis-Ariman 2012; Siaya and Hayward 2012) state that faculty international experience matters in developing and designing curriculum, and advising students with diverse backgrounds. Findings from the current study showed that there is a growing number of foreign-born faculty serving at community colleges with international experience in their profession. Such faculty population is a valuable resource for community colleges to prepare their students and campus resources diverse and global.

As seen in descriptive statistics, community college faculty reported positive attitudes toward internationalization and the importance of international experience in higher education. Green (2005) mentioned that international experience also helps students to be more knowledgeable and understanding of different cultures and languages. Foreign-born faculty members serve as a valuable resource extending worldviews to their students and campus community. Future research that highlights the differences among two faculty groups (foreign-born and US-born) will help colleges better serve the needs and challenges of faculty and students, and particularly toward campus internationalization. It is acknowledged that foreign-born faculty increase cross-cultural competence, global literacy, and the growing internationalization efforts at colleges (Mamiseishvili 2011, Raby 2012). In this context, college administrators (presidents, deans, chairs) may need to recognize the role that foreign-born faculty may serve on their campuses to contribute toward the internationalization mission.

Significance of the Study

This study may help faculty and administrators understand the perceptions of faculty regarding international experience and campus internationalization. This research may also help community colleges enhance internationalization efforts by strengthening study-abroad, international education, international/student diversity, and exchange programs on campus. Foreign-born faculty bring with them diverse perspectives and worldviews that potentially enrich the university in the global context (Kim et al. 2011). As colleges are changing their mission to include the internationalization of education, faculty has the potential to be role models in global and international education. The current study emphasizes the need for further understanding of the experiences and contributions of foreign-born faculty if institutions' missions are campus internationalization and the twenty-first-century knowledge production. This study may also contribute to future research in the field.

References

Adebayo, Akanmu, & Paracka, Dan (2010). *Faculty survey on internationalization.* American Council on Education. http://www.acenet.edu/news-room/Documents/Kennesaw-State-University-Faculty-Survey-International.pdf

Bacalis-Ariman, Patricia R. (2012). *The influence of international experience on faculty attitudes toward the infusion of global perspectives.* Unpublished doctoral dissertation, Alliant International University, Califonia.

Bales, Susan N. (2008). *How Americans think about the world.* http://asiasociety.org/education-learning/partnership-global-learning/making-case/how-Americans-think-about-world

Biddle, Sheila (2002). Internationalization: Rhetoric or reality? *American Council of Learned Societies Occasional Paper, 56.* http://www.acls.org/Publications/OP/56_Internationalization.pdf

Bissonette, Bonnie, & Woodin, Shawn (2013). Building support for internationalization through institutional assessment and leadership engagement. In Tod Treat & Linda Serra Hagedorn (Eds.), *The community college in a global context* (pp. 11–26). New Directions for Community Colleges. No. 161. San Francisco: Jossey-Bass Publications. doi:10.1002/cc20045.

Blair, Donna, Phinney, Lisa, & Philippe, Kent A. (2000). *International programs at community colleges: Research brief.* Washington, DC: Association of American Community Colleges. http://www.aacc.nche.edu/Publications/Briefs/Documents/01012001internationalcc.pdf

Bradshaw, Geoffrey W. (2013). Internationalization and faculty-led service learning. In Tod Treat and Linda Serra Hagedorn (Eds.), *The community college in a global context* (pp. 11–26). *New Directions for Community Colleges.* No. 161. San Francisco: Jossey-Bass Publications. doi:10.1002/cc20047.

Burdzinski, Donna R. (2014). *Attitudes about globalization, internationalization, and the role of student affairs administrators in internationalizing*

Florida's community and state colleges. Doctoral dissertation, University of South Florida (UMI No. 3615607).

Childress, Lisa K. (2010). *The twenty-first century university: Developing faculty engagement in internationalization.* New York: Peter Lang.

Czarra, Fred (2002). *Global education checklist for teachers, schools, school systems and state agencies.* http://www.globaled.org/fianlcopy.pdf

de Wit, Hans, Ferencz, Irina, & Rumbley, Laura E. (2013). International student mobility: European and US perspectives. *Perspectives: Policy and Practice in Higher Education, 17*(1), 17–23. doi:10.1080/13603108.2012.679752.

Fowler, Floyd J. (2014). *Survey research methods* (5th ed.). Thousand Oaks, CA: Sage Publications.

Green, Madeleine F. (2005). *Internationalization in U.S. higher education: The student perspective.* Washington, DC: American Council on Education. http://www.acenet.edu/news-room/Documents/Intlz-In-US-Higher-Ed-Student-Perspective.pdf

Green, Madeleine F., & Olson, Christa L. (2003). *Internationalizing the campus: A user's guide.* Washington, DC: American Council on Education.

Green, Madeleine F., & Siaya, Laura (2005). *Measuring internationalization at community colleges.* Washington, DC: American Council on Education. http://www.acenet.edu/news-room/Documents/Measuring-CommunityCollege.pdf

Harder, Natalie J. (2010). Internationalization efforts in United States community colleges: A comparative analysis of urban, suburban, and rural institutions. *Community College Journal of Research & Practice, 35,* 152–164. doi:10.1080/10668926.2011.525186.

Iuspa, Flavia E. (2010). Assessing the effectiveness of the internationalization process in higher education institutions: A case study of Florida International University. *FIU Electronic Theses and Dissertations* (Paper 316). http://digitalcommons.fiu.edu/etd/316

Johnson, R. Burke, & Christensen, Larry (2014). *Educational research: Quantitative, qualitative, and mixed approached* (5th ed.). Thousand Oaks, CA: Sage Publications.

Kim, Dongbin, Wolf-Wendel, Lisa, & Twombly, Susan. (2011). International faculty: Experiences of academic life and productivity in U.S. universities. *The Journal of Higher Education, 82*(6), 720–747. doi:10.1353/jhe.2011.0038.

Lin, Zeng, Pearce, Richard, & Wang, Weirong (2009). Imported talent: Demographic characteristics, achievement and job satisfaction of foreign-born full time faculty in four-year American colleges. *Higher Education, 57,* 703–721. doi:10.1007/s10734-008 9171-z.

Mamiseishvili, Ketevan (2011). Characteristics, job satisfaction, and workplace perceptions of foreign-born faculty at public two-year institutions. *Community College Review, 39*(1), 26–45. doi:10.1177/0091552110394650.

Mamiseishvili, Ketevan (2012). Academic and social integration and persistence of international students at U.S. two-year institutions. *Community College Journal of Research and Practice, 36*(1), 15–27. doi:10.1080/10668926.2012.619093.

Morgan, George A., Leech, Nancy L., Gloeckner, Gene W., & Barrett, Karen C. (2014). *IBM SPSS for introductory statistic: Use and interpretation* (5th ed.). New York, NY: Routledge.

NAFSA: Association of International Educators. (2014). In J. Steiner (Ed.), *Internationalizing the campus: Profiles of success at colleges and universities.* New York, NY: Author. http://www.nafsa.org/wcm/Product?prodid=417

National Science Foundation. (2014). *Science and engineering indicators.* http://www.nsf.gov/statistics/seind14/index.cfm/chapter-5/c5s3.htm

O'Hara, Sabine (2009). Vital and overlooked: The role of faculty in internationalizing U.S. campuses. In Peggy Blumenthal & Robert Gutierrez (Eds.), *Meeting America's global education challenge* (pp. 38–45). http://www.iie.org/~/media/Files/Corporate/Membership/StudyAbroad_WhitePaper6.ashx

O'Connor, Gavin C., Farnsworth, Kent A., & Utley, Mary E. (2013). Internationalization of general education curricula in community colleges: A faculty perspective. *Community College Journal of Research & Practice, 37*, 966–978. doi:10.1080/10668926.2010.515512.

Open Doors. (2014). *Special reports: Community college data resource.* http://www.iie.org/Research-and-Publications/Open-Doors/Data/Community-College-Data-Resource/International-Students/International-Students-Top-Host-Institutions-2013-14

Pascarella, Ernest T. (2001). Cognitive growth in college: Surprising and reassuring findings from the National Study of Student Learning. *Change, 33*(6), 20–27. doi:10.1080/00091380109601823.

Raby, Rosalind L. (1995). *Internationalizing the curriculum: Ideals vs. reality.* Paper presented at the annual conferences of the Association of California Community College Administrators, San Jose, CA, February 22–24.

Raby, Rosalind L. (2007). Internationalizing the curriculum: On-and off-campus campusstrategies. In Edward J. Valeau & Rosalind Latiner Raby (Eds.), *International reform efforts and challenges in community colleges.* New Directions for Community Colleges (138, Summer). San Francisco: Jossey-Bass. doi: 10.1002/cc.282.

Raby, Rosalind L. (2012). Reimagining international education at community colleges. *AUDEM: The International Journal of Higher Education and Democracy, 3*, 81–98.

Raby, Rosalind L., & Valeau, Edward J. (2013). Community college global counterparts: Historical contexts. *Research in Comparative and International Education, 8*(2), 110–118. doi:http://dx.doi.org/10.2304/rcie.2013.8.2.

Sandgren, David, Elig, Nick, Hovde, Peter, Krejci, Mark, & Rice, Mary (1999). How international experience affects teaching: Understanding the impact of faculty study abroad. *Journal of Studies in International Education*, *3*(1), 33–56. doi:10.1177/102831539900300104.

Siaya, Lauram, & Hayward, Frank. (2012). *Mapping internationalization on U.S. campuses: Final report*. Washington, DC: American Council on Education. http://www.acenet.edu/news-room/Documents/Mapping-Internationalization_on-US-Campuses-2012-full.pdf

US Census Bureau. (2013). *The foreign-born population in the United States*. http://www.census.gov/prod/2012pubs/acs-19.pdf

Watson, Connie Patricia (2014). *Community college internationalization: Faculty perspectives and practices*. Unpublished doctoral dissertation, Teachers College, Columbia University, (ProQuest No. 36218082014).

Wells, Ryan (2007). International faculty in U.S. community colleges. In Edward J. Valeau & Rosalind Latiner Raby (Eds.), *International reform efforts and challenges in community colleges* (pp. 77–82). New Directions for Community Colleges (138, Summer). San Francisco: Jossey-Bass. doi:10.1002/cc.284.

CHAPTER 4

Mentoring in an International Professional Development Program

Tod Treat

INTRODUCTION

As the link to postsecondary education and socioeconomic well-being strengthens globally, interest has developed in adopting the US community college model. The US community college model provides a mix of access, fluidity, and interactivity with industry that lends itself to development of curricula that meet the needs of multiple populations, varying lengths, and with recognized value in the workplace (Raby 2009). The driving forces that lead to international interest in the US community college include institutional adaptability, workforce development, an egalitarian ideal, and a student-centered orientation that is not always found in traditional higher education instructional methods (Valeau 2009). Approaches to adoption of the US community college include opportunities for study, faculty, and administrative professional development in US community colleges by international colleagues Cohen and Cohen (2013).

This study explores the role of mentoring of international faculty and administrators in the Community College Initiative Instructors and

T. Treat (✉)
Executive Vice President for Academic and Student Affairs at Tacoma Community College, Tacoma, WA, USA

Assistant Professor in Education Policy, Organization, and Leadership at University of Illinois, Champaign, IL, USA

© The Editor(s) (if applicable) and The Author(s) 2016   39
R.L. Raby, E.J. Valeau (eds.), *International Education at Community Colleges*, DOI 10.1057/978-1-137-53336-4_4

Administrators of Egypt (IAE) program developed and delivered by Community Colleges for International Development (CCID). CCID is a "global network of community, technical, and vocational institutions dedicated to creating globally engaged learning environments" (CCID 2015). CCID provides a variety of opportunities including institutional professional development, study-abroad and international study tours, technical training for international institutions, partnerships and development projects.

The IAE, sponsored by the US Department of State Bureau of Educational and Cultural Affairs (DoS ECA), provided faculty and administrators from Egyptian Technical Colleges an immersive experience aimed at developing:

- Enhanced understanding of the US community college, its mission and governance, and approach to meeting technical workforce needs
- Ability to better communicate in spoken and written English
- Ability to design technical curricula incorporating collaboration with industry and integration of teaching, learning, and technology

Over two years, 26 IAEs participated at five US community colleges, including pre-academic English at a central location. While each US community college developed unique approaches to providing professional development for the IAEs, the program substantively met the program aims as described in a previous publication (Treat 2010). Development of mentoring relationships between US community college faculty and the IAEs was a common element of the program delivery across the institutions. This paper explores the role of these relationships in more depth.

Mentoring

Mentoring has been recommended for a variety of higher education practices including leadership development, orientation and optimization of daily work skills, exposure to different contexts, feedback to challenges, and succession planning (Reille and Kezar 2010). For leadership development, a variety of diagnostic tools, inventories, formal activities, and reflections can be used to aid in the personal development of the participant in conjunction with coaching from the mentor (Eddy 2008). In particular, studies of the role of faculty in the development of faculty colleagues points to the development of social support, career development, and "models of teaching excellence," which are particularly important due to the learner-centered approach often supported in community colleges.

Elements of successful mentoring programs have been identified (Ennis-Cole and Lawhon, 2004; Zunz and Oil, 2009). These include administrative support, voluntary participation, broader programming to support professional development, careful matching of mentors and mentees, orientation for both mentors and mentees, flexibility, sharing of teaching resources, observations of teaching, recognition, and program evaluation for improvement (St. Clair 1994). The attributes of a good mentor generally include availability, flexibility, honesty, and collegiality, being a good listener, providing resources and perspectives about the institution, and helping mentees balance various faculty roles (Gaskin et al. 2003).

VanDerLinden (2005) posits mentoring in terms of social capital—the connections gained through shared practice, common understanding and values, and creation of social network and cooperative activity (Cohen and Prusak 2001). Social capital is gained through both internal and external activities and exhibits itself, at least generally, in the ability of an individual to organize activity among teams or groups based on expertise or interest, underpinned by a shared sense of purpose. Mentors play a particularly important role in exposing mentees to experiences directly or through introductions/recommendations.

In community college mentoring programs, the level of formality matters. In a study by Hopkins and Grigoriu (2005), mentees were shown to value support and desire structure, but not rigidity in the structure. Mentees value topic lists, for example, but want to retain the right to customize their learning in mentoring relationships. On the contrary, Vega et al. (2010) finds that structure is beneficial, particularly for mentoring minority faculty, and suggests that mentoring programs have the following components of specific goals with measureable outcomes:

- A defined time commitment each week or month
- Preparation of mentors
- Clearly articulated descriptions of clinical or internship experiences associated with the program
- Attendance expectations and records for supplemental events
- Measurement of use and outcomes
- Notetaking
- Surveying participations for continuous improvement

The literature on mentoring in the community college is focused on leadership or faculty development of community college employees, not international visitors. An increased interest in adoption of the US community college model internationally has led to creation of programs to facilitate mobility of international faculty to US community colleges for professional development. This study aims to fill the gap in the literature by providing an increased understanding of mentoring of international administrators and educators.

CONCEPTUAL FRAMEWORK

The framework of intercultural competencies provides a useful lens through which to consider mentoring of international administrators and educators. While various theories have emerged around cultural and intercultural competencies, the Association of American Colleges & Universities has codified competencies to include cultural self-awareness, knowledge of cultural perspectives and worldviews, empathy, highly developed intercultural communication skills, curiosity, and openness (AAC&U 2015).

As a qualitative study on mentoring of Egyptian administrators and educators, this study addresses cultural issues that may not be relevant to international programs elsewhere. Likewise, the mentors described in this study reflect highly technical programs from five geographically distributed community colleges. International professional development programs in nontechnical fields, of differing duration, or from different cultures may result in very different experiences and readers should weigh the findings of this study carefully when determining transferability to different contexts.

METHOD

The purpose of this study is to better understand the role mentoring plays in shaping the experiences and outcomes of international administrators and educators.

1. How are mentoring roles integrated into overall program models?
2. What knowledge and skills do mentors need to effectively serve international administrators and educators?
3. What are the implications of various mentoring roles on international professional development programs?

A case study approach was utilized to address these questions. Twenty-nine mentor–mentee relationships were developed in two cohorts participating in seven-month programs at five institutions disbursed geographically in Florida, Illinois, Iowa, Pennsylvania, and Washington. A multisite case study method was thus utilized to gain information. Individual interviews with IAEs and mentors, focus groups with college staff, presentation and document analysis, and participation in coordinator meetings were used to collect data. The data collection consisted of interviews with each IAE early in the program and again late in the program leading to over 40 IAE interviews. Institutional site visits led to over 15 focus groups, several individual mentor interviews, and several hours of conference participation.

Interviews were semi-structured. Care was taken to ensure that each participant experienced a similar line of inquiry to enhance the credibility of the study. The interviews were recorded and observer's notes taken. The interviews were coded using open coding and analyzed for emergent themes. Participants were advised of the protections and risks and voluntarily consented to participation. While the findings in this study have been reported accurately and honestly, care has been taken to protect the participants' identities. Thus, while the names of agencies are provided, the names of both individuals and colleges have been replaced with pseudonyms.

Characteristics of IAEs, Mentors, and Institutional Approaches

The characteristics of the educators were varied in terms of age, gender, position status, disciplinary background, and institution of employment. Twenty-one males and four females participated in the program. The IAEs in their 20s and lower 30s made rapid adjustments to American culture, engaged the program more fully, and made greater gains across the spectrum of goals (English; teaching, learning, and technology; community college concept). By contrast, the institutional approaches to program implementation and roles/backgrounds of mentors were quite varied as illustrated in Table 4.1. Institutional variation did not seem to affect overall program efficacy. In fact, institutional self determination within parameters was a strength of the program.

Each institution developed an organizational structure built upon its own culture and capabilities. Generally, chief responsibility for program implementation and staffing fell to a coordinator, but the coordinator's primary role at the institution varied considerably. The expertise of the coordinator, for example, might be in faculty development, or in interna-

Table 4.1 General approaches to mentoring at each community college

Institution	Primary coordinator role	Mentor roles
Midwest Grand	Director, Faculty Development Center	Department Chair Faculty, Welding Faculty, Plumbing
Steeltown	Dean, International Education	Faculty, IT Faculty, IT
Piney Tech	Coordinator, ESL	Department Chair, IT Faculty IT Faculty IT
Beachtown	Full time grants funded international educator	Faculty, IT Faculty, Engineering Technology Faculty, Culinary
Puget Sound	Director, Career and Employment Center	Faculty, Engineering Technology Faculty, IT Faculty, International Business

tional education. Furthermore, the coordinator might be responsible for all aspects of the program, including designing, implementation, reporting, and so on or might share these responsibilities with others in the organization. Finally, the role of the mentors might be narrow (instruction related, limited time and activity) or broad (cultural mentoring, general faculty mentoring, extended time and effort).

As outlined previously (Treat 2010), each institution took a different approach to providing professional development for the IAEs. In particular, some institutions utilized more formal mentoring relationships with an individual mentor, while others used an informal team approach to mentoring.

FINDINGS

Reliance on Mentor Guidance

The IAEs in both cycles of the program came to rely heavily upon their mentors, particularly early in the program cycle, in understanding the purpose of the professional development and the need to be actively engaged in it. In the hospitality program, for example, IAEs initially did not see the need to participate in food preparation, but only to observe students.

US Mentor 1. Well, probably that's part of the culture. They feel that they are not part of the student body. So, they're probably more comfortable just to observe some of the theory, for instance, handouts, PowerPoint presentations—get those information and observe how we present those information, and then when you go into the kitchen part, they kind of stay set back. Either they leave or taking some pictures. That's about it.

Over time, the mentor was able to establish a sense of purpose and engagement.

US Mentor 1. Actually, when I was teaching the baking class last term when they were around—they would get involved—if I was showing them how to roll up a Danish or something like that, they would actually try it and get involved in doing that. I welcomed to participate in just about whatever they wanted.

Eventually, IAEs began cooking and even washing dishes, a departure from common practice for instructors in Egypt.

Cultural Competency and Mentoring

The need for cultural competency was reinforced throughout the two years in which the program was offered. Successful mentors repeatedly showed sensitivity to the IAEs cultural differences. As examples, IAEs demonstrated a marked preference for home cooking as opposed to typical US food or food service where college dormitories were utilized. IAEs also practiced religious traditions, such as Ramadan, which sometimes required flexibility in meetings or instruction. Personal needs or conceptions of time required adaptation from mentors. Finally, the differences in the way Egyptians interact with one another sometimes required patience in developing trust between the mentor and mentee.

Culturally competent mentors understood these needs and adjusted their approach to accommodate the IAEs needs. Remarkably, however, cultural competence was not a result of training. None of the institutions developed specific programs for mentor cultural competence development. Instead, institutions selected mentors who (a) had prior experience or cultural roots in the Middle East, or (b) showed an openness to new ideas, flexibility, and curiosity.

Demonstrations of cultural competency sometimes came from unlikely places, such as faculty with no prior training or cross-cultural experience. For example, US Mentor 2 describes working with his Mentee (Mentee 2) and their discussions about gender and religion.

> *Author.* And you went to the Mosque with him.
> *US Mentor 2.* You heard about that. And it was very funny because we had made arrangements to get together and originally I said, "Let's go to my house and we'll show you traditional Christmas dinner." And he said, "No, no, no, you come to our house, and we'll do Christmas together." Okay fine. So we brought the food items and we were gonna finish things up, it was myself, my wife and my daughter and both my wife and my daughter are employed in the Lutheran church, and Mentee 2 looked at me and said, "Let's go to Mosque." And my wife and my daughter were excluded from that invitation. It was like okay, this is Christmas day this will be very different for me. And it really was. I learned a lot that day. It was the first opportunity that I had to witness, to observe a Muslim service, and it was very different.
> *Author.* Well, it speaks to a level of trust between you that I think reflects the spirit of the mentoring program, that you were in their home, they were in your home, they went to church with you, that you went to mosque with them. I mean, that's really a testament I think to what you were able to accomplish.
> *US Mentor 2.* I think most mentors should do it. It made the whole experience better for us. It was win–win.

US Mentor 2 was able to learn from Mentee 2 and vice versa, in part because of a commitment to openness, but also because of the presence of his own mentor, his wife, who transferred cultural competence through her work as a minister. In the following example, he expresses the need for counsel from a culturally competent mentor. He goes on to say that he frequently asked for guidance as issues arose for which he was poorly prepared to address.

> *US Mentor 2.* So my wife said, "These are things you've got to be aware of when you're dealing with [your mentee]." She was very good at bringing me up to speed. How important personal face is. That's a big, big deal, and I can damage that relationship if I wasn't careful.

US Mentors repeatedly spoke to the value of working with colleagues who had a deep understanding of Egyptian culture and Islam for advice, in addition to serving as mentors to the IAEs themselves.

Building a Community of Mentors (CoM)

The need for mentors for orientation, communication, and support was expressed repeatedly. One of the mentors who was involved in formal professional development workshops with the IAEs, suggested:

> I would have loved to have had just a before meeting to see the people that were involved, who are going to have that common contact, to be able to use them as resources, to maybe even call and chat about things, "Are you seeing this? Do you think—" it would have just been a great time to know who else was involved, I think. As far as ongoing meetings, I don't know how I feel about that, but certainly a before meeting would be of interest.

In some cases, communication was lacking between mentors on the same campus. In such cases, mentors were assigned roles, and did not even know who the other mentors were.

> I was talking to my person about some things and found out that one of the other mentors was talking—that we were repeating ourselves, and we could have just done that all at once, [so we suggested] having a meeting, periodically, of the mentors and the educators together, just to have kind of a lunch every three weeks or something, just so everyone's together—of the mentors and the educators.

Mentoring and Teaching

In addition to observations of instruction, many of the mentors engaged in explicit discussions about how career and technical education is delivered in US community colleges. For example, US Mentor 3, a plumbing faculty member, expressed how mentoring related to teaching methods, saying,

> US Mentor 3. Well, we met daily. Every morning he would come in about 20 minutes to the hour [and ask questions] from "What are we doing today?" through to questions he would have on, how I dealt with students, how I interacted with my students, which I think he found different. And it was very interesting early on, he would question me on my pedagogy. "When do you let a student struggle? Why do you let that student struggle? ... And he felt bad for the students":
> US Mentor 3. I want to go help [a US community college student]. If you really want to, but we shouldn't. Ivan needs to learn how to do that.

And if he struggles, he struggles. And we won't let him fall, we'll build a safety net for him, but he's got to struggle a little bit.

Author. Interesting. Did he talk much about how his shop works?

US Mentor 3. He did. He did relate some of the experiences, he compared and contrasted the shop space we have here compared to what he has back home. He has been giving some thought to how some of these technologies would fit into his shop, how he's going to develop his budget to be able to purchase some of the materials. And he feels in some ways overwhelmed, I think with the scope of the work that he sees down here versus what gets done in Egypt. I tell him he shouldn't. I tell him it's not going to be an overnight sensation, it's going to take him a long time, but you know, one small change per semester, will add up to large changes over the long run.

Discussions of teaching often became quite sophisticated as IAEs wrestled with methods of instruction and assessment and tried to conceptualize ways to import methods into technical institutes in Egypt. In one discussion, a US Mentor and IAE explored the nature of expertise and method of assessing it.

US Mentor 4. We did talk a lot about assessment, he was really interested in how I assessed a student's achievement ... As opposed to generalized testing, you know, that type of assessment, I would get the students into a lab atmosphere, where I could get closer, more one on one, and that's where we need to find out if they're actually capable of performing the tasks that they're going to need to perform. [And] he was wondering you know, like why did he get the grade that he got in my class, and that was part of the assessment.

Benefits of Mentoring

In the end, selection of individuals with a desire for learning about other cultures, patience in dealing with ambiguity, and expertise in the culture, or ability to lean on someone with that expertise, lead to deep relationships and development of shared understanding as expressed by US Mentor 5 who ended his interview by saying,

I really enjoyed this opportunity. I found Mentee 5 to be really receptive to the new ideas that he sees and he was willing to share, so it became a real communication back and forth. I felt that I was invited into their private lives into their home and you know, I wanted them to see how I live, the typical Midwesterner. I will miss him ... we are true friends.

This view was also expressed by US Mentor 4:

[My mentee] said to me last week—he said, "I want all your emails" and, of course, Facebook, "Because we will stay friends forever," and so I think that that gets to the heart of where you were going with all that. They are—they're giving out that. They are very thankful for the experience and thankful for the people that have been in their lives during this experience. I was pretty touched by that.

Mentoring Gone Awry

Over the two cycles of the program, there were cases in which the mentor–mentee relationship went very much awry. While the root causes in these instances were complicated, they speak to the care that must be taken in the selection and preparation of both participants and mentors. In one instance the mentor, a technical instructor, had no experience with international faculty and had not engaged in domestic mentoring either. The instructor was eager to engage in instructional settings—a major goal of the program—but failed to understand basic principles of mentoring, particularly the need to provide private and informal engagement opportunities. The lack of sufficient time and inability to engage informally left the IAE dissatisfied generally with the program overall, in spite of the fact that the program elements outside of mentoring were clearly in place institutionally. The opportunity to fully realize program aims was thus lost: the mentor relationship provides "glue" for related activities and grounds the overall program goals in a relationship of trust and openness. Breakdowns due to a lack of understanding of concepts might be resolved through mentor training and better communication regarding professional obligations in mentoring relationships.

In a second instance, a married male mentor with no international experience, little domestic mentoring experience, and no mentor training was assigned a divorced female a mentee. The formal elements of the relationships—observation of class, and transfer of technical elements of the program and curriculum—proceeded much as other mentoring relationships. However, the lack of understanding of Egyptian culture, Islam, and prior experience internationally led to a fear of informal relationship building that prevented meaningful development of trust and hindered full realization of learning outcomes. The faculty member expressed being "petrified" that he might do or say something that would be offensive, in spite of the fact that the participating female IAE expressed no concerns. Similar circumstances at other participating colleges, in which an internationally experienced male faculty member mentored a single female IAE and in which a female faculty mentor mentored a single male IAE, did not exhibit this challenge. Breakdowns due to lack of understanding of acceptable gender roles and interactions between genders could be mitigated through specific cultural competency training or assignment of mentors of same gender.

Finally, Beachtown Community College hosted IAEs in very different programs in year one (Hospitality/Administration) and year two (IT/HVAC). The program elements were substantially the same in each of the two years and included comparable housing situations, formal faculty professional development program participation, co-involvement with student activities relate to a parallel multinational CCID program, and the college leadership and program coordination. Two IAE participants were matched with mentors who had little prior experience and no cultural training. The participants themselves had low adaptability and disregard for program aims in favor of personal aims. The inability of mentors and mentees to adjust to *cultural dissonance* led to degradation of program satisfaction both on the part of IAE participants and the mentors.

One mentor in particular, who described himself as "an old country boy" with no international experience indicated frustration with many elements of the IAEs attitude and participation. He stated,

> *US Mentor 6.* It was all against his religion. He couldn't do it.
> *Author.* But in the formal course settings, was he an active participant?
> *US Mentor 6.* No, it seemed like he was more interested in whatever he could—like, obtain anything with his name on it. He was so adamant about his name. Everything had to have his full four names on it. Everything.
> *Author.* And so, you're frustrated. This wasn't a good experience for you at all.
> *US Mentor 6.* I will never do it again. Never.

US Mentor 6's experience was by far the most negative of all the mentors in the program. However, by the end of the interview, he conceded that he might consider mentoring an international faculty member again, if he is adequately prepared.

> It was just a rough one, I guess, for my first—[my supervisor] came to me he said "I'd like for you to do me a favor." And I first didn't want to do it. I said, "Nah, I don't think I'm capable." And he said "Yeah, you'll be fine." I have a really good rapport with the students, and it just didn't work out the way I wanted it to.

US Mentor 6 was willing to mentor, but doubted his ability. He was eager to "make a friend" from another culture, but ill-equipped to address complex issues leading to cultural dissonance between he and his mentee. His personal doubts and lack of formal preparation for this role are not uncommon. In fact, only a few of the mentors in the entire program were prepared to serve IAEs. Overwhelmingly, however, their collective spirit of giving, enthusiasm for teaching and for community college, and natural curiosities led to dramatic influence and life changing experiences.

US Mentor 7, a welding instructor at Midwest Grand, mentored a technical instructor from Egypt with very low English skills, in the first year of the program. US Mentor 7 had no prior international experience and, in many ways, had similar concerns to those of US Mentor 6. Unlike US Mentor 6 and his mentee, however, US Mentor 7 and his mentee developed an instant rapport and deep connection that led to dramatic progress toward program aims. US Mentor 7 had never been on an airplane, let alone out of the country, but accompanied a delegation on a follow-up visit to Egypt one year after his mentee returned. On a celebratory evening atop the Fulbright Commission office in Cairo, US Mentor 7 presented his mentee, who referred to US Mentor 7 as "his brother," with a flame painted welding mask in honor of their time together.

DISCUSSION

The purpose of this case study has been to explore the role of mentoring in developing quality international professional development opportunities in general, and more specifically, within the context of the US community college. Results suggest that, while the roles of mentoring vary, the importance of mentors is high for developmental progression of participants from reliance to self-directedness. In the presence of culturally competent mentors, participants in international professional development programs experience enhanced comfort, inquisitiveness, exploratory behavior, and learning outcomes (Treat 2010). In this study, the negative outcomes of lack of cultural competency also become apparent, as both the mentors and mentees experience severe frustration and lack of sense of worth in the relationship. On the other hand, culturally competent mentors provide transformational experiences in which enthusiasm, commitment, and friendships develop.

The mentoring relationships between IAEs and college faculty and staff established a foundation upon which program success could be built. In the best of cases, mentors provided both formal and informal guidance. At Puget Sound, where all of the IAEs initially were placed for intensive English as Second Language (ESL), two US mentors who were native to Middle East countries and fluent in Arabic provided considerable *cultural bridging* for IAEs. The guidance provided in the initial weeks of the program by these two mentors continued throughout the program, even as IAEs disbursed to other colleges.

The necessity of *cultural competence* was clearly visible in both successful mentoring relationships and those that were unsuccessful. While the mentors were universally respected and admired, many of the mentors took narrow approaches to their work—concentrating on teaching, learning, and technology at the expense of cultural, professional, and organizational mentoring. The institutions learned over time that out-of-classroom mentoring has great importance for the educators. Institutions recognized the need for specific mentor training in advance of international educators' arrival. A broad view of mentoring should be applied to all professional development programs, but has particular importance for international educators whose desire to learn extends far beyond the classroom. Such a view incorporates multiple roles (teacher, advisor, counselor, role model, cultural coach), varied support (institutional norms, rules, processes, curricula, access and openness, and help in documenting learning (Gaskin et al. 2003). In the case of international mentoring, prior cultural knowledge, flexibility, and patience are also traits that are needed. In one college, for example, two of the mentors were native speakers of Arabic and provided excellent "broad" mentoring to the benefit of educator satisfaction and learning.

A key finding in this study is the recognition that cultural competence can arise through informal means, given a propensity of the mentor to seek guidance. The *preconditions* for development of cultural competence can be found in faculty who lack cross-cultural experience, but who are open to new ideas, have excellent communications and team-building skills, flexibility, and patience, and who understand basic concepts of mentoring from prior experience in nonculturally different settings. Development of cultural skills are, however, extremely important and can be developed through access to *cultural guides* and norming/sharing activities in a *community of mentors* (CoM). This suggests a taxonomy of mentorship development that can include both formal and informal elements. Foremost in this taxonomy is selection of mentors whose openness, flexibility, and enthusiasm for new experiences will ensure capability for learning. Next, while formal training was not evident in this case, the desire by mentors for it clearly existed. Mentors want translatable mentoring skills, including deeper understanding of reciprocity in the relationship, recognizing time commitments and how to negotiate shared understanding of time, and developing broad concepts of learning, that incorporate in and out of classroom learning on both academic and nonacademic issues. Finally, training into culture, whether designed for formal or informal delivery, provides needed common threads for development of deeper mentoring and enhanced program outcomes.

Implications for Mentoring in International Professional Development Programs

The results of this study point to several factors for consideration in developing international professional development programs with mentoring components. These include:

- Affirmation of the importance of matching appropriate mentors and mentees
- Ongoing need for cultural competency training for mentors prior to mentee arrival
- Support requirements for mentor–mentee relationship
- Critical nature of mentor role in meeting program aims
- Policy and quality assurance in mentoring for international professional development

Culturally competent mentors are only one-half of the equation: building cultural competence in the participants in terms of readiness to accommodate program expectations and work with the mentor is also necessary. Preparing mentors–mentees includes both orientation to enhance readiness and matching of characteristics coupled with competency development.

Mentoring is a very effective means of development within international professional development programs. The connections gained through shared practice, common understanding and values, and creation of social network and cooperative activity and the ability of an individual to organize activity among teams or groups based on expertise or interest, underpinned by a shared sense of purpose. Mentors play a particularly important role in exposing mentees to experiences directly or through introductions/recommendations.

References

American Association of Colleges & Universities. (2015). *Intercultural knowledge and competence Value rubric.* http://www.aacu.org/value/rubrics/intercultural-knowledge

Cohen, Arthur M., & Cohen, Florence B. (2003). *The American community college.* San Francisco: Jossey-Bass.

Cohen, Donald, & Prusak, Laurence (2001). *In good company: How social capital makes organizations work.* Boston: Harvard Business School Press.

Community Colleges for International Development (CCID). (2015). http://ccidinc.org

Eddy, Pamela L. (2008). Changing the guard in community colleges: The role of leadership development. In Adrianna Kezar (Ed.), *Rethinking leadership in a complex, multicultural, and global environment: New concepts and models for higher education* (pp. 183–195). Sterling, VA: Stylus.

Ennis-Cole, Demetria L., & Lawhon, Tommie (2004). Teaching, technology, and support in the new millennium: A guide for new community college teachers. *Community College Journal of Research and Practice, 28,* 583–592.

Gaskin, Lynne P., Lumpkin, Angela, & Tennant, Keith L. (2003). Mentoring new faculty in higher education. *The Journal of Physical Education, Recreation and Dance, 74*(8), 49–54.

Hopkins, Ruth A., & Grigoriu, Elizabeth (2005). Mentoring community college faculty and staff: Balancing contradictions of informal program components and formal program structure. *Community College Review, 32*(4), 40–59.

Raby, Rosalind L. (2009). Defining the community college model. In Rosalind L. Raby & Edward J. Valeau (Eds.), *Community college models: Globalization and higher education reform* (pp. 3–19). Springer Science: Netherlands.

Reille, Audrey, & Kezar, Adrianna (2010). Balancing the pros and cons of community college "grow-your-own" leadership programs. *Community College Review, 38*(1), 59–81.

St. Clair, Karen L. (1994). Faculty to faculty mentoring in the community college: An instructional component of faculty development. *Community College Review, 22*(3), 23–35.

Treat, Tod (2010). Evaluating learning outcomes in an international professional development program. *Community College Journal of Research and Practice, 34*(1), 111–135.

Valeau, Edward J. (2009). The challenge of change: International adoption of community college models. In Rosalind L. Raby & Edward J.Valeau (Eds.), *Community college models: Globalization and higher education reform* (pp. 615–618). Springer Science: Netherlands.

VanDerLinden, Kim E. (2005). Learning to play the game: Professional development and mentoring. *Community College Journal of Research and Practice, 29,* 729–743.

Vega, William, Yglesias, Kenneth, & Murray, John (2010). Recruiting and mentoring minority faculty members. *New Directions for Community Colleges, 152,* 49–55.

Zunz, Sharyn J., & Oil, Karen R. (2009). A preliminary look at international students in MSW field placements at nonurban U.S. Campuses. *Journal of Social Work Education, 45*(1), 131–137.

CHAPTER 5

International Students' Struggles: Community College to the Rescue

Linda Serra Hagedorn, Shaohua Pei, and Lu Yan

INTRODUCTION

Each year the USA welcomes a large number of international students who enter the country with bright dreams of success and earning an American college degree. Although many will enroll in the country's most prestigious universities with confidence and high expectations of success, some will find the competitive atmosphere of American classrooms a challenging transition (Ramsay et al. 1999; Zhao et al. 2005). Some will be unprepared to live and learn in an all-English language environment, while others may encounter problematic cultural differences that interfere with their success. Some may encounter financial problems stemming in part from the higher cost of living in the USA as compared to their home countries. This chapter explores how international university students who initially started at four-year universities found assistance to these and other problems through the judicious use of community colleges.

L.S. Hagedorn (✉)
College of Human Sciences and School of Education,
Iowa State University, Ames, IA, USA

S. Pei • L. Yan
School of Education, Iowa State University, Ames, IA, USA

Background and Related Literature

International students suffer heavy pressures to maintain the good academic standing, necessary to keep their legal status as students in the US International students, as required by *the Student and Exchange Visitor Information System (SEVIS)* from the US government; *they* must maintain a cumulative 2.0 or higher grade point average (GPA) to maintain their F-1 student status visa in the USA. If grades fall below the acceptable level, they will be forced to return to their homelands (Hagedorn, 2014).

Some international students struggle with the American style of teaching that often includes critical analyses, working in groups, and independent thought. This style differs from the lecture-dominant and teacher-as-expert style more prevalent in most of their homelands (Poyrazli and Grahame 2007; Tran 2008). Asian students trained in the Confucian tradition that promotes harmony and consensuses often find it difficult to express their individual views, a practice that is typical in an American classroom. Some may be hesitant to ask questions, feeling that doing so will imply that they are inferior or not capable.

Culture

There is evidence that international students may be more stressed, anxious, and thus have a higher likelihood of becoming depressed compared to their native counterparts (Grey 2002). Many students come from cultures rich with shared aspirations with family. Although close familial ties typically bring comfort, they can also bring stress (Smith 1995). Some students may be studying in the USA not of their own choice but to honor family aspirations. This allegiance to family may also infiltrate the choice of major. In many countries especially Eastern Asia countries STEM majors bring more family pride than those in the humanities or arts, causing offspring to major in disciplines promoted by the family rather than to reflect personal desire or talents (Treiman 1977).

International students may encounter problems with social skills that are culturally rooted in their native countries (Ekman et al. 1987; Markus and Kitayama 1991; Russell 1994), and thus feel awkward and confused when trying to perform in group assignments.

Being far from home, international students may become homesick and some are unaccustomed to American food. In many colleges and universities, students cannot select their roommates (Smith-Barrow 2015) and may find themselves with others with very different eating habits and hygiene standards.

In short, many international students underestimate the culture shock that they will encounter when coming to the USA. They may have enjoyed the status of being top performing students in their home county and assume that this favorable status will follow them into their new adventure only to find themselves struggling both academically and culturally (Misara and Castillo 2004).

Language

For most international students language presents the most formidable barrier to academic success (Mori 2000). For this reason, international students may experience high levels of anxiety when facing oral presentations in classes, writing papers, reading articles, or preparing and taking essay tests (Grey 2002). Sandhu and Asrabadi (1991) explained that international students experience anxiety over their speaking accents, enunciation, and concerns regarding discipline-specific language. While there is ample evidence of the positive effects of intercultural friendship on improving international students' language proficiency (Gomez et al. 2014), generally speaking, native students may be unwilling and sometimes even hostile to providing assistance to international students to improve their language acquisition (Yeh and Inose 2003). Unfortunately, it is not just native students that may be less than sympathetic toward their language barriers; sometimes even the staff who work with international students may tire of dealing with students that are not as English proficient as they perceive necessary (Robertson et al. 2000).

Finances

Financial difficulties are often substantial concerns for international students. Although two-thirds of US undergraduate students pay their tuition with the assistance of federal grants (College Board 2014), 64.7 % of the international students rely solely on personal or family funds to pay their tuition costs (IIE 2014a, b), which is usually two-thirds higher than the in-state fee at public institutions. International students have very limited opportunities for scholarships or financial aid, and they are not eligible for any kind of federal student aid (Office of Student Federal Aid 2015). International students may be eligible for some student loans but only if they have a US citizen with an excellent credit history to co-sign; an almost impossible task for most students (International Financial Aid and Scholarship Search 2015). Many international students, like those from

China, come from middle-class families where their parents, grandparents, and other family members have sacrificed and saved to accrue sufficient funds to send their child abroad (Hu and Hagedorn 2013). Unfavorable monetary exchange rates may increase the cost of study even further. In spite of the limited funding resources, international students are required to be enrolled full time during their study (Lin and Yi 1997; Chin and Bhandari 2007), and can work only part time in on-campus authorized jobs (often difficult to get), thus restricting their opportunity to help support themselves while studying. Researchers have noted that some international students find themselves in financial dilemmas and may even be forced to choose between textbooks, food, or utility bills (Koyama 2010; Lee 2013).

THEORETICAL FRAMEWORK

In this chapter, we rely on the combination of Face Negotiation Theory and Identity Theory as guiding conceptual frameworks explaining why international university students may turn to community colleges for rescue and relief.

Face Negotiation Theory

The concept of face is related to honor, status, credibility, loyalty, competence, obligation, and respect (Ting-Toomey 1988). According to Ho (1994), face has three layers and they are related to the affective (related to shame and pride), the cognitive, and the behavioral. Although the concept of face is applicable to all cultures due to its universal relationship to self-esteem, pride, and self-worth (André 2013; Bargiela-Chiappini 2003; Mao 1994, Ho 1976; Zhang et al. 2014) people may frame and act upon face differently as determined by their cultures (Ting-toomey and Kurogi 1998).

Confronting academic difficulty or even the threat of academic dismissal can be devastating to international students. Similarly, financial difficulty that may threaten success will also bring the threat of losing face and positive identity. In many cultures, family honor overweighs individual will (Hu and Hagedorn 2013; Qian 2009; Stevenson 1992; Stevenson and Lee 1990). Failures must be borne not only by the student but also result in shame cast upon the entire family.

Identity Theory

Identity is deeply entwined with face (Mao 1994). Stryker and Burke (2000) and Burke & Sets (2009) defined identity as a set of meanings that standardizes individuals into different status and positions in society. Identity is activated through the process of self-verification. International students come to the USA with an emerging new identity as a successful college student working on a bright future. Most particularly for Asian and Hispanic students, identity is tied tightly to families and others who have provided the necessary supports that have allowed the student to come to the USA. Hence, identity is deeply entwined in a collectivist framework of family honor (Jetten et al. 2002) and dovetails tightly with the concept of face.

Dire situations evoke fear and a search for solutions. We propose that for some university students, turning to a community college for a course or for a semester or longer may be a viable option that can contribute to saving face and preserving a positive identity. This chapter will provide context and evidence of how students have utilized community colleges in various ways to respond to challenges and save face.

METHODS FOR GATHERING EVIDENCE

We approached this topic using an equal statues sequential mixed method design. Mixed methods, or a combination of both qualitative and quantitative inquiries, are believed to draw strengths and minimize some of the weaknesses of singular qualitative and quantitative methods (Johnson and Onwuegbuzie 2004). We first conducted qualitative interviews and used the findings to create a quantitative survey.

Guided by data from the Open Doors Study (Institute of International Education [IIE] 2014a) we began our sampling for the qualitative section by identifying universities with large numbers of international students that were also geographically close to community colleges that also had large numbers of international students. We requested interviews with admission officers in these institutions and were granted eight interviews. During the same time span, we also interviewed 18 international university students who had taken course(s) from the community colleges. This data was analyzed by the three co-authors using investigator triangulation (Denzin 1970).

We used the knowledge gained from our interviews to create a survey to more broadly gather information from university enrolled international students. A brief original online survey was emailed to all international undergraduate students at a large Midwestern University. The survey was designed to better understand the prevalence of their experiences taking courses at a community college as well as their general satisfaction with courses, faculty, and facilities of community colleges. The survey also allowed us to compare the assumptions and attitudes toward community colleges by both students who have taken community college courses and those who have not. Of the 365 usable surveys, 16 % of students had taken at least one community college course.

Descriptive analysis showed that students from over 50 countries took the survey, the top three origin countries were China (113 respondents, taking 33 % of the sample), India (78 respondents, taking 23 % of the sample,), and Malaysia (24 respondents, taking 7 % of the sample), followed by South Korea, Brazil, and Iran. The diversity of our sample mirrored that reflected by the Open Doors Data (International Institute of Education [IIE] 2014a, b).

We conducted a logistic regression to better understand the dichotomous variable of enrolling in a community college course (Agresti 2013). Using the independent variables of country of origin, university GPA, and time (in academic years) enrolled in the university, the equation was statistically significant (Chi-square = 21.76, df = 4, $p < .001$) and correctly sorted 83.7 % of the respondents. The findings indicated that students from China or Malaysia, with a lower university GPA and less time at the university were statistically more likely to enroll in a community college course. Among those who did enroll, the top reasons cited are presented in Table 5.1 (note students could choose more than one reason).

Overall, students reported moderately high levels of satisfaction with their community college enrollment. Table 5.2 provides the means and standard deviations of student ratings of satisfaction (1 = very unsatisfied to 5 = very satisfied).

Table 5.1 Top reasons for enrolling in a community college course

The course was offered during the summer	53.7 %
The course was less expensive than taking it at the university	53.7 %
I wanted to finish my degree earlier	31.5 %
The course was offered at a convenient time	25.9 %
I thought the course would be easier at the community college	24.1 %

Table 5.2 Means and standard deviations of satisfaction with community college enrollment

	Mean (s.d.)
Scheduling of classes	4.23 (0.89)
Course availability	4.18 (0.87)
Course difficulty	4.17 (0.94)
Class size	4.14 (1.02)
Quality of instruction	4.07 (0.91)
Access to computers	4.06 (1.17)
Personal Safety	4.03 (1.18)
Support from teachers	4.02 (1.06)
Costs	4.02 (1.00)
Registration for courses	4.00 (1.16)
Parking	3.79 (1.22)
Library	3.84 (1.14)

We were also interested in the attitudes and assumptions toward community colleges by those international students who had never taken a course at a community college. One out of five (21 %) indicated that they had considered taking a course at a community college. Although the majority of non-enrollers (79 %) acknowledged that the tuition is less at a community college, 45 % indicated that they felt that courses through a community college would be inferior to those offered at a university. In addition, 38.5 % indicated that they believed that community college faculty were less knowledgeable than university faculty.

RESCUES

We have identified seven basic issues encountered by international students and the resultant rescues that involved the use of community colleges. We have created vignettes that are representative of the problems cited and the use of the community college that can help alleviate the pressure. Each of these scenarios are based on our interviews with admission advisors and international university students and reinforced through our survey of international students.

Rescue One: Low Grades and the Threat of Academic Dismissal

If academically dismissed, international students will be forced to go back to their home countries and cast as a failure. While academic dismissal is most likely a distressing experience for all students, domestic or international, it is especially traumatic for international students. The stress of academic dismissal may be sufficient to evoke extreme depression and in some cases may even lead to suicide (Yang and Clum 1994). Simply put, this is a serious situation and the student who finds him/herself in this situation is in dire need of help (Wong 2013).

Of course, enrollment in a community college will not change grades but the generally smaller classes that may reflect more faculty attention can result in higher grades than those earned at a large university. Many of the university admission counselors indicated that they will recommend and in some cases actually direct students in academic difficulty to transfer to a community college when an international student is having severe academic problems. An academic advisor called it "a way to get back on track." Another advisor indicated that most of the students who transfer to the community college do manage to increase their GPA and ultimately transfer back to the university. An advisor from a university in a southern state indicated:

> These students tend to get more support in community colleges. For some international students this is the best answer. A semester or a year at a community college may allow them to develop academically as well as personally. I find that some students come to us very young. They have never been in a Western culture and just don't fit. They seem to be able to adjust easier at the smaller college.

Rescue Two: The "Bad" Course

It is common for all college students, both international and domestic, to be confronted with one course that seems impossible to pass. It may be that the course is required but the student has no interest in the subject. Or, it may be the method of teaching is one that does not work well for the learner. The course may have what seems to be unreasonable expectations. Or, from the standpoint of the student, the instructor is just not teaching in a way that promotes learning. The "bad" course could also be due to problems understanding the instructor. For example, it is not uncommon for American university students to report difficulties in understanding a professor or teaching assistant who speaks English with an accent. But for international students who struggle with the English language in general, add an unfamiliar accent and the lecture may be completely unintelligible.

Some international students will use the community college course as the rescue for that "bad course." The "bad course" problem was discussed by an admission advisor from a research university:

Certain majors require international students to take some courses like American history and American government. These students are intimidated by the rigors of the classes at <university> and the content is very different for them. Sometimes students think it would be easier to take it at the community college. Since <college name> offers it regularly, some students will enroll there.

The perspective from a university student was similar. Although this student ultimately decided against taking the course at a community college, she indicated that one course could stand out in memory as being exceptionally difficult and cause extreme stress. She related how she sought relief:

For me the hard course was Economics 101. There was so much reading. I asked about taking it at the community college, if it would be easier, you know or would the university be OK with it. But I decided to stay here and finish it. But I got a "C" and maybe I should have taken it at the community college. If I knew more about how I could take it at <college name> I would have done it. Now I know that other students have done that.

It is important to note that the authors do not want to indicate that courses at community colleges are less rigorous than the equivalent course at a university. However, these are stereotypes held by many. Key points to counter these stereotypes are to educate students and advisors that smaller classes at community colleges result in more faculty attention. Moreover, in that community colleges serve a more diverse student body, faculty are more accustomed to using a different variety of teaching methods.

Rescue Three: The Fear of Public Speaking (in English)

Fear of public speaking plagues many people (Slater et al. 2006). However, couple the natural reluctance to speak in public with the requirement that it be done in a foreign language in front of an audience of predominantly native speakers and many international students react with fear. Most universities have a public speaking course requirement, international students

fear the course and welcome a rescue from this uncomfortable requirement. We spoke to two creative students who used community college
courses to their advantage. In fact, we found that this fear of public speaking led to a network of knowledge of where to go to find relief. A somewhat popular response was to turn to a community college that offers
Speech as an online course offering.

We must also say that some universities have reacted to this rescue and
have established firm policies regarding the transfer of an online speech
course to fulfill the general education requirements. Some universities
refuse to accept the transfer credit for speech if it is being applied as a general education requirement and the course was taken online. A university
admission advisor reacted to this rescue:

> The online Speech course is problematic for us on a number of levels. We
> want these students to learn, not just tick off a requirement. We are work-
> ing with <community college name> about this issue. In their defense the
> students do have to give speeches, they do it online but it is just not the
> same.

Rescue Four: The Lure of the Internet

The ubiquity of online courses has impacted virtually all aspects of higher
education including international students. Although the F-1 visa regulations allow international students to take online courses they are limited
to only one course (3 credit hours) that can be counted toward a full
course of study per term. In other words, if an international undergraduate were to enroll for 4 courses (12 credits) in a single academic semester, only one online course could be counted toward full-time enrollment
status. In addition, some universities have specific rules on the number of
online courses that international students may take. With that said, the
online offerings of community colleges offer many advantages for students. As indicated in Rescue Three, taking a course online may be the
answer for that "difficult" course. But more often we found that university students signed up for community college online courses for convenience and savings in both costs and times. Especially appealing was
summer online courses that could be taken even though the student may
be out of the country thus allowing the student to go home for the summer and still be working on credits toward graduation. For international

students, any path to decrease the time to degree yields significant savings. For other students, taking summer courses and those online could translate into enrolling in one less course during the regular academic year and still graduating on time. This was viewed positively as it allowed the student to concentrate more fully on less courses. A junior student told us the following:

> I didn't want to waste the summer and not take some credits. The <university name> didn't have the courses online but <community college name> did. So, yes I did take the course.

The academic advisors rarely advised students to take online courses, but in virtually all cases acknowledged that students often did. In fact, several of the advisors clearly advised international students against online courses offered anywhere. A university advisor indicated, "I never advise international students to take an online course either here or any other college. International students get confused by online courses. They need the structure and the personal contact they get in regular face-to-face courses."

Rescue Five: The Need to Finish Quickly!

Benjamin Franklin is credited with the often-heard quote that "time is money." Indeed, the costs for a degree escalates for international students who find they must remain enrolled in college for longer than anticipated. As indicated earlier, for most international students the cost of an American degree is very high. Moreover, students and their families typically save and plan for the degree to take the traditional four years. International students and their families may not realize that while half of all bachelor's degree programs require the traditional 120 credits that can be completed in four years,[1] the other half of majors require a higher credit count (often 124 or 128 credits[2]); (Douglas-Gabriel, 2014; Johnson et al. 2009). It is a fact that in America many full-time college students take more than four years to complete a degree. This is so common that the US Department of Education tracks six-year graduation rates in addition to the traditional four years. The national non-profit organization Complete College America (2014) reports that only between 19 % and 36 %, depending on the type of institution, of four-year full-time college students will graduate in the traditional four years. For both domestic and international students, there are many reasons why a degree will take longer than anticipated including but not limited to the following:

- Need for remedial or less than college level courses
- Required course(s) not offered when needed
- Received inaccurate advisement from advisor or others
- Student choice of taking additional courses not required for the degree
- Addition of a study abroad experience or an internship (either required or optional)
- Need to retake failed or low-grade course(s)
- Transfer from another college or university

For international students, the need to take additional coursework in English as a Second Language or in an Intensive English program will add time to degree. Thus, it is not surprising that international students may take courses at a community college while co-enrolled at their university for the purpose of acceleration. Students may take a course at the community college that is not offered that semester at their university. Most universities offer a slim list of course offerings during the summer and hence taking a community college course during the summer term may make sense. Some students with a full load of university courses may add another course at the community college for pure acceleration.

While the advisors never recommended students take courses at a community college for the sole purpose of decreasing the time to degree, they did acknowledge that especially in the summer or in the case of a needed course was not being offered at a time the student needed it the community college presents a good alternative. Hence, this rescue, although not promoted by the university advisors, was important to the students who felt it enabled them to finish their degree before their financial support was depleted.

Rescue Six: Need for Help with English Language

Although all university students from non-English speaking countries have met at least the minimum acceptable score on the Test of English as a Foreign Language (TOEFL), International English Language Testing System (IELTS), or other required tests, in order to gain admission to the university, many to most students struggle with the English language. Students learn that it is very different to learn English in their home countries than to sit in class and listen to a college lecture, and to read college level texts and to interact with others solely in English.

Many community colleges have various programs that can assist students in need of assistance with English. While some community colleges offer academic English as a Second Language (ESL) programs that provide academic credit, others offer only an adult education program designed to assist the community who have problems with the English language. Some community colleges offer more extensive intensive English programs and others offer a combination of programs (Hagedorn and Li, in press). Most international university students cannot apply the credits from an ESL program for their degrees, and hence, there is no record of ESL enrollments from the perspective of the university. We were able to interview several university students enrolled in a community non-credit course. They all indicated that their biggest problem was understanding spoken English. They indicated no problems with understanding textbooks but it was lectures that seemed the most difficult. One student indicated:

> I have been in the US for two years and I am a sophomore. I come here to learn to understand English better and to have help. I can read English but it is hard to understand it. I come here for help.

Some of the advisors suggest to those international students having academic problems to take additional English instruction at the community college. Since in most non-credit community college English courses are free of charge, this rescue is one that is truly affordable.

Rescue Seven: Financial Savings

Throughout this chapter, we have identified many reasons why university international students enroll for a course or a full load at a local community college. However, in almost all cases, students had several intersecting reasons that brought advantages to enrolling in a community college. While not always the chief motivator, but typically among the mix of reasons, students and advisors cited financial benefits when referring to community college enrollments. International students understood that there could be significant savings to the bottom line of their degree if they took advantage of community college offerings. As indicated earlier, any process that could accelerate or decrease the time to degree saves money.

When citing the reasons for taking courses with a community college virtually all students indicated that the reason they could do it was the low costs involved. A student from China said it very clearly:

> Yes. I was very happy when I needed to take a government course it was at the community college and at a cheap cost. I told my parents that I needed money for this course so I could graduate and they paid for it.

Conclusion

All over the world, young people and their parents are making plans to attend prestigious US universities. However, not all of these students will be able to attend their "dream universities." In fact, for any number of reasons, a significant number will come to the USA to attend one of the country's community colleges. In addition, many international students who enrolled in universities will find their way to a community college when academic or other problems arise. Most international students do not understand the mission of community colleges when they first come to the USA since there are typically no parallels in their home countries. But through word of mouth and by recommendations of their advisors, some students will find these institutions to seek assistance, save face, and find a welcome rescue.

Notes

1. 120 credits are easily achieved with an average credit load of 15 units each semester for four years. However, most students will enroll for more than 120 hours if they need to take any kind of prerequisite or developmental or remedial course.
2. 2% of the degree programs require 140 credits or more (Johnson et al. 2009).

References

Agresti, Alan (2013). *Categorical data analysis*. New York: Wiley.
André, James St. (2013). How the Chinese lost 'face'. *Journal of Pragmatics, 55*, 68–85.

Bargiela-Chiappini, Francesca (2003). Face and politeness: New (insights) for old (concepts). *Journal of Pragmatics, 35*, 1453–1469.

Burke, Peter J., & Stets, Jan E. (2009). *Identity theory.* New York: Oxford University Press.

Chin, H. K. K., & Bhandari, R. (2007). *Open doors 2006: Report on international educational exchange.* New York: Institute of International Education.

College Board. (2014). *Trends in college pricing.* http://trends.collegeboard.org/college-pricing

Complete College America. (2014). *4-year Myth. Make college more affordable.* http://completecollege.org/wp-content/uploads/2014/11/4-Year-Myth.pdf

Denzin, Norman K. (1970). *The research act in sociology: A theoretical introduction to sociological methods.* London: Butterworths.

Douglas-Gabriel, Danielle (2014, December 2). *Why so many students are spending six years getting a college degree [Web log post].* http://www.washingtonpost.com/blogs/wonkblog/wp/2014/12/02/why-so-many-students-are-spending-six-years-getting-a-college-degree/

Ekman, Paul, Friesen, Wallace M., O'Sullivan, Maureen A., Chan, Anthony I., Diacoyanni-Tarlatzis, Irene K., Heider, Karl A., et al. (1987). Universals and cultural differences in the judgments of facial expressions of emotion. *Journal of Personality and Social Psychology, 53*, 712–717.

Gomez, A. Edwin, Urzua, Alfonso, & Glass, Chris (2014). International student adjustment to college: Social networks, acculturation and leisure. *Journal of Park and Recreation Administration, 32*, 7–25.

Grey, Marianne (2002). Drawing with difference: Challenges faced by international students in an undergraduate business degree. *Teaching in Higher Education, 7*, 153–166.

Hagedorn, Linda S. (December 2014). *International students from China: Motivations, challenges, and U.S. admission policies.* Paper Presented at the Annual Meeting of Iowa Educational Research and Evaluation Association, Ames, IA.

Ho, David Yau-fai (1976). On the concept of face. *American Journal of Sociology, 81*, 867–884. http://www.jstor.org/stable/2777600?seq=1#page_scan_tab_contents

Ho, D. Y. F. (1994). Face dynamics: From conceptualization to measurement. In Ting-Toomey, S. (Ed.), *The Challenge of Facework*, 269–286. New York: SUNY Press.

Hu, Jiayi, & Hagedorn, Linda S. (2013). Earning American college credits in China: New model of transfer college credit programs. *Journal of Interdisciplinary Studies in Education, 2*, 4–17.

Institute of International Education. (2014a). Community college data resource: International students: Top 40 host institutions. *Open Doors Data: Special Reports.* http://www.iie.org/Research-and-Publications/Open-Doors/Data/Community-College-Data-Resource/International-Students/International-Students-Top-Host-Institutions-2013-14

Institute of International Education. (2014b). *Open doors data: Fast facts 2014* [Data file]. http://www.iie.org/Research-and-Publications/Open-Doors/Data/Fast-Facts

International Financial Aid and Scholarship Search. (2015). *International student loans* [Data file]. http://www.iefa.org/international-student-loans. International students. *Journal of Counseling & Development, 78*, 137–144.

Jetten, Jolanda, Postmes, Tom, & McAuliffe, Brendan J. (2002). 'We're all individuals': Group norms of individualism and collectivism, levels of identification and identity threat. *European Journal of Social Psychology, 32*, 189–207.

Johnson, R. Burke, & Onwuegbuzie, Anthony J. (2004). Mixed methods research: A research paradigm whose time has come. *Educational Researcher, 33*, 14–26.

Johnson, L. Nate, Reldy, Leonard M., Droll, Mike, & LeMon, R. E. (2009). *Program requirements for associate's and bachelor's degrees: A national survey.* Complete College America. https://www.insidehighered.com/sites/default/server_files/files/Program%20Requirements%20-%20A%20National%20Survey%281%29.pdf

Koyama, Miki (2010). The collective voices of Asian international doctoral students in counseling psychology in the U.S.: Recommendations for faculty and training programs. *Dissertation Abstracts International Section A, 70.* (AAT 3392150).

Lee, Kin Cheung (2013). Training and educating international students in professional psychology: What graduate programs should know. *Training and Education in Professional Psychology, 7*, 61–69.

Lin, Jun-Chi G., & Yi, Jenny (1997). Asian international students' adjustment: Issues and program suggestions. *College Student Journal, 31*, 473–479.

Mao, Luming Robert (1994). Beyond politeness theory: 'Face' revisited and renewed. *Journal of pragmatics, 21*, 451–486.

Markus, Hazel R., & Kitayama, Shinobu (1991). Culture and the self: Implications for cognition, emotion, and motivation. *Psychological Review, 98*, 224–253.

Misara, Ranjita, & Castillo, Linda G. (2004). Academic stress among college students: Comparison of American and international students. *International Journal of Stress Management, 11*, 132–148. doi:http://dx.doi.org/10.1037/1072-5245.11.2.132

Mori, Sakurako Chako (2000). Addressing the mental health concerns of international students. *Journal of Counseling & Development, 78*, 137–144.

Office of Student Federal Aid. (2015). *Who gets aid [Data file].* https://studentaid.ed.gov/eligibility#basic-criteria

Poyrazli, S., & Grahame, K. M. (2007). Barriers to adjustment: Needs of international students within a semi-urban campus community. *Journal of Instructional Psychology, 34*(1), 28–45.

Qian, Nancy (2009). *Quantity-quality and the One Child Policy: The only-child disadvantage in school enrollment in rural China.* National Bureau of Economic Research [Data file]. http://www.nber.org/papers/w14973

Ramsay, Sheryl M., Barker, Michelle, & Jones, Elizabeth (1999). Academic adjustment and learning processes: A comparison of international and local students in first-year university. *Higher Education Research & Development, 18*, 129–144.

Robertson, M., Line, M., Jones, S., & Thomas, S. (2000). International students, learning environments and perceptions: A case study using the Delphi technique. *Higher Education Research and Development,* 19(1), 89–102.

Russell, James A. (1994). Is there universal recognition of emotion from facial expressions? A review of the cross-cultural studies. *Psychological Bulletin, 115*, 102–141.

Sandhu, Daya Singh, & Asrabadi, Badiolah Rostami (1991). *An assessment of psychological needs of international students: Implications for counseling and psychotherapy.* ERIC database. (ED350550).

Slater, Mel, Pertaub, David-Paul, Barker, Chris, & Clark, David (2006). An experimental study on fear of public speaking using virtual environment. *Cyber Psychology & Behavior, 9*, 627–633.

Smith, A. D. (1995). The formation of national identity. In Harries Henry (Ed), *Identity* (pp. 130 -131). Oxford: Clarendon Press.

Smith-Barrow, Delece (2015, March 3). 10 national universities where students usually live on campus. *U.S News Education.* http://www.usnews.com/education-tion/best-colleges/the-short-list-college/articles/2015/03/03/10-national-universities-where-students-usually-live-on-campus

Stevenson, Harold W. (1992, December). Learning from Asian schools. *Scientific Americans,* 267(6): 70–76.

Stevenson, Harold W., Lee, Shin Yin, Chen, Chaunsheng, Stigler, James W., Hsu, Chen-Chin, Kitamura, Seiro, & Hatano, Giyoo (1990). Contexts of achievement: A study of American, Chinese, and Japanese children. *Monograph of the Society for Research in Child Development, 55*, i+iii–vi+1–119.

Stryker, S., & Burke, P. J. (2000). The past, present, and future of an identity theory. *Social Psychology Quarterly,* 284–297.

Ting-Toomey, Stella (1988). Intercultural conflict styles: A face-negotiation theory. In Y. Y. Kim & W. Gudykunst (Eds.), *Theories in intercultural communication.* Newbury Park, CA: Sage.

Ting-Toomey, Stella, & Kurogi, Atsuko (1998). Facework competence in intercultural conflict: An updated face-negotiation theory. *International Journal of Intercultural Relations, 22*, 187–225.

Tran, Ly Thi (2008). Unpacking academic practices: International students in management and education disciplines in Australian higher education. *Higher Education Research and Development, 27*, 245–256.

Treiman, Donald J. (1977). *Occupational prestige in comparative perspective.* New York: Academic Press.

Wong, Paul T. P. (2013). Suicide risks among college students from diverse cultural backgrounds. *Directions in Psychiatry, 33,* 237–249.

Yang, Bin, & Clum, George (1994). Life stress, social support, and problem-solving skills predictive of depressive symptoms, hopelessness, and suicide ideation in an Asian student population: A test of a model. *Suicide and Life-Threatening Behavior, 24,* 127–139.

Yeh, M. Christine, & Inose, Mayuko (2003). International students' reported English fluency, social support satisfaction, and social connectedness as predictors of acculturative stress. *Counseling Psychology Quarterly, 16,* 15–28.

Zhang, Qin, Ting-Toomey, Stella, & Oetzel, John (2014). Linking emotion to the conflict face-negotiation theory: A US-China investigation of the mediating effects of anger, compassion, and guilt in interpersonal conflict. *Human Communication Research, 40,* 373–395.

Zhao, G. Chun-Mei, Kuh, George, & Carini, Robert (2005). A comparison of international students and American student engagement in effective educational practices. *The Journal of Higher Education, 76,* 209–231.

CHAPTER 6

International Students Immigrating to the Title IX Environment: A Qualitative Cultural Analysis of Community College International Students

Leah P. Hollis and Russell A. Davis

INTRODUCTION

International students bring their respective cultures and expectations to the USA; these expectations include their social constructs regarding relationships and the treatment of women. *International Business Times* reported alarming percentages of rape in several foreign countries. In South Africa, 28–37 % of adult men reportedly committed rape (Iaccino 2014). Sweden reported the highest European rape percentage with 63 rape cases per 100,000. In turn, a third of Swedish women endure sexual assault before their 20th birthday. Caribbean countries reported comparable data with approximately 48 % of adolescent girls facing sexual assault (Iaccino 2014). In regard to Asian countries, the United Nations revealed that 10 % of Asian Pacific men reported forced sex with a non-partner and 24 % reported forced sex with a partner.

L.P. Hollis (✉)
Community College Leadership Program, Morgan State University,
Baltimore, MD, USA

R.A. Davis
Community College Leadership Program, Morgan State University, Baltimore,
MD, USA

© The Editor(s) (if applicable) and The Author(s) 2016   75
R.L. Raby, E.J. Valeau (eds.), *International Education at
Community Colleges*, DOI 10.1057/978-1-137-53336-4_6

In Papua New Guinea, 59 % of men reported raping sexual partners (Fossett 2013). While these statistics may startle the American reader, these incidents are an unfortunate social norm for many global citizens.

Simultaneously, the USA remains a coveted place to seek an education. Given the potential cultural clash between the global mistreatment of women and American federal regulations prohibiting sexual assault, colleges and universities from all sectors have a responsibility to offer education thorough Title IX. Specifically, community colleges within the higher education arena have the responsibility to educate those with different cultural expectations that sexual violence against women is strictly prohibited. Therefore, this study's purpose focused on international students' experience and understanding Title IX at the community college.

LITERATURE REVIEW

Title IX and Sexual Violence

In 1972, the federal government enacted Title IX, a regulation for federally funded educational programs and activities to protect individuals from discrimination based on sex. During the 40-plus-year period since the legislation was passed, higher education has made inconsistent application of Title IX to campus culture. Typically, articles reflecting on Title IX benchmarks (Boyce 2002; Pauline 2012) focused on women's access to sports. Most researchers who focused on Title IX lawsuits examined the application of Title IX legislation and compliance with Title IX primarily in relation to sports opportunities and the threat to men's sports teams (Greendorfer 1998; Staurowsky 2003; Haglund 2005; Messner 2006; Edwards 2010).

However, MacKinnon's work (1979) explicitly linked sexual harassment to sex discrimination which not only changed the Supreme Court's interpretation of Title VII legislation, as shown in MacKinnon's work (1979), but it also changed the interpretation of Title IX language. If a student faced "unwelcomed conduct of a sexual nature ... " that compromised the student's access to educational opportunities, a Title IX violation potentially existed (US Department of Education 2011). Despite the link between Title IX and sexual harassment, several lawsuits blurred the connection between sexual abuse and Title IX.

For example, in the late 1990s *Wills v. Brown University, 184 F. 3d 20 – Court of Appeals*, Wills charged that her tutor, Adesogan, assaulted her. However,

Despite Wills's arguments ... the court took the position that absent a second physical assault by Adesogan on Wills ... Wills had no claim for sex discrimination against Brown occurring after December 9, 1992. In taking that narrow view of hostile environment discrimination, the district court failed to recognize that Wills's educational experiences at Brown could be altered significantly by a hostile educational environment resulting from Adesogan's assault on her and his continuing presence in the classroom (*Wills v. Brown University* 1999, p. 9/17).

In short, while the single assault was undisputed, the court believed that Wills had to endure a second assault to prevail in her Title IX charge. Further, the court denied Wills' motions to appeal the decision.

In *Brzonkala v. VA Polytechnic Institute* 1997, Brzonkala who was raped by two football players during her first semester had to extend her fight by appealing a lower court's decision. In the university's process, the assailants, Morrison and Crawford, were not found responsible for rape. Instead, they were found responsible for abusive language and suspended from the next year. The district court denied Brzonkala's Title IX charge at the appeal where the defendant argued:

[T]he hostile environment that Brzonkala alleged never occurred. Brzonkala left [Virginia Tech] due to her concern of possible future reprisal in reaction to her pressing charges. She did not allege that this future reprisal actually occurred (*Brzonkala v. VA Polytechnic Institute* 1997, p. 7/24).

In the initial trial, VA Polytechnic Institute successfully argued that Brzonkala leaving school nullified her claim of an ongoing problem. The University settled with Brzonkala in 2000 for an undisclosed amount.

In *Williams v. Board of Regents of Univ. System of Ga.*, 477 F. 3d 1282 – *Court of Appeals, 11th Circuit 2007*, Williams claimed that she was gang raped by three basketball players: Cole, Grant, and Thomas, and a football player: Williams. She appealed the original district court decision that denied her Title IX claims. The University of Georgia stated that student-on-student harassment required for the federally funded institution to have prior knowledge of the assailants' history. The court's opinion stated:

Therefore, we will not hold a funding recipient [the University of Georgia] liable solely because a person affiliated with the funding recipient discriminated against or harassed the plaintiff ... the discrimination must be "so severe, pervasive, and objectively offensive that it effectively bars the victim's access to an educational benefit" (*Williams v. Board of Regents of Univ. System of Ga.* 2007, p. 5/14).

The appeal upheld the district court's decision that William's case lacked standing, as she no longer attended the University of Georgia. In 2007, five years after the incident, the University of Georgia and Williams settled for an undisclosed six-figure amount.

The aforementioned lawsuits confirmed a history in which a "hostile environment" and institutional culpability presented extensive challenges for Title IX complainants invoking the prohibition for sexual violence language. Cases that ruled that a single instance of sexual assault did not invoke Title IX protections sent a message to institutions and women that prevailing in a Title IX case regarding sexual violence was a Herculean task.

In 2011, the White House issued the "Dear Colleague Letter" which reiterated the Title IX application to sexual assault, violence, abuse, and coercion. Student-on-student, employee-on-student, and third-party-on-student sexual violence were subject to the Office of Civil Rights' investigations. In 2014, the Office of Civil Rights reiterated its commitment to preventing sexual violence and proceeded with unprecedented transparency by providing a list of 55 colleges and universities under investigation for sexual violence.

Regardless of any school's readiness, the Office of Civil Rights required that each campus have a Title IX coordinator. Further, grievance procedures should be published and distributed to the campus community that includes how to report violations, the student's right to file a criminal complaint, possible remedies, support for the student, and potential sanctions for the perpetrator (US Department of Education 2014).

International Students Immigrating to Shifting American Culture

The Institute of International Education in partnership with the Bureau of Educational and Cultural Affairs reported an 8.1 % increase in international students' matriculation to American higher education in 2014 (United States Department of Education 2014). According to Ruiz (2010), more community colleges have turned their attention to the recruitment and retention of international students. While college campuses benefit from the diversity accompanying a student body with a global perspective, international students also bring challenges to the community college that emerge from cultural differences and language barriers.

International students face a convoluted learning curve. While learning their academic discipline, they also must learn the culture to which they have migrated. Within this context, international students face subtle discrimination and harassment (Ee 2013). Due to language barriers and cultural differences, they might not even understand the nuances, threats, or insults levied against them (Ee 2013). Additionally, they may be less likely to fully comprehend a cursory description of policies or procedures on campus.

Further, international students in general focus on their primary goal to stay in the USA. Their privilege to study in the USA is based on remaining in good academic standing. They often do not wish to be dissuaded from this focus, or may not realize that sexual or domestic violence is a reportable crime (Joshi et al. 2013). Some might avoid reporting violence for fear of deportation (Bauer et al. 2000).

Joshi et al. (2013) conducted a study of six international student coordinators who agreed to a 20-minute interview. The qualitative study revealed that international coordinators had little contact with international students regarding domestic or sexual violence. While many coordinators believed proper counseling referrals were important for international students, coordinators also admittedly avoided discussions on domestic violence. They believed that international students would not attend the orientation if programs advertised any sexual violence content. While this was a study of university coordinators, it provides insight to attitudes of the two-year international student coordinator.

Other studies confirm that international students may have substantial difficulty in developing appropriate interpersonal and intimate relationships. Popadiuk and Arthur (2004) specifically considered the experiences of Canadian women in forming intimate relationships. D'Abreua and Krahe chronicled how sexual scripts and aggression influence male Brazilian college students (2014). When international students harbor incomplete or misguided information about interacting with the opposite sex, they may become more vulnerable within intimate relationships. International students, however, found support in clear communication with faculty (Liberman 1994).

A 2013 doctoral study, Shenoy (2013) examined international students' knowledge regarding community college and their decision making process. In this study, many international students dreamt of earning an American education; they relied on family members community college information. Specifically, Shenoy (2013) confirmed that international students choose a community college because of a single person's recommendation, "the person whom they trusted and helped them get to the school..." (p. 96).

Another critical finding was that international students trusted the information the community colleges offered online (Shenoy 2013). International students respected official documents with the institutions' seal as a credible source. Further, the Shenoy study revealed that international students "did not understand placement tests, remedial classes, and the transfer processes" (p. 136). Despite their commitment to being informed, international students had inadequate, inaccessible or inaccurate information regarding the community college; in turn, Title IX policies fall in the same scope of compromised information.

THEORETICAL FRAMEWORK

Some researchers considered culture as an indication of organizational climate, practice and values (Schein 1997; Deverell and Olsson 2010). Cultural expectations consolidated, confronted, or changed the prevailing wisdom of an organizational community. As a result, individuals developed an environment that reflected the organization's values. Also, these organizational values were pinned to cultural and institutional hierarchy. In turn, the culture and respective values influence organizational efficiency (Schein 1997).

Based on external or internal pressures, such as changing personnel, shifting market conditions or new legislation, leaders may strive to manipulate organizational culture by establishing new traditions (Lucas and Kline 2008). Therefore, the responsibility to embrace Title IX policy and apply to students within the culture emerges from the campus leadership. Cultural changes implemented by leadership can explicitly embrace new policy implementation and weave the new practice into the organizational culture. In converse, leadership can diminish application of such changes to their organizational climate.

Nonetheless, these new obligatory practices will inform the organizational knowledge distribution, interaction, protest, and compliance throughout the institution. Theoretically, when certain practices or policies are implemented and embraced, they will create a cultural code. Any idea, concept, or procedures that leadership deems as "important" would then be woven into the norms and practices. While leadership typically sets the tone for the culture, the community can decide to accept, reject, or stand apathetic to changes (Addy 1995).

Within an American campus culture, international students grapple with American social norms and its impact on the organizational culture. Further, they strive to learn the application of policy and procedures and learn such from the campus community. Despite their unique position, international students are still expected to acquiesce and understand given their sheer presence in the culture (Hobbes 1982). Leadership sets the tone for when the culture is modified. In this regard, when a college provides only a cursory introduction to important policies, such as Title IX, students struggling to enter the campus culture will experience a limited understanding of emerging cultural changes. If international students are on the periphery and a critical policy is also on the periphery, a reasonable person could surmise that the policy will lack importance. Subsequently, the policy would not be integrated into the social norms for students, especially those on the margins. In short, when leadership is lax about establishing a culture to prohibit sexual violence, the culture often follows the lax norms set by leadership.

Problem Statement

Since the inception of the 2011 "Dear Colleague Letter," American higher education has faced increased scrutiny regarding its compliance with the existing language prohibiting sexual violence in the Title IX legislation (US Department of Education 2011). During, May 2014, 55 post-secondary institutions were under federal investigation regarding sexual violence, including one community college. In June 2015, 111 post-secondary institutions were under federal investigation regarding sexual violence; three of which were community colleges (Kingkade 2015).

The general problem is that community colleges are often absent from discussions regarding the impact of Title IX education on the 12.8 million students who were enrolled in community colleges in 2012. Discussions about sexual assault on campus have primarily focused on four-year schools (Anderson 2015). More specifically, 7 % or 896,000 of those community college students are not US citizens (American Association of Community Colleges, [AACC] 2014). However, recent discussions appear to highlight interventions for four-year schools and student-athletes, yet precious little information has emerged about the requirement to provide the required Title IX education for community college students or its more vulnerable subset of international students. Typically, the discussion on Title IX has been about women's access to educational opportunities in sports. Therefore, given the increase in international student enrollment, as confirmed by the AACC, and the heightened awareness of sexual assault cases as confirmed by the US Department of Education on account of unprecedented transparency on sexual assault investigations, logically, community colleges should have an enhanced commitment to educating the burgeoning international student population.

Purpose Statement

The purpose of this study was to explore the lived experiences of 10 international community college students regarding Title IX education on their respective campuses. This study also explored international students' understanding of Title IX legislation and its language prohibiting sexual violence. Such information may provide insight to community college leadership on best practices for educating international students about Title IX and its language prohibiting sexual assault.

Central Research Question

As the literature review confirmed, international students may experience difficulty in adjusting to American college culture, a culture that has intermittent support for protecting women against sexual violence. Hence, the central research question for this study was:

- How do community colleges educate international students entering American culture about Title IX and sexual violence?

Further, the study utilized the following sub-questions:

- What understanding do international students currently enrolled at community colleges have regarding Title IX's language about sexual violence?
- How does this understanding of Title IX govern their behavior?

RESEARCH METHODS

Research Sample

The sample for this study comprised a total of 10 international students: three men and seven women. Participants' time in the USA ranged from one academic term to five years. All participants were traditional-aged students born after 1990. They represented a cross-section of the global population representing Vietnam, Jamaica, Brazil, India, Germany, Liberia, Iran, Mexico, and Puerto Rico.

Qualitative research experts have offered guidance regarding sample size in qualitative research data collection. Ritchie et al. (2003) commented that the sample size in any qualitative study ought to be fewer than 50 participants. With regard to phenomenological studies, Creswell (1998) stated that at least five participants are required, while Morse (1994) Morse and Mason argued that at least six participants are required. Despite the range of acceptable sample sizes, the aforementioned qualitative research experts found that a sample size of 10 in a phenomenological study is viable and can support a saturation of data from which salient themes can emerge.

Limitations

Researchers of this study discovered that trust was a major component in recruiting international students. The typical incentives such as gift cards or food violated students' visas and could not be used to encourage student participation. Therefore, researchers were limited to their informal network of community college colleagues to contact international students.

Reliability and Validity

According to Creswell (2014), the researchers' maturity and experience contribute to study method reliability. Both researchers in this study had prior experience conducting qualitative research. Both researchers also serve as doctoral faculty and work directly with doctoral students in developing qualitative primary research.

The researchers worked as a team, coding data separately, then communicated their respective conclusions and emerging common themes. This crosscheck method "compares results that are independently derived" (Creswell 2014, p. 203). Seasoned researchers independently coding and then communicating a result before reporting the findings helps to strengthen validity.

Data Collection and Data Analysis

Researchers of this study designed a qualitative phenomenological method that explored the lived experiences of ten international students from nine different countries in winter of 2015. Researchers interviewed participants individually, in person or via Skype. All participants reviewed and signed an informed consent form prior to the interview. They were also advised verbally that their participation was voluntary and that they could withdraw from the study at any time. For all participants, English was not their primary language. While their English skills were strong, many struggled to translate thoughts specifically about sexual topics from their native language to English. Each interview lasted approximately ten minutes.

Once the researchers completed the data collection process, each researcher, in a separate process, analyzed and coded the notes for keywords and emerging themes. Individually, researchers determined themes and later convened to review notes and discuss their final thoughts regarding the emerging themes. The analysis not only included a review of themes from each question, the researchers also considered participants' awkward body language and drifting eye contact.

FINDINGS

The research proposed a central research question and two sub-questions. The respective findings from the sample in the form of emerging themes are presented next:

- How do community colleges educate international students entering American culture about Title IX and sexual violence?

Based on the responses of 10 international students, community colleges were not educating international students about Title IX. The central emerging theme from the interviews was that international students did not know about Title IX. They had never seen the policy or talked to anyone at the community college about the policy (see Table 6.1).

The interviewers also considered the following sub-questions

- What understanding do international students currently enrolled at community colleges have regarding Title IX's language about sexual violence?
- How does this understanding of Title IX govern their behavior?

International students revealed that they did not understand Title IX and its protection for students against sexual violence. In addition to not knowing about Title IX, international students' consistent reluctance to discuss relationships, sex, or violence was a second emerging theme. Many students hesitated when researchers introduced the term "sexual violence" in a question at the midpoint of the interview.

Question 5 of the interview asked, "What was your reaction to the news on sexual violence against women?" Students responded with drifting eye contact, fidgeting body language, and denying that they had heard such news reports. Three students were desensitized to the problem and commented sexual violence occurs regularly in their home country. None considered any of the news on sexual violence in relation to their respective community college settings (see Table 6.2).

In addressing the second sub-question, the aforementioned responses revealed a third theme that Title IX did not govern international students' campus behavior. International students in this study were unaware of any policies or procedures regarding sexual violence on the community college campus. In short, beyond lacking understanding, they also did not

Table 6.1 Question: Are you familiar with Title IX ? If so, how?

Response	"Do you mean I-9?"
Response	"I spent so much time on my visa, I didn't think about anything else..."
Response	"No, never heard of it."

Table 6.2 Question: What was your reaction to the news on sexual violence against women?

Response	"I don't watch the news—I don't see it."
Response	"I don't have TV."
Response	"Sex is on TV shows all the time."

Table 6.3 Question: What is your response to sexual violence in your home [native] community?

Response	"It just happens all the time at home."
Response	"I don't think about it at home...ah...ah I just don't think about it."
Response	"Women don't have a voice at home."

know their respective Title IX coordinators, how to report sexual assault, or their rights as students under Title IX.

A fourth theme revealed that students were unfamiliar with such protections for women and unaware of any procedures or processes for them in the event of sexual violence. Cultural nuances appeared to be part of the equation as some were desensitized based on experiences from their home communities (see Table 6.3).

A fifth theme showed that international students' culturally informed expectations also assigned blame on the victim of sexual assault. Regardless of gender, age, field of study, or country of origin, international students believed that the woman was primarily responsible for avoiding sexual violence. While they did not know about policies or protections, international students did think women needed to avoid situations that lead to sexual violence, or isolate themselves from the possibility of creating a situation that leads to sexual violence (see Table 6.4). Despite their youth, the participants aligned with more traditional beliefs about women and sexual violence. Their comments echoed patriarchal systems in which the women were primarily responsible to avoid sexual abuse. They did not consider a joint responsibility for women and men to avoid sexual violence.

These interviews suggested that international students emerged from patriarchal paradigms, which left women solely responsible for avoiding sexual assault. While all of the participants were in their early 20s, both genders echoed the sexist language heard in the USA during the 1950s and 1960s. In turn, educational leadership is tasked with bridg-

Table 6.4 Question: What is the responsibility of both men and women to avoid sexual violence?

Response	"Women need to protect themselves."
Response	"Women should be careful not to send mixed messages."
Response	"Can't avoid the situation, be yourself. It's someone's choice if they want to do that. It depends on their mind. I'm just not that kind of person."

ing the cultural gap between the social mores from which international students emerge, and the inclusive environments sought for American education.

DISCUSSION

Burns (1998) suggested that cultural shifts occur over centuries not decades. As applied to Title IX, US legislation on Title IX appeared in 1972. The 40 years since the passage of Title IX shows a painful history where even a single incident of rape or assault did not qualify as creating a hostile environment or jeopardizing the educational environment.

Since the needed clarity in the 2011 Dear Colleague Letter, colleges and universities must reconsider the application of the sexual violence language in the legislation. Hence, the culture is still shifting to fully educate campus citizens regarding the Title IX and its language prohibiting sexual violence. Further, as community college leadership guides the organizational culture of their respective institutions, they also need to spearhead Title IX education for the general population and international students in particular.

While the recruitment of international students continually brings an opportunity to diversify the community college experience, community colleges also need to ensure that international students are educated about Title IX and have access to relevant information online. Further, consistent with the Shenoy (2013) study, international students need a trusted staff member who will not only bring them information, but serve as a confidant to help immigrating students internalize the spirit of the Title IX policy and apply this information to their campus experiences.

Within the global consciousness that often blames women for being the target of sexual violence, America is shifting to empower the community in protecting all citizens from sexual violence. With regard to this task, community colleges should understand the dynamics facing international students, which include denial, isolation, and desensitization to the topic. With this in mind, leadership at community college campuses needs to develop an institutional culture that highlights the Title IX coordinator as an officer who can educate faculty. This coordinator can educate faculty, administrators, and advisors on best practices to connect with students, gain their trust, and subsequently educate them about Title IX's critical language.

RECOMMENDATIONS

Based on the emerging themes in this study, the researchers offer the follow recommendations:

1. Establish mentors who can gain international students' trust. As noted in the Shenoy (2013) study, an anchorperson is a critical figure for international students. Leadership at community colleges can create mentors for international students. These mentors, when charged by leadership, can galvanize campus culture regard the proper application of Title IX in regulation to preventing sexual violence.

2. Establish Title IX as a formal part of orientation for international students. International students from this study did not know about Title IX or where to find Title IX policy and supporting resources Making Title IX training a mandatory segment of orientation for all students, including international students, will begin a thorough Title IX education for international students. The Title IX coordinator could lead this segment and begin establishing trust with the international student population.

3. Provide Title IX information in several languages. While international students had strong English language skills, some also struggled to manage their reactions or communicate about sexual issues in English. Offering Title IX policies in multiple languages, both verbally and in print, can help international students' comprehension.

4. Include Title IX coordinator in mandatory Title IX programming. As students did not understand Title IX, they were also unfamiliar with the Title IX coordinator. Community colleges can develop

short videos that introduce the Title IX coordinator, explain Title IX, and offer relevant information in different languages.

CONCLUSION

International students bring a compelling diversity to any college community. The globalization of the workforce means that international students learn about American culture. Simultaneously, American students also have the chance to broaden their horizons by learning about other cultures through international students.

According to the US Department of Education's *Open Doors Report*, colleges will continue to recruit international students, as evidenced by the 72 % jump in international student enrollment since 1990. Given the fiscal crisis colleges face, and the fact that 65 % of international students are cash payers (Institute of International Education 2014), colleges will continue to focus on international student recruitment.

Hence, in the process of educating international students, community colleges have the opportunity to create communities in which international students are included, not isolated. University leadership has an opportunity to shift culture through Title IX programming. The opportunity transcends preventing sexual violence, but also includes an opportunity to build collaborative models across culture and gender, without fear of "mixed messages" or desensitized assumptions about women's safety.

While the numbers of international students are increasing, the volume of students still does not discount the trouble international students have adjusting to American culture. In turn, community colleges, like all sectors in higher education, need to make a concerted effort to gain the trust of international students and then educate them comprehensively about their Title IX rights and responsibilities regarding sexual violence.

REFERENCES

Addy, Cathryn (1995). *The president's journey; Issues and ideals in the community college*. Bolton, MA: Anker Publishing.

American Association of Community Colleges. (2014). *2014 Fact sheet*. Washington, DC: American Association of Community Colleges. http://www. aacc.nche.edu/AboutCC/Documents/Facts14_Data_R3.pdf

Anderson, Nick (2015). Schools facing investigations on sexual violence now more than 100. *Washington Post*. March 4, 2015. http://www.washingtonpost.com/news/grade-point/wp/2015/03/04/schools-facing-investigations-on-sexual-violence-now-more-than-100/

Bauer, Heidi Marie, Rodriguez, Michael, Quiroga, Seline, & Flores-Ortiz, Yvette (2000). Barriers to health care for abused Latina and Asian immigrant women. *Journal of Health are for the Poor and Underserved, 11*(1), 33–44.

Boyce, Ann (2002). Title IX: What now? *Journal of Physical Education, 73*(7), 6–7.

Brzonkala v. VA Polytechnic Institute, 132 F. 3d 949 – Court of Appeals, 4th Circuit, 1997.

Burns, James (1998). *Leadership*. New York: Harper Row.

Creswell, James (1998). *Qualitative inquiry and research design: Choosing among five traditions*. Thousand Oaks, CA: Sage.

Creswell, James (2014). *Research design: Qualitative, quantitative and mixed methods approaches*. Thousands Oaks, CA: Sage Publications Inc.

D'Abreau, Lylla, & Krahe, Barbara (2014). Predicting sexual aggression in male college students in Brazil. *Psychology of Men and Masculinity, 15*(2), 152–162.

Deverell, Edward, & Olsson, Eva-Karin (2010). Organizational culture effects on strategy and adaptability in crisis management. *Risk Management, 12*(2), 116–134. doi:http://dx.doi.org/10.1057/rm.2009.18.

Edwards, Amanda Ross (2010). Why Sport? The development of sport as a policy issue in Title IX of the education amendments of 1972. *The Journal of Policy History, 22*(3), 300–336. doi:10.1017/S0898030610000126.

Ee, Jongyeon (2013). 'He's an idiot!' Experiences of international students in the United States. *Journal of International Studies, 3*(1), 72–75.

Fossett, Katelyn (2013). *How does a country develop a 60 percent rape rate? The FP Group*.http://foreignpolicy.com/2013/09/11/how-does-a-country-develop-a-60-percent-rape-rate/

Greendorfer, Susan (1998). Title IX gender equity, backlash and ideology. *Women in Sport & Physical Activity Journal, 7*(1), 69.

Haglund, Rich (2005). Staring down the elephant: College football and title IX compliance. *Journal of Law and Education, 34*(3), 439–452.

Hobbes, Thomas (1982). *Leviathan*. United Kingdom: Penguin Classics/Cambridge University Press.

Iaccino, Ludovica (2014). Top 5 countries with highest rates of rape. *International Business Times*. http://www.ibtimes.co.uk/top-5-countries-highest-rates-rape-1434355

Institute of International Education. (2014). *Open Doors 2014*. Report on international educational exchange. http://www.iie.org/Research-and-Publications/Open-Doors/Data/International-Educational-Exchange-2014

Joshi, Manisha, Thomas, Kristie, & Sorenson, Susan (2013). Domestic violence and international students: An exploratory study of the practices and role of US university international offices. *Journal of College Student Development, 54*(5), 527–533.

Kingkade, Tyler (2015). *Colleges under Title IX investigations for sexual assault case – May 13, 2015*. US Department of Education, Office of Civil Rights. http://www.scribd.com/doc/265908119/Colleges-Under-Title-IX-Investigations-For-Sexual-Assault-Cases-May-13-2015

Liberman, Kenneth (1994). Asian student perceptions on American university instruction. *International Journal on Intercultural Relations, 28*, 399–414.

Lucas, Colleen, & Kline, Theresa (2008). Understanding the influence of organizational culture and group dynamics on organizational change and learning. *The Learning Organization, 15*(3), 277–287.

MacKinnon, Catharine (1979). *Sexual harassment of workplace women: A case of sex discrimination*. New Haven, CT: Yale University Press.

Mason, Mark (2014). Sample size and saturation in PhD Studies Using Qualitative Interviews. *Forum: Qualitative Research, 11*(3), 1–20.

Messner, Michael (2006). A place on the team: The triumph and tragedy of title IX. *Academe, 92*(1), 63–64.

Morse, Janice (1994). Designing funded qualitative research. In N. K. Denzin & Y. S. Lincoln (Eds.), *Handbook of qualitative research* (2nd ed., pp. 220–235). Thousand Oaks, CA: Sage.

Pauline, Gina (2012). Celebrating 40 years of Title IX: How far have we really come? *Journal of Physical Education, Recreation & Dance, 83*(8), 4–56.

Popadiuk, Natalee, & Arthur, Nancy (2004). Counseling international students in Canadian Schools. *International Journal for the Advancement of Counseling, 25*, 125–145.

Ritchie, Jane, Lewis, Jane, & Elam, Gillian (2003). Designing and selecting samples. In Jane Ritchie & Jane Lewis (Eds.), *Qualitative research practice. A guide for social science students and researchers* (pp. 77–108). Thousand Oaks, CA: Sage.

Ruiz, Eddy (2010). International community college students: Opportunities and challenges. *Journal of Applied Research in the Community College, 18*(1), 43–45.

Schein, Edgar (1997). *Organizational culture and leadership*. San Francisco, CA: Jossey-Bass.

Shenoy, Gloria (2013). *Information mismatch: What international students thought of their community college experience would be like* (Doctoral dissertation). Retrieved from ProQuest Dissertations and Theses. (UMI Dissertations Publishing, 2013. 3603444]).

Staurowsky, Ellen (2003). Introduction to Title IX theme: Title IX in the aftermath of President George W. Bush's commission on opportunities in athletics. *Women in Sport & Physical Activity Journal, 12*(2), 1–3.

United States Department of Education. (2011). *Office of Civil Rights*. "Dear Colleague Letter." http://www2.ed.gov/about/offices/list/ocr/letters/colleague-201104.pdf

United States Department of Education. (2014). *Office for Civil Rights revises sexual harassment guidance: Harassment of students by school employees, or third parties.* http://www.ed.gov/news/press-releases/us-education-secretary-announces-guidance-ensure-all-students-have-equal-access-???

Williams v. Board of Regents of University System of Georgia, 477 F. 3d 1282 – Court of Appeals, 11th Circuit 2007.

Wills v. Brown University, 184 F. 3d 20 – Court of Appeals, 1st Circuit 1999.

CHAPTER 7

Appreciative Advising with International Students in American Community Colleges

Yi (Leaf) Zhang

INTRODUCTION

International students in US higher education have received greater attention in the past decades as their enrollment continues to grow. According to the *Open Doors* report, during academic year 2013–2014, the total enrollment of international students in US higher education reached an all-time record of 886,664, of which 87,963 (10 %) attended Baccalaureate/Associate's Colleges and Associate's Colleges (Institute of International Education 2014). This important student population has benefited US higher education in many different ways, such as bringing a global perspective to domestic students who cannot afford to study abroad (Campbell 2012), and providing additional revenue to higher education institutions as public funds continue to diminish (NAFSA 2015).

Despite the benefits, international students often face many barriers when navigating through US higher education. They may have low English proficiency, are unfamiliar with the US culture, and lack financial support (Mori 2000; Hsieh 2007). They may also have a difficult time understanding college requirements due to limited exposure to the community college concept, since it mainly exists in North America (Cohen et al. 2014).

Y. Zhang (✉)
Department of Educational Leadership and Policy Studies,
University of Texas at Arlington, Arlington, TX, USA

© The Editor(s) (if applicable) and The Author(s) 2016   93
R.L. Raby, E.J. Valeau (eds.), *International Education at Community Colleges*, DOI 10.1057/978-1-137-53336-4_7

Although the difficulties international students experience pose new challenges to both students and institutions, the current discussion is often focused on issues of international students' adaptation and acculturation, and portrays them as problems and less capable (Mestenhauser 1983; Lee and Rice 2007; Charles-Toussaint and Crowson 2010). More attention should be given to how institutions could better respond to international students' needs and to maximize their learning outcomes.

Among all the available students' services on campus, this chapter selected academic advising because it is "perhaps the only structured campus endeavor that can guarantee students sustained interaction with a caring and concerned adult" who can assist them with a meaningful learning experience (Hunter and White 2004, p. 21). Therefore, the purpose of this chapter is to discuss how academic advisors could better help international community college students achieve such an experience. Specifically, this chapter focuses on the Appreciative Advising model because it is "a powerful tool for building rapport with students, discovering their strengths, unleashing their hopes and dreams, and devising plans to make those hopes and dreams come true" (Hutson and Bloom 2007, p. 4). Adapting the Appreciative Advising model, it is expected that community colleges could develop a more welcoming and enriching environment for international students.

This chapter was developed based on a thorough examination of existing literature regarding the development of academic advising in US higher education and particularly the practice of academic advising in community colleges. It then focuses on the significance of academic advising to students' learning outcomes in community colleges, followed by discussions of challenges of international students. Next, the chapter elaborates the Appreciative Advising model and how it can help academic advisors better assist international students in a community college setting. Finally, recommended actions are provided for academic advisors as well as community colleges to improve their practice of advising international students.

ACADEMIC ADVISING IN COMMUNITY COLLEGES

Academic advising has been viewed as an integral part of student success in community colleges. It was traditionally offered by faculty members in academic departments in four-year universities (O'Banion 1972). Community colleges were encouraged to adopt this faculty-only model in the 1960s, but O'Banion (1972) acknowledged unique characteristics of community colleges and proposed a five-stage model, which altered the world of academic advising and initiated conversations of the professionalization of the field in US higher education (Tuttle 2000).

With the development of academic advising, the faculty-only model has declined nationally across US institutions. According to the 2011 NACADA National Survey of Academic Advising, the faculty-only model was employed at 17.1 % of all institutions surveyed and only 8.8 % among two-year colleges. The most popular model used in two-year colleges was shared-split (39.3 %), where faculty and professional advisors share responsibilities, followed by self-contained (32.6 %), where advising is predominately offered by professional advisors (Carlstrom 2013).

Academic advising in the community college context is ever-challenging. Community colleges have a long history of attracting students with diverse backgrounds, such as transfers, adult learners, disabled, paraprofessional, honors, international, and student athletes (Cohen et al. 2014). Unlike four-year universities, which normally employ different personnel for different aspects of advising, advisors in community colleges often have to serve multiple roles responding to students' diverse demands (Jordan 2000; Tuttle 2000). This can be attributed to a lack of sustainable funding, resources, and trained personnel in community colleges (King 2002).

With limited resources, advisors in community colleges are normally responsible for a large number of advisees. The ratio of students to academic advisors or counselors averaged 1000 to 1, and, on some campuses, the ratio was as high as almost 2000 to 1 (MDRC 2010; Cohen et al. 2014). This indicates that many students in community colleges have limited access to advising sessions, if they are not totally excluded (Cohen et al. 2014).

Academic Advising and Community College Students' Success

According to NACADA (2003), academic advising is "a planning process" that aims to teach students "to understand the meaning of higher education, … to understand the purpose of the curriculum," and to enhance "students' intellectual and personal development toward academic success and lifelong learning" (n.p.). A large body of literature (Frost 2000; Habley 2004; Hunter and White 2004; Campbell and Nutt 2008; Bai and Pan 2009) demonstrates that academic advising, when done well, is positively associated with students' satisfaction, involvement, retention, and graduation. However, the majority of these studies were conducted in four-year universities and only a few (Seidman 1991; Flaga 2006; Bahr 2008) investigated academic advising in a community college context.

Academic advising in community colleges has positive linkage to students' persistence and retention. For instance, Seidman (1991) found that a higher percentage of community college students, who received advising before and after admissions, persisted in the program compared to those who only attended the traditional orientation program. Academic advising is also beneficial for students in remediation courses and transfer process. Bahr (2008) used data from 107 community colleges in California and claimed that receiving academic advising increased students' likelihood of remediating successfully in math and benefited students' long-term progress, including transferring to a four-year institution. Bahr also indicated that academic advising was more beneficial for underprepared students than their college-ready counterparts. In a more recent study of community college students pursuing transfer-based programs in (Science, Technology, Engineering and Math) STEM fields, Packard and Jeffers (2013) found that both advisors' knowledge and personal relationships with advisees were key to students' success in transfer. The students received critical information about transfer and were exposed to new knowledge or opportunities that they were originally unaware of.

Regardless of the significance of academic advising to community college students' success, many chose not to use advising services. According to the 2014 Community College Survey of Student Engagement (CCSSE) (2014), almost one-third of the students (32 %) *rarely* or *never* used academic advising services (n.d.). What these students missed is not just receiving course information, but more importantly, they failed to utilize the opportunity to enhance their learning experience for themselves. This may indicate there is a need to further investigate factors that prevent community college students from fully engaging themselves with academic advising, and to adopt more efficient advising strategies to encourage community college students to seek advisement.

Challenges Facing International Students

Prior research (Yi et al. 2003) suggested that international students experience challenges in US higher education primarily in academic studies, physical health, finances and tuition, employment after graduation, and personal and social issues. Numerous researchers (Yeh and Inose 2003, Andrade 2006) emphasized the importance of English proficiency to students' academic success and social adjustment. International students are often found to be unclear with writing technique and challenged with academic writing (Angelova and Riazantseva 1999). Additionally, international students tend to experience more homesickness and loneliness (Kegel 2009), and have more mental health concerns than their American counterparts (Kwon 2009). Although mostly conducted in four-year universities, the existing literature sheds light on the similarity of experiences that international students may encounter on community college campuses.

The review of the relevant literature suggests that the research on international students to date primarily outlined students' adjustment issues and implied that these students are deficient. Consequently, US colleges and universities emphasize that international students have to adapt, adjust, or assimilate themselves to the US culture and assume that the international students should take major responsibility for improvement (Perrucci and Hu 1995; Lee and Rice 2007). More than 30 years ago, Mestenhauser (1983) claimed that international students provide an important, yet convenient and low-cost resource for intercultural education and training on many US campuses, although this resource was normally overlooked or underused. In fact, many international students were perceived as "handicapped" or "deficient" due to low English proficiency and/or lack of academic preparation (p. 164). Unfortunately, negative perceptions about international students still exist on many campuses in recent years. For instance, Beoku-Betts (2004) suggested that international students may experience purposeful or unintentional marginalization in US colleges and universities. Lee and Rice (2007) revealed that international students confronted insults both in and outside the classroom by peers, faculty, and members of local community.

It is apparent that a more welcoming and enriching learning environment should be created on college campuses for international students. However, the challenge is to change the deficient view of key personnel across campus, such as academic advisors whose impact is critical to students' learning experiences. To make such changes means adapting advising strategies that recognize students' strengths and capabilities. This chapter introduces Appreciative Advising as a possible solution because this advising model is fully student centered and shows great promise in helping international students and other student subpopulations achieve academic success.

APPRECIATIVE ADVISING

Appreciative Advising, initiated by Bloom and colleagues (Bloom and Martin 2002; Bloom et al. 2008), was defined as "a social-constructivist advising philosophy that provides an advising framework for advisors to use in optimizing their interactions with students in both individual and group settings" (Bloom et al. 2008, p. 19). Appreciative Advising is not about being mindlessly happy or ignoring problems; rather, it helps "students optimize their educational experiences and achieve their dreams, goals, and potentials" (Bloom et al. 2007, p. 28).

Appreciative Advising tenets were developed primarily based on Appreciative Inquiry, which is an organizational change theory that "provides a positive rather than a problem-oriented lens on the organization, focusing members' attention on what is possible rather than what is wrong" (van Buskirk 2002, p. 67). It consists of four major concepts: Discover, Dream, Design, and Destiny. Based on the cycles, Appreciative Advising developed two more stages, which are Disarm and Don't Settle, and renamed the Destiny stage to Delivery to better represent the practice of academic advisement as a process.

Together, the six steps of Appreciative Advising clearly delineate a process of academic advising that focuses on students' strength and potential. More specifically, the first phase, Disarm, recognizes the importance of first impressions. During this phase, advisors attempt to establish a positive relationship using both verbal and non-verbal tools, such as greeting, being respectful, making eye contact, and smiling. During the Discover phase, advisors and students are expected to build rapport and work together to discover students' strengths, passions, and skills. The third phase, Dream, is about discovering students' dreams and hopes. During the Design phase, advisors and students work collaboratively on planning that can realize students' dreams. Next, students carry out their plans during the Deliver phase. The last phase is about students' continual development. Students are challenged and encouraged to pursue their fullest potential (Bloom et al. 2008).

Appreciative Advising has been used on many university campuses and applied to diverse student populations. For instance, in the University of North Carolina at Greensboro, the Appreciative Advising model led to an 18 % increase in the retention rate of first-time probation students and a statistically significant increase in GPA (Hutson and Bloom 2007). Researchers (Bloom et al. 2008) also found that adult learners in Eastern

Illinois University, with online or on-campus Appreciative Advising, were well satisfied with their degree programs, curriculum, and the quality of advising. The advisors also had a higher level of satisfaction with their job.

Although the research (Hutson and Bloom 2007; Bloom et al. 2008; Hall 2008) primarily highlighted its benefits for non-traditional students' academic studies, Appreciative Advising can likewise lead to similar positive outcomes for international students, since these students often share similar characteristics with and relate their college experiences to non-traditional students. Instead of using a problem-oriented lens, the Appreciative Advising model encourages advisors to emphasize international students' potential and to value their prior experiences. This approach could also motivate international students to appreciate their own strengths and to develop a meaningful educational career for themselves.

RECOMMENDATIONS FOR COMMUNITY COLLEGE ADVISORS

This section discusses how Appreciative Advising techniques could be applied to international community college students. Recommendations for academic advisors as well as community colleges are provided in each phase of the Appreciative Advising model.

Disarm Phase

The purpose of the Disarm phase is to make a positive first impression with students and create a welcoming environment to put students at ease. Advisors are encouraged to have conversations with students about their home countries, past experiences, interests and hobbies, academic goals, and other aspect of their lives. Advisors are also encouraged to share their own information with the students (Bloom et al. 2008).

It is sometimes easier for advisors to establish a positive first impression and to quickly build a good advisor-advisee relationship with domestic community college students, who are mostly from the local communities. However, it can be challenging to establish such a relationship with international students because they usually have a wide diversity of personal, cultural, and political backgrounds. To successfully engage these students in conversations, advisors need to have at least minimal understanding of cultural differences. For instance, a handshake is normally seen as a sign of warm welcome in the USA, but it may be considered inappropriate by some Islamic female students if a male advisor extends his hand for a shake

(Haddad and Lummis 1987). Moreover, in some Asian cultures, bowing is more widely used as a greeting gesture than handshaking (Matsumoto and Hwang 2013). Pronunciation of international students' names can be challenging, but it is important in establishing a positive first impression (Rhee and Sagaria 2004). Advisors could practice the pronunciation of the student's name prior to the meeting, ask the student to pronounce it during advising, or at least show interest in learning it correctly.

International students in community colleges are usually unclear about importance of academic advising in their academic success and unaware of available advising resources on campus (Upcraft and Stephens 2000; Zhang 2015; 2016). To have a better introduction, academic advisors need to introduce their responsibilities to international students during their first meetings and explain what they *can* and *cannot* do for the students. Equipped with sufficient knowledge about academic advising, international students would be more likely to use advising services in their time at the community college.

Discover Phase

The Discover phase focuses on building rapport with students and collaborating with them to discover their strengths, passions, and skills through asking positive, open-ended questions. Bloom et al. (2008) developed the Appreciative Advising Inventory to guide academic advisors through the Discover phase. The following are some examples of questions advisors might ask during advising sessions (pp. 44–45):

- Tell me a story about a time you positively impacted another person's life.
- Who are your two biggest role models? Why are they role models to you and what about them do you hope to emulate?
- What were you doing the last time you lost track of time? When time just flew by and you looked up at the clock and thought it must be wrong?

Specifically for international students, questions about their home country and transition can be asked to guide them to share more about their stories:

- Tell me about your journey to America.
- What challenges did you overcome to study in the USA?

- Tell me about a time you felt most proud to be from your home country (Palmer 2009, para. 10).

The researchers (Bloom et al. 2008) also suggested that advisors make encouraging comments and use positive follow-up questions to probe detailed responses.

Given the fact that many international students on community college campuses are English-as-a-second language (ESL) learners, academic advisors need to be more thoughtful about the use of jargons and slang terms (Zhang 2015; 2016). Academic advisors could confirm with the students by repeating, summarizing, or paraphrasing the statements made by international students (Palmer 2009). To overcome language barriers, academic advisors can encourage international students to tell their stories through drawing, painting, photos, or other forms of art. It has been confirmed (Howie et al. 2013) that art-based consulting and therapy is more helpful to explain one's experience when verbal expression is insufficient.

Unlike those in four-year institutions, many international students in community colleges have not yet claimed a specific major; many are still exploring their potentials. To fully uncover these students' strengths, academic advisors must avoid stereotypical views about international students, which could severely hinder the advisors from understanding the students' true abilities.

Dream Phase

In this phase, advisors and students work together to identify hopes and dreams for the future. Advisors use open-ended questions to guide students in imagining and detailing their ambitions (Bloom et al. 2008). Example questions include the following:

- Imagine that you are on the front cover of a magazine 20 years from now. The article details your latest and most impressive list of accomplishments. What is the magazine? Why have you been selected to appear on the cover? What accomplishments are highlighted in the article?
- When you were approximately nine years old someone asked you, "What do you want to be when you grow up?" what was your answer? What is your answer to that question now?

- Twenty years from now, what will your ideal work day be like? (Bloom et al. 2008, pp. 56–57)

Academic advisors need to understand that dreams are often private, personal, and kept secret. Without a trust relationship, dreams might not be easily shared by international students. Researchers (Cornett-DeVito and Reeves 1999; Zhang 2015) have found that advisors are more likely to establish a trust relationship with the students when they have richer intercultural experiences, such as studying abroad, traveling overseas, and participating in classes or other activities improving intercultural understanding. Thus, academic advisors should be encouraged to step out of their comfort zones and to obtain more knowledge in cross-cultural understanding through personal experiences or professional training (Clark and Kalionzes 2008).

Additionally, academic advisors should avoid being judgmental and be cognizant of their own bias and underlying prejudice. If international students sensed their experiences were undervalued or their achievements were not recognized, they would not open themselves up to discuss their dreams.

Design Phase

Once students' strengths are identified and articulated, advisors and students move to the Design phase. Students and advisors continue working together to develop a clear plan where the students' strengths and abilities can be used to realize the students' dreams. Advisors should encourage students to take actions and refer them to campus resources when necessary (Bloom et al. 2008). Example questions are:

- What can you do today that will bring you one step closer to your goal?
- What can you do this week (month, semester) that will get you started?
- Who and what resources can help your dream become reality? (Howell 2010, p. 26)

This phase can be challenging for students at all levels because it requests detailed plans and specific steps, but it could be even more difficult for international community college students since they are often unfamiliar with campus resources. For instance, some international community college students aim to gain a bachelor's degree, but do not know where and who on campus they should go to for guidance. Advisors may need to iterate the transfer process, such as what courses are transferrable, if there are any articulation agreements between the current community college and their target four-year institutions, what materials are needed for transfer, and when they need to apply for admissions. A timeline of transfer needs to be clearly and carefully planned, because if international students fail to transfer but have graduated from a community college, they may lose their legal status in the USA, which could lead to limited or no career and/or education opportunities.

Knowledge of immigration is another important component in developing plans for international students who plan to enter the workforce in the USA immediately after they graduate from community college occupational programs (Clark and Kalionzes 2008).

Oftentimes, these students do not have much knowledge about immigration regulations and how they can successfully obtain a legal working status. To better guide these students to realize their plans, advisors should at least know who and where they can refer these students to, when appropriate.

To provide students with information necessary to form their plans in a time-efficient manner, community colleges could create a "one-stop" service through collaborating with other professionals who work with international students on campus, such as international admission officers, multicultural center administrators, and international students' organization leaders. This collaboration can also benefit community colleges financially. Serving as an entity through which other student services are realized, academic advising can maximize various services available in community colleges without requiring new staff (O'Banion 1972).

Deliver Phase

The focus of this phase is to implement the plan that students designed with guidance of advisors to achieve their goals. The advisors continue guiding students to "revise, modify, and prioritize the plan" through positive feedback and active listening (Bloom et al. 2008, p. 96). Students may make mistakes, but advisors are there to help them to regroup and start over again. The following questions are examples that can be used to explore obstacles or resistances:

- What roadblocks have you hit? How are you dealing with them?
- Since our last meeting, what concrete steps have you taken to achieve your goals?
- What have you learned so far? (Howell 2010, p. 27)

Compared with American students, international students, especially those from Asia, tend to view advisors as authorities and may be afraid of talking about mistakes that they made during plan implementation or asking for additional assistance to revise their plans (McMahon 2011). Academic advisors should reassure international students of their capability, remind them of their goals and dreams, and continue emphasizing hope for the future. Advisors could also make follow-up sessions with international students and reiterate that they are expected to return to the advising office for help if they encounter any obstacles (Palmer 2009).

Advisors could also organize small group discussions among international community college students who speak the same language or those from a similar cultural background. Consequently, international students could feel more comfortable revealing their resistance in implementing their plans and feel more supported through peer advising (Diambra and Cole-Zakrzewski 2002).

Don't Settle Phase

This is the final step but it is designed to lead to the beginning of the next cycle: improvement or accomplishment in one area leads to another. Advisors continue to motivate students to think beyond their initial plans, to dream about something bigger and better, and to identify new plans that can realize their greater ambitions (Bloom et al. 2008).

Celebration with international students on what they have achieved could be a huge motivation for the students, since most of their family and friends are thousands of miles away. A sense of belonging in the host culture could improve student retention, provide a feeling of inclusion, and encourage them to aim at new goals (Moores and Popadiuk 2011; O'Keeffe 2013).

This is also the time for academic advisors to reevaluate opinions, attitudes, and cultural understandings that they hold. Such examination could help advisors understand their own cultural heritage, worldviews, and underlying assumptions, if any, about other cultures or nations. With understanding of their own biases and remaining open to diversity, academic advisors could better assist international students to achieve new success (Gudykunst 1993).

CONCLUSION

The enrollment of international students has been increasing in US community colleges over the past years (IIE 2014). It suggests that student support services must also grow to meet the demands of these students. International students face unique challenges when pursuing an educational career in the USA, but are often perceived as problems and expected to take major responsibilities to overcome their obstacles (Perrucci and Hu 1995; Mestenhauser 1983; Lee and Rice 2007). However, the literature of international community college students is limited in the ways that international students are understood, as well as how academic advising can be applied to respond to these students' needs and to guide them to overcome the challenges.

Appreciative Advising provides a five-step process that focuses on students' strengths and potentials in advising, but it is more than just a tool; it provides "a whole new way of thinking and of being" (Redfern 2008, conclusion session, para. 1). It provides a positive approach in advising international students in community colleges. Using the Appreciative Advising approach, academic advisors could play an important role in helping international students achieve success in community colleges and continue to influence their life journey even after they transfer to a four-year university. The practice of Appreciative Advising with international students should be encouraged on more community college campuses. However, to fulfill its potential, community college administrators need to provide more support for advisors; a critical one is to lower the student-advisor ratio. Appreciative advising requests the advisors to devote into a large amount of time to guide each individual student. With a high student-advisor ratio on many community college campuses, advisors might not have sufficient time to develop individual relationships with each student. Future researchers should conduct empirical studies to provide a fuller understanding of impact of Appreciative Advising on international community college students' success and its application for other underrepresented student populations.

REFERENCES

Andrade, Maureen S. (2006). International students in English-speaking universities. *Journal of Research in International Education, 5,* 131–154.

Angelova, Maria, & Riazantseva, Anastasia (1999). "If you don't tell me, how can i know?" A case study of four international students learning to write the U.S.way. *Written Communication, 16*(4), 491–525.

Bahr, Peter R. (2008). Cooling out in the community college: What is the effect of academic advising on students' chances of success? *Research in Higher Education, 49,* 704–732.

Bai, Haiyan, & Pan, Wei (2009). A multilevel approach to assessing the interaction effects on college student retention. *Journal of College Student Retention: Research, Theory and Practice, 11*(2), 287–301.

Beoku-Betts, Josephine A. (2004). African women pursuing graduate studies in the sciences: Racism, gender bias, and third world marginality. *NWSA Journal, 16*(1), 116–135.

Bloom, Jennifer L., Hutson, Bryant L., & He, Ye (2008). *The appreciative advising revolution.* Champaign, IL: Stipes Publishing Co..

Bloom, Jennifer L., & Martin, Nancy A. (2002). Incorporating appreciative inquiry into academic advising. *The Mentor, 4*(3) Retrieved from https://dus.psu.edu/mentor/old/ articles/020829jb.htm

Bloom, Jennifer L., Cuevas, Amanda E. P., Hall, James W., & Evans, Christopher V. (2007). Graduate students' perceptions of outstanding graduate advisor characteristics. *NACADA Journal, 27*(2), 28–35.

Carlstrom, Aaron H. (2013). Advising models. *Results of the NACADA 2001 national survey of academic advising. (NACADA monograph no. 25).* Manhattan, KS: National Academic Advising Association. http://www.nacada.ksu.edu/Portals/0/Clearinghouse/M25/M25%20Chapter%20chapter%205%20updated.pdf

Campbell, Nittaya (2012). Promoting intercultural contact on campus: A project to connect and engage international and host students. *Journal of Studies in International Education, 16*(3), 205–227.

Campbell, Susan M., & Nutt, Charlie L. (2008). Academic advising in the new global century: Supporting student engagement and learning outcomes achievement. *Peer Review, 10*(1), 4–7.

Charles-Toussaint, Gifflene C., & Crowson, H. Michael (2010). Prejudice against international students: The role of threat perceptions and authoritarian dispositions in US students. *The Journal of psychology, 144*(5), 413–428.

Clark, Evette C., & Kalionzes, Jane (2008). Advising students of color and international students. In V. N. Gordon & W. R. Habley (Eds.), *Academic advising: A comprehensive handbook* (pp. 204–225). San Francisco, CA: Jossey-Bass.

Cohen, Arthur M., Brawer, Florence B., & Kisker, Carrie B. (2014). *The American community college* (6th ed.). San Francisco, CA: Jossey-Bass.

Community College Survey of Student Engagement (CCSSE). (n.d.). *Key findings: Support for learners.* http://www.ccsse.org/survey/bench_support.cfm

Cornett-DeVito, Myma M., & Reeves, Kenna J. (1999). Preparing students for success in a multicultural world: Faculty advisement and intercultural communication. *NACADA Journal, 19*(1), 35–44.

Diambra, Joel F., & Cole-Zakrzewski, Kylie G. (2002). Peer advising: Evaluating effectiveness. *NACADA Journal, 22*(1), 56–64.

Flaga, Catherine T. (2006). The process of transition for community college transfer students. *Community College Journal of Research and Practice, 30*, 3–19.

Frost, S. H. (2000). Historical and philosophical foundations for academic advising. In V. N. Gordon & W. R. Habley (Eds.), *Academic advising: A comprehensive handbook* (pp. 3–17). San Francisco, CA: Jossey-Bass.

Gudykunst, William B. (1993). Toward a theory of effective interpersonal and intergroup communication: An anxiety/uncertainty management perspective. In R. L. Wiseman & J. Koester (Eds.), *Intercultural communication theory* (pp. 33–71). Newbury Park, CA: Sage.

Habley, Wesley R. (2004). *The status of academic advising: Findings from the ACT sixth national survey (Monograph No. 10).* Manhattan, KS: National Academic Advising Association (NACADA).

Haddad, Yvonne Y., & Lummis, Adair T. (1987). *Islamic values in the United States: A comparative study.* New York: Oxford University Press.

Hall, Lindsay R. (2008, July 23). Appreciative advising: How the academic centers for excellence at the University of South Carolina are using this breakthrough concept. *The Mentor: An Academic Advising Journal.* http://dus.psu.edu/mentor/old/articles/080723lh.htm

Hsieh, Min-Hua. (2007). Challenges for international students in higher education: One student's narrated story of invisibility and struggle. *College Student Journal., 41*(2), 379–391.

Howell, Nancy G. (2010). *Appreciative advising from the academic advisor's viewpoint: A qualitative study.* Unpublished doctoral dissertation, University of Nebraska, Lincoln.

Howie, Paula, Prasad, Sangetta, & Kristel, Jennie (Eds.) (2013). *Using art therapy with diverse populations crossing cultures and abilities.* London: Jessica Kingsley.

Hunter, Mary S., & White, Eric R. (2004). Could fixing academic advising fix higher education? *About Campus, 9*(1), 20–25.

Hutson, Bryant L., & Bloom, Jennifer L. (2007). The impact of appreciative advising on student success. *E-Source for College Transitions, 5*(1), 4–5.

Institute of International Education (IIE). (2014). International student enrollments by institutional type, 2004/05–2013/14. *Open Doors Report on International Educational Exchange.* http://www.iie.org/opendoors

Jordan, Peggy (2000). Advising college students in the 21st century. *NACADA Journal, 20*(2), 21–30.

Kegel, Karen (2009). *Homesickness in nternational college students.* Paper presented at the American Counseling Association annual conference and exposition, Charlotte North Carolina. http://www.counselingoutfitters.com/vistas/vistas09/Article_7_Kegel.pdf

King, Margaret C. (2002). Community college advising. *NACADA Clearinghouse of Academic Advising.* http://www.nacada.ksu.edu/clearinghouse/advisingissues/comcollege.htm

Kwon, Yangyi (2009). Factors affecting international students' transition to higher education institutions in the United States. *College Student Journal, 43*(4): 1020–1037.

Lee, Jenny J., & Rice, Charles (2007). Welcome to America? International student perceptions of discrimination. *Higher Education, 53*(3), 381–409.

Matsumoto, David, & Hwang, Hyisung C. (2013). Cultural similarities and differences in emblematic gestures. *Journal of Nonverbal Behavior, 37*(1), 1–27.

Mestenhauser, Josef A. (1983). Learning from sojourners. In D. Landis & R. W. Brislin (Eds.), *Handbook of intercultural training* (Vol. 2, pp. 153–185). New York: Pergamon.

McMahon, Patrick (2011). Chinese voices: Chinese learners and their experiences of living and studying in the United Kingdom. *Journal of Higher Education Policy and Management, 33*(4), 401–414.

MDRC. (2010). *Can improved student services boost community college student success?*NewYork:MDRC,http://www.mdrc.org/publication/can-improved-student-services-boost-community-college-student-success

Moores, Lisa, & Popadiuk, Natalee (2011). Positive aspects of international student transitions: A qualitative inquiry. *Journal of College Student Development, 52*(3), 291–306.

Mori, Sakurako C. (2000). Addressing the mental health concerns of international students. *Journal of Counseling & Development, 78*(2), 137–144.

NACADA. (2003). Paper presented to the Task force on defining academic advising. *NACADA Clearinghouse of Academic Advising Resources.* http://www.nacada.ksu.edu/Resources/Clearinghouse/View-Articles/Definitions-of-academic-advising.aspx

NAFSA. (2015). *Explore international education: The international student economic value tool.* http://www.nafsa.org/Explore_International_Education/Impact/Data_And_Statistics/The_International_Student_Economic_Value_Tool/

O'Banion, Terry (1972). An academic advising model. *Junior College Journal, 42*, 62, 64, & 66–69.

O'Keeffe, Patrick (2013). A sense of belonging: Improving student retention. *College Student Journal, 47*(4), 605–613.

Packard, Becky W. L., & Jeffers, Kimberly C. (2013). Advising and progress in the Community College STEM transfer pathway. *NACADA Journal, 33*(2), 65–76.

Palmer, Eriko (2009). Using appreciative advising with international students. *The Mentor: An Academic Advising Journal*. https://dus.psu.edu/mentor/old/articles/090909ep.htm

Perrucci, Robert, & Hu, Hong (1995). Satisfaction with social and educational experiences among international graduate students. *Research in Higher Education, 36*(4), 491–508.

Redfern, Kimberly (2008). Appreciative advising and the nontraditional student. *The Mentor: An Academic Advising Journal, 10*(4). https://dus.psu.edu/mentor/old/articles/081104kr.htm

Rhee, Jeong-eun, & Sagaria, Mary A. D. (2004). International students: Constructions of imperialism in the Chronicle of Higher Education. *The Review of Higher Education, 28*(1), 77–96.

Seidman, Alan (1991). The evaluation of a pre/post admissions/counseling process at a suburban community college: Impact on student satisfaction with the faculty and the institution, retention, and academic performance. *College and University, 66*, 223–232.

Tuttle, Kathryn N. (2000). Academic advising. *New Directions for Higher Education, 11*, 15–24.

Upcraft, M. Lee, & Stephens, Pamela S. (2000). *Academic advising and today's changing students*. In V. N. Gordon & W. R. Habley (Eds.), *Academic advising: A comprehensive handbook* (pp. 73–83). San Francisco, CA: Jossey-Bass.

Van Buskirk, William (2002). *Appreciating appreciative inquiry in the urban Catholic school*. In R. Fry, F. Barrett, J. Seiling, & D. Whitney (Eds.), *Appreciative inquiry and organizational transformation: Reports from the field* (pp. 67–97). Westport, CT: Quorum Books.

Yeh, Christine, & Inose, Mayuko (2003). International students reported English fluency, social support satisfaction, and social connectedness as predictors of acculturative stress. *Counseling Psychology Quarterly, 16*, 15–28.

Yi, Jenny K., Lin, Jun-Chih G., & Kishimoto, Yuko (2003). Utilization of counseling services by international students. *Journal of Instructional Psychology, 30*(4), 333–342.

Zhang, Yi L. (2015). Intercultural communication competence: Advising international students in a Texas community college. *NACADA Journal, 35*(2), 48-59.

Zhang, Yi L. (2016). An overlooked population in community college: International students' (in)validation experiences with academic advising. *Community College Review, 44*(2), 1–18.

CHAPTER 8

Study Abroad as Self-Authorship: Globalization and Reconceptualizing College and Career Readiness

Eboni M. Zamani-Gallaher, Raul A. Leon, and John Lang

INTRODUCTION

Reflecting on current trends impacting higher education today, it is unde-niable that pressure exists on institutions of higher education to fulfill the demands and expectations of students to acquire global competencies through curricular and co-curricular global experiences (Hovland 2009). According to the Center for Internationalization and Global Engagement (Center for Internationalization and Global Engagement 2012), one of the fundamental duties of US higher education is to prepare students "to live and work in a society that increasingly operates across international borders" (p. 5).

E.M. Zamani-Gallaher (✉)
Higher Education/Community College Leadership, University of Illinois at Urbana-Champaign, Urbana-Champaign, IL, USA

R.A. Leon
Higher Education and Student Affairs, Eastern Michigan University, Ypsilanti, MI, USA

J. Lang
Education Policy, Organization and Leadership, University of Illinois at Urbana-Champaign, Urbana-Champaign, IL, USA

© The Editor(s) (if applicable) and The Author(s) 2016   111
R.L. Raby, E.J. Valeau (eds.), *International Education at Community Colleges*, DOI 10.1057/978-1-137-53336-4_8

The literature signals that like nearly all institutions of higher education, community colleges are not isolated from the effects of globalization and they continue to evolve grappling with the idea of becoming global actors (Cohen 2011; Zhang 2011). Responding to globalization trends, community colleges continue to work effortlessly to become catalysts for greater educational access, in particular, promoting economic and occupational mobility for non-traditional students (Valeau and Raby 2007; Raby and Valeau 2009). Study abroad is one of the most commonly implemented practices to move internationalization efforts forward and has been offered at community colleges for nearly four decades (Raby 2008; Institute of International Education 2014a). This chapter threads together aspects of educational policy and research that may seem tenuous at first. To begin, we consider *study abroad* in terms of a theory of *self-authorship*. We then formulate self-authorship as its own kind of *college and career readiness*. Our reconceptualization of readiness calls for broadening what is deemed essential in being prepared for college and career, asserting that global literacy is a necessary competency (i.e., *global readiness*). Moreover, in this chapter we focus on underserved and overlooked students, students of color, among them, who often come from disadvantaged backgrounds that entail generations of marginalization.

Our argument is that study abroad entails self-authorship, which translates into an exceptional kind of readiness for college and career that is important, particularly for racially/ethnically diverse groups. Our aim is fourfold. First, we offer a theoretical framework for future research into the interconnections between study abroad, self-authorship, and readiness for students of color. Second, we deepen educational policy discourse on *readiness* by making a vital connection between study abroad and self-authorship. Readiness policies often envision broad horizons for students made possible in the confines of the classroom. We take a more expansive view of readiness by advancing a global mindset about educational opportunities and "classrooms" for students of color.

Importantly, we delve into the question of access to study abroad. Students of color are often left out of study abroad opportunities due to limited finances and inadequate program recruiting, as well as student fears and negative pressures by family and friends (Hembroff and Rusz 1993; Dawson 2000; Dessof 2006; McMurtrie 2007; Brux and Fry 2010). We do not tackle these problems directly. Instead, our third aim is to give study abroad programs and community college campuses a timely reason to address barriers by understanding study abroad as a vital kind of readiness education for students of color: readiness to return to campus to complete a degree and readiness to meet the challenges of a global environment. Fourth, our hope is to encourage research into the nexus of study abroad, as self-authorship, for underserved students as a question of global readiness for college and career.

Globalization, Educational Policy, and Study Abroad

In November 1979, the President's Commission on Foreign Language and International Studies issued a report, titled: "Strength through Wisdom: A Critique of U.S. Capabilities" (Fersh and Fitchen 1981). The Commission, comprised of "leaders in education, government, language and area studies, and business and labor" (Ibid.) advanced recommendations and themes that resonate today: students must acquire foreign language skills for a global community; students must prepare for global citizenship; and students must meet the challenges of a global economy. In present-day parlance, education entails global *readiness*, from college to career.

Notably, the Commission singled out community colleges for their particular role in international education in light of the diversity of student populations and their overall numbers in post-secondary education. Fersh and Fitchen report that the Commission "urges that community colleges ... enlarge their international commitment and enlarge the staff development necessary to strengthen their commitment to foreign language and international studies" (p. 14).

Recent educational policy continues to affirm and advance a commitment to global education as study abroad. In 2005, the Abraham Lincoln Study Abroad Commission proposed a "bold vision for the United States," namely, "Send one million students to study abroad in a decade" (Commission of the Lincoln Study Abroad Fellowship Program 2005, p. v). In the report, *Global Competencies and National Needs*, the Commission establishes that "study abroad is a powerful educational tool." The report continues, "Overwhelming numbers of graduates who have studied abroad agree that the experience enhanced their interest in academic work, helped them acquire important career 'skill sets,' and continued for decades to influence their perspective on world events" (p. vi).

Important for community colleges given their diverse student populations, the Commission called for greater participation by minorities, first generation students, and other diverse students. In addition, they recognized that traditional study abroad programs might not be suitable to fit the needs and expectations a growing population of non-traditional students, older than 25, working full-time, and often providing the majority of economic support in the household that enrolls in community colleges (McMullen and Penn 2011). In short, the Commission identified the benefits of study abroad for traditionally underserved students in higher education—American Indian, African American, Hispanic, low-income, among others—and the challenges that often attend their pursuit of an education, some of which we noted earlier.

The numbers help to illustrate the challenges and their effect on participation. In 2012–2013, White students made up nearly four-fifths of study abroad participants in the USA. By comparison for 2012–2013, Hispanics/Latino Americans made up 7.6 % of students of color who studied abroad followed by Asian/Pacific Islanders at 7.3 %, 5.3 % African Americans, 3 % mixed race, and American Indian/Alaska Native comprised 0.5 % (National Association of Foreign Student Advisers n.d.; Institute of International Education 2014b).

On a brighter side, research conducted on students of color underscores that study abroad is linked to higher retention rates (Metzger 2006), promotes positive changes in self-image, reassures academic and professional goals, builds positive attitudes about their roles in society, encourages students to be more involved with faculty, and increases community participation (Kuh 2003). These findings draw attention to the potential of study abroad as a promising educational initiative, and provide further reason to increase participation in study abroad by students of color.

A Closer Look at the Literature

Community colleges are not immune from the demands and effects of globalization. Instead, they continue to grapple with the need to become global actors and educators (Cohen 2011; Zhang 2011), in order to provide greater access, and promote economic and occupational mobility for traditionally underserved students (Valeau and Raby 2007; Raby and Valeau 2009).

Researchers have documented higher levels of student engagement; second-language gains, increased cross-cultural adaptability, and intercultural sensitivity are associated with study abroad (Black and Duhon 2006; Baker-Smemoe et al. 2014; Raby et al. 2014).

Unfortunately, very little is known about nexus of educational commitments—student access, readiness, and study abroad—at community colleges, let alone the role of self-authorship within this nexus. A review of the literature shows that research on study abroad and community colleges is limited to a fewer than a dozen publications—articles, chapters, reports, and dissertations (Emert and Pearson 2007; Raby and Valeau 2007; Raby 2008; Niser 2010; Amani 2011; Drexler and Campbell 2011; Willis 2012; Raby et al. 2014). When research examines this nexus, it more often focuses on quantity instead of quality: demographics (background and numbers) and geographic (the diversity of study destinations) (Raby et al. 2014).

One telling figure is the level of student participation in study abroad at community colleges, when compared with student participation at four-year institutions. While the former enroll nearly half of all undergraduate students in the country (American Association of Community Colleges 2015), community college students represent only 2 % of all college students studying abroad (Institute of International Education 2014a, b). Although a comparatively small number of community college students participate in study abroad, the literature notes that community-college study abroad students report gains in international literacy (Raby 2008; Arden-Ogle 2009; Amani 2011; Willis 2012); knowledge of the global economy (Niser 2010); citizenship skills (Frost and Raby 2009); intercultural awareness skills (Emert and Pearson 2007), strong connections with faculty, academic persistence, and success (Raby et al. 2014). However, as stated by Raby (2012), "it is alarming that study abroad remains a peripheral community college program" (p. 181).

Current Trends in Study Abroad

One strategic means of advancing the college completion agenda for a global knowledge economy has been increasing the number of graduates in career technical education (CTE), particularly science, technology, engineering, and mathematics (STEM) (Taylor et al. 2012; Zamani-Gallaher et al. 2015). Recent figures for study abroad participation indicate an increase among STEM majors of 8.8 % between 2011–2012 and 2012–2013 (Institute of International Education 2014a). In fact, 23 % of all study abroad participants are STEM majors, which accounts for the highest number of education abroad participants by field of study. This pattern of the majority of study abroad students pursuing STEM fields holds true for two- and four-year institutions (Institute of International Education 2014a). The growth in American students studying abroad has largely been in the STEM areas. This is the first time STEM majors outnumber study abroad students in other major fields. Oguntoyinbo (2015) attributes the growth of STEM students pursuing education abroad to the impact of globalization on the curriculum, the flexibility of offerings, as well as concerted efforts of faculty and administrators to raise student awareness of the value of international study opportunities. In short, those who major in STEM are more competitive in the labor market for better jobs and there are now more study abroad programs in STEM at community colleges and their four-year counterparts.

A Theory of Self-Authorship

In this section, we tie together the tenuous strands of study abroad, self-authorship, and global readiness—to mix metaphors and advance an educational policy nexus that we hope will offer a basis for community colleges to conceptualize, design, and promote study abroad with underserved students in mind. Furthermore, we endeavor to encourage new lines of research (given the dearth that is available on community college study abroad programming) that deepens our understanding of the value of study abroad in fostering individual global readiness by way of a truly global education.

When considering the expectations of what college degrees should provide, there is public consensus that a college education should produce high quality professionals, engaged citizens, critical thinkers, problem solvers, and above all, individuals who are able to succeed in a global, diverse, and interconnected world (Taylor 2004; Hadis 2005; Tillmann 2010). Unfortunately, and generating great distress, it is argued that many students lack these valuable skills, and graduates come out of college with limited exposure to diverse perspectives and lack the skills needed to cope with current challenges in our society (Baxter Magolda 2008).

Baxter Magolda (2008) notes that many graduates today have accumulated a bulk of knowledge, but lack the ability to make effective decisions, and have been trained only to follow directions. In Baxter Magolda's words, graduates have not developed self-authorship, defined as the "internal capacity to define one's beliefs, identity, and social relations" (Baxter Magolda 2008, p. 69). Baxter Magolda affirms that in their twenties, students struggle to answer three major questions associated with the development of self-authorship: Who am I? How do I know? How do I want to construct relationships with others? (Baxter Magolda 2009). Using the analogy of a roadmap, Baxter Magolda (2008) describes self-authorship as a developmental capacity process that embodies three phases (a) external formulas, (b) crossroads, and, (c) self-authorship.

The first phase, external formulas, describes a time in which individuals rely on external forces, voices, and authorities to define their identity, explore their beliefs, and establish their relationships with others. In this phase, individuals heavily rely on others (e.g., parents, teachers, bosses) to make decisions and to resolve issues.

The second phase, the crossroads, defines a point where individuals begin to make decisions on their own relying on their internal voice. In this phase, individuals are torn between following their internal voice and listening to external formulas, and begin to recognize the importance of listening and cultivating their internal voice.

The last phase is self-authorship. This is the culmination of the journey toward development, with individuals listening, cultivating, and trusting their internal voice. Following your intuition is a key determinant, with individuals gaining confidence on what to believe, how to view themselves, and how to act on relationships. At its core, the transition from authority dependence to self-authorship entails questioning trusted sources of authority, it requires that individuals acquire new perspectives, and it pushes individuals to construct new beliefs that serve as the foundation or philosophy of life.

Self-Authorship and Study Abroad

In her text, *Black Passports: Travel Memoirs as a Tool for Youth Empowerment*, Evans (2014) describes study abroad as a mechanism for holistic youth development, self-empowerment, and a sense of agency. Evans argues that education abroad for students of color in particular provides a foundation of knowledge and skills needed for college and career competence and opportunity to find voice. In some respects, study abroad is ready-made to foster and even provoke a student's endeavor of self-authorship. From the very beginning, a student draws on a combination of outside encouragement and an inner drive or predisposition to venture out into the world. For marginalized groups, personal characteristics such as race, gender, and ethnicity can affect the predisposition of participants to "seek particular experiences (e.g., jobs, relationships, travel)" (Baxter Magolda 2008, p. 282; Leon 2013).

Then, once overseas, a student is the proverbial stranger in a strange new land. A student may wrestle with the question of how to view himself or herself. Research on self-authorship claims that, introducing college students to complex situations, promote the developing of their identity.

Pizzolato (2005) calls these complex situations provocative experiences, which offer an ideal scenario for students to deal with the complexities of adult life. Research has demonstrated that students are not likely to develop self-authorship in college because "institutions of higher education did not provide sufficiently provocative experiences that disrupted students student's equilibrium such that they felt compelled to consider and begin to construct new conceptions of self" (Pizzolato 2003, p. 798).

Building New Relationships

Forming relationships is one of the main concerns that individuals must face in order to develop self-authorship. Baxter Magolda (2008) points out that "self-authorship enhances, rather than constraints, relationships" (p. 282). Baxter Magolda argues that self-authorship fosters relationships that are more authentic because these relationships often help individuals pursue their internal commitment by listening to their internal voice.

A student is confronted with different contexts and ways of thinking, challenging him or her to evaluate and construct knowledge and judgments about culture, identity, politics, morality, and everyday ways of doing things. In all study abroad as self-authorship can mean self-confidence and autonomy as the student fashions an internal identity separate from, but sensitive to external factors. One important element is to trust your internal voice, recognizing that reality is beyond your control, but individuals can use their internal voice to shape that reality (Baxter Magolda 2009). Baxter Magolda (2008) states that as individuals develop toward self-authorship, they begin to recognize and identify their own voice. This helps individuals establish beliefs, priorities, goals, and discover themselves, while nurturing relationhsips that are aligned with their own voice.

Study Abroad as Readiness

How then does self-authorship relate to readiness? Self-authorship and readiness may seem to be worlds apart. One has an existential, phenomenological, and psychological feel to it. The other concerns the real world of academic degrees and jobs, and income and well-being. A closer look shows just how similar and even aligned they are. To navigate a global environment, math (and reading and science) skills are necessary, but they are not nearly enough. In 2010, the Office of Community College Research and Leadership (OCCRL) helped to formulate the Illinois College and

Career Readiness (CCR) Pilot Program in more basic and vital terms. Drawing on David Conley (2005, 2007, 2009, 2010), OCCRL advanced the "Conley model," which entails four key concepts toward college and career readiness: academic behaviors; content knowledge; cognitive strategies; and contextual skills and awareness (Baber et al. 2010). The Conley model is the foundation for acquiring math skills, among others, *and* for using these skills meaningfully and effectively in the real world.

1. *Academic behavior* includes "the ability of a student to be organized, possess study skills, and work within a group dynamic."
2. *Content knowledge* includes "skills, concepts and principles" that are foundational to the subject at hand.
3. *Cognitive strategies* include "problem solving, interpretation, precision, and accuracy" (Ibid.).
4. *Contextual skills and awareness means* "college knowledge" (Conley 2010, p. 72), and includes understanding the "campus system" and learning to navigate college culture (Baber et al. 2010).

The blending of CCR and the Conley model means helping to foster capable and confident students who can apply subject matter to the world beyond the classroom. CCR as an exercise in global navigation suffers from a basic problem, however, since the classroom environment must stand in for the world. OCCRL (Bragg et al. 2011) spoke to this challenge by emphasizing a Conley model in which students are "co-facilitators in their learning and development," which must ultimately take them beyond the confines of the school. What kind of global horizon does the world around them inscribe and/or reinforce on a daily basis?

One consideration is the effect study abroad as a new kind of classroom conceived as an endeavor of self-authorship has for students of color. To illustrate the promise and the impact, we draw on a recent study by Leon (2013), *Examining the Concept of Self-Authorship: Black Males Who Study Abroad*. While Leon's focus was undergraduate students at a four-year university, his conversations with African Americans—Mark, Reggie, David, and Logan—who had just completed study abroad programs, introduce voices and lived experiences into our more abstract discussion. While the present chapter is merely a prelude and commentary for future research, we hope to show that the story of study abroad (i.e., its promise and effects) is best told by the students themselves as self-authors; and self-authorship as a kind of self-education, which is often the very best kind of education. The following highlights study abroad experiences drawn from a larger study of 20 African American males who were first time in any college attendees and community college transfer students at four-year institutions participating in study abroad (Leon 2013).

On Academic Behavior. One of the challenges at first was the whole independence aspect because like I said I'm a passive person generally and I'm a person that waits for instructions from somebody to tell me what to do, but that person wasn't there. It was a lot of me becoming more self-reliant. I got to cook for myself, went to the grocery store by myself, took myself to the hospital, it was just like one of those sort of things (Mark).

On Content Knowledge. When it comes to going to other countries, you hear a lot about it. But when you actually study abroad, you get to come to your own conclusions because you're actually seeing it first-hand and you can make your conclusions about what you see versus what someone told you (Mark). We went to Greece during the protest; it was immediately after the crisis. We went to the national bank, and you know, we had a better understanding of what was going on in Greece because we saw in the news the protests and riots, and everyone looks angry and you didn't have any idea of what was going, but things weren't like that, they were so different. The media portrayed the things very different from how they were and we were able to discover that in our own and form our own opinions (Reggie).

On Cognitive Strategies. When you go into study abroad, you have more interaction, especially with people that study abroad. The one aspect that changed it was that now I am less likely to judge people on their appearance, especially international students. Study abroad opened my eyes to other cultures, to what they go through, and what it is like to live there, it also changed my perspective in judging someone from their perception or you might think about them at first glance, you never know what people are like until you meet them (Reggie). I was more willing to make a decision on my own and not have a bunch of people backing you up, a group of people. Study abroad helped my individual thought process, helping me make decisions by myself without anyone telling me what to do (David).

On Contextual Skills and Awareness. Study abroad helped me to realize that I should be more adventurous, that you can take a risk, and the majority of time you will be okay. Through simple things like doing something on your own, meeting other people, you might not know how people will respond to you, but it will be fine (Reggie). I feel like the experience as a whole does that because you're there by yourself, you have to like recreate your group of friends and recreate everything and so much has to do with yourself image because you're meeting all these people for the first time and you can really kind of portray whatever you want. Study abroad is a really nice tool to help you deal with self-image (Mark).

On Career Readiness. I learned how to network. [Study abroad] opens up a door of possibilities for you. Just two weeks ago I got a job offer from over there and I'm over here, don't limit yourself (Logan).

Closing Thoughts

In 1839, at the age of 20, Herman Melville took to sea. For the next five years, he worked his way across the Atlantic and Pacific Oceans. He lived among the Typee on Marquesas Island, traveled to Tahiti, and ended up in Honolulu before he returned home to New England. He wrote along the way and for the rest of his life. From this brief biography, two facts seem clear. First, Melville's authorship of great novels was possible only through his travels. Second, his travels *were* his education—education as *study abroad*.

The epigram of this chapter is especially fitting given a concern for global readiness. Melville writes, "having little or no money in my purse, and nothing particular to interest me on shore ... " Translated into present-day educational policy, the concern is that underserved and marginalized students, often *students of color*, are especially not in the full fold of participation when it concerns study abroad programming.

Melville also charts a solution to the problem. In light of no prospects at home, he continues, "I thought I would sail about a little and see the watery part of the world." The challenge today is globalization. Even in Melville's day, the world seemed to be shrinking and intensifying through interconnection and competition between nations, economies, and people. Melville did not wait for the world to call upon him. Instead, he waded into the world in order to write his own story. Today, we might call this endeavor *study abroad*. Study abroad students have the opportunity for *self-authorship* and as a result *readiness* to face the world. In sum, considering "study away" opportunities (Sobania 2015) for global learning within one's local context fosters college and career readiness. With study abroad, community colleges can play an integral role in connecting the global and the local to develop students' competencies, which, in effect, contribute to their global readiness.

REFERENCES

Amani, Monija (2011). *Study abroad decision and participation at community colleges: Influential factors and challenges from the voices of students and coordinators*. Unpublished doctoral dissertation, George Washington University, Washington, DC.

American Association of Community Colleges. (2015). *Fast facts*. http://www.aacc.nche.edu/AboutCC/Pages/fastfactsfactsheet.aspx

Arden-Ogle, Ellen A. (2009). *Study abroad and global competence: Exemplary community college programs which foster elements of achievement*. Unpublished doctoral dissertation, Oregon State University, Corvallis, OR.

Baber, Lorenzo D., Castro, Erin L., & Bragg, Debra D. (2010). *Measuring success: David Conley's college readiness framework and the Illinois College and Career Readiness Act*. Champaign, IL: Office of Community College Research and Leadership, University of Illinois at Urbana-Champaign.

Baker-Smemoe, Wendy, Dewey, Dan P., Brown, Jennifer, & Martinsen, Rob A. (2014). Variables affecting L2 gains during study abroad. *Foreign Language Annals, 47*(3), 464–486.

Baxter Magolda, Marcia B. (2008). Three elements of self-authorship. *Journal of College Student Development, 49*(4), 269–284.

Baxter Magolda, Marcia B. (2009). *Authoring your life: Developing an internal voice to navigate life's challenges*. Sterling, VA: Stylus.

Black, H. Tyrone, & Duhon, David L. (2006). Assessing the impact of business study abroad programs on cultural awareness and personal development. *Journal of Education for Business, 81*(3), 140–144.

Bragg, Debra D., Barber, Lorenzo D., & Castro, Erin L. (2011). *Illinois' college and career readiness pilot initiative: Progress on implementation of Conley's comprehensive model. The Illinois Report 2011*. Institute of Government and Public Affairs, University of Illinois.

Brux, Jacqueline M., & Fry, Blake (2010). Multicultural students in study abroad: Their interests, their issues, and their constraints. *Journal of Studies in International Education, 14*(5), 508–527.

Center for Internationalization and Global Engagement (2012). *Mapping internationalization internationalization on US campuses: 2012 Edition*. Washington, DC: American Council on Education.

Cohen, Arthur M. (2011). Further views from professors, state directors, and analysts. *New Directions for Community Colleges, 156*, 87–100.

Commission of the Lincoln Study Abroad Fellowship Program. (2005). *Global competencies and national Needs: One million Americans studying abroad.* http://www.nafsa.org/Resource_Library_Assets/Public_Policy/Lincoln_Commission_s_Report/

Conley, David T. (2005). *College knowledge: What it really takes for students to succeed and what we can do to get them ready.* San Francisco: Jossey-Bass.

Conley, David T. (2007). *Toward a more comprehensive conception of college readiness.* Eugene, OR: Educational Policy Improvement Center.

Conley, David T., (2009, Spring). Rethinking college readiness. *Update on research and Leadership, 20*(2). Champaign, IL: Office of Community College Research and Leadership, University of Illinois.

Conley, David T. (2010). *College and career Ready: Helping all students succeed beyond high school.* San Francisco: Jossey-Bass.

Dawson, Nancy J. (2000). Study abroad and African American college students at Southern Illinois University at Carbondale. *African Issues, 28*(1/2), 124–129.

Dessoff, Alan (2006). Who's not going abroad? *International Educator, 15*(2), 20–27.

Drexler, Devi S., & Campbell, Dale F. (2011). Student development among community college participants in study abroad programs. *Community College Journal of Research and Practice, 35*(8), 608–619.

Emert, Holly A., & Pearson, Diane L. (2007). Expanding the vision of international education: Collaboration, assessment, and intercultural development. In E. J. Valeau & R. L. Raby (Eds.), *International reform efforts and challenges in community colleges, New Directions for Community Colleges, 138* (pp. 67–75). San Francisco: Jossey-Bass.

Evans, Stephanie Y. (2014). *Black passports: Travel memoirs as a tool for youth empowerment.* Albany, NY: SUNY Press.

Fersh, Seymour, & Fitchen, Edward (1981). *The community college and international education: A report of progress.* http://files.eric.ed.gov/fulltext/ED211153.pdf

Frost, Robert A., & Raby, Rosalind L. (2009). Democratizing study abroad: Challenges of open access, local commitments, and global competence in community colleges. In R. Lewin (Ed.), *Handbook of practice and research in study abroad* (pp. 170–190). New York, NY: Routledge.

Hadis, Benjamin F. (2005). Gauging the impact of study abroad: How to overcome the limitations of a single-cell design. *Assessment & Evaluation in Higher Education, 30*(1), 3–19.

Hembroff, Larry A., & Rusz, Debra L. (1993). *Minorities and overseas studies programs: Correlates of differential participation. Occasional papers on International Educational Exchange, 30.* New York: Council on International Educational Exchange.

Hovland, Kevin (2009). Global learning: What is it? Who is responsible for it? *Peer Review, 11*, 4–7.

Institute of International Education. (2014a, November 17). *Open doors 2014*. Open doors data: Community colleges data resource. http://www.iie.org/ Research-and-Publications/Open-Doors/Data/Community-College-Data-Resource/Study-Abroad

Institute of International Education. (2014b, November 17). *Open doors 2014: Report on International Educational Exchange*. http://www.iie.org/~/ media/Files/Corporate/Open-Doors/Open-Doors-2014-Presentation. ashx?la=en

Institute of International Education. (2014c, November 17). *Open doors 2014*. Open doors data: Fast facts. http://www.iie.org/Research-and-Publications/ Open-Doors/Data/Fast-Facts

Kuh, George D. (2003, March/April). What we're learning about student engagement from NSSE: Benchmarks for effective educational practices. *Change*, 24–32.

Leon, R. A. (2013, April). *Examining the concept of self-authorship: Black males who study abroad*. Research paper presented at the annual meeting of the American Educational Research Association, San Francisco, CA.

McMullen, M., & Penn, E. B. (2011). "Egypt in Transition": Uniting Service-Learning and Short-Term Study-Abroad. *Intercultural Education, 22*(5), 423–436.

McMurtrie, Beth (2007). Study-abroad numbers continue to climb, trips are shorter, report says. *Chronicle of Higher Education, 54*(12), A36.

Metzger, Christy A. (2006). Study abroad programming: A 21st century retention strategy? *College Student Affairs Journal, 25*(2), 164–175.

National Association of Foreign Student Advisers. (n.d.). *Explore international education: Trends in U.S. study abroad*. http://www.nafsa.org/Explore_ International_Education/Advocacy_And_Public_Policy/Study_Abroad/ Trends_in_U.S._Study_Abroad/

Niser, John C. (2010). Study abroad education in New England higher education: A pilot survey. *International Journal of Educational Management, 24*(1), 48–55.

Oguntoyinbo, Lekan (2015, June 18). Science and study abroad. *Diverse Issues in Higher Education, 32*(10), 10–11.

Pizzolato, Jane E. (2003). Developing self-authorship: Exploring the experiences of high-risk college students. *Journal of College Student Development, 44*(6), 797–812.

Pizzolato, Jane E. (2005). Creating crossroads for self-authorship: Investigating the provocative moment. *Journal of College Student Development, 46*(6), 624–641.

Raby, Rosalind L. (2008, September). *Meeting America's global education challenge: Expanding education abroad at U.S. community colleges*. Institute of International Education Study Abroad White Paper Series 3. New York, NY: Institute for International Education Press.

Raby, Rosalind L., & Valeau, Edward J. (2007). Community college international education: Looking back to forecast the future. In R. L. Raby & E. J. Valeau (Eds.), *International reform efforts and challenges in community colleges* (pp. 5–14). San Francisco, CA: Wiley Periodicals.

Raby, R. L., & Valeau, E. J. (Eds.) (2009). Community college models: Globalization and higher education reform. Netherlands: Springer.

Raby, Rosalind L., Rhodes, Gary M., & Biscarra, Albert (2014). Community college study abroad: Implications for student success. *Community College Journal of Research and Practice, 38*(2–3), 174–183.

Sobania, Neal W. (Ed.) (2015). *Putting the local in global education: Models for transformative learning through domestic off-campus programs*. Sterling, VA: Stylus Publishing.

Taylor, John (2004). Towards a strategy for internationalisation: Lessons and practice from four universities. *Journal of Studies in International Education, 8,* 149–171.

Taylor, Jason L., Linick, Matthew A., Reese, George C., Barber, Lorenzo D., & Bragg, Debra D. (2012, November). *Illinois' college and career readiness implementation evaluation: Year-five (2011–2012) results*. Champaign, IL: Office of Community College Research and Leadership, University of Illinois at Urbana-Champaign.

Tillmann, Martin (Ed.). (2010). *Impact of education abroad on career development*. American Institute of Foreign Study, Vol. 1. www.aifsabroad.com/advisors/pdf/Impact_of_Education_AbroadI.pdf

Valeau, Edward J., & Raby, Rosalind L. (Eds.). (2007). International reform efforts and challenges in community colleges. *New Directions for Community Colleges, 138,* 1–96.

Willis, Tasha Y. (2012). *Rare but there: An intersectional exploration of the experiences and outcomes of Black women who studied abroad through community college programs*. Unpublished doctoral dissertation, California State University, Long Beach, CA.

Zamani-Gallaher, Eboni M., Lang, John, Graham, Edmund, & Baber, Lorenzo D. (June 2015). *STEM college and career readiness report: 2014–2015*. Champaign, IL: Office of Community College Research and Leadership, University of Illinois at Urbana-Champaign.

Zhang, Yi (2011). CSCC review series essay: Education abroad in the US community colleges. *Community College Review, 39*(2), 181–200.

CHAPTER 9

Microaggressions and Intersectionality in the Experiences of Black Women Studying Abroad through Community Colleges: Implications for Practice

Tasha Y. Willis

INTRODUCTION

Community colleges have a unique opportunity to both increase access to and improve the quality of education abroad for underrepresented students. Their use of faculty-led programs (Raby 2008; Amani 2011) can be capitalized upon to reach students of color as well as first-generation and low-income students and to provide them with supportive environments that help maximize their learning experiences. However, despite the relative diversity of many community colleges, underrepresented minority students can still be marginalized on their home campuses, and by extension, when they study abroad.

Microaggressions and intersectionality are concepts particularly important to understand in considering community college and underrepresented students' study abroad experiences. Campus climate includes racial, class, age, and gender demographics and dynamics which can influence peer interactions, as well as student comfort and engagement with faculty, faculty's cultural competence or lack thereof, and the occurrence and han-

T.Y. Willis (✉)
College of Social Work, California State University, Los Angeles, Los Angeles, CA, USA

© The Editor(s) (if applicable) and The Author(s) 2016   127
R.L. Raby, E.J. Valeau (eds.), *International Education at Community Colleges*, DOI 10.1057/978-1-137-53336-4_9

dling of microaggressions related to the students' intersectional identities. Racial microaggressions are subtle insults aimed at people of color and may be verbal, nonverbal, and/or visual and may be automatic or unconscious (Solórzano et al. 2000). Such affronts, though often unintentional and/or minimized by others, have been documented by critical race scholars in the context of education for years (Solórzano 1998, 2000; Solórzano et al. 2000). They have been shown to come at psychic, emotional, and physical cost to the targeted individuals (Smith et al. 2011).

Microaggressions also occur against women, baring the importance of the concept of intersectionality, which offers insight into the interplay between varying forms of marginalization. Black feminist theorists Crenshaw (2005) and Collins (2000) highlight the double bind that women of color face in a sexist, racist, classist society. These scholars argue the intersection of these social forces must be considered for more meaningful and accurate analysis of oppression. These ideas are central to the guiding premise of this chapter, which offers insight and practice implications for practitioners committed to programming that meets the needs of diverse students—Black women among others—studying overseas. Additionally, it should be noted here that faculty-led study programs hold the potential to replicate or even amplify the campus climate abroad, for better or for worse.

Study Abroad: Benefits and Barriers

Study abroad has been linked with numerous developmental benefits among college students and is also identified as a high-impact practice that can lead to increased engagement and student success (Kuh 2011). However, most research to date has primarily centered on White, middle-class, female students at four-year institutions, perhaps, due in part to the fact that this population is overrepresented in the US study abroad (Jackson 2006; Kasravi 2009, Wick 2011; Willis 2012).

Students of Color Abroad: Barriers, Heritage-Seeking, and Beyond

While the literature on students of color abroad has not fully explored factors that influence how these students experience their time abroad, it does illuminate the importance of intersectionality in understanding these students' experiences abroad. The limited studies that do exist are primarily related to access (Comp 2008; Brux and Frye 2009; Penn and Tanner 2009) and heritage-seeking (Raymondi 2005; Guerrero 2006; Beausoleil

2008). Regarding Black students in particular, early research focused on ethnic identity development (Carey 2007; Harden 2007), intergroup relations (Landau and Moore 2001; Morgan et al. 2002), and intercultural gains (Day-Vines et al. 1998). More recent studies reflect similar themes of "empowerment," "agency," and "self-actualization" respectively (Jackson 2006; Wick 2011; Willis 2012). This budding body of literature highlights the importance of research on a wider range of experiences among Black students abroad, and also reflects a need for more inquiry into intersectionality and microaggressions in study abroad contexts.

Public Harassment of Women in Study Abroad

Given the wide cultural variances related to gender norms and tolerated behaviors, it is not surprising that women who study abroad have reported experiencing challenges when they encounter differences. Rawlins' (2012) most recent inquiry is representative of this body of literature, shedding light on how participants responded to, accounted for, and struggled to interpret public harassment. Instances of catcalling, men being more forward than students were used to, men following them home, and even exposing themselves publicly to women were more disconcerting and frightening than the same types of experiences at home, perhaps because they felt more vulnerable. Yet, Rawlins' participants expressed a strong desire to not misinterpret "innocuous behaviors as harassment" due to cultural differences because of being US Americans. Earlier researchers explored the experiences of White US women in Costa Rica (Twombly 1995), Japanese women in Canada (Fryer and Wong 1998), and a sole African American woman in Spain (Talburt and Stewart 1999). These studies touched upon the intersection of race, gender, and nationality.

Community College Study Abroad

Research on study abroad at community colleges is a small proportion of the wider literature on internationalization of their curricula. This larger body of literature ranges from the rationale for expanding global learning both on- and off-campus at these institutions (Frost 2007; Raby 2008) to models for doing so (Arden Ogle 2009; Frost 2007; Valeau and Raby 2007; Bradshaw 2013). Specific to study abroad, researchers have documented access issues (Niser 2010; Amani 2011), identity development (Drexler and Campbell 2011; Willis 2012), intercultural gains (Emert and Pearson

2007); and academic development (Sutton and Rubin 2010; Raby et al. 2014). In order to deliver more effective study abroad experiences for the rich diversity of community college students, this chapter seeks to derive practice implications from one sub-group of students: Black women who studied abroad through community college programs across the country.

METHODS

Through purposeful snowball sampling, I recruited 19 women, aged 19–62, who: (a) had at least one biological parent who was of Black/African/African American heritage, (b) had grown up in the USA, and (c) had participated in an educational program abroad at a community college. I conducted semi-structured, open-ended interviews with participants from Los Angeles, San Francisco, New York, and Arizona. The protocol consisted of 21 prompts aimed at answering four guiding research questions related to intercultural communication, global identity, race and ethnic identity, other learning outcomes, and potential microaggressions. Willis (2015) describes in detail how she utilized the constant comparative method, Atlas Ti, peer debriefing, member checking along with methods to enhance the trustworthiness of qualitative research as defined by Lincoln and Guba (1985).

FINDINGS

Though participants described their trips as positively life-transforming, they also faced disheartening and even painful encounters as a result of the climate for Black women, both in their host cultures and among their non-Black US peers. In fact, all participants cited instances of racial and gender microaggressions, regardless of whether Blackness was the norm (as in African countries) or not (the Mediterranean and the British Isles) in their host country.

US Peers: Stress Versus Support

In this study, nearly all participants traveled with US peers from their home institution on faculty-led programs, jointly housed either in homestays or in apartments and/or hotels. As a result, US peers played a significant role in shaping participants' experiences. This peer connection served as a cultural buffer and as a source of comfort for most students during the process of adjustment to the new environment. Most students had at least one other Black student on their program, which ultimately also proved helpful.

However, four participants were the only Black students in their groups. Although two reported having had previous experience being immersed in White and multiethnic settings, both still experienced some discomfort on their trips. Antoinette's quote reflects this group's experience:

> It was like I am a black dot on a White piece of paper. And it is like ... I didn't fear for my life, or anything. I wasn't afraid or anything like that, it was just like I don't have anyone that can share ... people who, you know, can understand.

Such isolation was often compounded by experiences of racial micro-aggressions perpetrated by US peers, host cultures or both. For example, though being the only Black student on a study abroad trip was itself challenging, Nyla (20) also cited specific actions by her US peers that heightened her feelings of isolation and marginalization:

> Just some of the comments that they would make were a little bit uncomfortable ... I mean I just let it slide. But at the same time, I started to distance myself from them. I noticed that I wouldn't hang out too much with them going out or I wouldn't hang out with them in a lot of large crowds.

When asked to compare her interactions with British people to those with her US travel peers, Nyla summarized by saying, "Most [negative] interactions or huge emotions came from just interacting with the students that came on the trip with different things they would say and everything." Unfortunately, even students who did have at least one other Black woman on their trip also experienced racial isolation.

Sabrina (age 19) recounted that in addition to her male cousin, who was with her in Italy, there were two other Black students present. She and the other Black woman (nearly 10 years older than Sabrina) were relieved to relate to each other and Sabrina "needed those moments." She explained that within their group, there seemed to be a divide between the White students and the students of other ethnicities. Her Black female friend in particular experienced isolation in her living arrangements, which were exacerbated in the larger group:

> It was the fact that she was in an all White girl apartment. And so they really didn't share different information with her. So if they would go to a party they wouldn't tell her ... So she would just kind of be left alone. And she was older. She was like 27 or 28 and they were like 22, 23. ... The White people would stay to themselves. ... And the rest of the people that were not White, we would be in a group. ... And so we would kind of discuss amongst ourselves as ethnicities, as the minority in a way ... that "How come they just don't hang out with us?" And we would invite them and they don't come. And they would go places and they wouldn't invite us. So we were just like "What?" We didn't understand we're like, "We're from the same school, like, what's going on?"

In this exemplar, the relevance of age, as well as race, should be noted as possibly playing a role in the lack of connection among students sharing the same apartment. This factor leads back to another intersectional consideration: Participants were not only of Black heritage but were also of a particular age and gender, which likely had a bearing on their experiences.

On a related and positive note, for most of the participants who went to Spain, the difficulty of feeling racially othered and older than other participants was largely mitigated by the presence of other mature, Black travel companions. In fact, Angel (49), a Los Angeles participant who participated in an earlier course in Spain and two years later recruited a cadre of Black women to travel with on her next trip, had a significant, positive impact on her peers. Two of three interviewees from the same program specifically cited Angel as a source of crucial predeparture information and in-country support. She helped prepare Betty (38) emotionally before the trip as a Black woman, and she was a source of comfort for Sage (24) when she encountered racial taunting by a Spanish school-aged child. Interestingly, the two oldest students in the study both described themselves as being in mentoring roles in relation to their peers, though Ruth (62) mentored young Latino students as she was the only Black woman on her program. Their life experiences likely served as helpful resources for them in managing their most challenging experiences abroad. Such age differences may be fairly unique to the community college experience, and because of their potential impact, they are important to note.

Microaggressions by In-Country Hosts

Notably, all 19 students experienced some form of microaggression, either from US peers, the host culture, or both. In this study, microaggressions occurred in all the three host regions (British Isles, Mediterranean, and West Africa) but were most pronounced in Spain and Italy, in reaction to the participants' intersectional identity as Black females abroad. These experiences offer evidence of gendered racism (Smith et al. 2011) toward participants while overseas, and ranged widely on a spectrum of severity. It is important to note that part of the challenge of microaggressions is that they can be very subtle, making them easy to discount by people who may not be experiencing them directly, yet they weigh on the receiver (Pierce 1995). For example, Alana (26) drew a comparison between the non-European places she studied (Morocco, Ghana, and India) and Spain:

> You know, it was like a subtle racism ... You'd go into the stores and people just have a certain attitude ... But then some people would say, "Well, they don't like you because you don't speak Spanish," and we'd be like, "Oh, okay, maybe that's what it is. Thanks, that explains everything," but, you know, sometimes that wasn't it, you know?

Alana expresses her frustration when her identification of a possible microaggression is dismissed. The elusive nature of microaggressions is troubling and as Smith et al. (2011) note, "consume[s] valuable time and energy that could be used for more creative, educative, professional or humanitarian goals" (p. 67).

More obvious on the spectrum, and beyond catcalls and being "hit on" as a Black woman in Italy, Sabrina, a vivacious and artistic 20-year-old, recounted being stopped by a policeman. He assumed she was a prostitute as she and a Filipina American girlfriend walked home late at night. Sabrina went on to describe the stereotypes and sexualization of Black women she experienced in Italy, which, thankfully, she had read about "doing her [own] homework" in advance at the behest of family and friends who had traveled. It should be noted that no students mentioned race being addressed as part of predeparture preparation offered by faculty or staff.

Racialized Sexual Harassment and Assault

Beyond the realm of microaggressions, several students were confronted with unwanted sexual behavior and even physical contact that, by US standards, would be classified as sexual harassment or assault.

A variety of students in the Mediterranean and British Isles expressed awareness that they received particular attention as a result of their intersectional identities. Betty (38) encapsulates the experience of many when she refers to how some men would call out to her and other Black women: "They definitely commented on my skin color. *Chocolate*, you know, stuff like that. ... *Morena* (*dark skin*). ... Sometimes it was okay and sometimes you could tell it was a little rude." These hypersexualized experiences for Black women is also seen in the literature for another Black woman in Spain who encountered more vulgar and sexualized catcalls than her White US female peers (Talburt and Steward 1999).

Intersectionality is also useful in helping to untangle another challenging situation encountered by two participants staying with the same family, which highlights language, skin color, age, and body shape, in addition to race and gender. Initially, Lanelle, (38), soft spoken and reserved, identified the language barrier as a concern within the context of her homestay experience, especially given that the other students housed in the same host family spoke more Spanish than she did. However, from Sage's (24) perspective (Lanelle's housemate) the fact that Lanelle did not speak much Spanish was compounded by the fact that their homestay mother seemed quick to draw comparisons between the two, blaming Lanelle's lack of Spanish skills on her darker complexion. Sage, who had traveled internationally before, spoke freely about race and racism during her interview.

In contrast to Sage, Lanelle did not initially attribute the rift between her and her homestay mother to race or skin tone in her interview. However, during a follow-up interview, she did clarify that though she could not be certain, she wondered if the homestay mother was used to younger students and/or may have been threatened by Lanelle's maturity and shapeliness as a Black woman, particularly as her husband lived in the home with them as well. Lanelle was flooded with memories of being scolded at the dinner table to the point of crying. She also hesitantly recalled an uncomfortable pattern that could be described as sexual harassment: Unlike her homestay peers who used weekends to travel, Lanelle often stayed home to save money and to recharge from the busy week. The homestay mother would leave and the host father would go into a room adjacent to Lanelle's and play pornography very loudly. Unfortunately, she did not feel comfortable addressing these issues with the program faculty until very late in the trip. This was largely because when she first shared that she was not given a key to the home (as the other students were on the first day), her program faculty unwittingly minimized the situation as a "simple mistake." She reflected upon her approach to coping with this daunting set of experiences: As a way to keep functioning during the trip, she minimized the racial undertones of her interactions and the pain that came with them.

This unsettling example highlights the relevance of intersectionality in understanding the possible experiences of Black women, as well as other students, studying abroad. Their diversity in physical phenotype, age, language skills, and personality, as well as their approach to managing race, discrimination, and even harassment, may contribute to their differing experiences in a host country among both hosts and US peers. It also explicates the emotional energy spent by recipients of such ambiguous experiences.

Less ambiguous and further on the spectrum of affronts is actual sexual assault, defined as any unwanted physical contact of a sexual nature. This was reported by several students and ranged from being groped to even grabbed by the hair. Yet another student, Sophie (20), described walking home at night by herself and being followed by a man on a bike, who was soon chased off by a bystander, who then himself "goes to do the whole hug and double cheek kiss and then he pulled me in for like a real kiss, and I like freaked out and just ran to my hotel room." Despite having a good rapport with her White male faculty, Sophie chose not to disclose this incident to him, so as not to worry him or risk "jeopardizing the program." These gendered moments were troubling for the participants in Italy in particular, and they spoke of the need to adjust to this cultural difference regarding what is publically condoned in that country. What is not clear is the extent to which these situations also involved race, or other aspects of participants' social identities given the cultural context.

PRACTICE, IMPLICATIONS, AND RECOMMENDATIONS

A tension ran between the two primary themes of the participants' study abroad experiences: On one hand, they described experiences that helped them become more self-actualized while on the other hand, they also recounted disturbing microaggressions and in several instances, harassment and assault attributed to their race, gender and/or other dimensions of their identities. By highlighting microaggressions, harassment, and assault, I do not seek to minimize the positive experiences study abroad afforded participants. Instead, my intention is to draw attention to the urgency of improving not only *access to* but also the *quality of* the experiences for marginalized students. As such, these findings highlight the potential that faculty-led community college education abroad programs hold.

Programs led by faculty from students' home campus could serve to better prepare and support students and to deepen their learning outcomes. Though most participants mentioned receiving some form of predeparture orientation, none mentioned issues of race being addressed during these sessions. More than a quarter of participants cited positive relationships with their faculty, who were instrumental in encouraging them to make the trip a reality. As such, faculty can intentionally foster such trusting relationships and thereby maximize their intervention and involvement with students for more targeted predeparture preparation, increased in-country support and deeper reentry reflection and learning. Three recommendations for practice are offered in the following section.

Critically Reflexive Programming

As demonstrated in this study, campus climate expands beyond physical borders. Thus, program leadership should consider the racial composition of courses in order to facilitate group cohesion. Orientations should include awareness-raising activities that directly broach personal identity, modeling openness, and building trust on these issues that are often otherwise taboo in daily discussions. In-country leadership should facilitate routine check-ins and inquire about how students are experiencing their identities in the host culture and among their peers, fostering a climate in which microaggressions and other sensitive issues are safer for students to address directly themselves or with support. In some cases, skillful faculty intervention may be warranted to (a) help a targeted student process painful emotions and regain focus on the overall experience, (b) facilitate learning and change behavior by a perpetrator in the group (whether student, faculty, or staff), and (c) to enhance overall group dynamics and learning for all students.

The reentry period should be looked upon as equally important. Ideally, a campus office of international programs would convene reflective reentry opportunities for debriefing. However, in lieu of this, faculty can also work toward these practices themselves, particularly if provided with some institutional support. For example, a for-credit reentry course can be offered or even required to increase returnee participation in reflection. This will also enable, even incentivize, faculty to follow through with reentry programming, which is otherwise challenging with their myriad other campus demands. Where institutional support is not feasible, offering at minimum several reentry debriefing sessions and directing students to online reentry resources would strengthen programs which otherwise often have minimal if any reentry reflection activities.

Critically Self-Reflexive Leadership

Issues of campus climate are widely discussed in the literature and among student and student affairs professionals within a US context (Hurtado et al. 1999; Locks et al. 2008). This study raises the notion that campus climate issues can travel with students abroad, particularly in diverse community college programs. If faculty and staff are well prepared to recognize and address these climate issues, including microaggressions in the group, they can have a positive impact on both the targeted students and those who unwittingly perpetrate these affronts. However, this requires faculty and staff to have the requisite knowledge, awareness, and skills to recognize microaggressions and other racial and diversity-related dynamics in the student group and host country. They must be critically reflexive (Sisneros et al. 2008) of their own practices and skilled in facilitating the dynamics of diverse groups, beyond the general intercultural training and experience they may already have from international exposure or study. Otherwise, they risk reifying the very dynamics they wish to avert.

Creativity in Collaboration

To successfully respond to microaggressions and intergroup tensions, many faculty and international office staff may find it useful and/or necessary to collaborate with other faculty and staff who have expertise in domestic diversity and student affairs. Attending professional development events offered by these experts or, at minimum, consulting with them during program development can offer study abroad leadership the opportunity to (a) explore their own levels of awareness, biases, and preparedness for addressing microaggressions of any kind, and (b) develop the necessary critically reflexive programming. Interdepartmental collaboration can be an excellent way to help prepare internationally focused faculty to address domestic diversity campus climate issues which reach beyond a campus' physical borders. It can also have other positive ramifications for education abroad beyond the scope of this chapter, such as reducing structural barriers and enhancing recruitment and reentry.

Conclusion

Study abroad for Black women and other marginalized students in community colleges is a powerful yet largely untapped resource, offering rich opportunities for growth. However, as promising as these outcomes are, they are only part of the whole story. In fact, an intersectional analysis reveals that race, gender, class, age, sexual orientation, and other aspects of social diversity, as well as a travel group's climate, shape student interactions with their peers and their in-country hosts. As leaders in education abroad, we have a responsibility to ensure that these dynamics are anticipated and addressed proactively. To do so, we must explore ways to enhance our faculty and programs' capacities to meet students' needs. In short, the late Dr. Maya Angelou would have us ensure that our students depart for their sojourns "hoping for the best, prepared for the worst, and unsurprised by anything in between" (1969, p. 308).

References

Amani, Monija (2011). *Study abroad decision and participation at community colleges: Influential factors and challenges from the voices of students and coordinators*. Unpublished doctoral dissertation, George Washington University, Washington, DC.

Arden-Ogle, Ellen A. (2009). *Study abroad and global competence: Exemplary community college programs which foster elements of achievement*. Unpublished doctoral dissertation, Oregon State University, Corvallis, OR.

Beausoleil, Amy (2008). *Understanding heritage and ethnic identity development through study abroad: The case of South Korea*. Doctoral dissertation University of California. Santa Barbara, Retrieved from Dissertation Abstracts International. (AAT 3330411).

Bradshaw, Geoffrey W. (2013). Internationalization and Faculty-Led Service Learning. New Directions for Community Colleges, 2013: 39–53. doi: 10.1002/cc.20047

Brux, Jacqueline M., & Fry, Blake (2009). Multicultural students in study abroad: Their interests, their issues, and their constraints. *Journal of Studies in International Education, 20*(10), 1–19.

Carey, Kami J. (2007). *The shifting character of social and ethnic identity among African-American sojourners*. Doctoral dissertation Howard University, Dissertation Abstracts International. (AAT 3283227).

Collins, Patricia H. (2000). *Black feminist thought: Knowledge, consciousness, and the politics of empowerment*. New York: Routledge.

Comp, David (2008). U.S. heritage-seeking students discover minority communities in Western Europe. *Journal of Studies in International Education, 12*(1), 29–37.

Crenshaw, Kimberle (2005). Mapping the margins: Intersectionality, identity politics, and violence against women of color. In R. K. Bergen, J. L. Edleson, & C. M. Renzetti (Eds.), *Violence against women: Classic papers* (pp. 282–313). Auckland, New Zealand: Pearson Education.

Day-Vines, Norma, Barker, Jeanette M., & Exum, Herbert A. (1998). Impact of diasporic travel on ethnic identity development of African American college students. *College Student Journal, 32*(3), 463–471.

Drexler, Devi S., & Campbell, Dale F. (2011). Student development among community college participants in study abroad programs. *Community College Journal of Research and Practice, 35*, 608–619.

Emert, Holly A., & Pearson, Diane L. (2007). Expanding the vision of international education: Collaboration, assessment, and intercultural development. In E. J. Valeau & Rosalind L. Raby. (Eds.), *International reform efforts and challenges in community colleges* (pp. 67–75). New Directors for Community Colleges No. 138(Summer). San Francisco: Jossey-Bass.

Frost, Robert A. (2007). Global studies in the community college curriculum. *Community College Enterprise: A Journal of Research and Practice, 13*(2), 67–73.

Fryer, Chad, & Wong, Lily (1998). Sexual harassment: Experiences of Japanese women studying in Canada. *TESL Canada Journal, 15*(2), 75–78.

Guerrero, Ernesto Jr. (2006). *The road less traveled: Latino students and the impact of studying abroad.* Doctoral dissertation, University of California, Los Angeles, Dissertation Abstracts International. (AAT 3249418).

Harden, Renata (2007). *Identities in motion: An autoethnography of an African American woman's journey to Burkina Faso, Benin, and Ghana.* Doctoral dissertation Bowling Green State University, Dissertation Abstracts International. (AAT 3262332).

Hurtado, S., Milem, J., Clayton-Pedersen, & Allen, W. (1999). Enacting diverse learning environments: Improving the climate for racial/ethnic diversity in higher education, 26(8). Washington, DC: George Washington University, Graduate School of Education and Human Development: ASHE-ERIC Report.

Jackson, Marilyn J. (2006). *Traveling shoes: Study abroad experiences of African American students participating in California State University international programs.* Doctoral dissertation, University of San Francisco, ProQuest Dissertations and Theses. http://search.proquest.com/docview/304909330?accountid=10351

Kasravi, Jinous (2009). *Factors influencing the decision to study abroad for students of color: Moving beyond the barriers.* Doctoral dissertation, University of Minnesota, Dissertation Abstracts International. (AAT 3371866).

Kuh, George D. (2011). *Inspiring success on a dime: Growing and enhancing high impact practices and high quality opportunities while maximizing resources.* [Powerpoint presentation]. NAFSA Region VI Drive Conference April 13, 2011, University of Riverside, California.

Landau, Jennifer, & Moore, David Chioni (2001). Towards reconciliation in the motherland: Race, class, nationality, gender, and the complexities of American student presence at the University of Legon. *Frontiers: The Interdisciplinary Journal of Study Abroad, 25,* 25–59.

Lincoln, Y. S., & Guba, E. G. (1985). *Naturalistic inquiry.* Beverly Hills, CA: Sage.

Locks, Angela M., Hurtado, Silvia, Bowman, Nicholas A., & Oseguera, Leticia (2008). Extending notions of campus climate and diversity to students transition to college. *The Review of Higher Education, 31*(3), 257–285.

Morgan, Rose M., Mwegelo, Desideria T., & Turner, Laura N. (2002). Black women in the African diaspora seeking their cultural heritage through studying abroad. *NASPA Journal, 39*(4), 333–353.

Niser, John C. (2010). Study abroad education in New England higher education: A pilot survey. *International Journal of Educational Management, 24*(1), 48–55.

Penn, Everette B., & Tanner, Jennifer (2009). Black students and international education: An assessment. *Journal of Black Studies, 40*(2), 266–282.

Pierce, Chester (1995). Stress analogs of racism and sexism: Terrorism, torture, and disaster. In C. Willie, P. Rieker, B. Kramer, & B. Brown (Eds.), *Mental health, racism and sexism* (pp. 277–293). Pittsburgh, PA: University of Pittsburgh Press.

Raby, Rosalind L. (2008). *Meeting America's global education challenge: Expanding education abroad at U.S. community colleges.* Institute of International Education Study Abroad White Paper Series 3 (September 2008). New York: Institute for International Education Press. file://localhost/from http://www.iie.org/en/Research-and-Publications/Publications-and-Reports/IIE-Bookstore/Expanding-Education-Abroad-at-US-Community-Colleges

Raby, Rosalind L., Rhodes, Gary M., & Biscarra, Albert (2014). Community college study abroad: Implications for student success. *Community College Journal of Research and Practice, 38*(2–3), 174–183.

Rawlins, Roblyn (2012). Whether I'm an American or not, I'm not here so you can hit on me: Public harassment in the experience of U.S. women studying abroad. *Women's Studies, 41,* 476–497.

Raymondi, Mary D. (2005). *Latino students explore racial and ethnic identity in a global context.* Doctoral dissertation, Dissertation Abstracts International. (AAT 3153765).

Sisneros, Jose, Stakeman, Catherine, Joyner, Mildred C., & Schmitz, Catheryne L. (2008). *Critical multicultural social work.* Chicago: Lyceum.

Smith, William A., Hung, Man, & Franklin, Jeremy D. (2011). Racial battle fatigue and the miseducation of black men: Racial microaggressions, societal problems, and environmental stress. *The Journal of Negro Education, 80*(1), 63–82.

Solórzano, Daniel (1998). Critical race theory, racial and gender microaggressions, and the experiences of Chicana and Chicano scholars. *International Journal of Qualitative Studies in Education, 11*(1), 121–136.

Solórzano, Daniel, Ceja, Michael, & Yosso, Tara (2000). Critical race theory, racial microaggressions, and campus racial climate: The experiences of African American college students. *Journal of Negro Education, 69*(1/2), 60–73.

Sutton, Richard C., & Rubin, Donald L. (May 2010). *Documenting the academic impact of study abroad: Final report of the GLOSSARI project.* Paper presented at the annual conference of NAFSA. Association of International Educators, Kansas City, MO.

Talburt, Susan, & Steward, Melissa A. (1999). What's the subject of study abroad?: Race, gender, and 'living culture.'. *Modern Language Journal, 83*(2), 163–175. doi:10.1111/0026-7902.00013.

Twombly, Susan B. (1995). Piropos and friendships: Gender and culture clash in study abroad. *Frontiers: The Interdisciplinary Journal of Study Abroad, 1*, 1–27.

Valeau, Edward J., & Raby, Rosalind Latiner (2007). *International reform efforts and challenges in community colleges.* New Directions for Community Colleges No. 138 (Summer). San Francisco: Jossey-Bass.

Wick, David J. (2011). *Study abroad for students of color: A third space for negotiating agency and identity.* Unpublished doctoral dissertation, received from author on June 26, 2011.

Willis, Tasha (2012). *Rare but there: An intersectional exploration of the experiences and outcomes of Black women who studied abroad through community college programs.* Doctoral dissertation, California State University, Long Beach, ProQuest Dissertations and Theses. Accession Order No. [3533746].

Willis, Tasha (2015). And still we rise: Microaggressions and intersectionality in the study abroad experiences of Black women. *Frontiers: Journal of Study Abroad.* September, 2015.

CHAPTER 10

Calls for Accountability: Measuring Internationalization at Community Colleges

Shawn Woodin

INTRODUCTION

Administrators and faculty members at community colleges increasingly recognize that globalization affects their missions and their students, and colleges respond through internationalization efforts (Raby and Valeau 2007). Local businesses and policymakers influence community colleges with certain expectations including, "meeting the challenges of a growing but diverse student population, serving as the training ground to respond to increasing industrial globalization, and meeting the immediate training or retraining needs of the local economy" (Walters and McKay 2005, p. 55). A key aspect of globalization is focused on helping student transformation into productive citizenship. Mellow and Heelan (2008) state that if "graduates of community colleges are not aware of global issues, and if we cannot help them to become the citizens and entrepreneurs who understand the intended and unintended consequence of out-sourcing and off-shoring, no college education will suffice" (p. 161). US workers face increasing competition for their jobs from workers all over the world, and higher education institutions must promote global skills (Milliron 2007). Dellow (2007) added, "community colleges must internationalize their occupational and technical programs

S. Woodin (✉)
President/CEO of the Southern Scholarship Foundation, Inc., Tampa, FL, USA

© The Editor(s) (if applicable) and The Author(s) 2016
R.L. Raby, E.J. Valeau (eds.), *International Education at Community Colleges*, DOI 10.1057/978-1-137-53336-4_10

143

because globalization is changing local communities and job prospects for students" (p. 44). Preparing small business owners to operate in a global marketplace is another responsibility of community colleges (Mellow and Heelan 2008). Institutional efforts to spur awareness of others' cultures, respect for differences, and develop appreciation of our own unique culture rises to overlap with preparation for technical workplace competitiveness.

How community college leaders internationalize campuses is crucial to effectively address the changing global and local economic characteristics of the communities served. Observed processes include strategic internationalization (Green 2002; Boggs and Irwin 2007; Harder 2010) and internationalizing the curriculum (Raby 2007; American Council on Education 2012); study abroad (Metzger 2006; Rose and Bylander 2007; Salisbury et al. 2009), partnerships (Le 2013; Treat and Hartenstine 2013) and recruitment of international students (Green and Siaya 2005; Fitzer 2007). While these descriptive approaches document methods, metrics for community colleges at an institutional level remain underdeveloped in the literature.

While calls for community colleges to respond to globalization through internationalization efforts grow progressively louder and emphasize the urgency, accountability measures remain amorphous. The continued lack of understanding by community colleges' leadership about the relevance of internationalization, absence of an institutional strategy, isolated and decentralized international programming, inadequate financial and human resources, and individual interests and attitudes presented obstacles community colleges must address when they internationalize (Green 2007). Quantifying institutional efforts allows college leaders to set benchmarks and evaluate efforts, and to create specific, measurable goals for integrating internationalization into strategic planning documents (Beerkens et al. 2010). Defining possible measurements of internationalization may aid college leaders in identifying the institutional levers that can catalyze the process. This study sought to identify the quantifiable variables to measure institutional internationalization at US community colleges and provide those for leaders as a basis for adaptation and adoption at their institutions.

QUANTIFYING INTERNATIONALIZATION

Measuring strategic internationalization at the institutional and sub-units level can provide administrators with data about this aspect of general performance, inform decisions about an institution's internationalization strategy and components, and help to advance international programs

(Green 2012). However, developing a set of indicators can be complicated by using terms that need extensive definitions, providing rules for measuring and calculating the desired value, and developing rules for how to deal with exceptions. In addition, existing metrics are not designed with the specific needs of community colleges.

Existing metrics primarily focus on university higher educational institutions. Using publicly available data, Horn et al. (2007) considered five dimensions of internationalization for US universities that include (a) student enrollment in internationally themed majors and student mobility flows; (b) faculty mobility flow; (c) faculty research; (d) institutional requirements for curricular programs; and (e) organizational support. Juknyte-Petreikiene (2006) identified four dimensions to measure internationalization at higher education institutions in Lithuania, including (a) academic programs, (b) research and scholarly collaboration, (c) external relations, and (d) extracurricular activities. Each dimension included 4–12 indicators. Unique to these indicators is the activity of partnerships with community groups and partnerships through international development projects. Iuspa (2010) developed ten indicators to assess Florida International University and similar to Horn et al. (2007) included the number of international students, participation in study abroad, international curricular content, faculty exchange activity, foreign languages, international development projects and offshore programs as metrics. Finally, a pan-Europe set of metrics for higher education institutions identified three purposes of measuring internationalization (Beerkens et al. 2010) that include (a) mapping where the institution stands in terms of internationalization, (b) evaluating internationalization efforts, and (c) setting an internationalization institutional profile for both internal and external stakeholders.

A recent monograph offered an analysis of institutional internationalization akin to a simplified process model that focuses on input and output dimensions of internationalization such as articulated commitment, goals, and vision statement, teaching and curriculum, research, budget, co-curriculum and campus life, structures, leadership positions, and staffing, international students, education abroad, faculty participation in international activities, and institutional assessment processes (Green 2012). While the paper described each of these components, it omitted specific metrics; nor did it specifically identify which types of higher education institutions the process model applies to.

The most notable study that quantified internationalization of community colleges was the Green and Siaya (2005) 2001 survey of 752 higher education institutions, including 233 community colleges. The resulting internationalization index had six dimensions: (a) articulated commitment, (b) academic offerings, (c) organizational infrastructure, (d) external funding, (e) institutional investment in faculty, and (f) international students and student programs. While community colleges were included in the survey, the instrument did not address areas critical to internationalization at community colleges, such as business/education partnerships or community education; yet it included areas such as international research partnerships and foreign language admission requirements. While the authors provided a useful foundation, the same survey instrument was also administered at four-year colleges and universities.

CONCEPTUAL FRAMEWORK

With such diversity of metrics, the Delphi study was designed to create something unique for community colleges. Informing this study, Bissonette and Woodin (2013) theorized a progressive model of community college internationalization. A college with little international capacity but interest would be at the disaggregated phase of the spectrum, while an institution with pervasive and coordinated internationalization activities would be at the integrated side of the spectrum as modeled in Fig. 1.

The model suggests that colleges with low capacity have institutional elements housed in specific departments (Bissonette and Woodin 2013). These include the seven elements of leadership and policy, partnerships, professional development, student services, co-curricular, curricular, and international development. Low capacity institutions will not demonstrate every element of internationalization. Other elements may exist but with a lack of institutional commitment, illustrated as dotted circles. Institutions demonstrating high capacity for internationalization move toward greater integration of institutional elements, greater institutional commitment, and leadership focus on internationalization illustrated as movement from left to right along a continuum.

According to Bissonette and Woodin (2013), the integrated side of Fig. 1 displays the ideal institutional environment for comprehensive internationalization. As representatives from departments with a role in internationalization actively engage with one another, communication crosses typical departmental lines and an institutional global education advisory committee spans the institution. This model displays the areas with equal importance. However, each institution that uses the model should prioritize

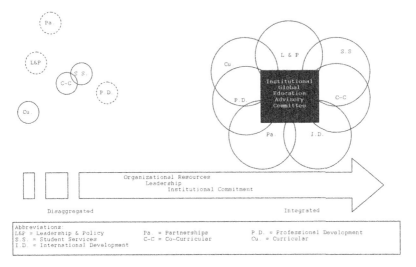

Fig. 1 Institutional progression of internationalization at community colleges (Bissonette and Woodin 2013)

its strategies to align to its mission. Elements overlap in a systemic manner. Moving clockwise or counterclockwise integrated internationalization creates, overlapping and interdependent institutional movement.

BENCHMARKING AT COMMUNITY COLLEGES

When a college chooses to pursue institutional internationalization, a set of reliable performance indicators will inform strategic decision-making. Strategic planning includes resource allocation among discussions by senior management, deans, chairs, and governing board members (Goho and Webb 2003). Mission statements clarify institutional goals, communicate a college's function to the public, and are required for accreditation (Lake and Mrozinski 2011; Walters and McKay 2005). In a data-driven environment, performance indicators are the basis to represent progress toward goals and accomplishments.

Learning from achievements in benchmarking and resource allocation, college leaders should adopt metrics of institutional internationalization for accountability as well. Shifting to a data-informed environment can transform institutional decision-making from reacting to trends to steering strategic decisions (Thornton 2005). Performance indicators designed to assess mission achievement may quantify outputs, and the indicators also can provided data for decision-making regarding institutional resource allocation for areas such as course and program alignment (Spiers et al. 2008). Using reporting tools for accountability purposes, performance-based strategic planning can link key goals with resource allocation and departmental accomplishments to achievements in other areas of the college (Billings 2005).

METHOD

Indicators of internationalization can be developed either "based on expert judgments and knowledge about internationalization" or stakeholder involvement (Beerkens et al. 2010, p. 24) and this study employed both as embodied by internationalization practitioners at US community colleges using the Delphi technique. The premise of the Delphi technique is that "group opinion is more valid than individual opinion" (Keeney et al. 2011, p. 3). Structured group communication controls feedback from individual members that might dominate a face-to-face group collaboration method, allows participants to review their responses in relation to other responses through subsequent rounds, and provides anonymity from other participants (Wilhelm 2001). The Delphi technique is subject to the biases of the researcher who identifies criteria for experts and decides who participates, creates the instruments, interprets the results, and draws the conclusions (Keeney et al. 2011; Wilhelm 2001). Even when consensus occurs on items with the Delphi technique, agreement is limited to the perceptions of the study participants. However, being reflective and maintaining the subjective aspects of the process may enhance the analysis and interpretation of the data (Mosselson 2010).

Through snowball sampling, this study identified 18 internationalization administrators at US community colleges in 12 states to validate potential metrics. Each participating panelist's experience included a minimum of the full-time equivalent of three years' internationalization at one or more community colleges in the USA; they each held institutional or individual membership in at least one international education professional association, and their primary responsibilities included at least 50 % time on international-related decision-making administrative duties within the preceding 24 months.

Metrics observed in the literature provided initial suggestions for consideration by the panelists. The study extracted indicators applied to four-year institutions from the literature, and the panelists modified and filtered the variables for applicability to community colleges. Round One included closed- and open-response questions to capture insights and additional items from panelists. The Round One closed-response questions asked experts about the importance of measuring specific aspects of internationalization at an institutional level. Final consensus to accept metrics occurred when 80 % or more of the expert panelists agreed on the specific indicator. Findings are limited to the group that participated, and are not generalizable to a larger population. Open-response statements were grouped together around similar ideas, resulting in unique indicators to quantify each variable for consideration in Round Two. Figure 2 displays the flow of the Delphi process.

Round Two Part One asked panelists to reflect on variables that did not achieve consensus in Round One to consider confirming or changing their original ratings. Round Two Part Two presented panelists with specific quantifiable indicators, or how to measure the variables that met consensus in Round One. Indicators that reached consensus from the panel became part of the set of metrics of institutional internationalization at US community colleges. Indicators that the panel did not accept at the pre-determined level of consensus were reconsidered in Round Three. Indicators that reached consensus in Round Three were captured in the final set of metrics for this study.

DISCUSSION AND CONCLUSIONS

This study drew on concepts of higher education internationalization (Green 2012) and community college internationalization (Bissonette and Woodin 2013) to provide a structure for the study's organization, and related literature provided initial content for panelists' consideration. Further content emerged from Delphi panelists' comments. Based on the perceptions of experts in the field the findings suggest how an institution may create a set of internationalization metrics.

Table 10.1 presents community college leaders with a set of metrics to benchmark and analyze institutional internationalization. Institutions that adopt the instrument will have an interest in building capacity for global engagement to develop a sense of awareness among students, faculty, and staff. This instrument will not inform leaders about what students learn,

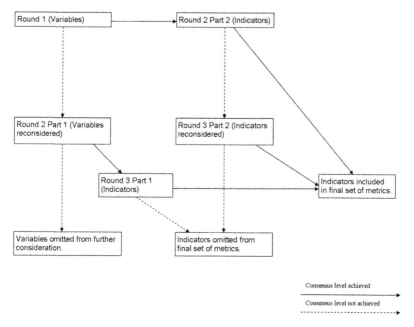

Fig. 2 Delphi method flowchart

rather it is intended to measure the resources required to internationalize a community college, and the activities undertaken toward that objective. The set of metrics consists of 79 indicators in broad categories. Leaders should first examine this instrument to determine which indicators relate to institutional priorities, and adapt the relevant items in the local and state context. Administrators should consider that internationalization is an ongoing process, and as such data should be collected and analyzed longitudinally.

Leadership and Policy

Along with an express institutional commitment, leadership support is a factor of import for institutional internationalization (Boggs and Irwin 2007; Harder 2010), which the findings suggest is quantified by frequency of leaders' participation in international activities as well as frequency of leaders' internal and external communications regarding

Table 10.1 Quantifying institutional internationalization: a tool for community college leaders

Leadership and policy

LP 1	Frequency of meetings with agenda items pertaining to international education per year.
LP 2	Frequency of participation in international activities per year.
LP 3	Frequency of internal and external communications about internationalization per year.
LP 4	Number of times the governing board requests updates on internationalization per year.
LP 5	Frequency of international education committee meetings per year.
LP 6	Existence of institution-wide international education committee.
LP 7	Percentage of college departments represented on the international education committee.
LP 8	Existence of internationalization explicitly in the mission or vision statement.
LP 9	Existence of a college policy to internationalize syllabi for each course.
LP 10	Existence of policies encouraging hiring and promotion of faculty with global competencies.
LP 11	Existence of policies encouraging hiring and promotion of staff with global competencies.
LP 12	Existence of policies that cover all aspects of internationalization.

Organizational resources

OR 1	Number of international activities per year.
OR 2	Number of people that attend international activities per year.
OR 3	Number of full-time equivalent (FTE) international programs staff members.
OR 4	Existence of an international student admissions counselor position.
OR 5	Number of Fulbright or similar awards per year.
OR 6	Number of faculty members that have hosted international students or visitors.
OR 7	Number of faculty members that have participated in institutional internationalization planning.
OR 8	Number of faculty members that have led study abroad programs.
OR 9	Number of faculty members that have internationalized curricula.
OR 10	Amount of funding from external sources for international activities.
OR 11	Amount of funding to internationalize the curriculum.
OR 12	Amount of funding for international travel.
OR 13	Amount of funding devoted to the support of international activities.
OR 14	Number of communication channels used to inform college community about internationalization (e.g. website, notice boards, streaming video, meetings, workshops, advisory boards, etc.).
OR 15	Number of internal communications per year devoted to internationalization.
OR 16	Frequency of attendance and presentations at international-focused meetings.
OR 17	Number of memberships in international-focused organizations represented by college faculty and staff.
OR 18	Percentage of college personnel involved in international conferences or projects.

(continued)

Table 10.1   (continued)

OR 19	Existence of internationalization as a priority in the strategic plan.
OR 20	Degree of inclusion in the strategic plan (e.g.—a separate item or section of the plan; a sub-topic or goal under a larger heading or item, or not mentioned at all).
OR 21	Existence of specific, identifiable international programs space.
OR 22	Existence of webpage for international programs.
OR 23	Number of international faculty exchanges.

Curricular

C 1	Number of world languages offered at the college, including credit and continuing education.
C 2	Percentage of students enrolled in world languages.
C 3	Percentage of faculty/staff/students familiar with 'Global Competency' or similar term.
C 4	Existence of institutional definition for 'Global Competency' or similar term applicable to all fields of study.
C 5	Existence of a global studies certificate or similar academic incentive.
C 6	Percentage of courses with specific international components shown in the syllabus meeting institutional criteria for internationalized syllabi.

Professional development

PD 1	Number of campus based professional development opportunities available for faculty per year.
PD 2	How many faculty members took advantage of the available campus based professional development opportunities per year.
PD 3	Number of international visitors on campus per year.
PD 4	Number of campus based professional development opportunities available for staff per year.
PD 5	How many staff members took advantage of the available campus based professional development opportunities per year.

Co-curricular activities

CA 1	Percentage of faculty members who have led study abroad programs.
CA 2	Number of faculty-led study abroad programs available.
CA 3	Number of students participating in study abroad programs.
CA 4	Number of study abroad programs completed per year.
CA 5	Number of countries represented in study abroad programs.
CA 6	Legal review as a step of approving study abroad policies.
CA 7	Existence of risk management plan.
CA 8	Existence of risk management training for faculty.
CA 9	Existence of travel insurance for all participants.
CA 10	Number of attendees/participants at internationally themed campus programs.
CA 11	Number of attendees at internationally themed events that involve the community.
CA 12	Number of internationally themed campus programs per year.
CA 13	Number of internationally themed activities that involve the community.
CA 14	Existence of study abroad as credited study that counts toward graduation.

Table 10.1   (continued)

CA 15	Number of attendees/participants at student-led internationally themed campus programs.
CA 16	Number of student-led internationally themed campus programs.
CA 17	Percentage of academic fields offering study abroad programs.
CA 18	Existence of international service learning programs.
CA 19	Existence of awards for international programs.
CA 20	Number of symbols of internationalization (flags, murals, photos, multilingual signage, etc.) on campus.

International student services

ISS 1	Existence of an ESL program that provides courses from beginner to intermediate to advanced in all skills of language acquisition: speaking, listening, writing, reading for domestic immigrant populations.
ISS 2	Existence of programs for visa holding international EAP students to interact with other college students.
ISS 3	Existence of an EAP program that provides courses from beginner to intermediate to advanced in all skills of language acquisition: speaking, listening, writing, reading for visa holding international students.
ISS 4	Existence of programs for domestic immigrant ESL students to interact with other college students.
ISS 5	Existence of dedicated international student advisor position for academics.
ISS 6	Existence of dedicated international student advisor position for non-academic issues.
ISS 7	Existence of separate orientation for international students.
ISS 8	Existence of support for professional development for international student advisors.
ISS 9	Number of international students advised per year.
ISS 10	Percentage of international students that take advantage of programs designed for integration.
ISS 11	Number of articulation agreements with four-year colleges that international students can follow.
ISS 12	Number of international students that transferred to domestic four-year institutions per year.
ISS 13	Existence of clearly identified pathways for international students to transfer to four-year colleges.

(continued)

internationalization. The findings suggest agreement with the importance of including internationalization as an integrated component of a community college mission or vision (Green 2012), and the panel supported existence of an explicit statement of internationalization in the mission or vision as a measure.

Organizational Resources

Financial resources to support international activities, and dedicated international staff, align with inputs indicated in the literature as catalysts for advancing institutional internationalization (Bissonette and Woodin 2013; Green 2012). Defining how to measure financial resources highlighted a paradox among the panelists; they agreed that a measurement should be the "amount of funding devoted to support international activities," while disagreeing that the "amount of revenue generated by the international unit" should be a metric, but preferring the "amount of funding from external {non-institutional} sources." The findings may suggest that the panelists viewed the college's budgetary allocation as a statement of institutional commitment, whereas their departmental contribution did not reflect the institution per se. The findings also prompt the question of who would be responsible to generate external funding for international activities if not the staff in the international unit.

The strategic planning process integrates a college's central theme into other elements of a college's plans (Kelly and Kaufman 2007). Panelists signaled agreement regarding internationalization, unanimously endorsing both the "existence of internationalization as a priority in the strategic plan" and the "degree of inclusion in the strategic plan" as measurable indicators. The finding is not surprising, and is noteworthy in its consistency with a similar level of support for an explicit expression in the college's mission statement under Leadership and Policy.

Finally, the panel agreed with all five measurements of faculty engagement in international efforts. As reported by the American Council on Education (2012), the only institutional type in which the faculty is as likely to stimulate internationalization as executives is Associate degree granting institutions. Faculty involvement to incorporate international perspectives will internationalize curricula, one of the seven areas within the conceptual model (Bissonnette and Woodin 2013). Given the pervasiveness of indicators throughout the study regarding faculty involvement, further findings referencing faculty are incorporated elsewhere as well.

Curricular

World languages presents an intriguing example of how any specific metric proposed in this study must be contextualized for a given policy environment. While the panelists reached consensus with "availability of world languages" as a variable, they did not reach consensus on inclusion of the "requirement of world language proficiency." In the context of Florida, in 2013 the legislature passed Section 48.1007.262 of Florida Statutes, creating a requirement that students within the Florida College System [formerly the Florida Community College System] must demonstrate foreign language competencies to transfer, with a provision to allow students whose primary language is not English to establish proficiency in their first language. The Florida requirement is instructive in that if administrators decide to adopt the metrics proposed here for specific institutional use, consideration of any indicator must be tempered by state and local contexts.

Among other noteworthy findings for the curricular category were the variables of "internationalization integrated into courses" and "institutional definition of 'Global Competency' or similar term." Community college students face obstacles to study abroad, and in order to expose students to global concerns faculty must internationalize the curriculum (Frost 2007; Raby 2007; Malkan and Pisani 2011). The expert panelists agreed unanimously to quantify the former variable by measuring the "percentage of courses with specific international components shown in the syllabus meeting institutional criteria for internationalized syllabi." Logically, incorporating international perspectives would link curricular components with institutionally defined global competencies, and the experts agreed that a set of indicators would include a measure of whether such a definition exists in an institution.

Professional Development

According to the model of community college internationalization (Bissonette and Woodin 2013), professional development overlaps with internationalization of the curriculum and with leadership and policy. Realizing the planned institutional path as reflected by the mission relies upon ongoing professional development (Walters and McKay 2005; Mak 2010). Findings indicated consensus for both variables, and the panel also supported measurements of on-campus professional development opportunities.

Co-Curricular

Study abroad featured heavily in the co-curricular category, and the panelists concurred that it be represented through 5 variables and 11 indicators.

Study abroad is one common strategy to internationalize at higher education institutions (Green 2002), including community colleges (Green 2002; Green and Siaya 2005). Among the five variables, faculty involvement in study abroad garnered the most consistent support from the experts with four distinct quantifiable indicators. This finding underscores the importance of faculty to community college internationalization, as also reported in other findings, and is common in highly active community colleges (Green and Siaya 2005).

Also noteworthy among the findings about co-curricular activities was a thread that underscored a community college's ties to the local community. The panelists agreed that the "number of internationally themed activities that involve the community" be measured; and the panel agreed that the "number of attendees at internationally themed events that involve the community" be part of an institutional set of metrics. Partnerships with community groups were noted among metrics used by Juknyte-Petreikiene (2006) in the Lithuanian context, but the aspect of community engagement as a part of internationalization is largely absent from literature focused on US institutions. These indicators add differentiation to the findings of this study from metrics proposed for other types of US higher education institutions.

International Student Services

Extending the theme of community engagement in the findings, the panel came to consensus on differentiated English programs for resident immigrants in the form of English as a Second Language (ESL) versus English for Academic Purposes (EAP) for non-resident alien students attending the institution with student visas. The findings also indicate panelists' support of programs designed to integrate both domestic immigrant students and non-resident international students to interact with other college students. From a pragmatic and college policy perspective, administrators should consider that in a classroom or co-curricular setting, native born students may not differentiate between immigrant and non-resident students while developing programs designed to foster interactions between students of different backgrounds.

Regarding transfer pathway programs from community colleges to four-year institutions, the panel reached consensus on the "number of articulation agreements with four year colleges that international students can follow" and the "number of international students that transferred to domestic four year institutions per year." These represent the only accepted metric alluding to partnerships, diverging from existing literature that emphasized the importance of international partnerships for community colleges (Le 2013; Treat and Hartenstine 2013). Implications of this finding for international education administrators are confounding, for international partnerships are foundations the implementation of study abroad, faculty exchanges, and many other international activities.

International Student Recruitment

The panelists did not reach consensus on a metric for international student recruitment. This finding is noteworthy given that much research in internationalization of higher education, and in particular community colleges, documents the importance of recruitment as an internationalization strategy (Green and Siaya 2005; Fitzer 2007). It is plausible that some of the experts participating in this study do not engage in active student recruitment, as at least five panelists known to the researcher work in institutions that do not pursue this strategy. In two instances, confirmed through personal communications with panelists at colleges in North Carolina and Tennessee, the institutions are prevented by state or local policies from actively recruiting international students. Also note that myriad variables and indicators in this study reference international student services which one might presume implies a method of attracting the students to a college.

RECOMMENDATIONS FOR FUTURE RESEARCH

Since this study involved a limited number of international education practitioners, a study that involves a combination of executives, faculty, and/or institutional research officials could further inform development of metrics. The study could be replicated, but within different geographic limitations such as a specific state. Finally, the findings included a perception that adequate funding be dedicated for internationalization, but also that the international education office should not be measured by how much revenue it generates. Further investigation about this seeming paradox could involve a qualitative approach to explain why this emerged, or whether it differs among internationalization experts and other stakeholders such as executives or governance board members.

Recommendations for Community College Leaders

This chapter identified quantifiable variables that represent institutional internationalization at US community colleges so that administrators may better understand and manage global engagement efforts. In summary, college leaders should adopt metrics of institutional internationalization for accountability while recognizing that internationalization is an ongoing process, and as such data should be collected and analyzed longitudinally. As the Florida and student recruitment examples demonstrate, if administrators decide to adopt the metrics proposed here for specific institutional use, consideration of any indicator must be tempered by state and/or local contexts. The proposed metrics should be examined for those elements that most closely align with the institution's mission and strategic plan to narrow the options. Leaders should also note the importance of faculties' role to internationalize an institution.

Concluding Thoughts

In an era of increasing calls for accountability, investing resources into efforts at community colleges should be documented with evidence. Institutional internationalization has historically been viewed at the fringe of college activities even today it remains underdeveloped in many community colleges. However, for those institutions that identify internationalization among its priorities there is need to measure the inputs and outputs.

With this study, an institution can develop benchmarks and monitor performance related to internationalization. Pragmatically, 79 indicators would overwhelm any institution, as internationalization is likely to be one of many aspects of institutional performance that executives, accreditation bodies, governmental agencies, and governing board members seek to measure. Institutions deciding to use the results of this study will necessarily wrestle with which indicators are most appropriate for the college.

Furthermore, networks or consortia of colleges may endeavor to create common metrics for collaboration, benchmarking, and innovation based on the findings of this study. State-specific metrics would provide comparative data for colleges operating within relatively similar regulatory and governance structures. Broader, national-level metrics could be developed by Community Colleges for International Development (CCID), Inc. as a benchmarking resource.

The larger issue of institutional learning outcomes intended through investment in internationalization remained beyond the scope of this study. Yet questions arise as to which internationalization strategies are most effective in fostering the intended learning goals. Perhaps with implementation of some of these metrics, institutional leaders can also develop assessment strategies to inform how investment in varying internationalization strategies creates a context for learning and how funding can be best directed for effective and efficient use of the scarce resources so common at US community colleges.

REFERENCES

American Council on Education. (2012). *Mapping internationalization on U.S. campuses: 2012 edition.* http://www.acenet.edu/news-room/Documents/MappingInternationalizationonUSCampuses2012-full.pdf

Beerkens, Eric, Brandenburg, Uwe, Evers, Nico, van Gaalen, Adinda, Leichsenring, Hannah, & Zimmerman, V. (2010). *Indicator projects on internationalization – approaches, methods and findings: A report in the context of the European project 'Indicators for Mapping and Profiling Internationalization' (IMPI).* European Commission. http://www.impi-project.eu/pdf/full_indicator_projects_on_internationalisation-IMPI%20100511.pdf

Billings, M. Frank (2005). Web-based strategic planning. *Community College Journal of Research and Practice, 29*(8), 609–610. doi:10.1080/10668920591005369.

Bissonette, Bonnie, & Woodin, Shawn (2013). Building support for internationalization through institutional assessment and leadership engagement. In Tod Treat & Linda Serra Hagedorn (Eds.), *The community college in a global context* (pp. 11–26). New Directions for Community Colleges. No. 161. San Francisco: Jossey-Bass Publications. doi:10.1002/cc.

Boggs, George R., & Irwin, Judith (2007). What every community college leader needs to know: Building leadership for international education. In Edward J. Valeau & Rosalind L. Raby (Eds.), *International reform efforts and challenges in community colleges* (pp. 25–30). New Directions for Community Colleges (138, Summer). San Francisco: Jossey-Bass.

Dellow, Don A. (2007). The role of globalization in technical and occupational programs. In Edward J. Valeau & Rosalind L. Raby (Eds.), *International reform efforts and challenges in community colleges* (pp. 39–45). New Directions for Community Colleges (138, Summer). San Francisco: Jossey-Bass.

Fitzer, John K. (2007). *Foreign students at California community colleges: Benefits, costs, and institutional responsibility.* Ph.D. dissertation, ProQuest Dissertations & Theses: Full Text. (Publication No. AAT 3261961).

Fla. Stat. § 48.1007.262. (2013). http://www.flsenate.gov/Laws/Statutes/ 2013/1007.262

Frost, Robert (2007). Global studies in the community college curriculum. *The Community College Enterprise*, *13*(2), 67–73.

Goho, James, & Webb, Ken (2003). Planning for success: Integrating analysis with decision making. *Community College Journal of Research and Practice*, *27*(5), 377–391. doi:10.1080/713838156.

Green, Madeline F. (2002). Joining the world: The challenge of internationalizing undergraduate education. *Change*, *34*(3), 12–21. doi:10.1080/0009138 0209601850.

Green, Madeline F. (2007). Internationalizing community colleges: Barriers and strategies. In Edward J. Valeau & Rosalind L. Raby (Eds.), *International reform efforts and challenges in community colleges* (pp. 15–24). New Directions for Community Colleges (138, Summer). San Francisco: Jossey-Bass.

Green, Madeline F. (2012). *Measuring and assessing internationalization*. Washington, DC: NAFSA; Association of International Educators. http://www.nafsa.org/resourcelibrary/Default.aspx?id=32455

Green, Madeline, & Siaya, Laura (2005). *Measuring internationalization at community colleges*. Washington, DC: American Council on Education.

Harder, Natalie J. (2010). Internationalization efforts in United States community colleges: A comparative analysis of urban, suburban, and rural institutions. *Community College Journal of Research and Practice*, *35*(1), 152–164. doi:10. 1080/10668926.2011.525186.

Horn, Aaron S., Hendel, Darwin D., & Fry, Gerald W. (2007). Ranking the international dimension of top research universities in the United States. *Journal of Studies in International Education*, *11*(3–4), 330–358. doi:10.1177/ 1028315306294630.

Iuspa, Flavia E. (2010). *Assessing the effectiveness of the internationalization process in higher education institutions: A case study of Florida International University*. Doctoral dissertation, ProQuest Dissertations & Theses. (Document ID 858857253).

Juknyte-Petreikiene, Inga (2006). Parameters of higher school internationalization and quality assessment. *Quality of Higher Education*, *3*, 92–122. http://search.proquest.com/docview/61802715?accountid=10920

Keeney, Sinead, Hasson, Felicity, & McKenna, Hugh (2011). *The Delphi technique in nursing and health research*. West Sussex: Wiley-Blackwell.

Kelley, Susan, & Kaufman, Roger (2007). Integrated strategic planning in a learning-centered community college. *Planning For Higher Education*, *35*(3), 45–55.

Lake, Rebecca, & Mrozinski, Mark (2011). The conflicted realities of community college mission statements. *Planning For Higher Education*, *39*(2), 5–14.

Le, Ann T. (2013). The history and future of community colleges in Vietnam. In Tod Treat & Linda S. Hagedorn (Eds.), *The community college in a global context* (pp. 11–26). New Directions for Community Colleges. No. 161. San Francisco: Jossey-Bass Publications. 85–99. doi:10.1002/cc.20050.

Mak, Anita (2010). Enhancing academics' capability to engage multicultural classes and internationalize at home. *International Journal of Teaching and Learning in Higher Education, 22*(3), 365–373.

Malkan, Rajiv, & Pisani, Michael J. (2011). Internationalizing the community college experience. *Community College Journal of Research and Practice, 35*(11), 825–841.

Mellow, Gail O., & Heelan, Cynthia (2008). *Minding the dream: The process and practice of the American community college.* Lanham, MD: Rowman & Littlefield Publishers, Inc..

Metzger, Christy (2006). Study abroad programming: A 21st century retention strategy? *College Student Affairs Journal, 25*(2), 164–175, 136.

Milliron, Mark D. (2007). Transcendence and globalization: Our education and workforce development challenge. In Edward J. Valeau & Rosalind L. Raby (Eds.), *International reform efforts and challenges in community colleges* (pp. 31–38). New Directions for Community Colleges (138, Summer). San Francisco: Jossey-Bass.

Mosselson, Jacqueline (2010). Subjectivity and reflexivity: Locating the self in research on dislocation. *International Journal of Qualitative Studies in Education, 23*(4), 479–494. doi:10.1080/09518398.2010.492771.

Raby, Rosalind L. (2007). Internationalizing the curriculum: On- and off-campus strategies. In Edward J. Valeau & Rosalind L. Raby (Eds.), *International reform efforts and challenges in community colleges* (pp. 57–66). New Directions for Community Colleges (138, Summer). San Francisco: Jossey-Bass.

Raby, Rosalind L., & Valeau, Edward J. (2007). Community college international education: Looking back to forecast the future. In Edward J. Valeau & Rosalind L. Raby (Eds.), *International reform efforts and challenges in community colleges* (pp. 15–25). New Directions for Community Colleges (138, Summer). San Francisco: Jossey-Bass. (pp. 5–14). doi:10.1002/cc.276.

Rose, Susan, & Bylander, Joyce (2007). Border crossings: Engaging students in diversity work and intergroup relations. *Innovative Higher Education, 31*(5), 251–264. doi:10.1007/s10755-006-9028-2.

Salisbury, Mark, Umbach, Paul, Paulsen, Michael, & Pascarella, Ernest (2009). Going global: Understanding the choice process of the intent to study abroad. *Research in Higher Education, 50*(2), 119–143. doi:10.1007/s11162-008-9111-x.

Spiers, Cynthia, Kiel, Dorothy, & Hohenrink, Brad (2008). The compass rose effectiveness model. *Community College Journal of Research and Practice, 32*(11), 909–912. doi:10.1080/10668920802394602.

Thornton, Robert H. (2005). Housatonic's national cobeta test of the community college strategic planner. *Community College Journal of Research and Practice, 29*(8), 631–632. doi:10.1080/10668920591005512.

Treat, Tod, & Hartenstine, Mary Beth (2013). Strategic partnerships in international development. In Tod Treat & Linda Serra Hagedorn (Eds.), *The community college in a global context* (pp. 11–26). New Directions for Community Colleges. No. 161. San Francisco: Jossey-Bass Publications. doi:10.1002/cc20048. (pp. 71–83).

Walters, Evon, & McKay, Shaun (2005). Strategic planning and retention within the community college setting. *College Student Affairs Journal, 25*(1), 50–63.

Wilhelm, William J. (2001). Alchemy of the oracle: The Delphi technique. *Delta Pi Epsilon Journal, 43*(1), 6–26.

CHAPTER 11

Building the Pipeline for Community College International Education Leadership

Edward J. Valeau and Rosalind Latiner Raby

INTRODUCTION

International educational programs play a key role in providing the skills needed for a competitive, globally competent workforce and for a citizenry who are cultured, transformative, and empowered to support reform at the local and global level. This educational focus was mentioned as a key role for community colleges in the 1947 Truman Commission Report, is a theme in President Barack Obama's "Race to the Top" initiative, and is supported by community college chancellors, presidents, Boards of Trustees, and associations. Astin and Astin (2000) describe transformative leadership as a pattern that involves individuals as "change agents" who seek to create intentional change within the institution. In the community college, strong leadership is needed at the faculty, mid-administrator level,

E.J. Valeau (✉)
Superintendent/President Emeritus Hartnell Community College District
Salinas, California

Co-Founder, the ELS Group, LLC

R.L. Raby
Educational Leadership and Policy Studies, Michael D. Eisner College of Education, California State University, Northridge, CA, USA

California Colleges for International Education, Los Angeles, CA, USA

University of Phoenix, Costa Mesa, CA, USA

© The Editor(s) (if applicable) and The Author(s) 2016   163
R.L. Raby, E.J. Valeau (eds.), *International Education at Community Colleges*, DOI 10.1057/978-1-137-53336-4_11

and executive officer levels, to turn their vision into action that stimulates and affects long-term and systemic change.

There is a strong body of literature that profiles community college leaders including their demographic, professional history, training needs, and leadership styles. The same cannot be said about community college international education leaders, even though they are on the front lines for organizing, evaluating, and advocating international outreach and programs. There is little care for where this leadership comes from, who they are, what skills are necessary for them to carry out their jobs effectively, and if they are prepared for leadership.

This chapter sets parameters for charting a profile of existing community college international education leaders to put them into view so that the pipeline can be strengthened. To achieve this intent, and because there is little to no information on the topic, we use the literature related to chief executive officers (CEOs) as a portal to anchor our study. In doing so, in no way are we suggesting any comparisons other than the fact that we can learn from what has been done in acquiring information to open a discussion on who are our nation's community college international education leaders.

POLICY DEVELOPMENTS TO BUILD LEADERSHIP

Since 2005, the American Association of Community Colleges (AACC) has made proactive leadership development a central focus of its mission. Competencies reports suggest that instead of developing leaders to maintain the inherited design, colleges now need to develop leaders to transform the design by reshaping the community college of today to meet the needs of tomorrow (AACC 2013). With such focus and external support services, emerging leaders can chart their own leadership progress, program developers can use curricula guidelines for training and development, and human resource departments can have direction for staff recruitment, hiring, and internal rewards. The AACC perceived framework is a "living document" that evolves over time to meet changing human and institutional needs.

Recognizing the urgency in turnover in the community college presidency, AACC in partner with the Association of Community College Trustees (ACCT) started a new leadership initiative, "Thriving in the Community College Presidency" (2015). Curricula now focus on Board-CEO relationships aimed at improving student outcomes and achieving dramatic gains in student success. Adding to the policy discussion and drawing a nexus between student outcomes and community college presidential leadership is the Aspen Institute College Excellence

Program (2013), which outlines steps needed to identify, select, and develop a new generation of leaders.

DATA ON COMMUNITY COLLEGE PRESIDENTS

The community college presidency has been widely studied (Moore et al. 1985; Weisman and Vaughan 2002; Eddy 2005; Duree 2007, ACE 2012). Collectively, these studies build an inventory of competencies appropriate to a leadership role and to ground future training. Some studies also chart the changing demands of the job and requirements needed to secure it (Kabala and Bailey 2001; Tackle 2012). Perhaps the most definitive work stems from George Vaughn's *Career and Lifestyle Survey* which, for 30 years, remains a prominent source for AACCs data collection (Vaughan 1986) on CEOs in its' membership. This survey profiles CEO demographics, workload, and professional development to understand the changing field. For example, data reveals that the average age of community college presidents was 51 years of age in 1984; 56 in 2001, and 58 in 2007 and that nearly all were either married or had a domestic partner (Weisman and Vaughan 2007). AACC (2013) concurs that the median CEO age has risen to 60 years, with half between the ages of 55 and 64; a quarter between the ages of 65 and 75; less than a quarter between the ages of 45 and 54. These studies suggest that 75 % of responding college CEOs are planning to retire within the next ten years thereby indicating a need to reinforce the pipeline.

Surveys also share professional profiles. Weisman and Vaughan (2007) found that 25 % of presidents had taken classes at the community college level while less said that they had earned an associate's degree. In terms of becoming a president, most had served their institution for several years and most were involved in academic affairs, while less than a small fraction worked in student services. Moreover, most CEOs have doctoral degrees and follow a traditional career path of graduate training, teaching, and appointment as department chair, promotion to dean, vice president, and finally president. Likewise, few CEOs move to presidency without having prior teaching experience and even fewer have their start in K-12 administration.

Regarding race, ethnicity, and gender, when historically compared to zero, these studies show some progress toward diversity. However, CEOs are still predominantly White and male (ACE 2012). The AACC (2013) study of 952 CEOs showed that nearly 80 % of the respondents identified themselves as White, 11 % as unknown, 6 % as Black, 3 % as Hispanic and 1 % as Asian American or Pacific Islander. When compared to student demographic data, which reveals that 50 % of students are White, 21 % Hispanic,

14 % Black, 6 % Asian or Pacific Islander, 1 % Native American, 2 % or more races, 4 % unknown, and 1 % non-resident Alien, (AACC 2015) there is still a need for advocacy for having leaders approximate their constituencies.

With demographic and professional knowledge, a richly informed discussion on leadership needs can emerge to help decisions makers prepare for succession planning in the area of international education more effectively. It is the understanding of who the leadership is and will be that is crucial for the next wave of college leadership.

METHODOLOGY

The *Valeau Lifestyle and Career Survey for International Education Leadership* is based on the Vaughn *Career and Lifestyle Survey for CEOs* and is designed to set in motion a new track for gathering data on the nation's community college international leadership. In summer 2015, we administered an online survey to eight community college LISTSERV that serve the field of community college internationalization and requested that those who work at a community college and have at least some of their duties involving international education respond. The survey had mostly open-ended questions to allow respondents an opportunity to provide their personal opinions. Since a survey of this type has not been done before, the open-ended questions allowed those in the field to define terms from their own viewpoints. A consistency of themes emerged from the answers that were coded to quantify descriptive statistics and to qualify the categorization of data that then can be used to ground future versions of the survey.

There is currently no single source that identifies how many community colleges are involved in international education (IIE 2015). One of the more reliable sources is the more reliable sources is the Institute for International Education (IIE) *Open Doors report* that in 2014 listed data from 336 community colleges. Our sample includes individuals at 84 colleges (representing 25 states) and as such, represents but an introduction to the field and does not speak to the generalizability of the data.

PRELIMINARY FINDINGS

The results of this study, which is still in progress, gives the reader a snapshot of institutional profiles, personal demographics, workload and titles, and professional development of community college international leadership at the mid-management level.

Institutional Profile

Half of the respondents come from colleges with a student population of 26,000 or more while the other half have less. When asked about the size of the international student programs, 48 % have less than 300 students and of these, 19 % have less than 100 students. Our sample thus includes those who work at various size institutions with mostly small international student programs.

Demographic Profiles

Our sample shows that the profiles of international education leadership are not similar to CEO profiles, and nor did we expect it would be. Unlike CEOs who are mostly married and male, only 79 % of international educators are married and most (73.8 %) are female. A sensitive demographic data element is inquiry of sexual orientation. 54 % of respondents answered this question and defined themselves as 71 % heterosexual/straight, 18 % as gay, 2 % as bisexual, and 9 % as other. More discussion on these variables are needed to understand whether the data point is of future value. Our intent in including it was to be inclusive and respectful of the changing demographics in our community college systems. In terms of race and ethnicity, findings are similar to CEO leadership, with the majority being White/Caucasian (66.7 %), Hispanic (14.1 %), Asian/Pacific Islander (12.8 %), African-American (3.8 %), multi-race (2.6 %), and American Indian/Native Americans (0 %). From this sample, international education leadership is far from representing their likely student populations and is dismally failing in placing African-Americans and Native Americans into leadership roles. Regarding age, there is a healthy range to support a leadership pipeline with 22.9 % between the ages of 31 and 40; 32.5 % between 41 and 50; 20.5 % between 51 and 60, and 19.3 % between 61 and 70. One respondent was unknowingly prophetic when their answer to the demographic questions was—who cares? At minimum, demographic data, especially when compared over time, has the potential to discover inequity patterns that can then be targeted for resolution.

Workload and Titles

96.4 % of the respondents work full-time, which has positive implications for what might appear to be a strong pipeline. Work titles include coordinator (67 %), executive or assistant director (22 %), dean, assistant dean or department chair (10 %), advisor/counselor (10 %), and faculty (9 %). Two respondents reported they were up for reclassification. When viewed as a whole, mid-management roles are evident and these individuals have the opportunity to make decisions related to influencing change. The data also reveals that when the titles are collapsed, 71 % of the positions are in traditional areas that would suggest upward mobility may exist for these individuals. Important to the field of international education is that 29 % of the titles had the word "international" or "intercultural" or "global."

Professional Development

The level of degree attainment is high among respondents with 60.8 % holding as their highest degree a Master's degree, 7.6 % an EdD, and 15.2 % a PhD. Very few degrees are in international education and tend to cluster around the liberal arts, social sciences, and for those with a doctorate, in education/higher education. The array of fields and discipline may suggest a minimal demand for those with higher education degrees in international education as a field of study.

Before coming to their current position, most respondents had served in a variety of roles in the community college including professor/faculty, English as Second Language (ESL) staff, international student advisor, director of international programs, department chair, and dean of instruction. 71.6 % moved into their current position from a position in their college that was not related to international education; 10.4 % moved from a position in their college related to international education; 9 % came from the non-profit or private sector of international education; and 9 % came from non-profit or private sectors outside the field of higher education, including the K-12 environment.

Respondents clearly indicate they are part of the professionalization of the field. For example, 38.8 % interviewed for their position which demanded knowledge of international education and 24.2 % were specifically asked to take on the responsibilities of the position and learned about international education on the job. Training and mentorship comes equally from the field of international education (43.2 %) and from the field of community college leadership (48.6 %). Finally, 49.2 % are not likely to move into another position within next three to five years, while 21.3 % are very likely to move. There is longevity for those working in international education with 34 % of respondents having spent 10–18 years in their current position, 28 % between 6 and 9 years, 31 % between 1 and 5.5 years of experience, and 7 % being in their position for under one year. The number of new positions is noteworthy and a reflection of the changing field itself.

CONCLUSION

The literature on the profile of community college CEOs serves as our portal to frame a serious and sustained conversation on the need for long-term planning related to community college international education leadership. They are arguably the gate keepers to strategic planning, curricula, and program offerings aimed at preparing students to become globally competent. Not only is there too little attention given to the demographics, job titles, and training needs of these individuals, but there is also no discussion on how they can become part of the community college leadership pipeline. The *Valeau Lifestyle and Career Survey for International Education Leadership* provides an initial profile as the preliminary results show as follows:

1. Small and large size community colleges have dedicated international education leaders. Many work at colleges with small international student programs. This is important because in the past, most of the full-time international positions were primarily at colleges with very large international student programs.
2. A range of individuals (from faculty to CEOs) are taking charge of international education for at least some of their duties. Unique to this survey is that so many of the respondents work full-time in jobs that are specifically devoted to overseeing international education. Fewer individuals have "international" as an additional assignment to their regular job requirements.
3. Community college international education leaders have higher education degrees and mostly rise through the ranks of the college. These leaders have mentors in one or both international education and community college leadership. Finally, these leaders have a high degree of commitment and involvement to their jobs.
4. Community college international education leaders do not reflect wider student population demographics. There is unequal gender, sexual orientation, race and ethnicity profiles among the individuals

participating in the study. Specifically colleges are dismally failing in placing and hiring African-Americans and Native Americans into leadership roles.

It is difficult to be dedicated to student success without the balance of leadership preparation. Although there is strong satisfaction for many who work in community college international education, these individuals can also become part of a cadre that feeds into the college leadership pipeline. We believe that as a result of these institutionalized administrative positions that international leaders can also be involved in programmatic change in all sectors of the college. However, in this process, it is critical to design specific support for these individuals so that as they move up the pipeline they still have the means to continue to advocate and actively support internationalization efforts.

For decades, those writing about community college internationalization have advocated that professionalized positions be created (Raby and Valeau 2007). It is evident that there is now a direction that we hope will support future growth in the field.

RECOMMENDATIONS

Using the *Valeau Lifestyle and Career Survey for International Education Leadership* as a theoretical guideline, we recommend the following:

1. National Associations need to increase their reach to make sure that succession planning and leadership training for international leaders is better focused and relevant.
2. CEOs and Boards must work more effectively to implement international education programming that respects the vision of their own international educators.
3. CEOs and Boards must recognize existing international educators as part of their college's leadership pipeline.
4. The pipeline for international education leaders must be monitored so as to ensure that new leaderships, due to retirements and transitions due to upward mobility, is readily available.
5. More attention must be devoted to diversifying the position of international education personnel especially as it pertains to African-Americans and Native Americans.

REFERENCES

American Association of Communities Colleges. (2013). *AACC competencies for Community College Leaders* (2nd ed.). Washington, DC: AACC. http://www.aacc.nche.edu/newsevents/Events/leadershipsuite/Documents/AACC/CoreCompetencies/web.pdf

American Association of Community Colleges. (2015). *Fast facts.* http://www.aacc.nche.edu/AboutCC/Pages/fastfactsfactsheet.aspx

American Association of Community Colleges and Association of Community College Trustees (ACCT) "Thriving in the Community College Presidency". (2015). http://www.aacc.nche.edu/newsevents/Events/leadershipsuite/Documents/CC%20Presidency%20Meeting%202012-13.pdf

American Council on Education (2012). *The American college president.* Washington, DC: Author.

Aspen Institute. (2013). *Crisis and opportunity: Aligning the community college presidency with student success.* http://www.aspeninstitute.org/publications/crisis-opportunity-aligning-community-college-presidency-student-success

Astin, Alexander W., & Astin, Helen S. (2000). *Leadership reconsidered: Engaging higher education in social change.* Battle Creek, MI: W.K. Kellogg Foundation. http://eric.ed.gov/?id=ED444437

Duree, Christopher (2007). The Challenges of the community college presidency in the new millennium: Pathways, preparation, competencies and leadership programs needed to survive Unpublished doctoral dissertation, Iowa State University, Ames Iowa.

Eddy, Pamela L. (2005). Framing the role of leader: How community college presidents construct their leadership. *Community College Journal of Research and Practice, 29*(9/10), 705–727.

Institute of International Education. (2015). *Open doors 2014. Open doors data: Community colleges data resource.* http://www.iie.org/Research-and-Publications/Open-Doors/Data/Community-College-Data-Resource/Study-Abroad

Kabala, Thomas S., & Bailey, George M. (2001). A new perspective on community college presidents: Results of a national study. *Community College Journal of Research and Practice, 25*(6), 793–804.

Moore, Kathryn, Martorana, S. V., & Twombly, Susan (1985). *Today's academic leaders: A national study of administrators in two-year colleges.* Center for the Study of Higher Education: University Park, PA.

Raby, Rosalind Latiner, & Valeau, Edward J. (2007). Community college international education: Looking back to forecast the future. In Edward J. Valeau & Rosalind Latiner Raby (Eds.), *International reform efforts and challenges in community colleges* (pp. 5–14). New Directions for Community Colleges (138, Summer).San Francisco: Jossey-Bass.

Tackle, Rahel (2012). *Compensation and benefits of community college CEOs: 2012.* Washington, DC: American Association of Community Colleges Research Brief. 2012-1. http://www.aacc.nche.edu/AboutCC/Trends/Documents/ CEOCompensationResearchBrief.pdf

Vaughan, George B. (1986). *The community college presidency.* New York: American Council on Education/Macmillan.

Weisman, Iris M., & Vaughan, George B. (2002). *The community college presidency, 2001.* Report No. AACC-RB-02-1; AACC Ser-3. Washington, DC: American Associations of Community Colleges.

Weisman, Iris M., & Vaughan, George B. (2007). *The Community College Presidencey: 2006.* http://www.aacc.nche.edu/Publications/Briefs/Documen ts/09142007presidentbrief.pdf

PART II

Case-Studies and Research Studies

Building a World-Class College: Creating a Global Community at Pima Community College

Ricardo Castro-Salazar, Kelley Merriam-Castro, and Yvonne A. Perez Lopez

It is the obligation of colleges and universities to prepare people for a global-ized world.

The American Council on Education Blue Ribbon Panel on Global Engagement (2011)

INTRODUCTION

When Pima Community College (PCC) in Tucson, Arizona, announced its goal to internationalize, local newspaper articles, emails to college adminis-trators, and social media bristled with critical commentary (Alaimo 2014).

R. Castro-Salazar (✉)
International Development, Pima County Community College, University of Arizona Center for Latin American Studies, Pima, AZ, USA

K. Merriam-Castro
Pima Community College, Pima, AZ, USA

Y.A. Perez Lopez
Cultural Foundations of Education, Syracuse University, International Development Department, Pima Community College District, Pima, AZ, USA

© The Editor(s) (if applicable) and The Author(s) 2016   175
R.L. Raby, E.J. Valeau (eds.), *International Education at Community Colleges*, DOI 10.1057/978-1-137-53336-4_12

A vocal group of concerned citizens questioned: Shouldn't *community* colleges focus on providing educational opportunities to their communities? Why should we "import" students from other countries? One illustrative email submitted to college administration asked: "We can't get our own states children to come to Pima why are we tying [*sic*] to get other country's kids here. Seems like our taxes should be spent on AZ kids first" (comment received July 2015).

In a state under the national spotlight for its harsh anti-immigration policies, these uninformed questions circulated in public forums once PCC announced its intentions to expand its international programs. In the face of this criticism, global-minded administrators, faculty, staff, and community members arose in support of internationalization. This chapter outlines the process by which PCC began implementing fundamental institutional changes across all six of its city-wide campuses in order to internationalize its college and curriculum in the face of an ambivalent local populace.

In contrast to Arizona's nativist stance, internationalization efforts emerged nationally after World War II in response to concerns surrounding the country's political and economic security (Hser 2005). Ongoing international conflicts led US officials to conclude that the general public should possess a basic understanding of global affairs (Burn 1980). In 1947, President Truman appointed a Presidential Commission on Higher Education tasked with defining the responsibilities of colleges and universities and concluded that higher education institutions should prepare students to participate not only as national citizens, but also as denizens in a newly expanding global community (Higher Education for Democracy 1947). Thus, since the mid-twentieth century, international education was understood as an essential component in maintaining national security, developing international collaborations, and producing global citizens (Hser 2005). These imperatives resonated with the nation's desire to retain its powerful international status: globally educated citizens would act as economic and political leaders, utilizing cultural and linguistic competency to manage global assets from anywhere in the world.

Far from decreasing with time, the importance of preparing an internationally competent workforce has increased due to rapid developments in transportation, communication, and economic globalization. Despite this, the concept of using the community college as the vehicle for preparing students for the global arena has met with resistance in Arizona. This may stem partially from a general misunderstanding of the function and goals of international programs. One broadly held belief is that internationalization focuses solely on bringing international students to college campuses and sending local students abroad. While some institutions have implemented study abroad programs as isolated units within their colleges (Altbach and Knight 2007), transformative internationalization efforts like PCC's involve substantial college involvement at all levels. This benefits all students, since teaching internationalized classroom curricula across subject areas while incorporating international students into standard courses provides opportunities for students who cannot travel to experience a diversity of perspectives, opinions, and experiences.

A second erroneous conception revolves around the idea that colleges internationalize solely for economic reasons—that is, to attract tuition dollars from out-of-state fees. These criticisms do not acknowledge the benefits of including diverse perspectives and experiences in a local college classroom, nor do they account for the multiplying benefits of additional programs and services that can be provided to local students, thanks to increased revenues. The most effective programs maximize the benefits of international tuition dollars, integrate internationalization into their overall college identity, values, and curriculum, and continually evaluate and respond to issues and concerns that arise globally (Altbach 2004). PCC's experience highlights how any institutional change toward internationalization must accompany a campaign to educate the local community on the importance of global education (Boggs and Irwin 2007, p. 26). For this reason, PCC's internationalization efforts include collaborating with local news channels and print media to reiterate the benefits of global exchange (Castro-Salazar 2015).

The benefits of internationalization resonate not only on campus and among the students who travel; they provide transformative benefits to surrounding communities. The American Council on Education (ACE), the American Association of Community Colleges (AACC), and the Institute for International Education (IIE) all advocate that international education become a priority for all institutes of higher learning (Sasser 2014). ACE affirms that a deeper understanding of and appreciation for cultures abroad provides a framework for greater intercultural relationships at home (1995, p. 11) and the Case Statement for Internationalization asserts that "in order for the United States to have a truly world-class higher education system, colleges and universities must be globally engaged and prepare students to be citizens of a multicultural community both at home and in a globalized world" (ACE 2015, para 2). To be effective, higher education must keep pace with global changes and prepare students for a diverse local community. To prepare local students for the twenty-first-century workforce, PCC has embraced the challenge of educating the local community, expanding exchange opportunities, and internationalizing its curriculum.

CONTEXT

PCC is one of the largest multicampus community colleges in the nation, with six main campuses, two satellite centers, and full-time student enrollments of over 52,000 in a city of just over 550,000 people (USCB 2010). PCC receives a large percentage of its funding through county tax revenues and is, therefore, highly responsive to the needs and concerns of the community. The college's six campuses, satellite centers, and continuing education programs function under a unifying district administration, the Pima County Community College District (PCCCD). Each campus houses a local administration team that reports to a campus president. Campus presidents oversee one or more campuses and any corresponding satellite units. The District offices are headed by a chancellor who is selected by and reports to an elected Board of Governors (BOG). The BOG consists of five publicly elected members who serve six-year terms as representatives of their district within Pima County. This board of citizen representatives from Pima County selects PCC's highest administrator and, through executive voting privileges, determine the mission and goals of the college.

PCC serves the population of all of Pima County, estimated at just over one million residents in 2014 (USCB PEP 2014). Similar to other border regions in the USA, non-Hispanic White (47.2 %) and Hispanic/Latino (41.6 %) form Tucson's two major demographic groups, with Black/African-American, Native American, Asian and other groups each claiming 5 % or less of the demographic pie (USCB 2010). In the 1990s, PCC was among the ten community colleges with the highest international student enrollment in the country, with a robust and well-staffed international program that actively recruited students and facilitated their stay. After September 11, 2001, a reduction in support for internationalization coupled with the discontinuation of international recruitment led to a decade-long decline in international enrollment.

Over a decade later, the selection of Chancellor Lee Lambert by the BOG and his installation in July 2013 signaled the beginning of a major effort to revitalize and reinvent PCC's international arena. Lambert joined PCC with a reputation as an initiator of international programs, and he immediately set a comprehensive, institution-wide vision of internationalization as a top priority for the college. Lambert's vision involved a transformative plan to be implemented across the entire district. Understanding that international education would remain in the margins unless it became part of the college's central mission (Raby 2012), he encouraged PCC administrators at both the district and the campus levels to reimagine the institutional planning process (Lambert 2014). He challenged them to produce a model where PCC would serve the needs of the local community while producing graduates who were competitive in the global economy.

Lambert articulated this vision in the Pima Community College Strategic Plan of 2014–2017, developed in collaboration with college personnel, supportive community members, current students and alumni. Strategic Direction 5 outlined the college's intent to *increase diversity, inclusion, and global education*. This strategic direction included among its objectives the establishment of a task force to develop and implement a college-wide internationalization plan. From the beginning of Lambert's term, PCC's BOG had endorsed internationalization as a concept. The critical component for converting theory into praxis lies in Lambert's success in obtaining BOG approval to invest significant institutional support in implementing the new directive. With BOG approval, he created a high-level administrative position, the Vice President for International Development (VPID) to spearhead an integrated approach to implementing the college plan and to manage the college's reinvestment in international outreach efforts. In January 2015, the newly instituted VPID began providing strategic planning, developing internal and external relationships, building support programs, representing the college to international constituencies, and providing leadership to raise the college's profile domestically and abroad.

STRATEGIC PLAN FOR COMPREHENSIVE INTERNATIONALIZATION

To prepare an internationalization program that met the needs of multiple constituencies in the college and the local community, PCC administrators determined that the implementation of the strategic plan should be broadly inclusive and democratic in nature. The following steps were implemented to achieve this goal:

Internationalization Task Force

One of the first tasks of the VPID was to create a *Chancellor's Internationalization Task Force* (ITF) to define and implement the specific objectives of the internationalization plan. An invitation to participate was sent to PCC faculty, staff, and the broader Tucson community. Despite the concerns raised by some vocal members of the broader community, college faculty and other community leaders showed enthusiastic support for the internationalization plan. In total, 84 individuals from the college and Pima County responded to the call, including PCC staff, faculty, administrators and students, and community members from the Office of the Mayor, Pima County, Visit Tucson Office, the Consulate of Mexico, and from the nearby four-year university. To maintain an inclusive, democratic process, all volunteers were officially incorporated into the ITF. To share the burden of commuting and to include all campuses, the location of the weekly meetings rotated throughout the district. The ITF spent the first 12 weeks discussing the state and context of the college, defining vision and mission statements for internationalization, delineating the possible lines of work and goals for internationalization, and identifying measurable objectives that would communicate the new international imperative. They also received feedback from an internationalization consultant from another successful international community college program. The size of the committee brought diverse perspectives into the plan, and helped quell concerns about local criticism by demonstrating broad-level support for internationalization across multiple educational, economic, and political sectors.

Vision and Mission Statements

Management theory emphasizes that organizations with Vision and Mission statements that are clearly understood and become integral parts of a strategic plan outperform other organizations (Ireland et al. 2008). Thus, the task force's first goal was to clarify Vision and Mission statements, ensure they were clearly understood, and integrate them into the broader strategic plan. The starting premise was that PCC's internationalization efforts fit naturally within the larger College Vision to "provide access to learning without the limits of time, place, or distance." Nevertheless, some ITF members suggested that the college should articulate a derivative, more specific vision for internationalization. After extensive analysis and discussion, this more focused vision statement was expressed in four words: *Global education without limits.*

The ITF also developed a mission statement for internationalization. ITF members suggested and debated multiple proposals before they arrived at a brief statement that incorporated PCC's international focus into the college-wide mission: *Developing communities through global education.* The plural term "communities" acknowledges that the "community" served by a community college is an overlapping network of groups, relationships, and interests that constitute a mosaic of aspirations, beliefs, interests and goals. These communities can be local, international, transnational, multicultural, and virtual. The new mission statement developed by the task force specifies that Pima Community College will provide educational resources for them all.

Goals

Pima Community College's international task force explored existing models as it identified measurable objectives for its strategic plan. Members reviewed, among many, a six-phase comprehensive internationalization plan outlined by ACE's Center for Internationalization and Global Engagement (CIGE 2012) as well as other approaches that encourage colleges to implement changes in process, activities, competency, and organization (Knight 1999). Drawing from these models and Chancellor Lambert's direction, the task force established seven strategic goals and lines of work for the college's internationalization efforts. The task force divided into seven subcommittees of approximately ten members each to work on these goals. Each group utilized SWOT Analysis to identify the college's Strengths, Weaknesses, Opportunities, and Threats in their assigned area. The subcommittees provided feedback to each other's SWOT summaries, and then developed possible actions and ideas for their respective goals that would later be developed into specific objectives. To prioritize their objectives, task force subcommittees discussed their proposals individually and filled out charts that outlined the desired accomplishment, relevance of the objective, performance indicators, expected outcomes, and timeframes. The subcommittees presented their ideas to the entire task force for feedback and suggestions. This continuous exchange of perspectives allowed all task force members to provide input into each stage of the strategic planning process. The end result of this process was the development and prioritization of measurable objectives that became the foundation of a widely supported strategic plan for internationalization. This allows PCC to evaluate the effectiveness of the programs as they are implemented, an essential step in maximizing educational outcomes (Van Damme 2001). The Internationalization Task Force (ITF) established goals, specific objectives, and milestones within them, allowing PCC to determine how well the institution is approaching each goal across all of the district campuses as it implements its internationalization plan. The seven strategic goals identified through this planning process included:

Infuse Global Knowledge and Competency Into the Curriculum. An essential component of comprehensive internationalization involves internationalization of all aspects of a college's curriculum (CIGE, cited in Helms and Ward 2014). PCC's strategic plan includes revisions to the general curriculum across content areas to incorporate internationalization at all levels of student learning. The college already assesses Student Learning Objectives (SLOs) across all content areas. Inserting internationalization goals into the already extant planning and assessment cycle allows PCC to incorporate a globalized curriculum and track its progress. In addition, an internal audit will be conducted to identify community and global initiatives already underway and to build upon curricular and co-curricular activities that already expose students, both domestic and international, to aspects of global competency.

Create a Language Institute. PCC's International Task Force came to the conclusion that establishing a language institute to serve local and international students must start by reconceptualizing English as a Second Language (ESL) offerings at the college. ESL programs are emerging as an important pathway for international students. The number of international students enrolling in ESL programs increased from 10,224 in 2003–2004 to 29,603 in 2010–2011 (Choudaha and Chang 2012). In 2013, ESL programs accounted for a 16.4 % increase of international student enrollment (IIE 2013). Moreover, the percentage of English language learners in public schools increased from 8.7 % in 2002–2003 to 9.1 % in 2011–2012. By 2014, this represented approximately 4.4 million students who required language programs (Kena et al. 2014). There is a clear local and international demand for access to English language instruction. Community colleges provide quality instruction with small class sizes and affordable tuition, providing a competitive advantage over four-year universities (Farnsworth 2005). Thus, PCC decided to revise and expand its existing credit and non-credit ESL offerings. PCC now offers short-term, long-term, and certificate programs to satisfy the diverse needs of local and global communities. A more ambitious language institute offering both transfer and non-transfer learning opportunities, and providing a central base for language instruction other than English will be explored as the ESL program expands.

Develop Community and Global Engagement Opportunities. The Chancellor, the Vice President for International Development, campus presidents, and other members of PCC have been actively involved in establishing relationships with local organizations to support international visitors to Tucson, as well as with international institutions and organizations to establish support networks for the development of new programs and opportunities abroad. PCC reinitiated relationships with local and international institutions where previous articulation agreements existed, and started to promote engagement by sending faculty and staff abroad as instructors or for professional development opportunities.

Develop a Study Abroad Program. Internationalization task force members listed essential components to establishing a robust study abroad program such as: identifying partnering institutions, planning occupational and transfer opportunities, providing language-learning opportunities, and planning international service learning, community service and internship opportunities. PCC faculty, staff and administrators are now actively engaged in establishing Memoranda of Understanding (MOUs) with institutions abroad to articulate the details of these relationships.

Identify Opportunities for Workforce Development in the International Arena. In 2014 Tucson was recognized as one of "America's Best Cities for Global Trade" (Global Trade 2014). In the twentieth century, Arizona's economic development evolved from the historical Five C's (cattle, citrus, copper, cotton, and climate) to the Five T's of technology, trade, transportation, tourism, and teaching. These five new dimensions rely on complex global networks where international strategic alliances and interdependence are inevitable, even for residents who would never consider leaving Tucson. PCC's plan strives to prepare future leaders from the local community who have the educational training and the cultural competency to be competitive in the global economy. International workforce development is a natural area of focus for the extensive socioeconomic relationship between Arizona and Mexico, where previous training programs have been implemented for the *maquiladora* industry and other economic sectors.

Provide International and Cultural Development for Faculty, Staff, and Administration. Preparing students for the global job market requires faculty who have optimal training and education in the internationalization of their field, thus, PCC will provide international language and cultural development opportunities for faculty, staff, and administrators. International programs such as the Core Fulbright US Scholar Program provide teaching and/or research grants to US faculty and experienced professionals in a wide variety of fields. PCC also provides professional development funds for faculty and staff, allowing them to take advantage of international courses and cultural immersion programs. PCC classrooms will benefit from the knowledge and experience faculty and staff bring from abroad as they internationalize their field.

Expand International Student Outreach and Recruitment. The entire community benefits from the cultural enrichment international students bring to campus. Furthermore, higher out-of-state tuition fees help support programs that benefit all students. As PCC's task force worked on strategic planning, the VPID began developing relationships and programs with global institutions to revive robust, sustainable international enrollments. The task force identified numerous recruitment strategies, including marketing, recruitment fairs, transfer agreements, and working with contracting agents. Educating international recruits on the concept of the community college will also play a role in these efforts, as the institution is often misunderstood in international sectors. Prospective international students must be educated on the role of the community college and the benefits, both educational and economic, it brings to the student academic experience.

First Steps

Even while this college-wide plan was being drafted, PCC began participating in international agreements. In fall 2014, the college welcomed 49 Mexican students as part of the *100,000 Strong in the Americas* Initiative. The *Bécalos* program was funded by *Fundación Televisa* (a large private foundation in Mexico), Santander Bank, and the Ministry of Education of Mexico (SEP). The rapid implementation of this program served as a pilot experience to help PCC establish new procedures and routes of communication. Participant and community feedback at the program's conclusion demonstrated how international exchange programs provide benefits for distant and local communities far beyond the individual student experience.

For example, before entering the program, the Mexican participants reported concerns about studying in Arizona. The current political status of many immigrants in the USA and the high-profile anti-immigrant legislation in Arizona worried many of the students, who feared they would face discrimination as a result of their citizenship. Despite these misgivings, students accepted their placement at PCC. PCC in turn provided the students with peer mentors, conversation sessions with local students, educational field trips, and professional development workshops in addition to their credit coursework. Participating in PCC's program transformed their initial negative perceptions, such as in the case of one student, who related in the December 2014 closing ceremony: "I felt sad because some of my partners ... were going to 'better' places ... Now, I realize that I was selected for the best place in whole America." [*sic*]. By returning to their home communities and relating their positive experiences in Arizona, students help quell some of the negativity and concern, and effectively become goodwill ambassadors in regions where US culture is poorly understood.

The presence of the international students on campus and in Tucson also provided benefits and learning opportunities for the local college and community. Interactions with the *Bécalos* students facilitated intercultural understanding and acceptance. One faculty member shared that he "felt the benefit of the program was it helped the Pima brand and ... it helped with my growth by exposing me to Mexican students from a region of Mexico I didn't know much about." Moreover, this experience served to connect our local students not only with their international peers but also with the broader PCC community in their role as local hosts. A peer mentor lauded her opportunity to interact with "every person I met along the way! The Bécalos students, the faculty, every new face ... I am so glad to have had the opportunity to be a positive influence." This successful reception of the Bécalos students resulted from a collaborative effort by PCC faculty, staff administrators, peer mentors, and the Tucson community to provide an enriching experience for the students. It provided an important opportunity for PCC offices to work together to implement an internationalized curriculum based on the students' needs and interests, and to create working relationships with other local and national organizations to provide cultural learning opportunities for the students while they were visiting Arizona. Institutionally, PCCCD developed a positive relationship with the US State Department that made it possible for the participants to obtain J-1 student visas. PCC had previously lost its ability to sponsor such visas due to lack of use and had not yet regained this privilege by the time the *Bécalos* students needed to matriculate. The college later applied for and reobtained authorization to become a J-1 visa sponsoring institution. Finally, the presence of this group of students from various regions of Mexico provided local PCC students, staff, and faculty the opportunity to know these students as individuals and learn more about their home regions, lived experiences, and cultural backgrounds.

As PCC entered the 2015–2016 academic year, it hired a new Director for International Programs and Recruitment, an Associate Director for International Student Services, an Associate Director for Admissions, Compliance and Operations, and an Assistant Director for Recruitment with a focus on Asia. The job descriptions for International Student Advisors were restructured and reclassified with a higher salary. These new positions support the implementation of PCC's Strategic Plan for Comprehensive Internationalization. Although the personnel were not yet in place in 2014–2015, already PCC had increased its international student enrollment under all types of visas to 246 students in the spring and 212 in the fall. A clear sign of progress was evident by the spring 2015, when PCC had an auspicious increase of 18 new F-1 students over the previous year. Furthermore, in the summer and fall 2015 the College hosted 103 international students under J-1 visas, including those in the renewed 2015 *Bécalos* program.

These numbers demonstrate that PCC's new course of action is reviving international enrollment, but these numbers represent only a small part of the college's comprehensive plan to transform the identity of the college into that of an internationalized institution. In addition to hiring new administrators and staff, increasing visa offerings, and launching a pilot international program, the college's administration also started promoting international professional development opportunities for faculty and staff, and advocated the incorporation of Global Learning Outcomes into the curricula through the regular SLO development process. These critical first steps provided objective measures of success as the college moved closer to the goals identified by the Internationalization Task Force. In the face of criticism from local reporters and some community members who poorly understand the benefits of internationalization at the community college, PCC established measurable performance indicators to demonstrate how a comprehensively internationalized college can provide an enhanced educational experience for all of its students and prepare its local workforce to be competitive in the global twenty-first century.

REFERENCES

Alaimo, Carol Ann (2014, November 29). PCC seeks students in China to offset losses. *The Arizona Daily Star.*

Altbach, Philip G. (2004). Globalization and the university: Myths and realities in an unequal world. *Tertiary Education and Management, 10*(1), 3–25.

Altbach, Philip G., & Knight, Jane (2007). The internationalization of higher education: Motivations and realities. *Journal of Studies in International Education, 11*(3–4), 290–305.

American Council on Education (1995). *Educating Americans for a world in flux: Ten ground rules for internationalizing higher education.* Washington, DC: American Council on Education In-House Press.

American Council on Education. (2015). The ACE case statement for internationalization. *Making the case for internationalization.* http://www.acenet.edu/news-room/Pages/Making-the-Case-for-Internationalization.aspx

American Council on Education Blue Ribbon Panel on Global Engagement. (2011, November). *Strength through global leadership and engagement: U.S. higher education in the 21st century.* http://www.acenet.edu/news-room/Documents/2011-CIGE-BRPReport.pdf

Boggs, George R., & Irwin, Judith (2007). What every community college leader needs to know: Building leadership for international education." In Edward J. Valeau & Rosalind Latiner Raby (Eds.), *International reform efforts and challenges in community colleges* (pp. 25–30). New Directions for Community Colleges (138, Summer). San Francisco: Jossey-Bass.

Burn, B. (1980). *Expanding the international dimension of higher education.* San Francisco: Jossey-Bass Publishers.

Castro-Salazar, Ricardo (2015, January 5). PCC reacting to imperatives for global education. *Arizona Daily Star.*

Center for Internationalization and Global Engagement. (2012). *Mapping internationalization on U.S. campuses. 2012 Edition.* American Council on Education. http://www.acenet.edu/news-room/Documents/Mapping-Internationalizationon-US-Campuses-2012-full.pdf

Choudaha, Rahul, & Chang, Li (2012, February). *Trends in international student mobility.* New York: World Education Services. www.wes.org/RAS

Farnsworth, Kent (2005). A new model for recruiting international students: The 2+2. *International Education, 35*(1), 5–63.

Global Trade. (2014, November). Global trader list. Export assistance. *Global Trade.* http://www.globaltrademag.com/list/export-assistance

Helms, Robin M., & Ward, Heather H. (2014, June). Internationalization in action. *ACEnet.* http://www.acenet.edu/news-room/Pages/Intlz-in-Action-June-2014.aspx

Hser, M. P. (2005). Campus internationalization: A study of American universities' internationalization efforts. *International Education,* 35(1), 35.

Institute for International Education. (2012). *International education as an institutional priority. What every college and university trustee should know.* http://www.iie.org/Research-and-Publications/Publications-and-Reports/IIE-Bookstore/International-Education-as-an-Institutional-Priority

Institute of International Education, Center for Academic Mobility Research. (2013, November). *Fall 2013 International student snapshot survey. A brief report.* file:///C:/Users/yperez11/Downloads/Fall-2013-Snapshot-Survey-International-Students%20(1).pdf

Ireland, R. Duane, Hoskisson, Robert E., & Hitt, Michael A. (2008). *Understanding business strategy: Concepts and cases.* Mason, OH: South-Western Cengage Learning.

Kena, Grace, Aud, Susan, Johnson, Frank, Wang, Xiaolei, Zhang, Jijun, Rathbun, Amy, Wilkinson-Flicker, Sidney, & Kristapovich, Paul (2014). *The condition of education 2014* (NCES 2014-083). Washington, DC: U.S. Department of Education, National Center for Education Statistics. Retrieved February, 2015, from http://nces.ed.gov/pubsearch

Knight, J. (1999). *A time of turbulence and transformation for internationalization* Research Monograph No. 14. Ottawa: Canadian Bureau for International Education.

Lambert, Lee (2014, July). *District-wide strategic plan.* Pima Community College. https://www.pima.edu/about-pima/strategic-plan/

Raby, Rosalind Latiner (2012). Re-imagining international education at community colleges. *Audem: International Journal of Higher Education and Democracy, 3,* 81–99.

Sasser, Jackson N. (2014, November). *Internationalizing community colleges.* *AACC21stcenturycenter.*http://www.aacc21stcenturycenter.org/article/internationalizing-community-colleges/

Truman Commission on Higher Education. (1947). Higher education for democracy: A report of the President's commission on higher education. *Establishing the goals.* http://courses.education.illinois.edu/eol474/sp98/truman.html

United States Census Bureau (USCB). (2010). *Quick facts 2010 pages.* http://quickfacts.census.gov/. Accessed June 30, 2015.

United States Census Bureau Population Estimates Program (USCB PEP). (2014). *Pima County 2014.* http://www.census.gov/popest/. Accessed July 7, 2015.

Van Damme, Dirk (2001). Quality issues in the internationalization of higher education. *Higher Education, 41,* 415–441.

Internationalization and the Influence of Environmental Factors

Deborah M. Sipe

INTRODUCTION

Community colleges in the USA have been significantly impacted in recent years by powerful global forces (Levin 2001; Siaya and Hayward 2003; Panel on Global Engagement 2011). These forces include the increased movement of goods, people, and information across borders. Research (Kedia and Daniel 2003; Hart Research Associates 2010) suggests that US colleges and universities need to acknowledge these forces and respond to changing market and civic needs by enacting significant organizational, policy, and curricular changes, often termed *internationalization*, to better prepare college students to be global citizens and globally competent. Results from national surveys and case studies (Harder 2010; Hudzik 2011) indicate that such changes are occurring in some US colleges and universities; however, quantitative research on internationalization in community colleges is very limited. The following pages describe recent quantitative research regarding internationalization in Oregon and Washington community colleges, with attention to organizational behaviors in the areas of governance and student support services that are responses to global forces.

D.M. Sipe (✉)
Teaching and Learning, Chemeketa Community College, Salem, OR, USA

© The Editor(s) (if applicable) and The Author(s) 2016   189
R.L. Raby, E.J. Valeau (eds.), *International Education at Community Colleges*, DOI 10.1057/978-1-137-53336-4_13

Historically, community colleges have been charged with responding to the needs of their communities (Levin 2001; Cohen and Brawer 2003). Research on community college internationalization efforts could (a) indicate whether these colleges have made changes resembling those suggested by research (de Wit 2002) that can better serve changing community needs, (b) provide guidance to other colleges contemplating such changes, and (c) assist community college policymakers in understanding how environmental factors may influence internationalization efforts.

In that spirit, this study explores two dimensions of organizational behavior in Oregon and Washington community colleges that research (de Wit 2002) suggests can be strong indicators of internationalization: governance and student support services. These states were selected because of the significant impact of two global forces—international trade and increased student diversity—on the region's economies, societies, and educational systems (Portland Business Alliance 2010; Institute for International Education 2011; Washington Department of Commerce 2011; US Census Bureau 2013). The study exposes a relationship between global forces that impacted Oregon and Washington community colleges between 1990 and 2013 and specific institutional changes and organizational behaviors in response to these forces.

Findings from the study examine the possibility of a relationship between the level of internationalization in these colleges and three environmental factors—setting, student demographics (in terms of ethnic diversity), and primary industry in the college's service area. The theoretical construct that informed this research was that of systems theory; community colleges, as systems, were viewed as being influenced by larger systems in which they operate.

Literature Review

Peer-reviewed journals, reports, dissertations, full text studies, and other works in higher education literature were reviewed to explore the existing limits of current research on internationalization in community colleges. Works that were 20 or fewer years old were used to provide the most current research on the topic; most of the reviewed research was published after 2000. A few slightly older works provided historical context. The review included quantitative and qualitative research studies and reports that focused on: (a) effective internationalization strategies and processes; (b) the internationalization experiences of individual colleges and universities; and (c) factors affecting internationalization. The time period of mid-1990s–2013 was selected after an initial review indicated that the onset of significant impact of global forces on education began in the early 1990s. The method used in the literature review to locate the data involved the use of the following key phrases: (a) internationalization in community colleges, (b) internationalization in higher education, (c) internationalizing higher education, (d) globalization in higher education, (e) globalization in community colleges, (f) international students in the USA, (g) and demographic trends in community colleges.

Defining Effective Internationalization

Before exploring internationalization in community colleges, it is important to clarify how the term was used in this study. Internationalization has been defined in various ways and its definition continues to evolve. Levin (2001) suggested that internationalization represented a set of organizational behaviors that higher education institutions employed in response to the impact of global forces. De Wit (2002) saw internationalization activities as falling into two main categories of organizational behaviors: (a) organizational strategies, which focus more on the governance, operations, support services, and human resource development of organizations, and (b) program strategies, which focus on development and implementation of specific programs. Organizational strategies were key; if internationalization was not thoroughly integrated into the organization's culture and processes, it was at risk of being marginalized or considered a fad. Siaya and Hayward (2003) and Hudzik (2011), after examining the experiences of both two-year and four-year institutions, echoed this perspective.

Raby (1996) discussed several aspects of internationalization in community colleges, including exchange programs, partnerships, and services. She concluded that support from top college administrators and a committed faculty (as indicators of governance) and the presence of a specific coordinator (as an indicator of support services) were essential to successful internationalization. Thus, the research suggested that for four-year and two-year institutions, the most effective internationalization efforts are comprehensive in nature and involve organizational behaviors and actions at the highest levels of the institution. In contrast, Green and Siaya (2005) noted, regarding the responses of 233 community colleges to the American Council on Education (ACE) 2003 institutional survey on internationalization, that less than one quarter included internationalization goals in their mission statements or strategic plans—evidence of internationalization at the governance level. McGill-Peterson and Helms (2013) analyzed the results of the most recent ACE national survey of the status of internationalization at US colleges and universities (Center for Internationalization and Global Engagement 2012) and noted that overall, US colleges and universities had made some progress in internationalization since 2003, but "many still lack the 'connective tissue' that shapes internationalization efforts into a coherent strategy" (p. 33) that is necessary for a deep and long-lasting impact.

Environmental Factors Affecting Internationalization

Limited research exists regarding the influence of environmental factors on internationalization in community colleges. Using the 2005 ACE study results (Green and Siaya), Harder (2010) investigated whether a relationship existed between the location of the college (urban, suburban, rural) and its level of internationalization. She explored this relationship along four dimensions of internationalization: (a) institutional support, (b) academic requirements, programs, and extra-curricular activities, (c) faculty policies and opportunities, and (d) international students. Her findings indicated that there were significant differences between location categories of community colleges as to overall internationalization efforts as well as regarding each of the four dimensions. I was unable to locate any other quantitative research effort that explored a possible correlation between environmental factors and internationalization efforts in community colleges.

METHODS

For the present study, I employed quantitative research methods to investigate two research questions. The first research question focused on organizational behaviors at the administrative level regarding two dimensions of internationalization—governance and support services—in Oregon and Washington community colleges. Research described earlier has suggested that administrative behaviors in these areas regarding internationalization are key to successful internationalization efforts. The first research question for the study was this:

To what extent do administrative actions and behaviors within community colleges reflect increasing attention to issues in internationalization?

The research question reflects a systems theory construct in that actions and behaviors with the systems of community colleges are seen as being influenced by factors in their environment, in this case, the impact of global forces. I used survey research methods to collect and analyze data regarding these two dimensions of internationalization (governance and support services). A ten-item survey inquired about (a) the presence or absence of three indicators of governance—the college's mission statement, policy statements, and the existence of a college committee focused on internationalization, and (b) support services for international and study abroad students. I disseminated the survey in summer 2013 via electronic mail to the president, vice president of instruction or chief academic officer, and international education director at each Oregon and Washington community college. I also conducted archival research regarding the presence or absence of (a) a college partnership with an international higher education institution (either a college or university), and (b) a relationship between the college and an internationally focused company in the community. This additional research was conducted to explore institutional actions outside of the organization itself that might indicate additional evidence of internationalization efforts. Points were assigned to the survey results and archival findings to arrive at an internationalization "score" for each institution.

The second research question was this:

To what extent are environmental factors related to a community college's level of internationalization?

I posed this research question to explore a possible relationship between three environmental factors and levels of internationalization revealed in the first part of the study. The second research question thus also reflected a systems theory construct in that it focused on the relationship between a college's internal operations regarding internationalization and outside environmental factors. For this part of the study, three independent variables were used regarding environmental factors: (a) setting, or population density in the college's service area (expressed as urban/non-urban), (b) type of primary industry in the college's service area, and (c) level of ethnic student demographic diversity at the college, to address the research question. I selected these environmental factors based on research from the literature review. As indicated earlier, Harder's (2010) research suggested that there is a relationship between population density in a community college's service area and its level of internationalization. Type of primary industry in the college's service area and student demographic diversity were chosen as additional variables because previous research (Levin 2001; Turner 2008) suggested that global economics and the increased movement of people across borders have strongly impacted community colleges. Service areas of many community colleges are strongly impacted economically by large companies who primarily sell their products abroad. Additionally, community colleges across the country have seen increased enrollments in the numbers of immigrants as well as the number of international students (Bevis and Lucas 2007).

This second part of the study used a correlational explanatory design (Creswell 2012) to test if the three independent variables were related to the dependent variable (internationalization score). Thus, the data collected to answer the first research question was also analyzed to answer the second question: to examine the possibility of a relationship between the level of internationalization in Oregon and Washington community colleges and three environmental factors. Single and multiple regression analysis methods were applied to the data to address the research question.

Data for Independent Variables

Archival data gathered regarding the three environmental variables yielded the following information. Two Oregon community colleges and 16 Washington community colleges were classified as urban because they were "physically located within Primary Metropolitan Statistical Areas (PMSAs) or Metropolitan Statistical Areas (MSAs), respectively, with populations exceeding 500,000 people according to the 2000 Census" (Carnegie Foundation for the Advancement of Teaching, 2010). Ten primary industries (i.e., industries employing the largest number of people in the college's service area, as indicated by US Census data) emerged in the colleges' service areas. To allow for easier data analysis, these industries were classified into one of four categories: agriculture, services, manufacturing, and government. Student demographic data from the Federal Education Budget Project (New America Foundation 2011) indicated that the level of student ethnic diversity (percentage of enrolled non-Caucasian students) varied between 7 % and 43 % across the colleges.

Data Analysis

For the first research question, the combined scores from the answers to the questions from the survey and the archival research provided each college's total internationalization "score" (with 17 as the highest possible score). These scores were then analyzed using descriptive statistical methods.

The second phase of the study consisted of (a) a series of simple regression analyses comparing each independent variable (environmental factor) with the internationalization scores (the dependent variable) to determine if any relationship existed, and (b) several multiple regression analyses to explore the interaction of the three environmental variables of population density, primary industry, and student demographic diversity. The general goal of the regression analyses was to determine the relationship between each independent variable and the dependent variable (the internationalization score), or interaction amongst the three independent variables and the dependent variable.

The more specific goals were to determine (a) which independent variable was the strongest predictor of the score, and (b) which interaction of independent variables had the greatest influence on the dependent variable.

Results

Forty-nine responses to the survey were received. Overall, 79 % (or 27 of 34) of Washington colleges and 76 % (or 13 of 17) of Oregon colleges responded to the survey. Of the 13 responding Oregon colleges, 11 were classified as "rural." Sixteen Washington colleges were classified as "urban" and 11 were classified as "rural." Five of the Washington community colleges also offered baccalaureate degrees, a group not listed in the Carnegie Classification system. However, each of these colleges is located in a densely populated area, so was considered "urban" for this study.

Descriptive Statistical Analysis

The median internationalization score for all institutions was 5, with the median of 2 for Oregon colleges and 7.5 for Washington colleges. It is interesting to note these findings confirm those from the 2012 report on the 2011 ACE national survey. The Center for Internationalization and Global Engagement (2012) and McGill-Peterson and Helms (2013) concluded from analyses of the overall findings from the national survey that many institutions do not have a focused, comprehensive strategy concerning internationalization that is necessary for a deep and long-lasting impact. The results of the present study, indicating few institutions with internationalization as a high priority, suggest a similar conclusion.

Various tests of significance were conducted on the response frequencies for each of the survey and archival data questions to investigate whether there was an association between the state (Oregon or Washington) and the score distribution. Test results regarding the responses to the governance questions on the survey pointed to a strong association between state and responses only on Question 2—the existence of a college policy statement regarding internationalization; Washington colleges more frequently answered "yes" regarding this question. Regarding support services for international and study abroad students, the Washington colleges more frequently provided the services described in most categories of the survey. Results of frequency analyses of responses regarding various manifestations of internationalization in governance showed a consistently higher percentage of Washington versus Oregon community colleges reporting college policy statements that addressed internationalization. However, less than half of the Washington colleges indicated that internationalization was referred to in their mission or policy statements or had internationalization committees. Only 15 % or fewer of Oregon community colleges indicated that internationalization was mentioned in their mission or policy statements or had internationalization-focused committees.

Linear Regression Analysis

The results of the analysis regarding a possible relationship between internationalization scores and setting (urban vs. non-urban) indicated a positive correlation—that is, there was a greater tendency for colleges classified as "rural" to have lower scores. In contrast, the scores for colleges classified as "urban" were somewhat evenly distributed across the range of scores (2 to 17). The results of the analysis regarding a possible relationship between internationalization score and student demographic diversity indicated no consistent correlation.

Analysis results indicated that "services" was the primary industry in the largest number of colleges. There was not enough evidence of an association between the type of industry in the college's service area and the college's internationalization score to reject the null hypothesis.

Multiple Regression Analysis

Two models were constructed to investigate the interaction amongst the three independent variables and the dependent variable. In Model 1, all interactions were considered and the indicator variables for all four primary industry categories (agriculture, government, manufacturing, and services) were included so that the effects could be quantified. Only a few colleges had agriculture as the primary industry and were only in rural areas, thus an effect of agriculture as an industry was difficult to determine; this was also the case for government as the primary industry in urban areas. The results from this analysis indicated that the only significant predictor was the interaction of services and Washington colleges.

In Model 2, in order to focus on more specific interactions, the primary industry of services was the only indicator included and the interaction between services and Washington was considered. The results of this model again showed services and Washington as a significant predictor variable, but more significant was the association between score and setting for Washington colleges with services as the primary industry. The most significant predictor variable across all the data was that of the interaction between services and Washington; Washington colleges with services as the primary industry were more likely to have higher internationalization scores.

CONCLUSION

Using quantitative research and analysis methods, this study focused on aspects of internationalization in Oregon and Washington community colleges, with specific attention to organizational behaviors in governance and student support services.

The research of de Wit (2002) and Hudzik (2011) indicated that internationalization efforts are most effective and long lasting when they were integrated into the major functions of the institution and the institution had adopted an international perspective. Results from the present study suggest that as yet there are relatively few Oregon and Washington community colleges that have embraced a comprehensive approach to internationalization, as defined by de Wit (2002) and Hudzik (2011).

Reflecting a systems theory construct, the present study also explored a possible relationship between levels of internationalization in Oregon and Washington community colleges and three environmental factors: population density, student demographics (as to ethnicity), and primary industry in the college service area. The results of the study suggested that there was a relationship between the level of internationalization at an Oregon or Washington community (as defined by the study) and environmental factors, thus confirming the research of Harder (2010) in her national study of community colleges and internationalization.

Findings

The research indicated that more Washington colleges (a) showed manifestations of internationalization through governance in policy statements, and (b) delivered services to international and study abroad students than did Oregon colleges. However, the median total internationalization score for colleges in both states (as defined by this study) was very low. This finding supports recent national studies, which indicated that internationalization was not a priority at most colleges and universities (Harder 2010; Center for Internationalization and Global Engagement 2012). These studies suggest, then, that the comprehensive internationalization suggested by de Wit and Hudzik is not yet a reality for most Oregon and Washington community colleges.

Findings from the present study also suggested that there was a relationship between the level of internationalization at Oregon and Washington community colleges and their location (rural vs. urban); there was a greater tendency for colleges defined as "rural" to have lower internationalization scores. There was insufficient evidence to indicate an association between student demographic diversity (as to ethnicity) and the internationalization score, or the type of industry in the college's service area and the college's internationalization score. However, statistical analysis of the study results also indicated that, when interaction amongst the three independent variables (density, demographics, and industry) was considered, the most significant predictor of a higher internationalization score was the interaction between Washington and "services" as the primary industry. That is, Washington colleges with services as the primary industry were more likely to have higher internationalization scores.

Practical Implications of the Research

Study findings presented specific information for administrators regarding internationalization at their institutions. Research described in the literature review suggests that (a) the most effective and long-lasting internationalization efforts are comprehensive in nature, (b) international trade has an enormous impact on the economies of Oregon and Washington, and (c) there have been numerous and nationwide calls by employers for workers who are global citizens and globally competent. Key administrators might consider how much their service areas are impacted by international trade and use that as a rationale for a more comprehensive internationalization approach, strengthening or better supporting their institutions' internationalization efforts. The findings from this study also allow administrators and policymakers to compare the internationalization efforts of their institutions with others. When coupled with national survey findings, the findings from the present study should assist college presidents and chief academic officers in Oregon and Washington community colleges in identifying where governance and policy changes can occur in their institution to enhance the comprehensive nature of their internationalization efforts.

The study also explored the relationship between levels of internationalization at Oregon and Washington community colleges with three environmental factors: setting (related to the population density in a college's service area), primary industry, and level of student demographic diversity. The findings from this part of the study indicate that rural community colleges in Oregon and Washington are less likely to undertake comprehensive internationalization efforts.

There are several questions for future research: Why are rural community colleges less likely to internationalize? What would encourage them to internationalize? Why are urban community colleges where "services" is a primary industry more likely to have made significant internationalization efforts? Given the importance assigned nationally to educating for global citizenry and the global workplace and the limited quantitative research regarding internationalization in community colleges, there is a need for much more research to be done.

References

Bevis, Teresa, & Lucas, Christopher (2007). *International students in American colleges and universities: A history*. New York: Palgrave Macmillan.

Carnegie Foundation for the Advancement of Teaching. (2010). *The Carnegie classification of institutions of higher learning*. http://classifications.carnegiefoundation.org/

Center for Internationalization and Global Engagement. (2012). *Mapping internationalization on U.S. campuses. 2012 edition*. Washington, DC: American Council on Education. *Bibliography of higher education*. http://www.higher-ed.org/HEUS/Bibliog/A.htm

Cohen, Arthur M., & Brawer, Florence G. (2003). *The American community college* (4th ed.). San Francisco: Jossey-Bass.

Creswell, John (2012). *Educational research: Planning, conducting, and evaluating quantitative and qualitative research* (4th ed.). Boston, MA: Pearson Publishing.

de Wit, Hans (2002). *Internationalization of higher education in the United States of America and Europe: A historical, comparative, and conceptual analysis.* Westport, CT: Greenwood Press.

Green, Madeline, & Siaya, Laura (2005). *Measuring internationalization at U.S. community colleges.* Washington, DC: American Council on Education.

Harder, Natalie (2010). Internationalization efforts in United States community colleges: A comparative analysis of urban, suburban, and rural institutions. *Community College Journal of Research and Practice, 35*(1–2), 152–164.

Hart Research Associates (2010). *Raising the bar: Employers' views on college learning in the wake of the economic downturn.* Washington, DC: Author.

Hudzik, John (2011). *Comprehensive internationalization: From concept to action.* Washington, DC: NAFSA: National Association of Foreign Student Advisors.

Institute for International Education. (2011). *Open doors 2011: Report on International Educational Exchange.* Washington, DC: U.S. Department of Education Bureau of Educational and Cultural Affairs.

Kedia, Ben L., & Daniel, Shirley (2003, January). *U.S. business needs for employees with international expertise.* Paper presented at the Needs for Global Challenges Conference, Duke University, Chapel Hill, NC. http://www.ducis.jhfc.duke.edu/archives/globalchallenges/pdf/kedia_daniel.pd

Levin, John (2001). *Globalizing the community college: Strategies for changes in the twenty-first century.* New York: Palgrave.

McGill-Peterson, Patti, & Helms, Robin (2013). Internationalization revisited. *Change, 45*(2), 28–32.

New America Foundation. (2011). *Federal education budget project.* www.febp.newamerica.net/ý

Panel on Global Engagement (2011). *Strength through global leadership and engagement: US higher education in the 21st century.* Washington, DC: American Council on Education.

Portland Business Alliance. (2010). *International trade summary.* http://www.portlandalliance.com/public_policy/reports_studies.html

Raby, Rosalind L. (1996). International, intercultural, and multicultural dimensions of community colleges in the United States. In Rosalind Raby & Norma Tarrow (Eds.), *Dimensions of the community college* (pp. 9–36). New York: Garland Studies in Higher Education.

Siaya, Laura, & Hayward, Fred (2003). *Mapping internationalization on U.S. Campuses.* Washington, DC: American Council on Education.

Turner, Yvonne (2008). *Internationalizing the university.* New York: Continuum International.
U.S. Census Bureau. (2013). *Quick facts.* http://www.immigrationpolicy.org/just-facts/new-americans-oregon
Washington Department of Commerce. (2011). The quick rundown. *Commerce Quarterly Trade Bulletin 2011,* 2(4). www.chosewashington.com/Pages/CommerceQuarterlyTradeBulletin.aspx

The Texas/Czech Republic International Connection: A Reciprocal Exchange of Faculty and Students

Juanita Gamez Vargas

INTRODUCTION

Community colleges provide international educational opportunities for a diverse group of students and, indirectly, for their faculty, staff, and administrators. Some of these educational opportunities consist of credit/ non-credit courses in foreign languages and study abroad. At Texas Community College (TCC), many of the students, faculty, staff, and administrators reflect the larger local community of Mexican-Americans, Czech-Americans, and African Americans. After the fall of the Berlin Wall, locals traveled to the new Czech Republic in hopes of reuniting with their families and to economically promote traditional Czech products. In 1995, two TCC instructors visited Masaryk University (Brno) to initiate talks of a reciprocal faculty and student exchange program. This informal discussion began TCC's international connection and the first of its kind in Texas.

This chapter is a case study of a reciprocal community college faculty and student exchange program with a Czech Republic university that has been in place for over 20 years. Bolman and Deal's (2013) four frames for

J.G. Vargas (✉)
Jeanine Rainbolt College of Education, Department of Educational Leadership and Policy Studies, University of Oklahoma, Norman, OK, USA

© The Editor(s) (if applicable) and The Author(s) 2016   203
R.L. Raby, E.J. Valeau (eds.), *International Education at Community Colleges*, DOI 10.1057/978-1-137-53336-4_14

decision-making were used for a comparison/contrast analysis. The findings will provide detailed descriptions of how the program's success fell under the four organizational frames. A discussion for future consideration for existing and new international exchange program initiatives is provided.

TEXAS COMMUNITY COLLEGE (TCC)

The TCC international exchange program started in 1995 when two faculty members were vacationing in Brno, Czech Republic. As Czech-Americans, they had discussed the limited potential for study abroad in Czechoslovakia. With the creation of the new Czech Republic, they decided the time had come to pursue an exchange program. Strolling by Masaryk University, they impulsively walked in, searched for and met with the business and economics faculty and discussed the possibilities of a faculty and student exchange program. Upon their return to TCC, they met with the community college president who was immediately receptive to the idea of providing an opportunity for the faculty and students to learn of the Czech Republic higher education system and social culture. This faculty and student exchange program was the first of its kind between Texas, Masaryk University, and the Czech Republic. Within three years, the exchange program had expanded to include the English departments at TCC and Masaryk University (MU).

In 1998, the Vice President of Academic Affairs asked a mid-level administrator to make an assessment of the program and to provide a summary of the activities and expenses and program improvement recommendations. The administrator met with the four TCC faculty involved with the program the visiting Czech business instructor, and business student and gathered relevant documents. The report provided a detailed list of accomplishments and problems associated with the coordination and communication between the two institutions. Although there was a reciprocal TCC and MU faculty and MU student exchange in business and economics, there lacked reciprocal exchanges with TCC students. Several Masaryk business students had attended TCC with their tuition fees waived and housing and employment provided; however, only one TCC business student had been able to attend MU resulting with many unforeseen problems. In addition, there was no written documentation supporting the selection method for who could participate. Moreover, there was no financial accounting for expenses and in-kind provisions by both institutions.

As a result, the primary recommendations made by the mid-level administrator were to develop a mission statement, an understanding of the federal laws associated with institutional faculty and student exchange programs, secure memorandums of understandings (MOU) between the two institutions and their respective departments, and operate under a structured budget.

Documents revealed the president had suspected a lack of program coordination and personal bias by the faculty in administering the exchange of faculty and students from the departments at TCC and MU. After reviewing the report on the program, the president assigned the mid-level administrator, who had developed the report, to begin coordinating the international exchange program and report directly to him. This administrator possessed strong administrative and organizational skills, oversaw multiple departments, served on the President's Council and was chair of the Multicultural Committee. The administrator coordinated the exchange program from 1999 till 2003. In 2003, the program returned to the President's Office until the president's retirement in 2009. After 2009, the program fluctuated between the President's Office and the Vice President of Student Services Office (VPSS).

I am using the four decision-making organizational frames of Bolman and Deal (2013) as the methodology to review the history of the exchange program, recognize the leadership of the president, and define the faculty-driven persistence for its success. The documents gathered focused on the exchange program from 1995 to 2005.

BOLMAN AND DEAL'S FOUR DECISION-MAKING FRAMES

Bolman and Deal (2013) identify four frameworks in institutional decision-making. They conclude that the frames work independently or can be used interchangeably in the decision-making process. The first frame, structural, places the appropriate personnel in administering the college's policies and procedures and in developing the goals and objectives of the program and/or project. The administrator ensures the program reflects the institution's mission, carried out without personal biases and capable of negotiating with or without external pressures.

The second frame, human resources, refers to personnel such as staff, administrators, and/or faculty and finding the appropriate person who can move the program forward with enthusiasm and a commitment to the college mission.

The third frame, political, refers to the political dynamics that exist regardless of the type of institution. These political dynamics range from internal and external forces, personal agendas, funding issues, and negotiating these dynamics while focusing on the college's goals and objectives.

The final frame, symbolic, describes organizational or cultural symbols. These symbols form over time and can separate or unite people and organizations. Symbols take the form of myths, values, rituals, stories, ceremonies, values, customs, images, and/or metaphors. At TCC, the college's symbols do not reflect the Czech culture although many of the students, staff, administrators, and board of trustees are Czech-Americans.

These four frames, separately or together, assist in making decisions in writing policy, establishing procedures, developing strategies and other administrative actions. The analysis of the international exchange program compares these four frames with the data (documents). The following section presents the methodology and findings.

METHODOLOGY

The analysis of the TCC/MU exchange program was a result of comparing the documents gathered with the four organizational decisions-making frames of Bolman and Deal (2013). The exchange program had a number of documents (executive summaries, hand-written private notes, annual reports, written interviews with TCC and MU faculty and students, financial reports, budgets, etc.) that were categorized against the four frames (structural, human resources, political, and symbolic). The analysis revealed what aspects of the program and frames made the program continue to remain successful. The analysis also created a second category of *lessons learned* that were compiled for the discussion section.

FINDINGS

TCC's reciprocal faculty and student international exchange program analysis fell under all four frames of Bolman and Deal's organizational decision-making with multiple intersecting frames. The analysis fell under two categories: the actions of the faculty and the college president. Although the analysis found the faculty's impact significant on establishing the international program, it was the administrative commitment and leadership by the college president that determined the success of the exchange program. The following section describes the first category of the TCC faculty's impact for the development of the international exchange program. The second impact of the president's leadership follows the faculty section.

TCC Faculty

The analysis revealed the four frames were not always evident as a deliberate organizational administrative decision-making endeavor. In fact, under the structural frame, the TCC faculty's initiation for the exchange lacked any formal structure. For example, in 1995, the TCC faculty decided impulsively to negotiate a faculty and student exchange program with Masaryk University business and economics faculty without the TCC administrations knowledge and/or approval. The lack of the structural frame reappeared in 1997 when the TCC humanities professor initiated an exchange with MU's English department head. Verbal agreements were made without any written follow-up documentation. From 1995 to 1999, little program formal documentation was found.

Under the human resources frame, the TCC faculty began the exchange program, assuming the president's secretary would handle visas and other related documents and expenses. From 1995 to 1999, four TCC faculty taught compressed classes at MU and assisted with coordinating the visiting Masaryk faculty and students. However, they became overwhelmed and the president decided to place a mid-level administrator in charge of the international exchange program. Formal record keeping was kept on the outcomes of the exchange program from 1999 to 2003 and became sporadic after 2003 when there were multiple changes in administrators overseeing the program.

The symbolic frame intersected with the human resource and political frame since the program was initiated by Czech-American faculty and supported by the majority Czech-American Board of Trustees. TCC's logo, campus symbols, and traditions did not reflect a cultural connection to the Czech-American population. Therefore, the college campus and local community reaction to the Czech Republic exchange program was positive. The TCC faculty and students met the MU faculty and students through classes and session presentations. The local community met the faculty when they toured the neighboring Czech businesses and agricultural venues.

The primary political frame findings revealed that since the two TCC instructor's efforts had been carried out without TCC knowledge or approval, they feared the president would not be interested in the Czech Republic exchange program and that they would suffer political backlash. Therefore, when the president's reaction was positive, they expressed relief. The secondary political issues were the efforts from the faculty to create interest in the exchange program beyond business and economics faculty and students. Over time, the faculty struggled to balance their five-plus course teaching loads, committee responsibilities, and worried the administration would not support the program if they could not sustain the program. Therefore, they hesitated to discuss any program issues with the president.

TCC President

The analysis revealed that the continued success of the program was focused on the president and college's mission to introduce ethnic and cultural diversity to a rural and suburban community. The analysis showed all four decision-making frames were evident in the actions taken by the president and administration.

Structural Frame. As described earlier, the TCC president was unaware of the actions conducted by the two faculty. When the president met with the tenured faculty in March 1995, he learned they had negotiated an exchange program with Masaryk University and that in a few months a business faculty with 10 students would be arriving at TCC. Agreeing to the exchange fell under the structural and political frame because the president had been encouraging faculty to engage in international and diversity outreach activities but had received few responses to mini-grant travel and credit-course proposals. This faculty initiative met his administrative agenda. Therefore, he sought approval and funding from the Board of Trustees for the program. The structural frame intersected with the political and symbolic frame because the exchange was with the Czech Republic and the president was aware of the significant Czech-American population on his Board, and among students, faculty, staff, and local community.

The structural frame continued into the fall semester of 1995 when the TCC president traveled with the two instructors to Masaryk University to meet with the Rector and faculty involved with the exchange program. He negotiated reciprocal costs and in-kind donations. Although the TCC faculty assured the president that they would be responsible for handling the exchange program, from 1995 to 1999 few documents were available demonstrating any formal agreements, goals and objectives, or measured outcomes for the program thereby suggesting a weak structural frame.

In 2000, the president asked an administrator for an assessment of the program and based on the results designated that administrator to assume coordinating the program. The assessment identified several structural administrative and organizational issues ranging from a lack of (a) a mission statement, (b) goals and objectives, (c) a systematic program evaluation, (d) financial accountability, (e) checks and balances in following federal and state laws, (f) protocol in selecting TCC and MU participants, and, (g) coordination of the MU faculty and student visits. Decision-making by the TCC faculty on these issues were uncoordinated and not documented. These structural issues intersected with the human resources frame because the faculty did not have time or the administrative knowledge to conduct or maintain these issues.

In 2001, after being extensively briefed by the four primary TCC instructors, the mid-level administrator, accompanied by the Vice President of Academic Affairs, traveled to Masaryk University to meet with the business, economics, and English faculty to negotiate future exchanges. The visit resulted in MOU delineating in-kind services and expenses. New student exchanges were negotiated creating a balance in exchanges between the two institutions. Therefore, adding administrative structure to the program provided balance in student and faculty exchange opportunities and an increase in program visibility.

Human Resources Frame. The analysis of the human resources frame revealed that by 1997, faculty's five-plus course load teaching and committee responsibilities impeded their ability to administer the program. They passed those responsibilities to the president's secretary. As a consequence, the president's secretary was overwhelmed with coordinating the exchange program's financial needs, Immigration and Naturalization Service (INS) regulations, travel documents, visas, housing, student employment and other details. As mentioned earlier, the president requested an assessment report that recommended that personnel familiar with higher education bureaucratic structure become responsible for handling the day-to-day operations of the program. The founding faculty would still serve on the advisory committee and the new administrator would diligently promote the program beyond the business, economic, and English departments.

The second finding under the human resource frame was learning of the increasing number of TCC employees and faculty volunteers who provided transportation, entertainment and served in various capacities for the visiting Czech faculty and students. For example, one faculty's family was visiting during the Easter Holy Week and needed transportation to the Catholic Church services. Seven Catholic staff and administrators volunteered to take them. The support from the TCC campus and local community met the human resources frame and the president's outreach agenda as well as his political agenda.

Political Frame. Initially, the president's approval of the international exchange program was a strategic political success because he wanted to promote diversity and international travel for TCC faculty and students. With the faculty initiating the reciprocal exchange, the president had support from the ground up rather than from the top down. In addition, the exchange was well received on campus and in the community because of the large Czech-American population among the faculty, students, staff, administrators and especially the college's Board of Trustees.

The analysis revealed other politically sensitive issues that did not meet the goals and objectives of the international exchange program. A few of these issues encompassed misappropriation of college funds, conflicts of interest, and a lack of diversity in the selection of TCC faculty and students participants. By assigning a trustworthy mid-level administrator in charge of the program, the president removed any political landmines.

Symbolic Frame. The analysis showed the symbolic importance of establishing a reciprocal international exchange with the Czech Republic. Many TCC students, faculty, staff, administrators and elected Board of Trustees were Czech-American. Czech symbols were evident with Czech worded bumper stickers in the college parking lots, annual Czech heritage festivals, bakeries, restaurants, and retail businesses. Finally, in the president's assessment report, it was shown that all visiting Czech economic and business faculty were introduced to Texan Czech-American agricultural and retail businesses. The final example was when several Czech-American families volunteered to house 10 MU business students for one summer.

These findings demonstrated that the international exchange program was initially successful for the TCC faculty and president. However, after the recession of 2008 and subsequent state and local budget cuts, the number and frequency of exchanges of TCC were impacted. In 2015, the program continued to host one MU faculty and one student every two to three years, dependent on funding. The discussion section addresses the major concerns in initiating faculty and student exchange programs.

DISCUSSION

The TCC/MU faculty and student international exchange was successful under all Bolman and Deal's four decision-making frames. Among the intersection of the structural, human resources, political and symbolic frames, the TCC president's leadership in supporting the exchange program was key for success. These four frames were evident even after the president transferred the program to a mid-level administrator who reflected the president's strong organizational skills (structure), shared a positive relationship with the faculty (human resources), and understood the political and symbolic dynamics of the exchange program. The overall finding confirmed that the leadership of the president made the program successful.

However, for community college presidents who are considering reciprocal international exchange programs, exploring such endeavors using Bohman and Deal's four frames of decision-making is advisable. The structural frame requires delegating the development and coordination of these exchanges to personnel who support the college mission, capable of developing goals and objectives, conducting evaluations of the program, financing issues, following state and federal regulations, and being transparent in all negotiations and decision-making. Finding a suitable administrator may be difficult especially in small- to medium-size community colleges (similar to TCC) where personnel balance multiple responsibilities. Following are discussion questions that may help in decision-making when considering a reciprocal international exchange program. The questions will stimulate discussion and are not exclusive.

Structural Frame

1. How does an international exchange for your students and faculty reflect the college's mission?
2. Will the president and Board of Trustees support the exchange program?
3. What are the direct and indirect financial costs to the institution in initiating and maintaining an exchange program?
4. Are there policies in place that support an exchange program?
5. What organizational structures need to be in place to support the exchange program—for example, housing accommodation, tuition waivers, administrative support and oversight?

6. Who will write the long-term business plan including a systematic evaluation of the program?

Human Resources

1. Are there faculty and students interested in an exchange program?
2. How will the college contribute financially to support the faculty and students in this exchange endeavor?
3. What are the qualifications of the person who will be in charge of the program?
4. Who will be in charge of the program at the participating foreign college?
5. Who will be responsible in negotiating the exchange agreements?
6. Who would be responsible for promoting and marketing the program's success?
7. Does the college have the resources (campus housing) to accommodate the international visitors, short-term and long-term?

Political Frame

1. What country would you be interested in pursuing an exchange program and why?
2. This program is not revenue generating. Therefore, why is a reciprocal international faculty and/or student exchange program important for the college in these financially difficult times?
3. Who will benefit from the exchange program?—for example, faculty, teaching discipline, student government/associations, honor students, administrators, board members.

Symbolic Frame

1. What country would you be interested in pursuing for the exchange program and why?
2. Is there a symbolic value or custom associated with the college and the desire to establish an international exchange program?
3. Are there symbolic values or customs associated with the college and the country selected in establishing an international exchange program?

4. Will the campus and local community recognize the symbolic value or significance of the international exchange program? How will this be communicated to them?

CONCLUSION

Community colleges provide international educational opportunities for students and faculty beyond the traditional foreign language credit/non-credit courses. At Texas Community College (TCC), many of the students, faculty, staff, and administrators benefitted from the unique reciprocal exchange agreement with Masaryk University in the Czech Republic. However, the program would have not been successful without the leadership of the president and ground-roots interest of the faculty. For other community colleges pursuing such endeavors, presidential leadership and faculty support is essential.

Acknowledgments I would like to acknowledge Maricela Oliva, University of Texas at San Antonio, for her insight and guidance.

REFERENCES

Bolman, Lee G., & Deal, Terrence E. (2013). *Reframing organizations: Artistry, choice and leadership* (5th ed.). San Francisco: Jossey-Bass.

Addressing Myths About International Students

Deborah Budd, Andreea Serban, Dianne G. Van Hook, and Rosalind Latiner Raby

INTRODUCTION

Despite no community college association ever officially opposing international students programs, for decades, anti-internationalists remain vocal in claiming that international students do not support the local mission of the community college, that international students take seats away from resident students, and that there are limited benefits to hosting interna-

D. Budd (✉)
San Jose/Evergreen Community College District, San Jose, CA, USA

A. Serban
Educational Services and Technology, Coast Community College District, Costa Mesa, CA, USA

D.G. Van Hook
Santa Clarita Community College District, Santa Clarita, CA, USA

R.L. Raby
Educational Leadership and Policy Studies, Michael D. Eisner College of Education, California State University, Northridge, CA, USA

California Colleges for International Education, Los Angeles, CA, USA

© The Editor(s) (if applicable) and The Author(s) 2016
R.L. Raby, E.J. Valeau (eds.), *International Education at Community Colleges*, DOI 10.1057/978-1-137-53336-4_15

tional students. Even with empirical evidence that proves otherwise (Fitzer 2007), community college administrators and some boards continue to use these myths to underfund, to undersupport, and to curtail the growth of international student programs. The result is that in 2014, only 309 of the 1200 US community colleges had documented international student programs (IIE 2014). This case study explores how practices at three California community college districts are building evidence to counter the aforementioned prevailing myths.

BACKGROUND

In 2013–2014, 26,375 international students studied at 92 of the 112 California community colleges. Some programs supported fewer than 10 students while others served over 3000 students. When comparing international students to the total community college student population, 56 % of colleges had less than 1 % international students; 20 % of colleges had 1–1.9 % international students; and 8 % of colleges had more than 7 % international students. Institutional support for these programs is not consistent and can result in a gain or loss of up to 400 students for a single campus in one academic year (CCIE, 2015). Administrators, as mentioned earlier, consistently refer to three international students myths as the primary reason for limiting support and for placing a self-imposed cap on international student admission.

METHODOLOGY

To unpack the international student myths, the authors developed ten open-ended questions to understand if the anti-internationalists concerns could be validated. The President of Berkeley City College, the Vice-Chancellor of the Coast District, and the Chancellor of the Santa Clarita District answered these questions based on their professional opinions. In addition, content analysis of district mission statements, descriptive statistics of international student programs, classroom seat analysis, and informal observations of classrooms and on-campus activities were used to substantiate claims.

The three districts are typical of California multi-college districts in which some of the colleges in the same district have large international student programs, while other colleges have smaller programs. These districts are also typical in that they have a multi-decade history of accepting international students and yet, over time, have had periods of inconsistent support for their programs. These districts are not typical in that the executive officers fully support internationalization and include in their vision the growth of international student programming.

The Coast Community College District includes Coastline College (CCC), Golden West College (GWC), Orange County College (OCC), serving Orange County with 45,000 students every semester. In fall 2014, the district hosted 1352 international students from 95 countries, of which over 1000 attended OCC. There is District office coordination for all three colleges and OCC and GWC have dedicated international student offices. International students represent 4.8 % of the total student head count at OCC and 0.43 % at GWC.

The Peralta Community College District includes Berkeley City College (BCC), College of Alameda (COA), Laney College (LC), and Merritt College (MC), serving the San Francisco Bay with 30,000 students each semester. In fall 2014, the district hosted 851 international students. In the 1990s, a centralized District office eliminated campus offices that were then reopened at BCC and LC in spring 2014. International students represent 5 % of the total student head count at BCC and 0.69 % at MC.

The Santa Clarita District includes College of the Canyons (COC) and Valencia Campus (VC), and is located north of Los Angeles, serving 31,000 students each semester. In fall 2014, COC opened a comprehensive International Services and Program Center which hosted 165 international students who represented 0.67 % of the total student head count.

Table S4.1 illustrates enrollment patterns at these districts over 17 years.

COUNTERING COMMUNITY COLLEGE INTERNATIONAL STUDENT MYTHS

This section uses the executive officer opinions and campus observations along with corresponding district data to answer questions that highlight three themes: (a) how does international student enrollment fit into the California community college mission?; (b) is there evidence that international students divert funds away from resident student needs?; and (c) is there evidence of economic, cultural, and academic benefits for resident students as a result of international students studying on campus?

Irrelevance of International Students to College Mission. The most widely held myth is that international education counters the community college mission of serving the local community. There is no documentation

Table S4.1 International student programs over time

District	1998–1999	2005–2006 #'s	2010–2011 #'s	2014–2015 #'s
Coast District	Coastline: NA Golden West: 133 Orange Coast: 829	Coastline: 479 Golden West: 140 Orange Coast: 639	Coastline: 94 Golden West: 78 Orange Coast: 970	Coastline: 55 Golden West: 92 Orange Coast: 1190
Peralta District	Peralta Community College District: 379	Peralta Community College District: 505	Peralta Community College District: 937	District: 851 Berkeley City: 452 Alameda-96 Laney-261 Merritt-42
Santa Clarita District	College of Canyons: 25	College of Canyons: 100	College of the Canyons: 163 Valencia: 0	College of the Canyons: 155 Valencia: 7

Data obtained from CCIE State of Field Reports: 1999; 2006; 2011; 2015

that actually states this as being true. Instead, policy set by the American Association of Community and Junior Colleges (Gleazer 1976), the Joint Statement policy set by the American Association of Community Colleges and Association of Community College Trustees (2006), and State legislation, such as the California International Education Policy Resolution (2002) all firmly endorse international education as being in alignment with the mission of community colleges.

The three case study districts have policies that not only define international students as compatible with the community college mission, but clearly explain how international students support the mission to promote student success and to bring the campus closer to achieving its goals of increased diversity. The Coast District mission is, "To serve the diverse educational needs of its local and global communities" (Board Policy 1200 District Mission 2014). Peralta District mission is "to empower students to achieve their goals, develop leaders, and provide accessible and high quality educational programs to meet the needs of their multi-cultural communities" (Peralta Strategic Plan 2015). Santa Clarita fulfills its mission, by "embracing diversity, fostering technical competencies, supporting the development of global responsibility, and engaging students and the community in scholarly inquiry, creative partnerships, and the application of knowledge" (Mission Statement 2015). COC revised its mission to reference global responsibility and to simply reaffirm the District's pre-existing reasons for being so committed to boosting the number of international students. It is the link to student success and diversity that makes internationalization a comprehensive component of the mission of each of the districts and which firmly counters this myth.

International Students Prosper at Domestic Student Expense. This myth claims that international students take resources and seats away from needy resident students. There is no proof that this actually happens and yet public misconception drives this myth (Ng 2007; Fitzer 2007). An economic analysis and a seat analysis are used to counter this myth. An economic analysis shows that profit, no matter how small, can benefit the general fund that is then used to benefit all students. At the three districts, this profit ranges from $1,012,200 to $23,712,800 (NAFSA/IIE 2014). More specifically, the tuition/fees from 15 international students (about $75,000) can pay for selected budget line-items and special projects that help infrastructure needs, increase student support staff, subsidize resident students through jobs and scholarships, and pay for more class sections in which both resident and international students enroll (about 300 international students can pay for 25 additional sections of high-demand and honor courses). In addition, 135 international students (about $655,910) can fully fund an office and staff for student support services (CCIE 2015). The Peralta District (851 students) uses extra funds to help with additional student support and special programs. OCC (1190 students) uses extra funds to enable staff to travel abroad to foster relationships with international higher education organizations. GWC (92 students) uses extra funds for specific outreach programs and the COC Proyecta Project (95 students) uses extra funds to create on-campus jobs for domestic students.

A seat analysis as defined by Fitzer (2007) was applied to each district and confirmed Fitzer's findings that international students do not displace domestic students because international students tend to "fill up existing classes" (Fitzer 2007, p. 152). Similar to Fitzer, we found that even at the colleges with large international student enrollments of over 500 students, most classes still had few international students enrolled. Moreover, at those districts where physical capacity is highly impacted, using the seat-analysis method, we found that international students still do not take seats away from domestic students (Raby et al. 2015).

Resident students do not benefit from interactions with international students. This myth claims a resident student has little to gain from international students. A cultural analysis and an academic analysis are used to counter this myth. Each executive officer shared personal stories of resident and international students who have built friendships that filtered into future social and economic relationships and that continue to serve as a basis for people-to-people diplomacy. Informal campus observations by the executive officers found that intercultural learning is enhanced when faculty or designed campus activities build discussions that take advantage of intercultural knowledge so that, as one student stated, "Students can learn from and with those who have different cultural backgrounds which increases the caring environment of the college." At the Coast district, the *American Council in Education Internationalization Lab* is targeting new curriculum and pedagogical practices in and out of class to enhance intercultural learning. At the Peralta district, the *World Student Organization* connects staff, faculty, and international students to each other and the *Global Leadership Program* fosters global awareness by supporting community outreach activities (such as Tsunami victim support and Walk Around the World Events). At the Santa Clarita district, the *Passport Program* sponsors activities that build multi-cultural and international skills for all students, faculty, and staff. These designed activities foster intercultural communication that enhances learning for all students.

An academic analysis shows how the strong academic standing of international students contributes to overall district academic prestige. The average completion rate for California residents is 46.8 % (California Community College Student Success Score Card 2015). At all three districts, these numbers are enhanced because international students complete their studies in two years due to their taking 14–17 units (instead of minimum of 12 unit load). At COC, 99 % of international students transfer within two years. At the Coast District, course success rates for international students are 10–15 % higher than the rates for the general student population and there is a higher rate of students in "Good Academic Standing" (81 % compared to 73 % for the general student population). At Peralta District, more than half of international students have over a 3.5 Grade Point Average (GPA), and there is a large number who are in student government and who win prestigious awards. International students contribute to BCC and LC being ranked # 1 and # 3 of in the transfer acceptance rate to the University of California, Berkeley.

The increased academic prestige enhances each district's reputation as an institution of excellence in academic and career skills preparations that then benefits all students.

CONCLUSION

The case study of the Coast District, Peralta District, and Santa Clarita District shows evidence that counters anti-international student myths. Each district defines international students as a contributor to achieving the mission of student success and diversity. Each executive officer maintains a vision to build sufficient support linkages including professional staff networks, coordinated campus activities, and partnerships with the local community for jobs, internships, and defined social activities. Noted benefits from international student programs include economic, intercultural, and academic benefits for students, for faculty, and for the college's academic reputation. In fact, these benefits were evident for district colleges with large as well as with small international student enrollments. Moreover, the size of the international student program at these districts is not a deterrent to building new avenues to increase directed campus programs aimed at enhancing international and resident student interactions. Finally, and of critical importance, is that each district has public support for internationalization by their executive officer.

For this study, specific questions guided each executive officer to articulate their own vision, explore college documents, and conduct a seat analysis and also economic, cultural, and academic-based analysis to see if international student myths had validity at their districts. At each of these three districts, findings reveal that the connective tissue between international education and other college programs helps to align international student programs with the mission of the colleges and their districts, build opportunities for student success, and ultimately prove that there is no validity to the myths of international students.

REFERENCES

American Association of Community Colleges and Association of Community College Trustees. (2006). *Building the global community: A joint statement on the role of community colleges in international education.* Washington, DC: American Association of Community Colleges. www.aacc.nche.edu/Content/NavigationMenu/ResourceCenter/Services/International/AACCACCT_Joint_Statement.pdf

California Community Colleges Student Success Score Card. (2015). *Statewide Transfer.* http://scorecard.cccco.edu/scorecardrates.aspx?CollegeID=000#home

California Colleges for International Education (CCIE). (2015). *State of the field reports: 1999; 2006; 2011; 2015.* www.ccieworld.org/annualreports

California Education Code Section 66011-66027.5. (2002). California International Education Policy Resolution (12kb), *Educational Code Section* 66015.7.www.leginfo.ca.gov/cgi-bin/displaycode?section=edc&group=66001-67000&file=66011-66027.5

Coast Community College District Mission. (Board Policy 1200. District Mission, 2014). http://www.cccd.edu/aboutus/Pages/Mission-and-Vision-Statements.aspx

Fitzer, John K. (2007). *Foreign students at California community colleges: Benefits, costs, and institutional responsibility.* Ph.D. dissertation, ProQuest Dissertations & Theses: Full Text. (Publication No. AAT 3261961).

Gleazer Jr., Edmund J. (1976). Editorial. *Community and Junior College Journal,* 46(7), 5–7.

Institute of International Education. 2014. *Open doors 2014: Community College Data Resource International Students.* http://www.iie.org/Research-and-Publications/Open-Doors/Data/Special-Reports/Community-College-Data-2013-14

NAFSA/IIE. (2014). *The international student value economic tool.* National Association of Educators (NAFSA), Institute for International Education (IIE) and Indiana University, Office of International Services. http://www.nafsa.org/Explore_International_Education/Impact/Data_And_Statistics/The_International_Student_Economic_Value_Tool/

Ng, Jacob (2007). Campus politics and the challenges of international education in an urban community college district. In Edward Valeau & Rosalind Latiner Raby (Eds.), *International reform efforts and challenges in community colleges.* (pp. 83–89). New Directions In Community College Series, No. 138 (Summer, 2007). San Francisco: Jossey-Bass.

Peralta Community College District. (Peralta Strategic Plan, 2015). http://web.peralta.edu/strategicplan/

Raby, Rosalind Latiner, Budd, Deborah, Serban, Andreea, & Van Hook, Dianne (2015). International student mobility at California Community Colleges. In Krishna Bista & Charlotte Foster (Eds.), *International student mobility, services, and policy in higher education.* New York: IGI Publisher.

Santa Clarita Community College District. (Mission Statement, 2015). http://www.canyons.edu/Offices/PIO/Pages/keyinfo/Mission.aspx

Global Certificates: Bringing Intentionality and Ownership to Comprehensive Internationalization

Paloma Rodriguez

INTRODUCTION

For a number of years, Santa Fe College has worked on internationalizing its curriculum as a way to reach all students. In fall 2013, the institution went a step further by launching an International Studies Certificate, a distinction program that combines an internationalized curriculum with experiential learning, career development, and student-centered projects. Although it is too early to evaluate the full impact of this initiative, two years have sufficed to reveal the program's extraordinary potential to bring cohesion, shared ownership, and intentionality to our comprehensive internationalization efforts. This case study examines the history, current practices, and impact of this program at Santa Fe College.

The launch of the International Studies Certificate was preceded by over a decade of intense faculty-driven activity and curricular internationalization, a process greatly supported by three US Department of Education Undergraduate International Studies and Foreign Language grants and the presence on our campus of four Fulbright Scholars. The impetus to provide

P. Rodriguez (✉)
International Education, Santa Fe College, Gainesville, FL, USA

© The Editor(s) (if applicable) and The Author(s) 2016
R.L. Raby, E.J. Valeau (eds.), *International Education at Community Colleges*, DOI 10.1057/978-1-137-53336-4_16

223

students with global literacy came from a variety of academic, sociocultural and cross-cultural, political, and economic pressures that demanded the redefinition of our educational goals (Hudzik 2011). The need to create globally minded citizens who can coexist and interact effectively in an increasingly interconnected world and who can successfully join a globalized job market are some of the tenets that guided our efforts. Another was our commitment to access. As Raby and Valeau (2007, p. 10) point out, "community colleges educate a larger proportion of minority and low-income students than any other postsecondary institution." The recognition that for so many of our students global literacy will happen now or never turned comprehensive internationalization into an imperative for us. Yet, the events of 9/11 were perhaps the most powerful catalyst of our current initiatives. They served as a stark reminder that isolationism is no longer an option and that the global and the local are inextricably connected. It was this realization that compelled Santa Fe College President Jackson Sasser to initiate the internationalization process in 2002 (Sasser 2014):

> After 9/11, we launched our international initiative for reasons that hold true today: conflict is less likely when individuals from different cultures take the opportunity to learn from one another.... For our students to succeed in today's globalized society and economy, community colleges need to weave international perspectives into every program. That way, all of our students—whether they are from our local community, out of state or across an ocean—can have an international experience (para 2–3).

The curriculum internationalization process that resulted from this call for action closely followed well-established best practices (Raby 2007) and succeeded in several areas. Santa Fe now offers over 50 international courses in a variety of disciplines, including some not traditionally associated with global content (i.e., Math and Biology). It has also diversified and grown the number of foreign language offerings, created courses with a non-Western focus, and infused global perspectives across the curriculum not just through course content, but also by making involvement in international development projects and teleconferencing with foreign students a regular part of the coursework. Yet the curriculum alone does not capture the breadth of student learning, nor is it always the most effective tool to achieve the attitudinal change we demand from our global learners. In fact, involvement in co-curricular activities seems to lead to higher gains in all global perspective measurements (Braskamp and Engberg

2011). At our institution, the vision for an integrative approach toward internationalization had already been formulated by our current Provost, Edward Bonahue, when in 2008 he wrote:

> Those institutions that have most successfully promoted global competency ... have sought to internationalize their student and academic programs in tandem. In this way, international education initiatives within an institution may be united into an integrated, coherent initiative that consistently reminds students of their past, present, and future connection with a global community. (p. 209)

In an effort to bring permanent systemic change and create a meaningful and intentional pathway toward global learning that included not just curricular components, but also co-curricular experiences, the International Education Committee at Santa Fe College worked for over a year to design an International Studies Certificate.

Since the mid-1990s several institutions have embarked on this path (Stearns 2009) and a variety of models were available to us. While some programs sought to recognize the overseas experiences of their students, others had a more flexible approach and allowed for validation of domestic and on-campus activities. Among the options available, the International Education Committee at Santa Fe College followed more closely the model of existing undergraduate certificate programs in area studies in four-year institutions in the state of Florida. It also paid special consideration to the learning outcomes of the University of Florida's Quality Enhancement Plan (2014) *Learning Without Borders: Internationalizing the Gator Nation*, which was under development at the time. Since 60 % of our Associate of Arts (AA) degree students transfer to this institution, it was determined that the alignment of learning objectives between the global certificates of both institutions would be beneficial to students. In the end, the committee agreed to create a program that requires students to take twenty credits in courses with international content, including eight credits in a foreign language, and participate in a series of international events, clubs, and activities, with the option and encouragement to study abroad. As a capstone project, students produce an electronic portfolio—a personal website—where they reflect on their international activities and learning, link coursework and co-curricular experiences with career goals, and create a professional digital identity. Upon completion, students receive a lapel pin and a transcript notation reflecting their achievement.

Despite the short time that the International Studies Certificate has been implemented at Santa Fe College, our brief experience signals the potential that this type of program holds for the advancement of comprehensive internationalization at community colleges. Global Certificate programs present an all-encompassing alternative to curricular internationalization alone and function as an umbrella under which international initiatives coalesce and gain intentionality and exposure. They also provide a dynamic structure where new ideas find a home. More importantly, they naturally lead to the implementation of strategies that are key for the advancement of comprehensive internationalization: they facilitate the creation of cross-campus partnerships, encourage the engagement of a variety of stakeholders, promote shared ownership, build on institutional strengths, and make international education an essential part of the institution rather than an add-on (Hudzik and McCarthy 2012). An analysis of the campus-wide impact of the program will illustrate these points.

CAMPUS-WIDE IMPACT

Since fall 2013, Santa Fe College students have embraced the program with enthusiasm. Just one month after the launch, 700 students had expressed interest in it, demonstrating that they identify global literacy as a relevant aspect of their education. About 200 students are actively pursuing the certificate now, and in spring 2015, only a year and a half after launching the program, 19 students graduated with this distinction. Although the program is open to all students (there are no Grade Point Average (GPA) or other requirements for acceptance), those who have completed it so far represent a select group that excels academically, is actively engaged in student clubs, and is highly interested in pursuing international experiences. In fact, 74 % of these graduates have studied abroad, 42 % are Honor students, and 26 % are international (F1 visa) students. Given the short life of the program, it could be argued that these individuals graduated first because they were more advanced credit-wise than their uninvolved, non-traveling counterparts. As more students in the mainstream manage to complete the curricular and co-curricular requirements, and our tracking and engagement strategies improve, we hope that the number of graduates that will come from outside of this elite group will increase.

Growth of Experiential Opportunities

Since students receive credit for their engagement in experiential opportunities with an international focus, participation in these venues has grown significantly on our campus. Among student organizations, for example, "World Travelers," a club dedicated to promoting and raising funds for study abroad, has seen its membership base tripled in the last year. Other groups, such as the recently formed "Asian Corner" have now more than 70 participants. The importance of heightened student engagement is not simply a matter of quantity. Student organizations sponsor and advertise international activities, recruit and mentor new students, and take an active role in the development of new aspects of the program. For instance, a number of student clubs including the Model UN team and several organizations of international students have initiated a proposal for the creation of an international/domestic student exchange or "Buddy Program." This initiative will launch in fall 2015 creating an intentional bridge between these populations on our campus, while offering at the same time an additional means to gain credit toward the International Studies Certificate.

The co-curricular credit incentive has generated greater interest in study abroad as well. Although the International Studies Certificate was designed to provide alternative on-campus opportunities for those unable to travel overseas, the program has led to a 26 % increase in participation in education abroad. In the 2014–2015 academic year 64 % of all the study abroad participants were also pursuing the International Studies Certificate. In several of the programs nearly all the students (83 %) were prospective graduates. The integration of study abroad into a larger academic program has helped redefine it in the eyes of the students as a valuable educational pursuit and a career enhancement opportunity, rather than a summer vacation. Now more students are interested in having this experience.

International Events On-Campus and Outreach to Local Community

The program has not only served as validation for student engagement initiatives, it has also compelled the institution to grow the number of international events on-campus to ensure enough opportunities to obtain co-curricular credit. From the handful of mostly disconnected activities that were available before launching the program, Santa Fe College is now offering an average of 30 international events per year (film festivals, lecture series, performances, round tables, and cultural celebrations) that are open to the campus at large and attended by hundreds of students. Although different departments and units organize these activities, they are all coordinated and advertised as qualifying events for the certificate by the Office of International Education. The effort to centralize marketing operations and to co-sponsor activities has resulted, not just in greater opportunities to gain global perspectives for all students, but in increased cross-campus partnerships. In fact, having the needs of the program as a focal point has brought an unprecedented sense of common purpose to our campus collaborations and has rendered comprehensive internationalization a meaningful goal for an increasing number of stakeholders.

In addition, the reach of the college's internationalization initiatives has extended to the local community in more permanent and purposeful ways. International events taking place at local museums and institutions have become part of the landscape of offerings that Santa Fe College students consider as co-curricular options. The coordination of marketing efforts between the Office of International Education at Santa Fe College and the University of Florida International Center has been particularly fruitful, as it has allowed students and faculty in both institutions to learn about events they can attend beyond their campuses. For many Santa Fe College students this exposure acts as a powerful springboard for their future academic success in a four-year college. Additionally, community organizations, such as the Gainesville chapters of Sister Cities International and the United Nations Association, have become regular partners in the organization of events at our campus.

Impact on Academic Programs

Beyond improving our event offerings, the International Studies Certificate has allowed us to increase enrollment in international courses, incorporate international content into existing academic initiatives, and provide venues to better serve the international students on our campus. Despite overall declining enrollments at the college, the number of students taking three international courses or more has increased by 3 % since the launch of the program, while interest in foreign languages courses is holding steady despite the alarming national trends. Among the academic initiatives infused with international content, the Research in Undergraduate Education Festival is noteworthy. At this annual college-wide symposium, students who present research on international topics are rewarded with co-curricular credit toward the program. As a result, the festival displays a growing number of projects that feature the many faces of our internationalization efforts, from research conducted in study abroad programs to projects developed in international on-campus courses. This enriches the festival and validates the international interests and experiences of the students, in addition to making study abroad opportunities visible and relevant to a campus-wide audience.

The Honors program has been another vital academic partner. Since the International Studies and Honor Certificates purposefully share many co-curricular requirements, students can easily graduate with both distinctions. Those less committed can still enjoy an internationalized Honors track by choosing international opportunities to accrue points toward the program. Another group increasingly interested in the International Studies Certificate are the international students on our campus. For them the program is not just an added distinction; it constitutes an empowering validation of their own international identity. For instance, after an international student attended a lecture on the challenges of working abroad presented by a senior manager of a multinational company, he wrote this on his eportfolio:

> At this point I felt completely connected to the speaker because I am from Bolivia. I am actually studying overseas right now. Feeling lonely is, I believe, one of the most challenging and tough experiences that I have ever experienced in my life.

For these students, the program offers a valuable opportunity not only to reflect on their experiences in the USA, but also to expand their global perspectives beyond the borders of their host country:

> What surprised me the most was that I was able to compare my own country, Bolivia, to Nigeria and I could find out some surprising similarities that finally proved to me that even though both are completely different countries located in separate continents, they have some common social problems.

As community colleges seek to increase the number of international students on their campuses, they may want to consider Global Certificate programs as a way to ensure the effective integration of these individuals in campus life. By inviting their participation in co-curricular activities along with domestic students and by asking that they reflect on their life in the USA, these programs present an opportunity to validate the unique identity and contributions of these students as well as ensuring that they truly learn from their experience abroad.

FOSTERING A GLOBAL IDENTITY THROUGH ACTIVE LEARNING

ePortfolios: Promoting Ownership and Reflection

The real value of the International Studies Certificate—both as a collaborative campus-wide endeavor and as a transformative learning experience for the students—becomes evident in the program's capstone project: the student electronic portfolios. In the process of creating these personalized websites, students connect their learning, reflect on their international interactions, and assess their own progress in areas such as cultural self-awareness, openness, and perspective taking. In addition, students incorporate career development elements. ePortfolios, however, are not simply a collection of items or the digital equivalent of a reflective essay. Neither are they an excuse to use technology. Instead, they represent a powerful pedagogical shift that places the learner at the center. ePortfolios promote active learning, metacognition, integration of learning, and identity development (Light et al. 2012). By selecting the work that best demonstrates their skills and academic achievements for their eportfolios, students actively engage in an exercise of self-assessment and ownership of learning. This stands in contrast with traditional methods of instruction in which the teacher is the sole judge of their work.

In the process of gathering and connecting these materials, students approach their learning holistically and transcend the educational silos that separate curricular from co-curricular experiences. For example, in her eportfolio a student makes the following connections between class content and her recent experience participating in a discussion on marriage in China organized by a student club:

> In class, we have contrasted marriage as an economic contract versus marriage as an emotional choice. It is one thing to consider these practices abstractly and without context. However, speaking to a peer, hearing first hand their beliefs, and being able to ask them questions is a far more meaningful way to understand the perspective of someone different.

In the student eportfolios, coursework, career, and experiential learning come together allowing students to contemplate themselves as whole individuals as they engage in making meaning of their own journey. In fact, the most important contribution of eportfolios to the creation of global citizens is their role in promoting identity development. In their eportfolios, students answer the questions that are central to their development: How do I know?, Who am I?, How do I relate to others? (Braskamp and Engberg 2011). By reflecting on the role they play in the construction of reality and their own learning, and by considering their values and purpose in life in the context provided by their international courses and experiences, students truly develop a global identity. For example, 75 % of students self-reported in the exit survey that working on their eportfolios had strongly encouraged them to reflect on who they are and how they fit in the world.

The use of eportfolios has had a positive impact on the overall academic quality of our programs. By allowing students to take ownership of their learning, we have added intentionality. Rather than listening to an international lecture to simply earn attendance credit, or relying on the "study abroad magic" to happen, our students depart with a mission to engage in experiences, reflect on them, showcase them in a professional manner, and measure their own progress. This has made attendance to international events on-campus and study abroad participation more purposeful and engaging for them.

Assessment

Although students complete an exit survey where they self-report their perceived gains, eportfolios provide direct evidence of learning and in this sense constitute an indispensable source of feedback for the program. The assessment of such a comprehensive project, however, is difficult, and to meet this challenge we are currently developing soft rubrics and reflective prompts based on the AAC&U VALUE rubrics for Global Learning and Intercultural Knowledge and Competence (2010). Although this aspect of the program still needs to mature, our initial evaluation of essays about both on-campus and study abroad experiences shows that engaging in reflection is deepening our students' learning in significant ways:

> My time in China helped me overcome relying on stereotypes to assess other people or customs. This is only possible by having your assumptions challenged on a daily basis, because it forces you to think critically as you trust your own experiences over outside representations. Relying on stereotypes is a shortcut to thinking. This is a perspective I truly believe goes along with studying abroad.

Career Development

Along with prompting reflection, ePortfolios are a remarkable platform for the incorporation of career development elements into Global Certificate programs. They allow students to display, along with their résumés, what employers value even more than specific majors: transferable skills (Hart 2013). ePortfolios not only allow students to demonstrate that they possess these abilities; they also provide an extraordinary visualization of the kind of experiences that influence employers the most when making hiring decisions. Among them are being involved in extracurricular activities such as student clubs and holding leadership positions (National Association of Colleges and Employers 2015). This is exactly the kind of involvement we encourage our students to feature in their eportfolios along with the skills acquired in the process:

> The responsibilities of my position [in the World Travelers Club] taught me how to become more organized and dependable. I began to grasp the importance of managing time wisely ... I became more aware of maintaining a professional image ... I became much more comfortable with public speaking.

With the help of career development materials and software, we train our students to tailor their narratives to meet the requirements of particular career paths or to target specific skills. For instance, four out of five employers identify team-work and the ability to solve problems with people whose views are different from one's own as critical skills (Hart 2015). This is how one of our students demonstrates she possesses these highly sought abilities:

> One of the biggest challenges for me was learning to work with people whose personalities and leadership styles differed from my own. I learned to be more patient and open to understanding other points of view ... I also learned how to compromise.

Employers' views toward the value of eportfolios as an evaluation tool for prospective job candidates could not be clearer: 80 % consider these projects fairly or very useful for hiring purposes, as opposed to the 45 % who feel that transcripts alone are enough (Hart 2015). Providing opportunities for students to attain and display valuable job skills is essential to the community college mission to prepare students to join the workforce.

It is also very appealing to the increasingly pragmatic mentality of today's learners. Indeed the visibility and career applications of eportfolios have increased the social desirability of our international initiatives among our students and other important decision makers.

ALIGNMENT WITH INSTITUTIONAL MISSION AND VALUES

The connection of the International Studies Certificate to the institution's mission and core values has been enhanced by the use of eportfolios: they constitute a learner-centered pedagogy, instill professionalism, engage students in a meaningful use of technology, promote lifelong learning through the acquisition of metacognitive skills, and reinforce general education learning outcomes such as critical thinking and written communication. More importantly, they promote academic achievement by having a documented positive impact on retention and success (Eynon et al. 2014). This alignment with institutional priorities renders the International Studies Certificate program valuable to the college well beyond its role as an instrument to advance global literacy and intercultural proficiency. ePortfolios not only make these connections possible, but thanks to their visible and shareable nature, they also make them resoundingly clear to external audiences. In this sense, eportfolios have been crucial for the advancement of comprehensive internationalization on our campus. As academic departments, student affairs professionals, and administrators have seen their own contributions to student learning reflected in the eportfolios, support for internationalization has grown.

MOVING FORWARD TOGETHER

Although Global Certificates are not a new concept, community colleges have started to adopt them with increasing eagerness in recent years. Among statewide enterprises, the North Carolina Global Distinction initiative created by the University of North Carolina-Chapel Hill as a viable Global Certificate model for community colleges is clearly noteworthy (http://worldview.unc.edu/). Currently nine community colleges in the state are part of this partnership. In Florida, another group of eight state colleges with existing programs have engaged through the Florida Consortium of International Education in an ongoing conversation about the common requirements of Global Certificate programs in the state and the alignment of their learning outcomes. However, most programs are just in a nascent state. A February 2015 national survey of 21 community colleges with an interest in Global Certificates showed that 48 % of respondents were still in the planning stages (GCLC 2015), while the rest had not been running more than two or three years.

As more colleges embark in this journey, it is important that we share experiences, resources, and strategies that lead to building a shared knowledge of best practices. Community Colleges for International Development Inc. (CCID) in partnership with Santa Fe College has formed a Global Certificate Learning Community. The group has a website (http://www.gclc.net/) featuring a catalogue of programs, information about requirements, materials provided by member institutions, and survey reports. The community communicates through a listserv where members exchange ideas and learn from each other. Individuals or institutions with an existing program or an interest in developing one are welcome to join this community through the website and participate in this emerging yet potentially transformative conversation.

CONCLUSION

The International Studies Certificate at Santa Fe College is a young program, but in a short period it has shown a transformative nature that anticipates extraordinary potential for the continuous advancement of our comprehensive internationalization efforts. Perhaps the question is not so much about how many students will graduate with this type of distinction, but how else we could achieve this kind of impact. How else could we add this sense of common purpose to our campus partnerships? How else could we add intentionality to participation in study abroad, student engagement, and campus events? How else could we invite reflection, deep learning, and attitudinal change in our students? Perhaps the most crucial question of all is how else we can move forward, if not by embracing innovative pedagogical models that help us meet our student where they are. We believe that Global Certificate programs coupled with eportfolios are proving to be a valid strategy to accomplish these goals. The observations of one of our graduates offer perhaps the most eloquent testimonial that the program has set in motion a powerful wave of change:

> Along the way, I have observed my fellow club members achieve outstanding personal growth, develop a passion for international education, and build

close friendships with one another. Seeing them blossom into dedicated, globally-conscious individuals has been overwhelmingly fulfilling for me.

References

Association of American Colleges and Universities. (2010). *VALUE rubrics*. Washington, DC: Association of American Colleges and Universities. https://www.aacu.org/value/rubrics

Bonahue, Edward T. (2008). Internationalizing the Community College. In Kenneth J. Osfield (Ed.), *Internationalization of student affairs and services: An emerging global perspective* (pp. 207–212). Washington, DC: NASPA: Student Affairs Administrators in Higher Education.

Braskamp, Larry A., & Engberg, Mark E. (2011, Summer/Fall). How colleges can influence the development of a global perspective. *Liberal Education, 97*(3/4),34–39.https://www.aacu.org/publications-research/periodicals/how-colleges-can-influence-development-global-perspective

Eynon, Bret, Gambino, Laura M., & Török, Judit (2014). What difference can ePortfolio make? A field report from the Connect to Learning Project. *International Journal of ePortfolio, 4*(1), 95–114.

GCLC Report. (2015). *International sudies/global scholar certificate programs survey report*. CCID-Santa Fe College, February 2015. http://www.gclc.net/reports/

Hart Research Associates. (2013). *It takes more than a major: Employer priorities for college learning and student success*. Washington, DC: Association of American Colleges and Universities. https://www.aacu.org/leap/presidentstrust/compact/2013SurveySummary

Hart Research Associates. (2015) *Falling short? College learning and career success*. Washington, DC: Association of American Colleges and Universities. https://www.aacu.org/leap/public-opinion-research/2015-survey-results

Hudzik, John (2011). *Comprehensive internationalization: From concept to action*. Washington, DC: NAFSA, Association of International Educators.

Hudzik, John, & McCarthy, JoAnn S. (2012). *Leading comprehensive internationalization: Strategies and tactics for action*. Washington, DC: NAFSA, Association of International Educators.

Light, Tracy Penny, Chen, Helen L., & Ittelson, John C. (2012). *Documenting learning with ePortfolios: A guide for college instructors*. San Francisco: Jossey-Bass.

National Association of Colleges and Employers. (2015). *Job outlook survey*. https://www.naceweb.org/surveys/job-outlook.aspx

Raby, Rosalind (2007). Internationalizing the curriculum. In Edward Valeau & Rosalind Raby (Eds.), *International reform efforts and challenges in community colleges* (pp. 57–66). New Directions for Community Colleges (138, Summer). San Francisco: Jossey-Bass.

Sasser, Jackson (2014). Internationalizing community colleges. *AACC Global Connections.* American Association of Community Colleges, November 2014. http://www.aacc21stcenturycenter.org/article/internationalizing-community-colleges/

Stearns, Peter (2009). *Educating global citizens in colleges and universities: Challenges and opportunities.* New York, NY: Routledge.

University of Florida. (2014). Quality enhancement plan. *Learning without borders: Internationalizing the Gator nation.* http://assessment.aa.ufl.edu/quality-enhancement-plan

STUDY 6

Innovative Approaches to Study Abroad at Harper College and Fox Valley Technical College

Opal Leeman Bartzis, Kelly J. Kirkwood,
and Thalia M. Mulvihill

INTRODUCTION

Community colleges have an imperative to attend to building the global citizen (Raby and Tarrow 1996) as do all institutions of higher education. Despite the fact that community college students now comprise approximately half of the American higher education student population, only about 1 % of the American students engaged in study abroad are from community colleges Institute of International Education (2014). The reasons attributed

O.L. Bartzis (✉)
Vice President of Academic Affairs, Institute for Study Abroad at Butler University, Indianapolis, IN, USA

K.J. Kirkwood
Adult, Community, and Higher Education at Ball State University

Study abroad at the Rinker Center for International Programs at Ball State University, Muncie, IN, USA

Thalia M. Mulvihill
Social Foundations and Higher Education, Women's & Gender Studies Program and the Honors College, Ball State University, Muncie, IN, USA

© The Editor(s) (if applicable) and The Author(s) 2016   237
R.L. Raby, E.J. Valeau (eds.), *International Education at Community Colleges*, DOI 10.1057/978-1-137-53336-4_17

to this are many, and they mainly revolve around the distinct characteristics and needs of the typical community college student demographic.

Characteristically, community college students are engaged in degree programs which are brief, sequentially organized with regard to curriculum, and structured with little room for activities that may not satisfy (or appear to satisfy) specific degree program requirements. They frequently maintain one or more jobs while attending college, a fact which prevents them from being able to leave the country for extended periods of time. Many community college students are financially challenged and the expense of study abroad is a real or perceived barrier. Direct association between low study abroad participation rates and the financial constraints of community college students have been made (Ruffer 2010). Similarly, Chieffo (2000) found that concern for personal finances was the chief reason cited by community college students who opted not to study abroad.

The ideal study abroad experience, therefore, would be structured in direct response to these realities of the community college student life. Such a program would be brief enough to allow the student to maintain family responsibilities and to incur a job break that would not have significant impact on personal finances. The program would be priced affordably and would represent high educational and professional value, positioned as an enrichment to the student's degree program and an enhancement to career preparation. As noted by Brennan et al. (2005), linking career opportunities to the determination to study abroad is crucial because of the distinctive vocational focus of community college students.

The following programmatic review from two community colleges, informed by a case study framework, examines two different ways colleges have approached internationalization. This lens is particularly appropriate for understanding internationalization in a community college setting, as it involves the collection and analysis of multiple forms of data (Yin 2013) in order to understand and interpret each case as a bounded system (Creswell 2013). Primary and secondary sources informed the case study data collection and analysis process through faculty interviews, email correspondence, and review of strategic planning, enrollment, and participation data.

REVIEW OF WILLIAM RAINEY HARPER COLLEGE PROGRAM

William Rainey Harper College (Harper College 2015) is a comprehensive community college located in Palatine, Illinois. The institution was established in 1965 and opened for the first students in 1967. The school serves approximately 40,000 students within the suburban Chicago region. Harper College students have access to associates degrees, workforce training, continuing education, professional certification, developmental education. Nearly 15,000 students are enrolled in credit-bearing coursework. According to the most recent institutional profile (2015) 49 % of Harper students have a transfer mission, 18 % are engaged in career preparation, 8 % are earning a General Education Development (GED) certificate, and 25 % have other intent. Harper College has developed an innovative and comprehensive means of internationalizing the community college experience through a faculty-driven approach.

The Office of International Education's Global Focus initiative (Global Focus) is a three-year cycle of interdisciplinary programs and area studies centered on a particular region of the world. The first cycle began in spring 2014 and was scheduled for completion in fall 2016. Programs in each of the three years are guided by an annual theme. For example, in year one, the theme was regional and cultural diversity. Year two was focused on economic development. Year three will cover sustainability. While meant to provide structure to the initiative, the themes are intentionally broad. Each year the Global Focus is marked by a sustained semester or year-long project in the targeted region. The goal is to educate students for leadership in an increasingly complex global society, as outlined in their mission statement. This is accomplished through investment in faculty, staff, and students.

The program was developed under the leadership of Dr. Richard Johnson, Coordinator of International Studies and Professor of English and Humanities, in conjunction with the Academy for Teaching Excellence, the International Studies and Programs Committee, and the Office of the Provost. According to Dr. Johnson, initial efforts to engage students and faculty in international education at Harper did not lead to the desired internationalization outcomes. As a result, a group of external global education consultants were hired to review Harper College's international strategy and provide feedback. This review led to a new strategic plan and clarified vision. The regional focus concept emerged as a way to build momentum in a clear, consistent, and sustainable manner. The Global Focus initiative was implemented in January 2014 after nearly three years of planning.

To better understand the Global Focus initiative at Harper College, it is important to describe the sequential and intentional structure of the program. Year one launched with an overseas faculty development program. This was designed to provide select Harper College faculty members with a core understanding of both international education and the target region. Faculty members from across all disciplines were invited to submit applications to participate in a Faculty International Field Seminar.

These faculty members came from Anthropology, Astronomy, Biology, Geography, History, Humanities, and Literature. Faculty applicants were asked to include a description of a proposed project that would infuse host regional content into an existing Harper College course.

The Faculty International Field Seminar was comprised of two parts: a pre-departure on-campus course and a summer overseas field experience. During the on-campus course, faculty members met four times, for a total of ten hours, on the Harper College campus, from March through May. In these meetings, the faculty members learned how to identify global learning outcomes, utilize new types of assessment, and infuse a course with global content, regardless of the discipline. The pre-departure course was taught by Mukila Maitha, Assistant Professor of Geography at Harper College. In preparation for their field experience, the group learned about the history, socio-economics, and politics of the region and attended two community events. The first was a movie screening and lecture by a survivor of the Rwandan genocide. The second was an all-day seminar on peace and social justice at the Illinois Holocaust Museum and Education Center. Faculty who were selected for the seminar was also expected to give guest lectures and participate in global programming related to the initiative on campus, after their return from the field seminar. The faculty members had the opportunity to earn three graduate equivalency credits (GEC) through the Harper College Academy for Teaching Excellence for their participation.

Once abroad, the faculty members met with colleagues at partner universities in the target countries and had the chance to develop and refine their curriculum projects based on these field experiences. Sustained contact with colleagues abroad enriched the course infusion process and provided the Harper College faculty with subject-matter experts for consultation during the fall course implementation stage.

The redeveloped globally infused courses were piloted at Harper College in the fall term of 2014. In keeping with the regional focus, students who enrolled in these courses engaged in poster sessions and campus panel discussions related to the region during spring 2015 International Education Summit. Other programming efforts, such as films, book discussions, and a lecture series were shaped by the regional focus and the current year's internationalization theme.

Year two, spring and fall of 2015, built upon the faculty development efforts. In the fall of 2015 Harper College hosted a Fulbright Scholar-in-Residence. Professor Jimrex Byamugisha of Makerere University in Kampala, Uganda, spoke in a variety of outlets, providing guest lectures, classroom visits, and engaging with the local community. He was the fifth Harper College scholar-in-residence in the past 15 years.

The third year, 2016, culminates with a short-term student study abroad experience in the target region of West Africa, making use of newly developed faculty expertise and strengthened international partnerships. By year three, faculty and students will be well prepared to engage and make meaning of this type of experience, as a continuation of their on-campus education. The study abroad program combines two different Harper College classes into one travel group. Students enrolled in the spring 2016 "Cultures of Africa" and "Geography of the Developing World" courses will travel to Uganda and Rwanda in the months of May and June. These courses run as late-start blended courses for the second half of the spring semester. This structure specifically meets the needs of community college students, who require shorter programs due to cost and time commitments. Recruitment for this phase was set for summer and fall 2015.

By the end of the three-year cycle, the internationalization effort will have grown from a core group of faculty, to the curriculum and culture of the campus, reaching students and faculty organically, infusing the campus with expertise via the regional and thematic activities. Although still in progress, the initial outcome from the Global Focus initiative has been profound. Efforts to measure the outcomes indicated 455 Harper College students were reached as of spring 2015, through 20 different infused course sections. An additional 670 Harper College students, faculty, and staff were reached through 21 campus programs, developed as a result of the initial Faculty International Field Seminar. With limited funding, and small cohort of eight faculty members, the effort has an exponential and immediate impact at Harper College. This program model could easily be replicated at other institutions program on a small or large scale.

The Global Focus initiative at Harper College is unique for several reasons. First, faculty are the initial target of the learning, rather than students. The initiative has achieved internationalization through faculty development rather than student mobility. An effort to isolate internationalization to student mobility risks diminishing return as students who have reaped the benefit of education abroad eventually graduate or move on from the institution. Faculty members remain on campus and have broad reach, years after the completion of the program. Second, the Global Focus initiative replaces broad internationalization efforts with global knowledge focused on a specific region. The Harper College approach embraces the reality that a global education is a vast and imprecise concept. Instead, the institution has found a way to ensure their students have exposure to non-Western perspectives, regardless of their area of study.

Not unlike Harper College, Fox Valley Technical College (FVTC) has been creative in its approach to internationalization, recognizing the power of faculty involvement and at all times keeping the distinct nature of the student body at the fore of program planning.

REVIEW OF FOX VALLEY TECHNICAL COLLEGE PROGRAM

FVTC is located is Appleton, Wisconsin, where it serves a district that encompasses the counties of Calumet, Outagamie, Waupaca, Waushara, and Winnebago counties. It began offering workforce development training to the community in 1912. Offering more than 200 associate degree, technical diploma and certificate programs, approximately 50,000 people receive training from FVTC annually; 10,000 students are enrolled in degree-declared programs, and 900 students participate in apprenticeship programs.

An examination of FVTC's evolving approach to study abroad reveals programmatic options that are a direct reflection of its institutional mission, to "provide high-quality education and training that support student goals, a skilled workforce, and the economic vitality of our communities" (Fox Valley Technical College 2015) and its collective vision of being "a model of innovation and distinction in technical education, recognized as an outstanding gateway to rewarding careers" (Fox Valley Technical College 2015). Within FVTC's statement of values, the following statement regarding diversity is of particular importance to this discussion: "We value an educational environment that attracts and supports a diverse student/staff community and fosters global awareness" (Fox Valley Technical College 2015).

In recent years, the number and variety of study abroad options at FVTC has expanded. A portfolio that once included a handful of short-term faculty-led options now encompasses not only short-term faculty-led programs, but also summer, semester, and academic year study through their membership in the International Student Exchange Program (ISEP) and a unique set of options known as "international professional field study programs." The focus on FVTC as part of this multiple-case study is, thus, two-fold: the ways in which FVTC has developed study abroad in recognition of institutional mission, vision and values, and the implementation of a specific type of study abroad option, the international field study program, which speaks to the distinct needs and circumstances of its unique student population.

Study abroad programs develop through the establishment of direct relationships with institutions abroad or through relationships with overseas-based program providers, typically beginning with exploratory conversations occurring during educational visits to FVTC by a team of students and faculty from the host country. Four such cultural exchange programs are currently in operation, in the Netherlands, Ireland, Germany, and Jamaica, and there are plans to add more.

Structurally, the programs include exposure to sites of historical and cultural interest, but the focus is always on the disciplinary nature of the program within the local context. Students participating in the nine-day Business and Culture in Ireland international field study program, for example, examine technology, innovation and modernization, touring Irish firms of varying types and sizes and meeting with local professionals to discuss their opportunities and challenges. Similarly, the international field study program in the Netherlands program entails experiences that are designed to be vocationally and culturally relevant to participants, as they explore off-shore wind farms, investigate varied approaches to sustainability embraced by the Dutch, and visit local businesses. Recognizing the time constraints of the average community college student, the Irish program is nine days in length and the Dutch program lasts two weeks. In appreciation of the importance of educational value, each program carries three general elective credits, an allocation that is determined through pre-departure and on-site course assignments and in recognition of the contact hours and intensive nature of the program itself.

However, perhaps the most vivid example of FVTC international programming that responds to institutional and student motivations is the Health Care Immersion in Jamaica international field study program. As part of this one-week experience, students complete 24 hours of clinical experience in local health care settings, interacting with Jamaican health care professionals and learning about issues of local and global importance within the context of the Jamaican culture. This program is unique among FVTC offerings in that it is incorporated directly into their health care degree and professional programs, yielding one credit of elective credit from the academic department of sponsorship. In future Health Care Immersion programs students will enroll in a one-credit intermediate clinical course as a requirement of the program.

As explained by study abroad coordinator Aaron Gorenc, in recognition of the needs of their students and a desire to augment the scope of their academic offerings, study abroad at FVTC aims to comprise three main

244 O.L. BARTZIS ET AL.

components: academic, professional, and cultural. They want the international experiences they develop to be relevant to the student's course of study and directly related to job attainment, and they consider cross-cultural awareness and communications skills to be among those employability essentials. Also of importance, FVTC study abroad programs are priced as affordably as possible and international partners for programming are selected in large part based on their ability to offer reasonably priced services.

For FVTC, awareness has been a challenge. Many faculty have simply had little experience with study abroad and have not been accustomed to thinking of their teaching areas in terms of international possibilities. A few faculty members led the earliest short-term programs abroad and additional faculty has followed their example in recent years. As faculty directors are responsible for recruiting students at FVTC, some of the newer programs directed by faculty who are still gaining international experience and study abroad promotion experience have struggled to reach minimum enrollments and, thus, program cancellations have occasionally occurred.

However, a unique faculty mini-grants program providing internal financial support for faculty development of short-term study abroad is poised to make a significant impact on study abroad at FVTC. Through the institution's curriculum development office, faculty can receive funding to support the internationalization of their courses in myriad ways, including the creation of course-embedded or stand-alone study abroad experiences, and the positive effects of this program area already being seen, as a result of increased knowledge levels and the confidence which is afforded through financial support. The mini-grant program for internationalization directly demonstrates that the institution is prepared to support initiatives that directly complement their mission, vision, and values.

As with any important endeavor, the support of stakeholders is critical to success. Within the community college system, we see that one section of stakeholders, the faculty, is particularly capable of exerting influence through their support. Chan (2013) noted that international programming at community colleges promotes global citizenship and global responsibility and aids students in critical and complex thinking skills, but also implored that faculty must become more engaged in increasing study abroad participation. Similarly, Paus and Robinson (2008) found that faculty have the greatest influence on students' decision to participate in study abroad, and thus their knowledge of study abroad and facility with international programming is critical.

In the last seven years at FVTC, faculty involvement has increased and due to an expanding portfolio of programs and increased promotional efforts, student participation in study abroad has grown from approximately 25 to 80 students annually. A portfolio which previously consisted of one language immersion program now includes two language immersion programs and four international field study programs. Other full summer, semester or year-long opportunities for individual students are also offered through a program provider relationship. Finally, a growing number of faculty-directed programs now satisfy general elective and major-specific elective requirements, and student recruitment goals are being realized. The FVTC approach is replicable based on the simple formula of linking study abroad to institutional goals, supporting faculty efforts to embrace internationalization, and ensuring that program design has recognition of student needs such as affordability, awareness of time constraints, and the value of professional and technical training at its core.

Conclusion and Recommendations

The positive impacts of study abroad on college students are many (Raby et al. 2014), ranging from improved academic performance and persistence (Ashford 2011) to increased disciplinary knowledge, intercultural competence, and social growth (Meyer-Lee and Evans 2007). The kinds of experimentations in fostering study abroad within institutional contexts as described earlier are important ways to enable students to enjoy these benefits and more. Thoughtfully designed programs, which must include active faculty involvement, and innovative approaches to funding can make study abroad a reality for community college students. Continued research on this topic in the form of case study analysis is suggested. In particular, the creation of a collection of mini-cases from a broad array of community college study abroad programs is recommended.

References

Ashford, Ellie (2011). Colleges urged to take advantage of study abroad. *Community College Times.* www.communitycollegetimes.com/Pages/Campus-Issues/Colleges-urged-to-take-advantage-of-study-abroad.aspx

Brennan, Michael, Frost, Robert, Hagadorn, Emily, Martin, Marie, & Natali, Jeanne (2005). Education abroad and the career development of community college students: Four case studies. In M. Tillman (Ed.), *Impact of education abroad on career development: Four community college case studies II* (pp. 7–16). Stamford, CT: American Institute for Foreign Study Publications.

Chan, Roy Y. (2013). *The emerging role of community colleges in international education and study abroad: A case study of Santa Monica College Associate's Degree (A.A.) Program in Global Studies.* Paper presented at the Forum on Education Abroad Tenth Annual Conference, San Diego, CA, April 2, 2014.

Chieffo, Lisa P. (2000). *Determinants of student participation in study abroad programs at the University of Delaware: A quantitative study.* Newark, Delaware: Doctoral dissertation.

Creswell, John W. (2013). *Research design: Qualitative, quantitative and mixed methods approaches.* Thousand Oaks, CA: Sage.

Fox Valley Technical College. (2015). www.fvtc.edu. Accessed 30 April 2015.

Harper College. goforward.harper.edu. Accessed 30 April 2015. p. 238

Harper College (2015). *2014 Fact Book.* http://goforward.harpercollege.edu/about/leadership/planning/pdf/2014-Fact-Book.pdf#page=10

Institute of International Education. (2014). *Open Doors Report 2013 (2014).* www.iie.org/Who-We-Are/News-and-Events/Press-Center/Press-Releases/2014/2014-11-17-Open-Doors-Data

Meyer-Lee, Elaine & Evans Joy (2007). Areas of study in outcomes assessment. In M. C. Bolen (Ed.), *A guide to outcomes assessment in education abroad* (pp. 61–70). Carlisle, PA: Forum on Education Abroad.

Paus, Eva, & Robinson, Michael (2008). Increasing study abroad participation: The faculty makes the difference. *Frontiers: The Interdisciplinary Journal of Study Abroad, 17*(1), 33–49. http://frontiersjournal.com/documents/PausRobinson FrontiersvolXVIIFall2008-3.pdf

Raby, Rosalind L., Rhodes, Gary M., & Biscarra, Albert (2014). Community college study abroad: implications for student success. *Community College Journal of Research and Practice, 38*(2–3), 174–183.

Raby, Rosalind Latiner, & Tarrow, Norma (Eds.). (1996). *Dimensions of the community college: International and inter/multicultural perspectives.* Garland Studies in Higher Education Volume 6, Vol. 1075. New York: Garland Pub., Inc.

Ruffer, Carly (2010). *Recruitment initiatives in higher education: A comparison of study abroad and enrollment management procedures.* Master's Theses. Paper 490. http://ecommons.luc.edu/luc_theses/490

Yin, Robert (2013). *Case study research: Design and methods.* Thousand Oaks, CA: Sage.

Partnering for New Possibilities: The Development of a Global Learning Certificate

Katherine Cierniak and Anne-Maree Ruddy

INTRODUCTION

While overseas partnerships are often seen as a facet of the internationalization process, an examination of the literature indicates that partnerships with the goal of the internationalization of campus curricula are much less common between domestic institutions. In 2012, a large research institution, Indiana University (IU), and Indiana's community college system (Ivy Tech), comprising of 30 campuses in 14 regions, entered into a unique partnership aimed at campus internationalization. The three-year initiative, Global Learning Across Indiana (GLAI), is funded by the US Department of Education's Undergraduate International Studies and Foreign Language (UISFL) grant. The core aims of this collaborative initiative are to develop a Global Learning Certificate (GLC), to offer Arabic language classes, and to internationalize the curriculum statewide

K. Cierniak (✉)
Educational Policy Studies, Indiana University, Bloomington, IN, USA

A.-M. Ruddy
Center for Evaluation and Education Policy, Indiana University, Bloomington, IN, USA

247

R.L. Raby, E.J. Valeau (eds.), *International Education at Community Colleges*, DOI 10.1057/978-1-137-53336-4_18

throughout the Ivy Tech campuses. By examining the initial outcomes of this partnership, this study contributes to the conversation on the process of internationalization in higher education and in particular the benefits of collaboration between domestic institutions. Specifically, this study investigates two key questions: To what extent has the initiative served to internationalize curricula on Ivy Tech campuses? Is this a replicable and recommended model for institutions seeking to form partnerships to internationalize? Through attaining the perspectives of faculty associated with the collaborative initiative via survey data and reviewing relevant documents, this study offers insight into collaborations between domestic institutions and the experiences of key stakeholders in their efforts to internationalize the curriculum of their institutions.

COMPREHENSIVE INTERNATIONALIZATION

Institutions that have gone through the process of internationalizing have identified strategies and approaches they believe reflect their mission. As such, institutions of higher education internationalize using a variety of approaches, reflecting the institution's underlying philosophy and definitions of internationalization. Clearly defining and establishing a shared understanding of the terms on each campus is imperative (Olson et al. 2006; Dewey and Duff 2009; Coryell et al. 2012; American Council on Education 2012). Further, a shared vision and agreed-upon vocabulary is likely to result in a higher degree of investment from administrators, faculty, and staff. Once a shared understanding of internationalization has been established at the institution it "must operationalize within and across academic programs and administrative functions" (Coryell et al. 2012, p. 91). Two prominent approaches in internationalizing the curriculum in higher education institutions are "importing" and "infusing" (Coryell et al. 2012). Importing may entail rigorous recruiting of international fee-paying students and be seen as "McDonaldalization" of state education as the purpose is to be efficient, calculable, and under state control (Coryell et al. 2012). Therefore, imported curricula often reflect government efforts to internationalize the curriculum, but in a manner that focuses on the state's role in the global knowledge economy, rather than the role of higher education institutions (Coryell et al. 2012). By comparison, an infusion approach is characterized by "permeating the existing curricula with diverse perspectives and knowledge gleaned from professional practices across cultures" (Coryell et al. 2012, p. 80, citing Whalley et al. 1997).

The "infusion" approach is consistently cited as an element of successful global citizenship education programs (Skidmore et al. 2005; Olson et al. 2006; Miller 2002; Battistoni et al. 2009; ACE 2012). Further, utilizing an "infusion" or integrated approach to global learning necessarily requires the participation of the institution as a whole (Miller 2002; Skidmore et al. 2005; Olson et al. 2006; Battistoni et al. 2009; ACE 2012). Successfully integrating global content across the curriculum depends on both administrative leadership and active networking among staff and faculty (Green and Siaya 2005; Skidmore et al. 2005; Olson et al. 2006; Dewey and Duff 2009). Centralized efforts are necessary to "mobilize campus-wide support for internationalization" as well as to set it as an institutional priority (Skidmore et al. 2005, p. 191). While campus leadership shapes the vision and provides the necessary resources, an infused approach requires collaboration across disciplines, involving the entire community in a dialogue about global learning, and local engagement in order to reflect global experience (Raby and Valeau 2007; Battistoni et al. 2009). Dewey and Duff (2009) state, "Passion for internationalization is not enough. If it is an institutional strategic priority, internationalization requires resources, support, and strategic coordination ... Internationalization must be addressed systemically and systematically" (p. 503).

PARTNERSHIPS: INTERNATIONAL AND DOMESTIC

ACE (2012) and Community Colleges for International Development (CCID 2015) outline a number of different types of international partnerships that typically occur between two or more institutions of higher education focused on international education. These international partnerships range from simple friendship and cooperation agreements, to dual degree programs, to collaborative research endeavors between international institutions (Egron-Polak and Hudson 2014). The type of partnership established between institutions will depend on the motivations and goals of the institutions involved.

Many partnerships related to international activities between domestic community colleges or K-12 schools and large research universities are geared specifically toward outreach activities conducted by the university. For example, Michigan State University's summer institute for community college and technical college faculty, cosponsored by Center for International Business Education and Research's and Wisconsin International Outreach Consortium comprised of two University of

Wisconsin campuses and Madison College, both emphasize outreach efforts (WIOC 2011a b, c). Outreach efforts are also emphasized by the University of Minnesota in their Global R(ace) E(thnicity) M(igration): Building on Interdisciplinary Strengths program as "Global REM faculty provide the cultural expertise needed by the university to work effectively with increasingly diverse communities in the Twin Cities and beyond" University of Minnesota, n.d..

A Collaborative Approach to Internationalizing the Curriculum

The IU and Ivy Tech GLAI project built on earlier work conducted by single campus locations of both institutions in the Internationalization Collaborative Across Bloomington (ICAB) project. To prepare faculty and staff for the new GLAI program elements and to facilitate campus and curricular internationalization, key IU and Ivy Tech faculty worked collaboratively to design and then provide professional development for a core team of 20 Ivy Tech faculty and staff. Each year of the three-year initiative (2013–2015) this cohort has the charge to develop strategies for incorporating international learning objectives into their courses and on campus. In the first year of the initiative, IU and Ivy Tech faculty were recruited to participate in the initial professional development workshops. This team outlined the requirements for the Global Studies Certificate, developed the Arabic I course, and developed learning outcome goals for the redesigned Course Outlines of Records (CORs). Dedicated personnel at Ivy Tech and IU played key roles in implementing and leading the initiative.

In the second year of the initiative (Fall 2014), the first redesigned global courses were taught on campus, while the Arabic 2 course was developed. Requirements for the Global Studies Certificate were finalized and approved for statewide implementation. In the third year of implementation (Fall 2015), the Global Learning Certificate will be available to Ivy Tech students system-wide and will be promoted across the state. Also, Arabic 1 and 2 will be taught, and a new cohort of faculty and staff will participate in professional development workshops to internationalize new courses and design supplemental resources for the Global Studies Certificate. (See Table S7.1). Internationalizing the curriculum at Ivy Tech with the assistance of IU is one of the key components of the initiative including the integration of global learning outcomes and less commonly taught languages at Ivy Tech campuses throughout the state.

Table S7.1 Phases of the global learning across Indiana initiative and related activities

Phase	Activities	Institution
Year 1	Faculty and staff recruited	Ivy Tech
	Professional development workshops conducted	Ivy Tech & IU
	Requirements of Global Learning Certificate outlined	Ivy Tech & IU
	Learning outcome goals developed	Ivy Tech & IU
	Arabic I course developed	Ivy Tech & IU
Year 2	Internationalized courses offered on campus	Ivy Tech
	Arabic 2 course developed	Ivy Tech & IU
	Global Learning Certificate requirements finalized and approved	Ivy Tech
	Additional faculty and staff participate in professional development	Ivy Tech & IU
Year 3	Arabic 1 and 2 courses taught	Ivy Tech & IU
	Global Learning Certificate available system-wide	Ivy Tech
	Additional faculty and staff participate in professional development	Ivy Tech & IU

This initiative aims to effectively prepare Ivy Tech students to transfer to four-year institutions, such as IU, where they will be more likely to graduate and further their international studies and language instruction. This approach of a mutually beneficial collaboration was structured to provide systemic change at Ivy Tech with professional development primarily conducted by IU's Center for the Study of Global Change. The IU Global Center also supervises the project coordinator. While a one-way flow of university outreach to the community college is evident in a number of activities, the ongoing level of engagement and collaboration between IU and Ivy Tech faculty and staff explicitly benefits both institutions. Ivy Tech benefits by efforts to effect systemic change and for IU the benefit is of forming strategic domestic partnerships and developing international opportunities for domestic students. Both institutions potentially benefit from the collaboration with the opportunity to work toward their internationalization goals.

THEORETICAL FRAMEWORK

In understanding a domestic partnership, the factors which led to the partnership and the processes involved in the collaboration, collaboration theory is particularly informative (Gajda 2004; Gray and Wood 1991; Huxham and Vangen 2005). This research draws upon the definition provided by Wood and Gray (1991): "Collaboration occurs when a group of autonomous stakeholders of a problem domain engage in an interactive process, using shared rules, norms, and structures, to act or decide on issues related to that domain" (p. 146). A problem domain refers to "the way a problem is conceptualized by the stakeholders" (Gray 1989, p. 5). The problem domain for those involved in the GLAI initiative is the need to prepare young adults to live and work in an increasingly globalized society.

In addition to examining the reasons organizations enter into a collaborative alliance, collaboration theorists also consider collaboration as a process which occurs in stages (Gajda 2004; Gray 1989; Hogue 1993; Peterson 1991). In this study, Gray's (1989) three-phase model of collaboration: problem setting, direction setting, and implementation is utilized. Collaboration theorists also posit that the personnel involved in a collaboration play a crucial role, particularly in establishing a climate of trust among collaborators (Gajda 2004; Gulzar and Henry 2005; Gray 1989). Gajda (2004) argues, "Collaboration depends upon positive personal relations and effective emotional connections between partners" (p. 69).

Beyond the factors which facilitate collaboration, some factors can serve as obstacles to collaboration. These may include institutional disincentives, historical and ideological barriers, power disparities, differing perceptions of risk, and political and institutional cultures, among others (Gray 1989). Additionally, Gray (1989) identifies two objective factors for evaluating the success of a collaboration: whether or not an agreement was reached and whether it was implemented.

Methodology

A case study approach was used for this study. Utilizing different types of materials for data collection allows for gaining a detailed and balanced picture of a given situation (Altrichter et al. 2008). In order to gain a holistic understanding of the process of the first year of the implementation of the collaborative initiative, a survey was administered to the first cohort of 20 faculty at the conclusion of the year one professional development activities (2013) and a follow-up survey was given a year later in 2014. This chapter draws upon this survey data. In addition, a content analysis of relevant documents including the mission statements of both IU and Ivy Tech, as obtained from each institution's website; Ivy's Tech's application for the UISFL grant; and relevant information gathered from IU's Center for the Study of Global Change's GLAI initiative and program websites was conducted. (See Table S7.2).

An inductive analysis technique was used to manually develop codes and categories from the data (Patton, 1980). Such an approach allowed the examination of patterns of meaning across the various groups within the institutions. We identified three emerging themes in the documents and survey data related to the concepts of strategic expansion/partnerships, organizational change and global learning. These themes were continuously revised throughout the data analysis process.

Survey participants were invited to participate in the study based on their experience with or role in the GLAI as well as their willingness to participate in the study. The Center for Evaluation and Education Policy (CEEP), an independent evaluator at IU, constructed and administered two surveys using Qualtrics survey software. These surveys were based on key concepts from the grant proposal and program website information rooted in mission statements and strategic plans. Respondents had two weeks to complete each survey. The post-workshop survey yielded a response rate of 100 % and the follow-up survey yielded a response rate of 30 %.

Respondents were asked to indicate on a Likert-style scale the level of support received for internationalization efforts, the extent to which they have integrated global content into courses taught, and their experiences with the professional development workshops. Survey participants were also asked to provide answers to open-ended questions about their experiences with the GLAI initiative and internationalization efforts on their campuses. Data were coded using Qualtrics and manually cross-checked by both researchers.

In December 2015, the study expanded to include feedback from the second cohort of faculty and administrators and assessed second-year implementation data. In 2016, student surveys and interviews will be

Table S7.2 Documents for analysis	No.	Year	Document
	1	2005	University Mission Statement
	2	2008	University International Strategic Plan
	3	2010	Community College Mission Statement
	4	2010	Community College Strategic Plan
	5	2012	Collaborative Grant Application (UISFL)
	6	2013	Program websites

incorporated into the study, so that the last year of the study will include data collected from administration, faculty, and students.

Findings

Our analysis of the data identified three emerging themes related to the concepts of strategic expansion/partnerships, organizational change, and global learning. This section discusses each theme in detail in reference to key documents and survey data. While the first two phases of the collaboration are understood in the context of both institutions key documents, the outcomes of the collaborative efforts are best understood through survey data collected after the first year of implementation. The numbers in parentheses refer to the specific document(s) where the theme being discussed is evident.

Strategic Expansion/Partnerships

The theme of strategic expansion/partnerships is evident in documents 2, 4, and 5 (as shown in Table S7.2). IU policy documents outline a series of goals which include plans to form strategic partnerships internationally and domestically. Strategies that aim to improve "far more than education at the university" (2) and efforts to foster collaboration across disciplinary and campus boundaries by "meeting the changing educational and research needs of the state, the nation, and the world" (1) are articulated. Another strategy outlined by IU is the expansion of international outreach activities and services to the citizens of the State of Indiana (2). Equally, Ivy Tech indicates a strategy to expanding partnerships with four-year colleges and universities (4). This emphasis is manifested in the grant application (5) where a clear commitment to the partnership by both institutions is outlined. A clear goal of the partnership is for both Ivy Tech and IU to develop a model of internationalization best practices that can be coordinated with and implemented by others.

Gajda (2004) argues that the ability to effectively collaborate depends upon the positive interpersonal relations among collaborators. Survey respondents reported a positive and beneficial aspect of participating in the GLAI. Of the 15 post-workshop respondents ($n = 15$) two (13 %) described those involved in the partnership as supportive and encouraging. One respondent stated, "The support from the GLAI staff to implement global teaching objectives has been incredibly valuable." For five

(33 %) of post-workshop respondents, forging new relationships with fellow collaborators was an important aspect of the partnership. For instance, one respondent reported that "developing professional relationships with colleagues from across the state" was a major benefit of participating in GLAI. Similarly, eight (53 %) of post-workshop respondents noted that meeting with others who share similar goals was beneficial. These respondents indicated that "meeting/working with people who embrace diversity" and "meeting others who are working to develop global courses" have been beneficial aspects of participating in GLAI. One respondent stated that the direct connection with colleagues who view global learning as important was valuable. This respondent further noted, "Now, thanks to GLAI, my message is endorsed by a program that encourages students to see things from a global perspective."

Organizational Change

The theme of organizational change is evident in documents 1–6 (found in Table S7.2). The documents articulate that there are structural and organizational changes that need to take place in order to coordinate campus-wide internationalization initiatives. These documents outline organizational and structural changes for university policies and programs (2, 4–5). Processes involved in the direction setting phase of collaboration are described in the grant document (5) and outlined in the grant's Project Timeline, including: the agenda for the collaboration, the tasks to be accomplished in each of the years of the GLAI, as well as the procedures for completing them (pp. 9–10). Also in the direction setting phase, collaborators organized subgroups of stakeholders in addition to organizing the leadership/administration of the initiative. This administrative subgroup included the project coordinator, the codirectors, and the lead person in developing the Arabic curriculum. The coordinator works with the codirectors to organize the workshops and assists with the development of the Arabic curriculum, the internationalization of the Ivy Tech Course Outlines of Records (CORs), and the faculty and staff reviews of various global learning instruments.

Survey respondents indicated the level of support they received regarding their involvement in GLAI and ultimately their efforts to affect organizational change to internationalize the curriculum. Respondents were asked to rate the level of support they received regarding their involvement in GLAI and ultimately their efforts to affect organizational change by internationalizing their curriculum. Of the 20 (100 %) respondents, the majority (95 %, 19) indicated receiving support from the administration with a total number of 11 (55 %) of respondents indicating they felt supported and eight (40 %) indicating they were somewhat supported from the administration. Regarding support from the faculty, half of respondents (50 %, 10) indicated being very supported and approximately two-fifths of respondents (35 %, 7) feeling somewhat supported. All respondents (100 %, 20) indicated they felt supported from the GLAI staff.

Despite the acknowledgement of support, the most cited challenge of the first year of implementation and instituting organizational change was gaining administrative buy-in. Of the 15 faculty members who responded to this post-workshop survey question, six respondents (40 %) indicated that administration challenges were the most difficult aspect of participating in GLAI. For instance, one respondent indicated that it was a challenge to get the CORs past the curriculum committee. Another noted that it was not possible to get the administration program chairs to add international language to a particular course. Consequently, one respondent argued that it may be instructive to find a way to demonstrate the need of curricular internationalization to administrators. One respondent stated:

> In order to effect real change at the regional level, top administrators must buy-in. On those campuses where the chancellors, VCAAs and VCSAs are supportive of global learning, GLAI efforts have been truly forwarded. Where this support is lacking or missing altogether, internationalizing the curriculum and global learning–for faculty, staff, and students–are only occurring for isolated individuals.

Similarly, another respondent argued for first gaining administrative support for the initiative as a means of affecting systemic change:

> I would suggest including or starting with administrators as opposed to faculty to implement systemic change. As an instructor, it is easy to get me interested in and passionate about something, but that doesn't always translate into systemic attention, even if the system has verbalized support and interest.

One faculty member suggested that increased dialogue across regions with administrators would facilitate gaining the buy-in and support needed.

In addition to inquiring about faculty experiences with GLAI and the impact of the initiative on their teaching, the post-workshop survey (*N*=20) asked faculty about the impact and potential for change at their home campuses. Respondents indicated the extent to which they agreed with the following statement: "There is sufficient engagement to effect curricular change at my campus." Despite an effective collaborative effort, nearly one-third of faculty felt that there was not sufficient engagement to effect curricular change at their campus. Though positive elements to the partnership are noted, these responses indicate that those engaged in a collaborative partnership may also encounter barriers to collaboration or disincentives to collaborate which can limit the impact of the collaborative effort (Gray 1989).

Global Learning

Documents 1–6 (in Table S7.2) reflect the theme of developing international opportunities for domestic students with the intended aim of providing opportunities for global learning and thus preparing global citizens. Documents outline a series of goals which include plans to increase participation, develop greater diversity in international activities and increase financial support for students, faculty, and staff, eliminate or reduce structural barriers to student participation in study abroad (2, 4, 5). Mission statements, for instance, are intended to reflect an institution's vision for education and should be one that is "deeply rooted in the institution's identity and practices" (Meacham and Gaff 2006, p. 6). Both IU and Ivy Tech's mission statements summarize organizational values aimed at enhancing global education opportunities for faculty and students at the university (1, 2) and the community college (3, 4). Ultimately, implementation of the collaborative project is intended to move both organizations forward in fulfilling their responsibility of preparing graduates for lives in the interconnected and complex world of the twenty-first century (5).

With an intention to implement the global learning priorities the majority of faculty members, (90 %) reported in the post-workshop survey (*N* = 20) that they were prepared to teach toward internationalized outcomes based on their involvement in the GLAI. Similarly, 95 % agreed or strongly agreed that they intend to apply the knowledge and skills gained through their GLAI experience in the course they internationalize. Equally, 95 % of faculty reported that they either agreed or strongly agreed that they intend to integrate global learning outcomes into their overall teaching. In the follow-up survey ($N = 6$), 100 % of respondents indicated that they are teaching toward internationalized outcomes, applying their knowledge and skills gained through their GLAI experience and integrating global learning outcomes.

Faculty provided responses to open-ended questions regarding the impact of the GLAI professional development workshops. One respondent stated, "The most valuable part has been hearing about ideas/suggestions for what to try and peoples' experiences in what they have tried. It just generates creativity and innovation." Another respondent similarly stated that sharing ideas was a particularly valuable part of the workshop experience, "This always pushes me to consider new ways to teach my classes." Finally, one Ivy Tech faculty member noted gaining a great deal of energy from the discussions in the workshop and that this has included learning about new materials, assignments, and opportunities which can be incorporated into the classes the faculty member teaches.

In addition to the sharing of ideas, respondents also noted that the sharing of resources was a beneficial aspect of participating in the professional development workshops. One respondent noted that the materials provided of assignments and assessments from other faculty were especially helpful. Similarly, another respondent stated, "The sample activities presented were very useful, as were the resources. I will be implementing a number of these activities and resources in my courses in the future."

Some participants also commented that learning new strategic approaches was a valuable element of the professional development workshops. For instance, one participant indicated that the sharing of successful international learning outcomes by other faculty was helpful. Another stated that learning to work in a backward course design was useful.

Additional Findings: Project Personnel

In many collaborative endeavors, the presence of an individual such as a convener, mediator, or leader can play a key role in facilitating collaborative efforts (Gray 1989; Sharfman et al. 1991; Wood and Gray 1991). Such an individual may be a major force in moving the collaboration forward and motivating the stakeholders involved (Gray 1989; Sharfman et al. 1991; Wood and Gray 1991). In the case of the GLAI initiative, three respondents particularly emphasized an appreciation for the project coordinator and their work with the project. One faculty member stated, "I want to offer a big thank you to [project coordinator] for all [they] have done to bring this program into view and to make the process of our engagement so rewarding." In addition, the faculty member explained that the project coordinator had served as a good guide for the project, and that the work undertaken by the project coordinator had facilitated positive outcomes. The faculty member stated, "The results we obtain are a credit to [the project coordinator's] resourcefulness and encouragement."

DISCUSSION AND CONCLUSION

Through the GLAI Initiative, IU and Ivy Tech has utilized many of the recommended strategies and approaches to internationalization. The initiative is clearly reflected in both institutions' key documents, adopts an infusion approach, calls upon university personnel at all levels, provides financial support and training for internationalization efforts, and evaluates the effectiveness of its programs. Equally, both institutions benefit from the collaborative initiative by working toward meeting their institutional internationalization goals.

Collaboration theorists posit that collaboration is a process, and that different stages of collaboration can be identified (Gajda 2004; Gray 1989; Hogue 1993; Peterson 1991). When examining Ivy Tech's application for the UISFL grant (5), elements of the problem setting and direction setting phases outlined in Gray's (1989) stages of collaboration can be detected in the narrative. During this first stage of the collaborative process, IU and Ivy Tech found a common definition of the problem, committed to collaborate, and identified the stakeholders involved. Ivy Tech and IU entered the collaboration in order to collectively solve a problem in a specific domain (Gray 1989; Trist 1977, 1983).

In fact, it was this common definition of a problem that served as the impetus for IU's and Ivy Tech's Bloomington campuses to commit to collaborating and submit an UISFL grant application with an intent to not only concentrate internationalization efforts in Bloomington, but reach Ivy Tech campuses statewide. In the problem setting phase of the collaboration, IU and Ivy Tech identified the stakeholders of the collaboration. In particular, the first cohort of faculty, staff, and administration of Ivy Tech were identified as stakeholders and those which would be most crucial to implementing the changes systemically and systematically across Ivy Tech's campuses.

Yet, as indicated by the first year participants, despite clearly articulating internationalization in key documents, including faculty and staff throughout the project and allocating dedicated personnel, difficulties arose in the first year of the implementation phase of the project with a challenge of administrative and faculty buy-in. Members of the GLAI initiative anticipated these challenges and strove to overcome these barriers by "having faculty, trained in internationalization, engage with administrators, staff, and others who are responsible for promoting international education on campuses" (5, p. 8). Indeed, members of this collaborative initiative made efforts to infuse global content systemically, and acknowledged that in order to do so personnel at all levels must be involved (ACE 2012; Battistoni et al. 2009; Coryell et al. 2012; Dewey and Duff 2009; Skidmore et al. 2005) but as indicated, barriers still exist.

Institutions of higher education seeking to internationalize may find that developing and adopting an international curriculum is often a process that requires a significant time investment, as institutions determine working definitions of global learning and internationalization and identify how to operationalize these definitions. Some institutions seek out partnerships, both overseas and in the USA, as they seek to expand their international offerings. A domestic collaborative partnership such as the case outlined here may be appropriate and ultimately beneficial to both parties. This partnership to internationalize curricula at the nation's largest single-accredited statewide community college system with a multi-campus public research institution as a collaborator may serve as a guide for future partnerships between domestic institutions. An agreement between the two institutions was reached and as stated in the narrative of the UISFL grant application (5), "Participants from both institutions determined that internationalization must become integrated with the other learning outcomes of each course and that ideally, curriculum must be redesigned to support these global learning outcomes" (p. 4). The initiative in its initial phase has been implemented but faculty voices regarding obstacles to successful implementation need to be heard if the initiative is to achieve its goals.

References

Altricher, Herbert, Feldman, Allan, Posch, Peter, & Somekh, Bridget. (2008). *Teachers investigate their work: An introduction to action research across the professions.* New York, NY: Routledge.

American Council on Education. (2012). *Mapping internationalization on U.S. Campuses. 2012 edition.* http://www.acenet.edu/news-room/Documents/MappingInternationalizationonUSCampuses2012-full.pdf

Battistoni, Richard M., Longo, Nicholas V., & Jayanandhan, Stephanie R. (2009). Acting locally in a flat world: Global citizenship and the democratic practice of service-learning. *Journal of Higher Education Outreach and Engagement, 13*(2), 89–108.
Community Colleges for International Development. (2015). http://ccidinc. org/
Coryell, Joellen E., Durodoye, Beth A., Redmon-Wright, Robin, Pate, P. Elizabeth, & Nguyen, Shelbee (2012). Case studies of internationalization in adult and higher education: Inside the processes of four universities in the United States and the United Kingdom. *Journal of studies in international education, 16*(1), 75–98.
Dewey, Patricia, & Duff, Stephen (2009). Reason before passion: Faculty views on internationalization in higher education. *Higher Education, 58*(4), 491–504.
Egron-Polak, Eva, & Hudson, Ross (2014). *Internationalization of higher education: Growing expectations, fundamental values.* Paris: International Association of Universities.
Gajda, Rebecca (2004). Utilizing collaboration theory to evaluate strategic alliances. *American Journal of Evaluation, 25,* 65–77.
Gray, Barbara (1989). *Collaborating: Finding common ground for multiparty problems.* San Franciso, CA: Jossey-Bass.
Gray, Barbara, & Wood, Donna J. (1991). Collaborative alliances: Moving from practice to theory. *The Journal Applied Behavioral Science, 27,* 3–22.
Green, Madeleine, & Siaya, Laura (2005). *Measuring internationalization at community colleges.* Washington, DC: American Council on Education.
Gulzar, Laila, & Henry, Beverly (2005). Interorganizational collaboration for health care between nongovernmental organizations (NGOs) in Pakistan. *Social Science & Medicine, 61,* 1930–1943.
Hogue, Teresa (1993). *Community-based collaboration: Community wellness multiplied.* Chandler Center for Community Leadership. Retrieved from The University of Vermont, National Network for Collaboration website: http://www.uvm.edu/extension/community/nnco/collab/wellness.html
Huxham, Chris, & Vangen, Siv (2005). *Managing to collaborate: The theory and practice of collaborative advantage.* London: Routledge.
Meacham, Jack and Gaff, Jerry G. (2006). Learning goals in mission statements: Implications for educational leadership. *Liberal Education, 92*(1), 6-13.
Miller, Margaret A. (2002). Editorial: American higher education goes global. *Change, 34*(3), 4.
Olson, Christa L., Green, Madeleine F., & Hill, Barbara H. (2006). *A handbook for advancing comprehensive internationalization: What institutions can do and what students can learn.* Washington, DC: American Council on Education.
Patton, Michael Q. (1980). *Qualitative evaluation methods. Beverly Hills,* CA: SAGE Publications.

Peterson, Nancy L. (1991). Interagency collaboration under part H: The key to comprehensive, multidisciplinary, coordinated infant/toddler intervention services. *Journal of Early Intervention, 15*(1), 89–105.

Raby, Roslalind L., & Valeau, Edward J. (Eds.). (2007). *International reform efforts and challenges in community colleges.* New Directions for Community Colleges, No. 138. San Francisco, CA: Jossey-Bass.

Sharfman, Mark P., Gray, Barbara, & Yan, Aimin (1991). A context of interorganizational collaboration in the garment industry: An institutional perspective. *The Journal Applied Behavioral Science, 27,* 181–208.

Skidmore, Drake, Martson, Jan, & Olson, Gretchen (2005). An infusion approach to internationalization: Drake University as a case study. *Frontiers: The Interdisciplinary Journal of Study Abroad, 11,* 187–203.

Trist, Eric (1977). Collaboration in work settings: A personal perspective. *The Journal Applied Behavioral Science, 13,* 268–278.

Trist, Eric (1983). Referent organizations and the development of interorganizational domains. *Human Relations, 36,* 269–284.

University of Minnesota. (n.d.). *Global R(ace) E(thnicity) M(igration): Building on interdisciplinary strengths program.* http://www.globalrem.umn.edu/about.html

Wisconsin International Outreach Consortium (WIOC). (2011a). *Home.* Reterived 2013, September 20, from http://www.wioc.wisc.edu

Wisconsin International Outreach Consortium (WIOC). (2011b). *Events: Event archive.* Reterived 2013, September 20, from http://www.wioc.wisc.edu/events/archive.html

Wisconsin International Outreach Consortium (WIOC). (2011c). *Events: Upcoming.* Reterived 2013, September 20, from http://www.wioc.wisc.edu/events/index.html

Wood, Donna, & Gray, Barbara (1991). Toward a comprehensive theory of collaboration. *Journal of Applied Behavioral Science, 27*(2), 139–162.

Creating and Enhancing a Global Consciousness Among Ethnic Minority Students in Community Colleges

Reyes L. Quezada and Paula A. Cordeiro

INTRODUCTION

In his 2009 address to Congress, President Obama stated, "Our children will compete for jobs in a global economy that many of our schools do not prepare them for." If Pk-12, community colleges, and universities are not preparing students to compete in a global economy, then experiences outside of school play a larger role in this process. According to the National Survey for Student Engagement (2007) study abroad is one of the best ways to provide a high-impact college experience that leads to significant and personal and intellectual growth (Mullens and Cuper 2012). Study abroad programs, either sponsored by a school or private company prepare students for employment in a global economy by providing learners with opportunities for firsthand experiences developing intercultural relations and honing foreign language skills. However, not all students have equal access to this type of experiential international education.

Many institutions of higher education (IHEs) have refocused their recruitment efforts by highlighting international opportunity type programs

R.L. Quezada (✉) • P.A. Cordeiro
School of Leadership and Education Sciences, University of San Diego, San Diego, CA, USA

© The Editor(s) (if applicable) and The Author(s) 2016   263
R.L. Raby, E.J. Valeau (eds.), *International Education at Community Colleges*, DOI 10.1057/978-1-137-53336-4_19

in order to attract students to their campuses. Community colleges are no different as they too, provide more international short-term courses and internship opportunities in many content areas. The purpose of providing these types of opportunities is to attract more students, who, in turn, become more globally conscious and globally minded citizens. However, community college students face challenges related to participate in these types of opportunities that other IHE students may not. These challenges include the expense of travel, time constraints (having one or two jobs), family commitments, never having traveled previously, or the belief that study abroad is for "others" (Comps 2007; Sweeney 2013).

We focus on the challenges faced by community college ethnic minority students to participate in international opportunities. Specifically, we outline and analyze community college study abroad practices as they relate to internationalization. The hope is that this analysis will guide further involvement by more ethnic minority students in study abroad. We begin with a discussion that the case for internationalization has been made in the three education sectors', Pk-12, community colleges, and at IHEs in undergraduate, graduate, and advanced programs. This is followed with a discussion of various methods of enhancing diversity in community college study abroad programs through featured case studies from five community colleges across the USA. Interviews with study abroad program directors and review of program websites were conducted and analyzed. We conclude by suggesting that further efforts are needed to enhance the opportunities for participation of ethnic minority community college students in study abroad and other internationalizing efforts.

INTERNATIONALIZATION OF HIGHER EDUCATION IS PART OF THE LANDSCAPE

According to NASFA (2010), internationalization is the process of integrating and infusing intercultural dimensions, global perspectives, and foreign language development into the ethos and outcomes of postsecondary education. Study abroad is only one aspect of this process. In the past 20 years, IHEs have increased internationalization and study abroad efforts in both program development and course offerings. The greatest increase is realized at doctoral institutions followed by masters, baccalaureate, and community colleges (Whissemore 2012). Why this increase? We know that education abroad is important to both students and IHEs. One key reason is the impact that technology has had on our ability to communicate with the global community. For example, social media has increased interactions across borders, which, in turn, has an impact on social and political outcomes worldwide. A second reason for the increase in focus on internationalization is the changing demographics in the USA. In some states, ethnic minority populations are now the majority population, particularly in our Pk-12 system and in community colleges (Longview Foundation 2008). Education abroad prepares our ethnic minority students to engage with multinational and multilingual ethnic groups both at home and abroad. The third reason education abroad has gained traction in the USA is that former third world countries are being transformed into powerhouses with strong economic and scholarly indicators (McKeown 2009; National Academy of the Sciences 2010; Zhang 2011).

The Need for Internationalization

According to the 2014 Open Doors Report on International Exchange there were 5907 community colleges students who participated in study abroad programs in the 2012–2013 academic year (including summer) which represents only 2 % of the total number of students studying abroad. Although the majority of students in community colleges are ethnic minority students, study abroad student demographic participation at the community college level for 2012–2013 was 66.6 % White and 33 % were ethnic minority students. Of these 16.8 % were Hispanic, 7.6 % were Black or African American, 5.1 % Asian, Native Hawaiian or other Pacific Islander, 4 % American Indian or Alaskan Native and 3.5 % were multiracial.

Promising and Inclusive Practices

It is evident that there is sufficient literature advocating for IHE, including community colleges to increase international study abroad and/or to internationalize the curriculum in order for our community college graduates to become globally minded citizens. Further, there is a greater need to recruit ethnic minority students in the participation of study abroad programs as a way of raising their participation in global opportunities. Many types of programs have been designed to attract ethnic minority students, such as short-term and faculty-led education abroad programs. These types of programs have increased ethnic minority students' participation as they address some of the barriers encountered (Raby and Valeau 2007; Zhang 2011). This recruitment approach has also increased the number of faculty and ethnic minority students from various disciplines and in various countries other than Europe who participate in study abroad (Forum on Education 2009). Therefore, as Raby and Rhodes (2004) argue, effective education abroad programs are those that take into account the specific needs of ethnic minority students and non-traditional students, such as re-entry students who are returning to school after an extended period of time, students seeking a career change, retirees, or displaced workers.

Efforts by Community Colleges to Internationalize

Many community colleges have had a long-standing tradition of providing international experiences for their student populations. For the most part it has been through study abroad programs aimed at enhancing foreign language fluency of students. According to The National Survey for Student Engagement (2007), "The amount of time one is abroad is not as important as whether a student has had such an experience" (p. 17). A review of the literature found that many community colleges have created or developed their own study abroad programs offering two types of international opportunities. Some programs offer and administer courses specifically through a study abroad program or international studies office. Other community colleges have joined a consortium with universities or private companies in the USA and abroad to pool resources and partner with host country universities or agencies.

Even with these partnership programs, the number one barrier for ethnic minority students to study abroad is still the financial hardship it brings to individuals and families. To combat this economic barrier, the US Department of State, Bureau of Educational and Cultural Affairs sponsors the Gilman International Scholarship Program in order to achieve a much higher rate of diversity in student participation (IIE 2010–2011). Although Gilman scholarships include students from four-year schools, the focus of the scholarship is on community college students. These scholarships work to diversify, not only the kinds of students who study abroad, but also the countries and regions where students would study, such as in developing nations.

METHODOLOGY

Community College Study Abroad Program Selection

We highlight five community college districts that have demonstrated success and have institutionalized study abroad through institutional or a faculty-led model. These programs are not necessarily the exemplars, nor are they the only ones offering students international opportunities to learn. Rather, we base their inclusion on the IIE Open Doors 2012–2013 report that ranked the top 20 programs in the USA. We reviewed the top 25 college/district websites and then narrowed selection to those sites that had a high number of ethnic minority students enrolled in a specific community college campus or as a community college district.

Because many of the study abroad programs did not ask students to identify their ethnicity in the study abroad application, we did not know if high numbers of ethnic minority students participated in study abroad. Instead, our data is based on the candor of the conversations from each of the program's directors. Part of the challenge in selecting colleges for inclusion here is that one could hypothesize that community colleges serving large numbers of ethnic minority students will, in turn, have proportional numbers who study abroad. However, that hypothesis may not be supported. There are many community colleges with a large population of ethnic minority students that do not have a study abroad program or there is minimal participation by students, and in particular ethnic minority students.

Data Collection

A two-pronged process was followed for data collection. First, we conducted a thorough archival data analysis of the programs' websites. The program text was extracted directly from these websites. Secondly, the program directors or designees were emailed or contacted by telephone and an interview was held in which they explained their respective programs. A summary of conversations from telephone interviews was reported with each of the study abroad program director or a college designee who may have been a faculty member. In addition, for one case, an in-person site visit and personal interview was conducted.

Each director or designee described his/her programs, key features, effective recruitment efforts, and challenges as well as recommendations they had to promote study abroad or international education programs. A particular focus of the interviews and analysis of the websites was that all of the community colleges selected did not keep accurate records or track the ethnic makeup of students in study abroad programs. Therefore, one may question how community colleges report ethnic data regarding study abroad to Open Doors or other agencies requesting information.

In order to provide consistency in the reporting of each of the community college case study we provide subheadings in the following areas: (1) Demographics, (2) Study Program Description, (3) Design and International Sites, and (4) Recruitment Practices.

Riverside Community College District (RCCD)

Demographics. RCCD is comprised of three community colleges (Riverside City College, Moreno Valley College, and Norco College). In fall of 2014, the total district enrollment for all programs was over 40,000. Although the district's mission does not reflect learning and teaching from a global perspective, it has a very diverse student body that reflects the surrounding population and workforce. In 2011, the student population was comprised of 27 % Caucasian, and 73 % ethnic minority students, 47 % of students Hispanic, 10 % African American, 8 % Asian/Pacific Islanders, and 8 % other ethnicities. (http://www.rccd.edu/services/studyabroad/Pages/index.aspx). According to data reported in Open Doors in the 2012–2013 academic year, 81 RCCD students studied abroad.

Program Description. The Riverside Study Abroad program has two full-time, district-funded positions: a director and an assistant director, as well as an assigned financial aid counselor. According to Jane Schall, Director of RCCD's, International/Study Abroad program, because of today's complex world and competitive job market, the decision to study abroad may be one of the best decisions students ever make. Most of their students who study abroad rate their experience as one of the most important of their undergraduate careers. All of the programs are designed to include projects, educational studies, and activities that encourage an individual to learn, understand, and care about the world beyond his or her community, and to transcend culturally conditioned, ethnocentric perspectives, perceptions and behaviors. The RCCD believes that meaningful international education not only increases one's knowledge; it also enhances one's wisdom and affinity with humanity.

Design and International Sites. Throughout the years, the RCCD commitment to international education has been reflected in a wide variety of programs and activities. Semester-long programs in Ireland, Italy, and England provided students with opportunities to make progress toward their general education and transferable courses' objectives. At the same time students were able to develop an understanding and appreciation for international issues. The RCCD's two-week Summer Study Tour program, offer students, as well as college faculty, staff, and members of the community, an opportunity to travel abroad in cultural excursions designed for all ages and professions. RCCD's summer educational programs in recent years have included journeys to the Czech Republic, Hungary, Italy, Greece, Turkey, Morocco, and Kenya.

RCCD has been at the front of the community college study abroad curve. Following Santa Barbara City College's pioneering efforts to provide study abroad in China, in 2010, the RCCD was the first community college system this century to offer a full semester program in China. In addition, according to program director Schall, in 2013 23 ethnically diverse students and three faculty members traveled to Japan on a two-week tour provided by the Japanese Consulate, again being the only community college in the nation to be included in this endeavor. A long-term benefit of these founding efforts has been that many former study abroad students have returned to their foreign study site to attend universities, obtain higher degrees, and/or to establish careers.

Recruitment Practices. Recruitment practices that RCCD employs for the outreach and recruitment of ethnic minority students include supporting students to complete their Free Application for Federal Student Aid (FAFSA) early in the process. Research shows that completing the application to subsidize travel (in other words, lack of finances) is the number one barrier as to why ethnic minority students are less likely to participate in study abroad programs. RCCD study abroad program has a designated financial aid counselor who specifically works with students to get financial aid. Another strategy that is used is "intentional recruitment" whereby informational sessions are provided when ethnic minority students' are gathered in groups out on the quad during class break, or in lunch areas. During this time they are asked and informed about study abroad. This "on the spot" recruitment strategy by the director or assistant director is employed to see if community college students have thought or know about study abroad opportunities and programs. This strategy targets a population who often does not make inquiries, seek, or stop by the international study abroad office for information. Many ethnic minority students have the perception that those types of programs are "not for me" and only for more affluent students (Jackson 2005).

Austin Community College (ACC)

Demographics. ACC is focused on student success and providing afford-able, flexible pathways to help students reach their education goals, learn new job skills, or advance their career. It has 11 campuses, and as of spring 2015, an enrollment of 39,474 students including 46.39 % Caucasian, 7.7 % Black, 28.83 % Hispanic, 4.92 % Asian, 1 % of both American Indian/Alaskan Native and Hawaiian Pacific Islander. According to data reported in Open Doors report in the 2012–2013 academic year data, 68 ACC studied abroad.

Program Description. According to William Hayden, Director of ACC Study Abroad, students can experience and learn from different cultures through the many types of study abroad opportunities provided. The study abroad office includes a full-time director and a half-time assistant direc-tor. There is a separate office called, the International Students Office, that works specifically with incoming foreign students.

Design and International Sites. Although ACC does not provide a full semester study abroad experience for students, short-term, 3–5 week courses are of great interest to students. These courses are conducted pri-marily in the summer.

ACC also supports its faculty by allocating $2000 funding for the development of study abroad courses, for the purposes of exploration for a study abroad course, as well as a one-year sabbatical leave. ACC has many unique study abroad courses such as American Sign Language where stu-dents provide interpretation during a one week Caribbean cruise. They also have from 10 to 15 different study abroad courses during the sum-mer, including vocational education courses from multiple disciplines. A joint summer study abroad program has been added as part of their hos-pitality and tourism program. ACC is also moving toward the integration of international courses with a math, science, engineering, and technology (STEM) focus.

Recruitment Practices. ACC's recruitment efforts include giving class presentations, posting flyers and posters throughout campus, speaking to students in different courses and on multiple campuses. A component of their program is allowing community members to participate in their short-term study abroad course. Another component is the development of partnerships with other universities that bring students to Austin from abroad for short-term courses in multiple disciplines, including tourism and hospitality.

The ethnic representation in study abroad courses average 65 % White, 30 % Hispanic, and 5 % other—Asian and African Americans. Based on Mr. Hayden's personal experience in directing the study abroad program, it appears that fewer African American students participate in study abroad. He reported that they either do not view study abroad as important, or have trepidation about leaving the USA since few in their families have traveled abroad. In comparison, Hispanics and other groups have families in their home country or their parents' home country, and therefore, may have traveled abroad for family trips. As expected, the challenges to recruiting ethnic minority students include the financial hardships students face, work responsibilities, and family obligations. ACC now provides more information through social media, particularly regarding financial aid as well as on scholarships for students. In addition, brochures advertising study abroad are in multiple languages to attract a more diverse student and community population. ACC is also utilizing their study abroad alumni to assist in recruitment efforts, in particular ethnic minority students.

City College of San Francisco (CCSF)

Demographics. Founded in 1935, California's City College of San Francisco has evolved into a multicultural, multicampus community college that is one of the largest in the country with 38,041 students enrolled during the 2013–2014 academic year. Their ethnic representation includes 29.84 % Asian, 22.37 % Hispanic, 25.26 Caucasian, 8.40 % African American, 5.58 % Filipino, and the others are American Indian/Native Alaskan or unknown. According to data reported in Open Doors report in the 2012–2013 academic year data, 116 CCSF students studied abroad.

Program Description. According to Jill Heffron, coordinator of study abroad at CCSF, there is a full-time coordinator and a part-time staff member. Heffron has been coordinator at CCSF study abroad for 20 years and has seen the program flourish throughout her tenure. This 2015–2016 academic year they no longer have a full semester study abroad program, but hope to re-establish it in the future. Their faculty-led programs are conducted only during the summer. When CCSF had semester study abroad programs, students tended to be younger and their parents paid for their participation, currently, CCSF has an older student population. Student participation in study abroad has been diverse, although low for Asian and Pacific Islander students when compared to the overall population. In the 2012 academic year the ethnic student participation was approximately 60 % White, 30 % Hispanic, 8 % Asian, and 2 % African American. In 2013, there were 138 students who studied abroad and the ethnic representation was 60 % White, 18 % Hispanic, 8 % Southeast/Asian, and 17 % African American.

According to the coordinator, there are several reasons why ethnic minority students' students do not participate in CCSF study abroad programs. These include lack of financial resources and aid, family responsibility, and an inability to leave for an entire semester. Therefore, only short-term study abroad options are viable for this segment of the population.

Design and International Sites. CCSF has been a leader in study abroad education since 1985. Thousands of CCSF students, faculty and staff, students from other colleges and universities, and citizens of the Bay Area and beyond have participated in their programs. The college offers short-term programs (summer and winter) in a variety of locations around the world. They also provide online resources about non-CCSF programs for students to study, work, and volunteer abroad. (http://www.ccsf.edu/en/educational-programs/school-and-departments/school-of-international-education-and-esl/study-abroad.html).

Recruitment Practices. CCSF's main recruiting strategy in attracting ethnic minority students is through personal outreach by "intentionally" targeting and speaking to ethnic minority students. Other forms of recruitment include traditional class presentations, faculty presentations, and alumni presentations. Students are highly encouraged to apply for scholarships, in particular the Gillman Scholarship, where students are required to write two essays plus conduct a follow-up project once they return to the college.

Maricopa Community College District (MCCD)

Demographics. The Maricopa Community College District (MCCD) is located in Arizona. According to the MCCD website (https://mcli.maricopa.edu/international) the district's mission states, "MCCD excels in teaching, learning, and empowering individuals to succeed in our local and global community." MCCD seeks to create an environment where teaching and learning is augmented and enhanced by international study and work opportunities for faculty and by student-centered educational opportunities that prepares students for successful participation in the global community.

According to data reported in Open Doors report in the 2012–2013 academic year, 106 MCCD students studied abroad. The ethnic representation included 53 % Caucasian, 22 % Hispanic, 7 % African American, 6 % Asian/Pacific Islander, 4 % American Indian/Alaskan Native, and 8 % other.

Program Description. Yvonne Schmidt, Project Director at Mesa Community College, (MCC) (part of the Maricopa Community College District) has one full-time, district-funded position. At this point MCC only provides short-term and summer (3–4 weeks) courses. They usually have about 100 students participating in multiple summer courses. Only MCC degree candidates can receive financial aid, and therefore, students are also encouraged to apply for the Gillman Grant and a local Maricopa Community College Grant that is available only to ethnic minority students.

Design and International Sites. Programs the college supports include Study Abroad, Global Forums, Internationalization of the Curriculum Workshops, Faculty Professional Development Abroad, International Partnerships, Student Global Leadership Training, and International Travel Review. In 2015, short-term courses traveled to Ireland, Mexico, Namibia, France and various European countries. Six program faculty, from different disciplines, led the courses.

Recruitment Practices. MCC's recruitment efforts include continuous class presentations, use of the web, social media, and direct student contact. All students have to complete a pre- and post-reflective essay as well as attend a mandatory pre-orientation meeting or workshop. Based on the director's experience in recruiting ethnic minority students, financial hardship and taking time away from work are the two major reasons ethnic minority students participate less in study abroad.

Miami Dade Community College (MDCC)

Demographics. Florida's Miami Dade Community College system website describes how it is one of the largest and most ethnically diverse colleges in the nation. It has seven campuses, two centers and more than 165,000 students from across the world. Miami Dade first opened its doors in the 1960s, amidst the strain of desegregation and the influx of thousands of Cuban refugees. Its ethnic makeup constitutes 71 %, Hispanic; 18 %, Black non-Hispanic, 7 % White non-Hispanic; and 4 %, other ethnicities. According to data reported in Open Doors report in the 2012–2013 academic year data, 200 MDCC students studied abroad. The Dade Community College system supports global awareness in a section of its core Mission Statement, as well as in one of its eight vision points (http://www.mdc.edu/main/about/mission_vision.aspx).

Program Description. MDCC provides comprehensive international experiences to its students through the Office of International Education (OIE) and its many support programs. OIE's mission is to actively promote international and intercultural understanding and to enrich the academic and cultural environment of MDCC by creating programs to sustain the exchange of people and ideas. The OIE vision statement states that MDCC (students, faculty, and staff) is a diverse community of learners who have a broad worldview, have an understanding and appreciation of other cultures, and actively practice global citizenship, as a result of the educational experiences offered by the OIE.

Design and International Sites. The Study Abroad office administers faculty-led programs in more than 30 countries. MDCC students are eligible for international study abroad by living and studying in more than 25 different of these 30 countries. MDCC also offers faculty-led study abroad programs in architecture, science, business, nursing, foreign languages, among others.

Recruitment Practices. Joanne Michaud, Program Manager for the OIE, stated that MDCC works to ensure that standards of quality are maintained that will best support their students while at college as well as in future endeavors. Their best form of recruitment is "Word of Mouth," either from a student who has participated in a program, or from a faculty member. The opportunity to hear of the experiences firsthand really plays a role in promoting a program.

MDCC serves a population consisting of a majority of underrepresented students. However, they do not require their students to provide ethnic affiliation on the program application. In order to minimize the challenges that students might have in applying to study abroad, students begin preparing for their program abroad at least a year in advance. This is done in order to ensure that they are aware of all the costs and steps related to completing a program successfully. This not only relates to ethnic minority students or any particular group; rather, all students are always actively searching for scholarships to help fund their programs (email communication, April 17, 2015). The college also connects study abroad with history and ethnic studies courses with the ethnicity of the population (Latino/a students with parent or grand/great grandparent home country). To recruit ethnic minority students they include innovative practices supporting ethnic minority students by focusing on State Student Support Services (EOP & S), and one of the Federal Trio Programs (Special Support Service).

EFFECTIVE STUDY ABROAD PROGRAM PRACTICES

Several effective study abroad program practices emerged from the data collected. Each community college district supports global awareness in its mission or vision statements. Therefore, it lets the school community and students it serves know that internationalization is valued. Each study abroad program at the five community colleges had at least one full-time director or coordinator and the district allocates funds because they are viewed as an important position. The position provides continuity as well as advocacy for the program. Each program was pro-active in encouraging students to apply for the Gillman scholarships that helped students with the number one reason as to why they do not participate in study abroad—that is, financial reasons.

Other effective general practices in promoting study abroad in those programs that have been in existence for many years is that they created and developed excellent partnerships with host universities as well as with local agencies, organizations, schools, the community, and with host families. In order to prepare community college students for the intercultural experience, many colleges have an application procedure with requirements to encourage students to make a commitment to participating in the study abroad program. In many cases, students undergo extensive preparation for the cultural and educational experience. Students are required to attend study abroad orientation meetings and in some cases parents are invited or required to attend in order to support their sons and daughters. For numerous students, and in particular ethnic minority students, this is the first time they will have traveled abroad. Several programs have students attend take a course or workshop where they learn about program requirements, learn about the host country, its history, its customs, its people, and study their educational system.

DISCUSSION

For these five community colleges the most effective program specific practices that assisted them in the recruitment of ethnic minority students include (1) personal attention-making "intentional-target specific" ethnic minority group/student contacts, either individually or making presentations in specific courses such as ethnic studies course; (2) assistance in applying for financial assistance—the community colleges made sure ethnic minority students had assistance in completing their federal financial aid application as well as provided information on other available scholarships such as the Gillman scholarship or other community/district scholarships (IIE 2015); (3) targeted recruitment. Colleges make an effort to convince ethnic minority students of the advantages of studying abroad by connecting the experience to their personal and professional growth aspirations of becoming global citizens of the world. Alternative course design includes types of study abroad courses designed met different type of student's needs such as including both short-term and full-semester study abroad courses. This type of design allowed community college students with less financial resources or with employment or family commitments with greater potential to participate. In some cases, colleges made it a point to have study abroad courses in countries where the financial incidental costs for students are less and also integrating vocational education courses and not only degree required courses. These community colleges went beyond providing an educational tourism approach to both recruitment efforts and in program course offerings.

If we are to prepare community college students to be competitive in a global arena and as global citizens, community college campuses must not only provide study abroad programs (as the numbers of students participating is minimal and even more by ethnic minority students when compared to the general population), but colleges must also internationalize their curriculum and provide other forms of rich international learning experiences. This means community college faculty teaching in degree or non-degree programs must themselves be global learners and global citizens in order to promote and model internationalization efforts (Global Teacher Education 2013).

Community colleges in the USA enroll a more diverse student population than four-year institutions, as well as a greater immigrant population. As stated earlier, the need to prepare culturally proficient community college students to become national as well as global citizens is imperative.

However, current and prospective community college instructors and administrators themselves need to be comfortable as citizens of the world (Asia Society 2014; Quezada 2014; Quezada & Cordeiro 2015). Therefore, study abroad can be one method for our ethnic minority students to attain cultural and global competencies, in many cases this includes language competency (Stewart 2012; West 2012).

In summary, we learned from the community colleges that they should consider initiating new or improving current study abroad or international type programs and experiences for students at their local community college, and that it is worth initiating one if a program does not exist. Of most importance, we learned that improving the participation of ethnic minority community college students in international education or study abroad programs is a must if we are to provide a level playing field in order for them to compete in today's global economy and to become globally competent citizens.

REFERENCES

American Council on Education (2008). *College-bound students' interest in study abroad and other international learning activities.* Washington, DC: American Council on Education. p. 21

Asia Society. (2014). *Teacher profiles: Qualities of a 21st century teacher.* http://asiasociety.org/education/international-studies-schools-network/teacher-profile

Comps, David (2007). What we know about diversity in education abroad: State of the research. In C. A. Herrin, S. Dadzie, & S. A. MacDonald (Eds.), *Proceedings for the colloquium on diversity in education abroad: How to change the picture* (pp. 48–52). Washington, DC: Academy for Educational Development.

Forum on Education Abroad (2009). *Standards of good practice for short-term education abroad programs.* Carlisle, PA: Dickinson College.

Global Teacher Education. (2013). *What is global competence?.* http://www.globalteachereducation.org/what-global-competence

Heyl, John D., & McCarthy, JoAnne (2003). International education and teacher preparation in the U.S. Paper Presented at the National Conference for Global Challenges and U.S. Higher Education: National Needs and Policy Implications. Duke University.

Institute of International Education. (2014). Open doors 2014: International students in the United States and study abroad by American students are at all-time high. Institute of International Education, Inc. New York, NY.

Institute of International Education. (2015). *Supporting non-traditional students to study and intern abroad.* Gillman Web Symposium Series. http://www.iie.org/giman

Institute of International Education. (2014). *The benefits of studying abroad*. http://www.iie.org/en/Research-and-Publications/Open-Doors

Institute for the International Education of Students. (2010–2011). *The benefits of studying abroad*. https://www.iesabroad.org/IES/Student/alumniSurveyResultsStudents.html

Jackson, Marylin J. (2005, Fall). Breaking the barriers to overseas study for students of color and minorities. *IIE Networker*, 16–18. http://www.iienetwork.org

Longview Foundation. (2008). *Teacher preparation for the global age – The imperative for change*. Longview Foundation for Education in World Affairs and International Understanding, Inc. Silver Spring, MD.

Mckeown, Joshua S. (2009). *The first time effect: The impact of study abroad on college student intellectual development*. Albany, NY: State University of New York.

Mullens, Jo B., & Cuper, Pru (2012). *Fostering global citizenship through faculty-led international programs*. Charlotte, NC: Information Age Publishing, Inc.

National Academy of Sciences. (2010). *Rising above the gathering storm, revisited: Rapidly approaching category 5*. Washington, DC: The National Academies Press. http://www.aps.org/policy/reports/upload/rags-revisited.PDF

National Association of Foreign Student Advisors. (2010). *The changing landscape of higher education*. Washington, DC: Association of International Educators.

National Survey of Student Engagement. (2007). *Experiences that matter: Enhancing student learning and success*. http://nsse.iub.edu/NSSE_2007_Annual_Report/docs/withhold/NSSE_2007_Annual_Report.pdf

Omoregie, Norah (2007). The globally competent teacher in secondary level education. Education, 128(1), 3–9.

Quezada, Reyes L. (2014). *Internationalization of teacher education: Creating global competent teachers and teacher educators for the 21st. Century*. UK: Routledge.

Quezada, Reyes L., & Cordeiro, Paula (2015). *Internationalization in teacher education in the U.S.: Innovative programs and practices to meet the global challenges of tomorrow's schools*. New York: Rowman and Littlefield.

Quezada, Reyes L., & Cordeiro, Paula (2007). Internationalizing colleges of education: Educating teachers for global awareness. *Teacher Education Quarterly*, 34(1), 3–8.

Raby, Rosalind L., & Valeau, Edward J. (2007). Community college international education: Looking back to forecast the future. *New Direction for Community Colleges*, No. 138 (pp. 5–14). San Francisco, CA: Jossey-Bass. doi:10.1002/cc.276.

Raby, Rosalind L., & Rhodes, Gary (2004). *Barriers to student participation in California community colleges*. Sacramento: Chancellor's Office of the California Community Colleges.

Stewart, Vivian (2012). *A world-class education: Learning from international models of excellence and innovation.* Alexandria, VA: ASCD.

Sweeney, Karyn (2013, Fall). Inclusive excellence and underrepresentation of students of color in study abroad. *Frontiers: The Interdisciplinary Journal of Study Abroad 23*, 1–21.

West, Charlotte (2012). *Toward globally competent pedagogy.* NAFSA: Association of International Educators. www.nafsa.org/epubs

Whissemore, Tabitha (2012, August/September). Efforts to internationalize community college campuses must improve. *Community College Journal, 83*(1), 8–9.

White House. (2009). *President Obama's speech to joint session on Congress.* http://www.whitehouse.goc/the_press_office/Remarks-of-President-Barack-Obama-Address-to-joint-Session-of-Congress/

Zhang, Yi (2011). CSCC review series essay. Education abroad in the U.S. Community Colleges. *Community College Review, 39*(2), 181–200. doi:10.117/0091552111404552.

Community College Study Abroad and Implications for Student Success: Comparing California and New Jersey Community Colleges

Gary M. Rhodes, Janice M. Thomas,
Rosalind Latiner Raby, Amparo G. Codding,
and Andrea Lynch

G.M. Rhodes (✉)
International Education, California State University at Dominguez Hills, Torrence, CA, USA

J.M. Thomas
International Education Center, Brookdale Community College, Brookdale, CA, USA

R.L. Raby
Educational Leadership and Policy Studies, Michael D. Eisner College of Education, California Colleges for International Education

College of Humanities and Sciences, Southern California Campus, University of Phoenix, Costa Mesa, CA, USA

A.G. Codding
Bergen Community College, Bergen, NJ, USA

A. Lynch
Business and Technology and Study Abroad, Mercer County Community College, Mercer County, NJ, USA

© The Editor(s) (if applicable) and The Author(s) 2016   281
R.L. Raby, E.J. Valeau (eds.), *International Education at Community Colleges*, DOI 10.1057/978-1-137-53336-4_20

Introduction

The percentage of community college students who complete a program to earn a degree or certificate is less than 50 % and the time it takes most community college students to complete their program is generally longer than three years (AACC 2015). Research shows that when specific programmatic changes are introduced to the community college environment there is evidence for success (Crosta 2013). The California Community College Student Outcomes Abroad Research Project (CCC SOAR) conducted a multivariate regression analysis on students who studied abroad and those who did not to see if the programmatic change of studying abroad influenced student success (Raby et al. 2014). Bergen Community College and Brookdale Community College in New Jersey used a variation of the CCC SOAR methodology to assess the impact of study abroad on student success (Thomas et al. 2015). The importance of this study is that by using a similar process in three different contexts there is an increased reliability in the findings. The ensuing analysis is significant because it adds to the growing body of literature which supports the positive impact of study abroad on student success:

Community College Student Success and Study Abroad

Community College and Student Success

Community colleges are increasing student success by introducing new curricular and co-curricular initiatives into their colleges. Examples include control of age of entrance (Calcagno et al. 2007), control of initial enrollment intensity (Stratton et al. 2006), and frequency with which students access student services (McClenney et al. 2012). Each programmatic change has resulted in varying levels of impact on student success.

Study Abroad as a Form of Academic Engagement

College-impact models, such as Astin's Theory of Student Involvement (1984), Tinto's Theory of Academic and Social Integration (2010), and Pascarella's Model for Assessing Change (1985) identify environmental conditions that strongly impact student learning. The greater the student engagement, the greater the potential for achieving learning goals that lead to positive college outcomes. Study abroad not only engages students (Gonyea 2008), but also is a high-impact college experience that leads to significant personal and intellectual growth (Kuh 2008). Mullens and Cuper (2012) found that "the amount of time one is abroad is not as important as whether a student has had such an experience" (p. 17).

Community College Study Abroad and Student Success Measures

Empirical research shows specific benefits that result from studying abroad by community college students in terms of academic knowledge gained (Amani 2011), personal skills and self-confidence development for students of color (Willis 2012), and increased cross-cultural awareness (Arden-Ogle 2009). The literature shows that community college students regard studying abroad as an opportunity of a lifetime (Drexler and Campbell 2011; Raby 2008).

RESEARCH QUESTION

Research Question. Is student participation in study abroad associated with increased markers of student success?

METHODOLOGIES

The CCC SOAR study used an unadjusted raw data analysis and a multivariate regression analysis on cohorts of first-time California community college students from fall 2004 to fall 2009. Each cohort was tracked from entrance to completion for a three-year consecutive sequence. Since students self-select into study abroad, statistical adjustment through Poisson regression helped to statistically control for differences and eliminated confounding variables that were identified by the California Community College Chancellor's Office Research Unit as being statistically associated with moderate academic achievement and attainment. Outcome variables examined success as tracked throughout the first three years of attendance flagged at one-year and two-year retention. Permission was given to the Research and Planning Group for California Community Colleges (RP Group) to obtain data from California Community College Chancellor's Office Management Information System (COMIS), a longitudinal student data system that identifies student characteristics, student course activity and outcomes, and course inventories (Willett et al. 2013).

Bergen community college and Brookdale community college in New Jersey used a variation on the CCC SOAR methodology and tracked cohorts from entrance to completion for a three-year consecutive sequence. At Brookdale, the director of International Education worked with the office of Planning and Institutional Effectiveness to identify first-time students (full- and part-time, degree and non-degree) who had studied abroad for academic credit from fall 2001 to fall 2010. These students were compared to first-time students who did not study abroad along the following student success indicators: 1st year and 2nd year retention, completion of college-level Math and English, transfer rate and graduation rate. The Center for Institutional Effectiveness at Bergen identified all students who participated in study abroad programs from spring 2003 to summer 2014 and provided an analysis of participant profiles that included demographic information, program majors and success indicators of 1st year and 2nd year retention, graduation, cumulative Grade Point Average (GPA), and cumulative credits earned. A follow-up analysis focused on the three-year graduation rates of first-time, full-time degree seeking students in entering cohorts from fall 2001 to fall 2011 to compare study abroad students with students who did not study abroad.

Samples

The CCC SOAR sample included all first-time students from 16 California community college districts, which included 36 colleges. The sample included a total of 476,708 students, of whom 1906 did study abroad and 474,802 who did not. Brookdale's sample included a total of 221 study abroad students and a comparison group of 40,319 who did not study abroad. Bergen's initial analysis included 51 study abroad students, with no comparison on success indicators to the general population. Follow-up analysis yielded 42 study abroad students and a comparison group of 25,186 who did not study abroad.

Methodology Limitations

There are noted limitations to this comparative study. First, the CCC SOAR data is compiled from only 16 of the 72 California community college districts. Second, both CCC SOAR and New Jersey samples include only first-time college students who represent only one population of community college students. Third, the New Jersey colleges did not subject their samples to multivariate regression methods and as such were not able to consider other intervening control factors other than study abroad. Finally, the three studies were conducted independently and in some cases measured different variables which make it more challenging to conduct precise comparisons.

RESULTS

Data provides a context for understanding that study abroad is a contributing factor for community college student success.

Descriptive Statistical Data

Students in both the CCC SOAR and New Jersey studies have similar profiles. The majority of study abroad students were women. Brookdale reported a higher percentage of male study abroad participants (42 %) compared to 33 % for Bergen and 34 % for CCC SOAR. Age at the time of the study abroad experience was difficult to capture for all studies. At Brookdale, the average age of study abroad students in the first term of enrollment was 19.1 compared to 21.5 in the non-study abroad group. Bergen measured the current age of former study abroad participants and determined that 80 % were between the ages of 20 and 30. In the CCC SOAR sample, based on their age in their first term, the median age of study abroad students was 20 years old, 8 % were 55 or older, and 42 % were an average of 28 years of age. Ninety-one percent of study abroad students at Brookdale were on degree programs compared to 82 % of the general student population and 83 % of study abroad students were full-time as compared to 70 % of the general student population. The majority of study abroad students in all three studies were white. Brookdale sent slightly more Hispanic students abroad (9.5 %) than were enrolled in the general population (9.0 %). Table S9.1 profiles gender and race of study abroad and non-study abroad students.

Successful Completion of Transfer Level English and Math Within Three Years

CCC SOAR showed that students who studied abroad had a statistically higher rate of successfully completing a transfer level English and/ or Math course within three years of enrollment. The data showed that

Table S9.1   Gender and race profiles

Race and ethnicity	Bergen Community College		Brookdale Community College		CCC SOAR	
	Study abroad	Non-study abroad	Study abroad	Non-study abroad	Study abroad	Non-study abroad
Female	67 %	NA	58 %	51 %	66 %	49 %
Male	33 %	NA	42 %	49 %	34 %	51 %
White	57 %	NA	84.2 %	73.2 %	52 %	32 %
Hispanic	29 %	NA	9.5 %	9.0 %	21 %	26 %
African-American	0	NA	2.3 %	9.5 %	3 %	10 %
Asian/Native Hawaiian/ Pacific Islander	12 %	NA	1.8 %	4.4 %	10 %	17 %
Filipino	–	–	–	–	1 %	3 %
American Indian/ Alaska Native	0	NA	0	.3 %	1 %	1 %
Multiracial	0	NA	NA	NA	.5 %	NA
Do Not Know	2 %	NA	2.3 %	3.6 %	13 %	11 %

even students whose first college English or Math course was classified as remedial and who studied abroad successfully completed a transfer level English course at a rate 1.08 times greater and a Math course at a rate 1.19 times greater than those who did not study abroad. For Hispanic students, the number who completed a transfer level English course was 2.6 times greater than those who did not go abroad to study. Brookdale found comparable results in which 88.2 % of students who studied abroad completed college-level English as compared to 58.1 % of the general population and 67.9 % of students who studied abroad completed college-level Math as compared to 32.6 % of the general population.

Number of Transferrable Units Completed Within Three Years

The CCC SOAR study showed that students who studied abroad completed 12.46 additional transferrable units within three years of college enrollment when compared with students who did not study abroad. This is essentially an additional full-time semester's worth of units compared to their non-study abroad counterparts. At Bergen, students who enrolled in study abroad courses had mean cumulative degree credits of 61.4 which did not include remedial credits.

Effect of Study Abroad on Transferring Within Three Years

The CCC SOAR data revealed that students who studied abroad had a 47 % greater likelihood to transfer to a four-year institution and that Hispanic students had a 54 % higher transfer enrollment if they studied abroad compared to Hispanic students in the sample who did not study abroad. Brookdale had comparable results as 51.6 % of students who studied abroad transferred to a four-year university as compared to 23.7 % of the general student population.

Earning a Degree or Certificate Within Three Years

The CCC SOAR study showed that students who studied abroad earned a certificate or a degree within three years at a rate 1.35 times greater than their peers who did not study abroad. For Hispanic students, the gain was 2.0 times greater than Hispanic students who did not study abroad.

At Bergen, 55 % of study abroad students versus 14 % of non-study abroad students graduated within three years. Of the students who studied abroad, 61 % graduated with a degree or certificate within three years. Of those who did not graduate within the year following their study abroad semester, 53 % were retained to the following year. Of those who did not graduate within the two years following their study abroad semester, 29 % were retained to the following year.

At Brookdale, indicators that study abroad had a positive impact on student success were also evident. The one-year retention rate for study abroad students was 91 % as compared to 57.7 % for the general student population. The two-year retention for study abroad students was 52 % as compared to 35.5 % for the general student population. The graduation rate within three years for study abroad students was 47.1 % as compared to 15.4 % for the general student population. Table S9.2 examines the comparative markers for success.

DISCUSSION

The comparison of data from California and New Jersey community colleges raises important questions about the role that community college study abroad has in meeting the completion agenda. Data shows that first-time community college students who study abroad excel on a range of success measures when compared to those who did not study abroad in the same time frame. Analysis from raw data without regression and from multivariate regression shows impact in terms of persistence, completion of English and Math requirements for transfer, transfer units completed, ability to transfer, and graduation. When subject to regression analysis, the impacts are still statistically significant. A future step is to apply to the New Jersey community colleges a multivariate regression analysis to determine if the noted impacts are still significant after controlling for other potentially intervening factors. In addition, as more community colleges apply the CCC SOAR methodology, a better understanding of the depth of impact of study abroad on retention and success will emerge.

Studying abroad influences life choices, especially when those programs emphasize international learning outcomes. Raby et al. (2014), using the CCC SOAR qualitative data found that students in self-reporting reflections noted that they were more engaged in their college studies after studying abroad than before they left and that the mere act of participation in study abroad was identified as a defining element that elevated later success. Data from Mercer County Community College in New Jersey also shows that the type of class activities experienced during study abroad can deepen commitment through purposeful tasks, extended and substantive interactions with faculty and peers, defined interaction with people who are different than themselves, application of what students learn in different settings, and life changing experiences. Harper and Quaye (2009) note that the "participation in educationally effective practices, both inside and outside the classroom, leads to a range of measurable outcomes" (p. 3). Our study shows that when college-impact models, like study abroad, are purposefully planned and when students are placed in cohorts that include reflection as a learning activity, success often occurs. Although community college study abroad is a purposefully planned college program, additional research is needed on the impact from implementing intentional efforts to support student success in pre-departure, while abroad, and re-entry activities. It is the contention of the authors that such intentional efforts will significantly enhance overall student success gained by the study abroad experience.

CONCLUSION

Community colleges have long emphasized open access. However, it is also known that not everyone who starts at a community college completes their educational program. The Community College Completion Report (AACC 2015) articulates a commitment by six national commu-

Table S9.2 Comparative success markers

Outcome within 3 years	Bergen Community College			Brookdale Community College[a]			CCC SOAR—w/out regression[b]			CCC SOAR with regression[c]		
	SA	Non-SA	Difference	SA	Non-SA	Difference	SA	Non-SA	Difference	SA	Non-SA	Difference
Completion of English level	–	–	–	82.2 %	58.1 %	24.1 %	77.3	29.6 %	47.6 %	16.6 %	15.4 %	1.2 %
Completion of math level	–	–	–	67.9 %	32.6 %	35.3 %	46.6	17.6 %	29.0 %	7.6 %	6.4 %	1.2 %
1 year retention	61 %	–	–	91 %	57.7 %	33.3 %	88.7 %	57.7 %	31.0 %	62.4 %	55.9 %	6.5 %
2 year retention	–	–	–	52 %	35.5 %	16 %	72.0 %	39.7 %	32.3 %	45.0 %	36.5 %	8.6 %
Transfer units completed	61.4 %	–	–	–	–	–	48.6	24	24.6	37.6	25.1	12.5
Transferred to 4-years	–	–	–	51.6 %	23.7 %	27.9 %	39.9 %	14.4 %	25.5 %	11.8 %	8.0 %	3.8 %
Earned degree or certificate	55 %	14 %	41 %	47.1 %	15.4 %	31.7 %	16.6 %	5.3 %	11.3 %	3.6 %	2.7 %	0.9 %

[a] Brookdale Community College raw number comparisons (without regression)

[b] CCC SOAR raw number comparisons (without regression)

[c] CCC SOAR multivariate regression

nity college organizations to boost student completion by 50 % by 2020. While the report does not identify study abroad as a particular strategy, it does call for the need to improve student engagement. The findings of the CCC SOAR and New Jersey Community Colleges research show that community college study abroad can contribute to the completion agenda as a result of student engagement.

This comparative study shows that study abroad shares many of the defined elements that promote academic engagement and success and as such has implications to community college policy. The data suggests a statistically significant increase in academic achievement for students who study abroad and suggests that these programs be recognized as part of a mix of strategies that the college adopts specifically to counter historic achievement gaps. To maximize the potential to make a positive impact, colleges need to utilize the potential of study abroad to its fullest capability by ensuring the availability of programs, designing intentional support by staff and faculty and ensuring that adequate logistical, human, and financial resources are in place. In doing so, as colleges more broadly recognize study abroad as an academic program, it will lead to enhance overall learning and that can lead to academic persistence and success.

REFERENCES

Amani, Monija (2011). *Study abroad decision and participation at community colleges: Influential factors and challenges from the voices of students and coordinators.* Unpublished doctoral dissertation. George Washington University, Washington, DC.

American Association of Community Colleges. (2015). Community College Completion: Progress toward goal of 50% increase. Washington, DC: AACC Press.   www.aacc.nche.edu/AboutCC/Trends/Documents/completion_report_05212015.pdf

Arden-Ogle, Ellen (2009). *Study abroad and global competence: Exemplary community college programs which foster elements of achievement.* Unpublished doctoral dissertation, Oregon State University, Corvallis, OR.

Astin, Alexander W. (1984). Student involvement: A developmental theory for higher education. *Journal of College Student Personnel, 25*(4), 297–308.

Calcagno, Juan Carlos, Crosta, Peter, Bailey, Thomas, & Jenkins, Davis (2007). Does age of entrance affect community college completion probabilities? Evidence from a discrete-time hazard model. *Educational Evaluation and Policy Analysis, 29*(3), 218–235.

Crosta, Peter M. (2013, July). Trends in enrollment patterns among community college students. *Community College Research Center Analytics*. New York: Columbia University. http://ccrc.tc.columbia.edu/

Drexler, Devi S., & Campbell, Dale F. (2011). Student development among community college participants in study abroad programs. *Community College Journal of Research & Practice*, 35(8), 608–619.

Gonyea, Robert M. (2008, November). *The impact of study abroad on senior year engagement*. Paper presented at the Annual Meeting of the Association for the Study of Higher Education, Jacksonville, FL. Retrieved March 10, 2012 from http://cpr.iub.edu/uploads/Gonyea_StudyAbroad.pdf

Harper, Shaun R., & Quaye, Stephen J. (2009). Beyond sameness, with engagement and outcomes for all: An introduction. In Shaun R. Harper & Stephen J. Quaye (Eds.), *Student engagement in higher education: Theoretical perspectives and practical approaches for diverse populations* (pp. 1–15). New York, NY: Routledge.

Kuh, George D. (2008). *High-impact educational practices: A brief overview*. Washington, DC: American Association of Colleges and Universities. http://www.aacu.org/leap/hip.cfm

McClenney, Kay C. Marti, Nathan, & Adkins, Courtney 2012. Student engagement and student outcomes: Key findings from *CCSSE* validation research. http://www.ccsse.org/aboutsurvey/docs/CCSSE%20Validation%20Summary.pdf

Mullens, JoBeth, & Cuper, Pru (2012). *Fostering global citizenship through faculty-led international programs*. Charlotte, NC: Information Age Publishing.

Pascarella, Ernest T. (1985). Students' affective development within the college environment. *Journal of Higher Education*, 56(6), 650–663.

Raby, Rosalind Latiner (2008). *Meeting America's global education challenge: Expanding education abroad at U.S. community colleges*. Institute of International Education Study Abroad White Paper Series 3 (September 2008). New York: Institute for International Education Press.

Raby, Rosalind Latiner, Rhodes, Gary M., & Biscarra, Albert (2014). Community college study abroad: Implications for student success. *Community College Journal of Research and Practice*, 38(2-3), 174–183.

Stratton, Leslie S., O'Toole, Dennis M., & Wetzel, James N. (2006). *Are the factors affecting dropout behavior related to initial enrollment intensity for college undergraduates?* (IZA Working Paper #1951). Bonn, Germany: Institute for the Study of Labor. Retrieved from http://ssrn.com/abstract=880426

Thomas, Janice M., Codding, Amparo & Lynch, Andrea (2015). *Moving from a culture of anecdote to a culture of evidence: Assessing the impact of international education programs*. Presentation at Community Colleges for International Development (CCID) Annual Conference, Newport Beach, CA.

Tinto, Vincent (2010). From theory to action: Exploring the institutional conditions for student retention. *Higher Education: Handbook of Theory and Research, 25*(2), 51–89.

Willett, Terrance, Pelligrin, Nathan, & Cooper, Darla (2013). *Study abroad impact technical report.* Berkeley, CA: RP Group.

Willis, Tasha Y. (2012) *Rare but there: An intersectional exploration of the experiences and outcomes of Black women who studied abroad through community college programs.* Unpublished doctoral dissertation. California State University, Long Beach.

Transformative Learning Through Education Abroad: A Case Study of a Community College Program

Ashley Brenner

INTRODUCTION

Identified as a "high-impact" educational activity (Kuh 2008), study abroad is recognized as an integral component of the American undergraduate experience. Over 85 % of American universities currently provide some sort of study abroad opportunity to their students (Whalen 2008). Despite the pervasiveness of such programs, in the 2012–2013 academic year, community college students comprised only 2 % of American study abroad participants (Institute of International Education 2013).

To accommodate their students' needs and foster greater participation, community colleges typically offer short-term rather than long-term education abroad programs (Frost and Raby 2009). The duration of a long-term program is one academic or calendar year whereas a mid-length program is one semester or one to two quarters. Short-term programs are considered those lasting less than eight weeks (Institute of International Education 2009). I dub the program in this study "very short-term" because of its two-week duration.

A. Brenner (✉)
Community College of Philadelphia, Philadelphia, PA, USA

© The Editor(s) (if applicable) and The Author(s) 2016   293
R.L. Raby, E.J. Valeau (eds.), *International Education at
Community Colleges*, DOI 10.1057/978-1-137-53336-4_21

Although a substantial body of research delineates the impact of studying abroad for undergraduates, most of this research has focused on students at four-year institutions. Considerably fewer studies have documented the study abroad experiences of community college students, who comprise a growing portion of the college-going population. Furthermore, most of the research conducted on short-term study abroad programs, whether at two-year or four-year institutions, investigates programs whose duration exceeds one month (Jones et al. 2012).

Dwyer (2004) posits that "more is better" in regard to program length, arguing that thoughtfully planned programs should last at least six weeks. However, as the participants in this study asserted, six weeks would be an unrealistic duration for them to study abroad particularly because of financial constraints. Dwyer also suggests that whether the positive outcomes associated with longer study abroad programs "would hold for the increasingly popular 1-5 week programs is unknown" (p. 161). Thus, the current study aimed to address this void by investigating a two-week program.

Theoretical Context

To understand how community college students make sense of their experiences abroad, this research utilized Kiely's (2005) transformative learning model for service-learning as a lens. Developed from investigating the experiences of students engaged in week-long service-learning programs, Kiely's model comprises five learning processes: contextual border crossing, dissonance, personalizing, processing, and connecting.

Contextual border crossing encompasses four contextual dimensions—personal, structural, historical, and programmatic components—that can promote or restrict transformative learning. Dissonance refers to the discrepancy between a participant's viewpoint and experience of the new context. According to Kiely, low-intensity dissonance, such as trying to communicate in another language, often invokes instrumental or communicative learning that facilitates a participant's adaptation to the new environment. High-intensity dissonance, such as encountering extreme poverty, triggers stronger reactions from students and compels them to reconsider their prior frames of reference.

Moreover, Kiely's notion of personalizing underscores the role that emotions play in shaping learning. Cognitive processing of one's experience occurs formally and informally through social and individual reflection. Connecting, an affective element, involves students forging relationships with host country community members and program participants to empathize with others' challenges and understand disparate perspectives.

Although the program in this case study did not have a service-learning component, Kiely's transformative learning model for service-learning offered a useful lens for investigating transformational learning processes. Kiely developed this framework to understand short-term immersive international experience, in other words, a context with numerous parallels to this study abroad program. Furthermore, researchers have focused on the outcomes rather than processes of transformative learning, resulting in a "theoretical 'black box' regarding the contextual and process mechanisms" that promote learning (p. 5). By enabling a finer analysis of factors and their interaction, Kiely's model discourages researchers from ascribing learning to nebulous concepts such as culture shock or socioeconomic dissonance, which conceals the complex relationship among context, dissonance, and learning.

Moreover, Kiely's theoretical framework provided analytical power to leverage due to its emphasis on non-reflective modes of learning. The model's "identification of a dialectical relationship among non-reflective learning processes of personalizing and connecting and rational forms of learning entailed in processing" underscores the essential role that affective and visceral elements play in promoting or inhibiting transformative learning (Kiely 2005, p. 15). Furthermore, this insight "counters the dominant reflective tradition and Western cultural bias embedded in Mezirow's (1991, 2000) model," which privilege rational forms of learning and undervalue non-cognitive learning processes (p. 15). Particularly as formal reflection did not compromise a key component of this program, the students engaged in and experienced myriad non-reflective forms of learning, which supported their transformative learning.

Definition of Key Terms

This study examined how participants' biographies shaped their perceptions of their experiences abroad. One's *biography* envelopes what Kiely (2005) identifies as the personal aspects of contextual border crossing; in this sense, *biography* includes "personality traits, social roles, professional background, knowledge, skills, beliefs, values, interests, needs, learning styles, expectations, motivations, desires, fears, and sense of efficacy" (p. 9). In other words, *biography* refers to the participant's life experiences, assumptions, and beliefs that shape his or her frame of reference and interpretations of studying abroad.

In foregrounding the role of contextual qualities in shaping learning, this research relies on Kiely's transformative learning model as it provides insight on "how the relationship among at least four major contextual factors (e.g., program characteristics, historical relationships, personal biographies, and structural dimensions) affects the type, intensity, and duration of dissonance and the kinds of learning that result" (p. 15). Drawing on Mezirow's work, Kiely identifies three forms of learning: communicative, instrumental, and transformative. *Communicative learning* entails understanding the meaning that another individual conveys in regard to both concrete and abstract matters such as emotions, beliefs, and ethics. *Instrumental learning* involves attaining and applying knowledge and skills to more efficaciously complete tasks and solve problems (Mezirow 2000). Thirdly, *transformational learning*, involves the shifting of perspectives, for instance, in regard to spiritual, political, or moral dimensions. Kiely (2005) notes, "The ideal end result of transformational learning is that one is empowered by learning to be more socially responsible, self-directed, and less dependent on false assumptions" (p. 7).

According to Kiely, low-intensity dissonance, such as trying to communicate in another language, often invokes instrumental or communicative learning that facilitates a participant's adaptation to the new environment. High-intensity, such as encountering extreme poverty, triggers stronger reactions from students and compels them to reconsider their prior frames of reference. In this sense, high-intensity dissonance fosters enduring learning as students try to reconcile contradictions and make sense of social and economic injustices.

Program Component

Participants. Bannockburn Community College (BCC), a pseudonym to protect the identity of those involved, is the site for this study and is located in a large mid-Atlantic city. Seventeen participants went on the 2013 Peru program including eight students, seven BCC faculty participants, and two faculty leaders. The sample for this study included all eight BCC students. As Table S10.1 shows, the students hailed from diverse backgrounds, particularly in regard to age, race, educational attainment, and prior international experience.

BCC offered seven scholarships to Peru. Students on scholarship paid tuition and a $750 program fee, which included airfare. Edith was the only non-scholarship student, so she paid the full program cost. Although

Table S10.1 Demographic information for student participants

Name	Age	Gender	Race	Status at BCC	Degree(s) obtained
Alyssa	21	Female	Black	Graduate in May 2013	AA in Liberal Arts
Alan	21	Male	White	Current Student	High School Diploma
Brian	25	Male	White	Current Student	High School Diploma
Edith	78	Female	White	Continuing Education Student	ABD in German; MA in German; BA in Political Science
Cara	25	Female	Black and White	Graduated in May, 2013	BA in Business Management; AA in Culture, Science and Technology
James	25	Male	White	Current Student	High school diploma
Loren	24	Female	Black	Transferring to four-year university	High school diploma
Sebastia	19	Male	Latino	Current student	High school diploma

she could afford the program, Edith almost could not participate because she needed to take care of "a husband who's sinking rapidly into dementia and old age frailty" (Edith pre-program, May 15, 2013).

Seven BCC faculty members participated in the program as participants and intermixed with the students for the classes, homestays, and activities. The college required each of these faculty members to make a $300 donation to subsidize the students' travel. BCC's International Center director explained, "It is unusual for us to accept so many participants who are not students, but their required donation will help us to fund our study-abroad programs" (personal communication, November 18, 2012). Although I interviewed the program's faculty leaders, I did not interview the faculty participants; thus, the additional faculty participants were excluded from this study's analysis.

Two BCC faculty members co-led the program. Maura, a part-time faculty member in the History department, taught Interdisciplinary Studies 130: Introduction to Study Abroad (IDS 130); Charles, a full-time faculty member in the Foreign Languages department, served as the instructor of record for the Spanish classes, though instructors from Instituto, a language school based in Latin America, actually taught these courses.

Coursework. All participants were required to enroll in the one-credit IDS 130 course and a three-credit Spanish course; these courses were only open to program Participants. Maura explained that the IDS course had three purposes: to provide practical and logistical information, to orient participants to the specific sites they would visit, and to familiarize them with the history and the culture. The IDS class met for ten hours before departure, three hours while in Peru, and two hours the week after the participants returned. Upon arrival in Peru, the students took a diagnostic Spanish test and placed into three different levels. The Spanish course consisted of approximately 40 hours of instruction over the 10 days in Peru.

In addition to teaching the Spanish classes, Instituto facilitated the extracurricular activities and a weekend excursion to Machu Picchu. After the morning Spanish classes, the students spent the afternoon participating in various guided outings such as a city tour, visits to museums and Incan sites, and horseback riding. In the evening, students returned to their homestays for dinner with their host families, and then they had free time, which often involved studying or socializing with one another.

Homestays. Instituto also assigned the students to homestay families. Charles, the program co-leader, considered Insituto "an integral part of this because they help us organize this whole thing. We actually have our homestays selected through the school because they vetted these families" (Charles pre-program, April 18, 2013). Although Instituto described the families as middle-class, the sizes and furnishings of the homes revealed considerable differences in socioeconomic status. For instance, some houses had six bedrooms, each of which had a flat screen television, whereas others had no televisions or hot water.

Research Questions

In exploring the transformative capacity of short-term study abroad programs for community college students, this study asked three questions:

1. How do participants describe their perceptions of their experiences studying abroad?
2. How do participants' biographies impact their perceptions of their experiences?
3. How do programmatic features influence participants' perceptions of studying abroad?

Methods

This study utilized participant-observation, interviews, and document analysis as its primary sources of evidence. I conducted three semi-structured interviews with each student participant: before, during, and after the program. The semi-structured interviews aimed to elicit rich descriptions and interpretations of the participants' experiences.

In addition, I reviewed several types of documents, which included the IDS 130 course assignments and the students' program application essays. The students also submitted five photos that represented meaningful experiences from the program.

To analyze the data, this study utilized the constant comparative method. Glaser and Strauss (1967) methodology involves a continuous and systematic process of data collection and analysis. The transcribed interviews, field notes, and documents provided a comprehensive portrait of students' experiences studying abroad. Kiely's transformative learning model guided the coding of these documents.

RESULTS

This section provides the answers to the research questions undergirding the study.

Question 1: How Do Participants Describe Their Perceptions of Their Experiences Studying Abroad?

Without exception, the participants reported that they deeply benefited from studying abroad, but they often struggled to pinpoint exactly what generated learning. Other students considered the experience so profound that they believed portraying it in words would somehow devalue it. For instance, Alyssa contended, "It's hard to communicate just what it felt like being in a whole different country... I don't even like talking about it in just normal words, normal vocabulary. It would kind of diminish it" (Alyssa, post-program, June 27, 2013). Providing students with more structured reflective opportunities may have enhanced their capacity to articulate their learning. Several students commented that they lacked sufficient time to process their experiences. For instance, Edith asserted that because of the compact nature of the program, "there's no time for process and it's just one activity replaces another, and then I forget a lot of my feelings about the first activity" (Edith, during-program, May 29, 2013). Cognitive processing, which represents an important learning process in Kiely's theoretical framework, may have been facilitated through activities such as journaling, presentations, observations, and community-based research (Kiely 2005).

Despite the inadequacy of their words to convey their experiences, the students continually referred to the connections they forged and the immersive Spanish classes as yielding the most impactful learning experiences. The students also consistently reported two outcomes: the program instilled in them the desire and confidence to travel abroad, and it catalyzed them to reassess their lives.

Connecting facilitated learning. Students' perceptions of their connection to other individuals affiliated with the program provided deep sources of satisfaction or stress, which enriched or inhibited learning. Kiely describes the process of connecting as an "affective learning dimension" in which students make meaning of their experience through understanding and empathizing (p. 14). Although when describing connecting, Kiely often refers to relationships that students form with community members, in this program, most of the participants reported establishing their most meaningful bonds with other group members. These connections can be characterized as fast-forming, intergenerational, and caring.

Traveling, studying, and living together accelerated the forging of relationships. James believed that friendships among group members developed so quickly "for the same reason that I got close with people that I've played on sports teams with or in the army and experiences like that, because it is a unique shared experience" (James, during-program, May 30, 2013).

The group's intergenerational nature provided participants the opportunity to interact with individuals in varying life stages. Despite being more than 50 years older than the rest of the students, Edith felt integrated in the group. She remarked: "I was just astounded at how generous and close and open the students were... I could ask any of them, 'Could I hang out with you tonight?' and I would enjoy it" (Edith, during-program, May 29, 2013).

Another distinctive feature of group was that "everybody kind of took care of everybody" (Cara, during-program, June 23, 2013). For instance, Sebastiano frequently assisted Maura up and down the stairs; Brian carried other participants' heavy suitcases; and Cara held Edith's pinkie finger to help her balance at Machu Picchu. Furthermore, Cara noted the program brought together a diverse group of students who "wouldn't necessarily have met in school" and created a context in which they could care for one another in ways that they typically would not have (Cara, post-program, June 23, 2013).

Although Alyssa did not develop intimate friendships with other group members, she cultivated close relationships at her homestay. Alyssa characterized her host mother as particularly nurturing as she gave Alyssa a cell phone to use if she got lost, waited up for her at night, and made sure she ate breakfast. Alyssa described: "I love our relationship. It's like a mother-daughter relationship, very comforting" (Alyssa, during-program, May 29, 2013).

Immersion Spanish classes challenged and motivated students. Although initially overwhelmed by the Spanish classes' intensity, through the support of Instituto's nurturing instructors, the students believed their language skills improved remarkably in just two weeks. James explained how the students transitioned from feeling unsettled to experiencing a sense of accomplishment: "By the third day, it seemed like everyone was really astonished and excited about the fact that they were understanding someone that was only speaking Spanish to them" (James, during-program, May 30, 2013). Successfully grappling with this linguistic challenge increased students' confidence in their communicative abilities and enabled them to interact more with Peruvians, whether at their homestay or in public, which likely further developed their linguistic abilities.

Studying abroad fostered curiosity and self-reflection. This program stoked the students' curiosity about exploring other parts of the world. To that end, the students resolved to travel, work, study, and live abroad in the future. Several students conveyed expanded perceptions of the world, seeing it as vaster and, consequently, the USA as smaller. For instance, Alyssa explained that studying abroad "just makes the rest of the world so much larger than we grew up in... I feel like the world really is bigger than Bannockburn, and I can't wait to get out and explore it" (Alyssa, post-program, June 27, 2013).

Students also consistently reported that living with unfamiliar people, communicating in a different language, and overcoming unanticipated challenges incited them to reevaluate their own lives, including their personal characteristics, relationships, values, and American culture. For instance, Brian asserted: "My views of myself have totally changed" (Eckhart, during-program, May 29, 2013). Not only did students reflect on their own attributes, but they also reassessed American cultural values, particularly in regard to happiness and material resources. By reexamining their own culture and nationality, students engaged in the learning process that Kiely characterizes as "structural border crossing."

Participants adopted a more critical perspective of American consumerism as they distinguished between the concepts of having a high standard of living and high quality of life. Many students questioned how Peruvians had fewer material resources than Americans yet seemed to lead more fulfilling lives. This incongruity astonished Brian; he remarked that he was struck by "how happy everyone I've encountered in Peru have been for what they have, and seeing how miserable people are in Bannockburn and like how much we have. It's kind of a sickening thing" (Brian, during-program, May 30, 2013).

The students described the Peruvians they encountered as more oriented toward people rather than materials. Loren explained that at her homestay, even though her host father worked three jobs, he came home every day for lunch to spend time with his wife before returning to work. Loren contrasted her homestay experience with her residence in Bannockburn, which she described is "not really a home. It's just where I sleep, so it's completely different... I like it here a lot better... their values are in the right place" (Loren, during-program, May 29, 2013). As the students questioned their taken-for-granted assumptions about their own lifestyles, their perspectives of the USA generally became more critical.

Question 2: How Do Participants' Biographies Impact Their Perceptions of Their Experiences?

The most salient biographical features, which incorporate life experiences, assumptions, and beliefs that shape interpretations of studying abroad, included students' expectations, investment in the program, prior travel experience, degree of introversion, and linguistic confidence.

Expectations. The participants' high expectations for studying abroad may have contributed to their positive views of the program's impact. Prior to the program, the students anticipated that studying abroad would be transformative. For instance, Brian predicted, "The opportunity to learn and live another culture will surely be life changing" (Brian, pre-program, May 13, 2013).

Investment. Moreover, the students' considerable investment in the program may have impacted their opinions of studying abroad. Many students saved money for months or worked additional hours to pay the program fee. For instance, Loren regularly commented in interviews on "how hard I worked to get here" (Loren, during-program, May 29, 2013). As such, the students wanted to take advantage of every opportunity in

Peru. Sebastiano asserted: "I don't want to say, 'Oh, I wish I could have went there'" (Sebastiano, during-program, May 30, 2013). All of the students seemed to share this attitude, and during their limited free time, they went to museums and even organized outings to a soccer game and wildlife sanctuary. These supplementary experiences likely shaped their views of the program.*Prior travel experience.* Another biographical feature that prominently impacted students' perceptions of their experiences concerned their previous international travel experience. Edith, Alan, and James had all traveled abroad prior to the program, and they were the only participants who expressed a desire to spend less time with the group and be placed in a homestay without other English speakers. For example, Alan yearned for deeper immersion in Peruvian culture. In regard to the program, he stated:

> It was supposed to be this full Spanish immersion thing, and I was forced to live with someone who always wanted to speak English. Then I was forced to go on these trips where you speak in English the whole time or you're getting lectured in English, or at the very least having someone translate everything. (Alan, during-program, May 30, 2013)

Alan clarified, however, that had he not traveled independently before the program, he would have wanted to live with an English-speaking roommate and spend considerable time with the group.

The more novice travelers conveyed less concern for independence. They did not complain about the amount of time spent in group activities and reported enjoying living with other English speakers, who acted as interpreters and companions. For instance, Brian volunteered at an orphanage with his English-speaking housemates, and Alyssa described the friendships she developed with the two American sisters at her homestay as a program highlight.

Introversion. Introversion served as an additional biographical trait that shaped students' understandings of their experiences. Alyssa and Loren identified themselves as introverted and both described trying to find their places in the group as stressful. Loren viewed the program as an opportunity to try on a new persona and "practice" being less introverted, whereas Alyssa withdrew from the group and developed friendships at her homestay. The more extroverted students did not seem to grapple with these internal conflicts about their position in the group, and they quickly formed intimate friendships with other students.

Linguistic Confidence. The students' perceptions of their language proficiency seemed to more powerfully influence their interactions with Peruvians than did the students' actual linguistic ability. For instance, since James, Alyssa, Cara, Alan, and Sebastiano all tested into the same level of Spanish class at Instituto, their language proficiency levels were likely comparable. However, Cara demonstrated less confidence than her class-mates. She noted that until her housemate James got sick, which forced her to travel around Cusco without him, she did not know how to direct taxi drivers to her homestay because she had always relied on him to communicate. Those who felt more confident revealed a greater willingness to interact with people outside the group whereas those with less linguistic confidence felt more comfortable insulated with English speakers.

Question 3: How Do Programmatic Features Influence Participants' Perceptions of Studying Abroad?

In Kiely's model, programmatic factors comprise one of four elements in the process of contextual border crossing. The most impactful programmatic aspects in this study, which included the intensive Spanish classes, homestays, location, and compacted nature, intersected in numerous ways to shape learning.

Intensive Spanish classes. The intensive language courses at Instituto initially overwhelmed several of the students, who questioned their abilities to succeed in Spanish-only classes. Ultimately, the linguistic development that the students made astonished the instructors and students alike. James described, "My Spanish vocabulary and confidence grew exponentially" (James, post-program, June 19, 2013). The students' language progress increased their confidence not only in their ability to communicate but also in their capacity to learn.

Homestays. The living arrangements in this program enabled students to practice their Spanish and learn about Peruvian culture. Kiely (2005) explains that relationships students develop with members of the host community provide a face to "abstract and detached" concepts and social problems (p. 12), resulting in "personalized" learning. For instance, rather than learning about the stringent birth control policies in Peru in a strictly intellectual manner, Sebastiano understood the impact of such policies on his host mother's family through conversations with her (Sebastiano, during-program, May 29, 2013). This example reveals the intersection of the learning processes, particularly dissonance, personalizing, and connecting.

Program location. This specific program location also influenced the students' perceptions of studying abroad. In particular, several students identified their encounters with nature, such the Andes Mountains and the ancient ruins of Machu Picchu, as sublime or spiritual experiences. Moreover, James described his experience hiking Machu Picchu: "The struggle of the walk plus the sunrise over the mountains combined to create a spiritual experience in a very spiritual place" (James, during-program, May 29, 2013). This spiritual dimension may not have manifested if the program had not included opportunities to engage directly with the natural or ancient world.

Compact program. The compact nature of the program likely shaped how students responded to uncomfortable situations. Recognizing the program's limited duration, the students could disregard undesirable aspects of their experiences. For instance, Loren chose to ignore the racial discrimination she perceived. She noted that when she shopped with Brian and Alan, store clerks catered more to them and the White European shoppers than to her (Field notes, May 24, 2013). She explained how she coped with racial bias: "In the beginning of the trip, I noticed it, but during the end, I didn't really care because I was having a good time" (Loren, post-program, June 21, 2013). Loren may have demonstrated more tolerance for this unequal treatment because she knew that she would soon be departing.

RECOMMENDATIONS FOR PRACTICE

With a clearer understanding of how contextual features and their interaction shape learning outcomes, community college faculty and administrators can design and implement more effective programming. To that end, this section outlines key recommendations that may inform community colleges' study abroad decision-making about participants, coursework, and living arrangements.

Participants

Community colleges should aim to recruit a diverse range of participants for their study abroad programs. The students identified the relationships they forged with dissimilar others as edifying and as increasing their self-confidence. For instance, Edith described that being "totally accepted by" the other participants who, due to their ages, "could have been my grandkids... gave me confidence to be myself as an elderly person" (Edith, post-program, June 28, 2013).

Community colleges should also consider inviting additional faculty members to participate in study abroad programs. The additional faculty members' required donations reduced the program fee for students. By sharing their experiences upon returning to the college, these faculty members may also contribute to the program's "ripple effects."

Coursework

Pre-departure course meetings should prioritize relationship-building, so reserved students may feel more comfortable in the group. In addition, faculty should consider integrating more formal opportunities for reflection. Although reflection may be considered a best practice in the field of study abroad, Maura expressed misgivings about the structure of the IDS 130 course, noting, "There's never enough time to do everything" (Maura, during-program, May 30, 2013). Several students commented that they yearned for more time to process their experiences. Reflection topics should investigate the impact of gender, race, and class on participants' experiences. In pre-departure coursework, faculty might also explore ways to prepare students for the racial and gender bias they may encounter in an international context.

Because supplementary coursework provides vital opportunities to prepare for, process, and reflect on the study abroad experience, community colleges should investigate flexible options to address logistical constraints at their particular institutions. BCC's academic calendar and the students' disparate work schedules presented considerable limitations to scheduling the IDS 130 course meetings. A hybrid format in which students meet both online and face-to-face may increase student attendance and participation.

Furthermore, this research reveals the effectiveness of community colleges collaborating with local institutions to administer study abroad programs. The students' identification of Instituto's Spanish classes as one of the most challenging and gratifying aspects of the program lends support to "outsourcing" the language classes to accommodate students of varied proficiencies. Addressing the learning needs of the BCC students at three different Spanish levels would have been onerous for any single instructor.

Living Arrangements

Based on this study's findings, community colleges should consider including a homestay placement. The relationships students forged at their homestays offered sources of connection, particularly for students who felt detached from the group. The homestay also challenged students to speak Spanish with native speakers and diminished the insular nature of group travel.

RECOMMENDATIONS FOR FUTURE RESEARCH

The diversity of participants in this study points to the need for future research to consider how the structural features of race, class, and gender impact students' perceptions of their study abroad experience. In this sense, this study echoes Malewski and Phillion's (2009) call for researchers to investigate how these characteristics shape interactions with members of the host community and lead to "unique learner experiences" (p. 58). Such research holds particular importance given the disparate ways in which host country members may respond to study abroad participants based on these characteristics.

Moreover, this study underscores the need for longitudinal research to investigate if or how learning outcomes evolve over time. The BCC students cited behavioral changes they intended to make as a result of studying abroad; however, a longitudinal case study would be necessary to document whether students actually enact such changes.

CONCLUSIONS

This research portrayed the study abroad experiences of community college students, a population largely excluded from study abroad literature. All of the students reported that studying abroad challenged them in myriad ways and enriched their lives. Confronting social, academic, intercultural, and even physical challenges provided students with confidence and a heightened lens through which to examine the world and their position in it.

This study lends support to the value of short-term study abroad programs, particularly those lasting only two weeks. This study's findings also underline the need for further research investigating the learning processes and outcomes associated with very short-term education abroad programs. Rather than ask what constitutes the ideal duration for a study abroad program as some researchers have (e.g., Dwyer 2004), a more relevant and meaningful inquiry would investigate how to make a one- to two-week program most impactful. Reframing the question in this way acknowledges the realities of many community college students' lives. This study's findings demonstrate that the impact of short-term study abroad programs should not be underestimated.

REFERENCES

Dwyer, Mary M. (2004). More is better: The impact of study abroad program duration. *Frontiers: The Interdisciplinary Journal of Study Abroad, 10,* 151–163.

Frost, Robert A., & Raby, Rosalind L. (2009). Democratizing study abroad: Challenges of open access, local commitments, and global competence in community colleges. In Robert Lewin (Ed.), *The handbook of practice and research in study abroad: Higher education and the quest for global citizenship* (pp. 170–190). New York, NY: Taylor & Francis.

Glaser, Barney G., & Strauss, Anselm L. (1967). *The discovery of grounded theory: Strategies for qualitative research.* Chicago: Aldine.

Institute of International Education (2009). *Open doors 2009: Report on international education exchange.* DC: Washington.

Institute of International Education. (2013). Community colleges: Study abroad, 2012/13. *Open Doors Report on International Educational Exchange.* http:// www.iie.org/Research-and-Publications/Open-Doors/Data/Community-College-Data-Resource/Study-Abroad/Study-Abroad-Characteristics-2012-13

Jones, Susan R., Rowan-Kenyon, Heather T., Mei-Yen Ireland, S., Niehaus, Elizabeth, & Skendall, Kristan Cilente (2012). The meaning students make as participants in short-term immersion programs. *Journal of College Student Development, 53,* 201–220.

Kiely, Richard (2005). A transformative learning model for service-learning: A longitudinal case study. *Michigan Journal of Community Service Learning, 12*(1), 5–22.

Kuh, George D. (2008). *High-impact educational practices: What they are, who has access to them, and why they matter.* Washington, DC: American Association of Colleges & Universities.

Malewski, Erik, & Phillion, Jo Ann (2009). International field experiences: The impact of class, gender and race on the perceptions and experiences of preservice teachers. *Teaching and Teacher Education, 25,* 52–60.

Mezirow, Jack (2000). Learning to think like an adult: Core concepts of transformative theory. In J. Mezirow & Associates (Eds.), Learning as transformation: Critical perspectives on a theory in progress (pp. 3–33). San Francisco, CA: Jossey-Bass.

Whalen, Brian (2008). The management and funding of US study abroad. *International Higher Education, 50*, 15–16.

Ensuring Social Success: A Case Study of International Students' Social Experiences at Austin Community College

Sharon Miller

INTRODUCTION

Austin Community college located in Austin Texas, boasts 11 separate campuses spread across a metropolitan area that encompasses five counties and 4278 square miles (Metropolitan Areas, 2008) and served 37,294 students during the spring of 2014. Of these students, 4.7 % were classified as international students. ACC does not offer any on-campus residential areas, meaning that all students commute to and from the different campuses. Over 77 % of the students attend part-time and only one-quarter are in the traditional college age bracket of 19–21 years old (Austin Community College 2014).

Although each campus contains an admissions office, the International Students' Office (ISO) is located on only one campus. Nevertheless, this campus does not host a significantly higher number of international students nor is it the most centrally located campus in the area. Currently, the ISO's main purpose is to assist incoming international students with visa and immigration issues and provide an international students' orientation

S. Miller (✉)
Austin Community College, Austin, TX, USA

© The Editor(s) (if applicable) and The Author(s) 2016
R.L. Raby, E.J. Valeau (eds.), *International Education at Community Colleges*, DOI 10.1057/978-1-137-53336-4_22

at the beginning of each semester. Neither ACC nor the ISO provide any housing assistance for incoming students beyond basic tips on choosing the appropriate type of housing, precautions on lease negotiations, and a link to apartment locators around the city. ACC Student Life, which is present on every campus, hosts a variety of events throughout the semester, yet, of the sixty clubs, only six have an international component, such as working with an international charity or creating events targeted at international students.

ACC provides many of the benefits that international students look for when choosing to attend a college in the USA, such as lower tuition, less restrictive English proficiency requirements, smaller class size, and transferability of credits to four-year institutions (American Association of Community Colleges 2008). Nevertheless, as ACC increases its efforts in international student recruitment, it is necessary to determine how international students develop social support networks that they need in order to have a truly successful sojourn.

International students attending ACC face different social challenges than those who choose to attend one of the many residential, four-year universities in the area, such as the University of Texas (UT). Unlike UT which has on-campus housing and on-campus locations in which international students can gather and meet domestic students, there is no on-campus accommodation for any of the 11 ACC campuses. There are also significant differences in the demographics between international students and domestic students attending community college (Hagedorn and Lee 2005). ACC serves a large non-traditional student populations, like older students, students with families, and students who work full-time, who have other obligations that keep them from staying on campus once their classes are complete. Furthermore, the domestic students who are of traditional college age most likely grew-up in the Austin community and already have an established social group, potentially making it more difficult for international students to develop friendships with them. These are just a few of the many factors that may affect an international student's ability to engage on a social level with local students and truly become part of the community that the ACC serves.

Theoretical Framework

Anderson et al. (2012) defined a transition as any "event, or non-event that results in changed relationships, routines, assumptions, and roles" (p. 39). Due to the fact that an international student's arrival at ACC would constitute a significant transition, Schlossberg's Transition Theory and Goodman's 4 S's (Situation, Self, Support, Strategies) provide two theoretical frameworks through which to explore the factors that affect an international student's ability to develop relationships and form a social support network.

Schlossberg's Transition Theory suggests that when examining an individual's movement through a transition, it is necessary to look at not only the type of transition (anticipated or unanticipated event or a non-event) but also the perspective of the individual, the context in which the transition takes place, and the impact the transition has on the individual (Anderson et al. 2012).

While Schlossberg's Transition Theory seeks to understand the factors that can affect how an individual manages a transition, Goodman's 4 S's can be adapted to help identify the factors that could impact a student's ability to develop relationships that can help mitigate cultural stress. Situation refers to the external factors surrounding the transition. Self relates to the factors that are attributed specifically to the individual, such as gender, ethnicity and culture, perceived language abilities, and personal outlook. Within the context of this model, support refers to the social support networks that the students begin to develop upon their arrival at ACC. Finally, strategies relate to the responses an individual may employ in order to manage a transition (Evans et al. 2010).

Research Methods

Utilizing the database of the ISO, a recruitment letter containing a link to the Letter of Informed Consent and a request to participate in a face-to-face interview was sent to 284 international students who were currently enrolled at ACC on F-1 student visas and had been attending ACC for at least one full semester. The first 13 students who indicated that they were willing to take part were invited to participate in the face-to-face interview.

The interview questions were based on the aforementioned theoretical framework and was divided into three sections: the international students' experiences upon arrival into the Austin area, the international students' experiences developing friendships, and the international students' perceptions of themselves.

Presentation of Data

Of the 13 students who participated in this research study, eight (62 %) were female and five (38 %) were male. Six participants identified as Hispanic/Latino, three as White, two as Asian, one as two or more races, and one as other. Ten of the participants were between the ages of 18 and 21, one was between 22 and 25, one was between 26 and 30, and finally, one was between 41 and 45.

When asked who helped them settle into the community, eight of the thirteen participants claimed that they had family members or close friends already living in the area. Two of the participants came to Austin with at least one good friend or family member. For these students, the fact that they already had a social connection to Austin was the reason that they chose to study at ACC. As one student said;

> That's something, like that pushed me to come here to Austin, my dad wanted me to study abroad but go to a place where I knew somebody...It was going to be a big change, so he didn't want me to be by myself.

Only three of the thirteen respondents arrived into Austin completely on their own with no social support networks in place.

In regard to working with advisors and registering for classes, five of the thirteen respondents said that their advisors helped them through the process and provided them with adequate assistance. The others felt that the location of the international students' office was too far and did not feel that regular admissions advisors could help in their particular situation, especially when dealing with the Texas Success Initiative (TSI) assessment test scores. One respondent explained, "I failed the TSI but passed the ESOL and like only international advisors know what's the deal when that happened, so talking to a regular advisor doesn't help that much" (Participant 216, March 17, 2015). Two participants described situations in which they felt their advisors did not want to help them causing them to seek assistance elsewhere. No matter their experiences working with general admissions advisors or international student advisors, none of the 13 participants said that they contacted the international students' office or an advisor for any issues beyond paperwork, immigration and visa issues, or finding legal employment.

Although all the respondents attended the international students' orientation prior to the start of their first semester and believed it provided necessary information about attending ACC, only a few of the participants believed it assisted them in developing friendships with other students. Several students mentioned an activity during which a microphone was passed around the room so that each student could introduce themselves. Two students explained how this activity made them feel at ease and one said it was an opportunity to "get a sense of all the places, all the diversity there is." Nevertheless, other students felt that more could have been done to encourage interactions amongst the students attending the international students' orientation. One student suggested that time be allowed for students to walk around after the introductions were completed, so that they could talk to people from similar regions. Another suggested that upon arrival students be grouped by nationality or country of origin, not just for the social aspects of being able to converse in the same native language, but also so that students who spoke better English could help explain things to those who were struggling to understand. Two students suggested that the orientation provide more information about student groups or clubs that could provide opportunities to meet other people outside of the orientation.

When asked how they met their first friend at ACC, seven of the thirteen participants claimed they met them in a class, two responded that they had met their friend during the international student orientation, one met her first friend through her brother, and one met her first friend at a party. Two claimed that they had not met any friends at ACC. The fact that many students change campuses, take different classes, transfer to another university, or graduate and move away, seemed to be a large barrier for international students developing deeper friendships. One participant said,

> I made some friendships, but I find it really hard to keep them, my friends, like, I lose a lot of friends because they just disappear, because they move to a different state or they move to a different city, and we just lose contact.

Nevertheless, five of the participants did develop and maintain close friendships with students they met in their classes and that continues to be one of the main ways they meet new people and develop new relationships.

When asked about participating in assigned group work during classes, all but one of the interviewees agreed that assigned group work helped them build some type of relationship with the other students in their class. Although for several of the respondents these types of friendships might never move beyond acquaintances, the ability to acknowledge and wave to these classmates while on campus did provide a connection to ACC. One student explained: "If we see each other on campus, we say hi, it's just like you know who you're sitting in a classroom with and I like that it's kind of closer."

Joining different clubs at ACC was one way that half of the participants attempted to engage with other students on campus. One participant managed an international student organization at ACC and developed most of her close friendships through it. She said, "I have a group of friends, like girlfriends, we have a group of five and I met them through my organization and a UT organization called START." However, two participants stated that they were completely unaware that the ability to join clubs on campus at ACC was even an option. Another student said, "I didn't know that Austin Community College had clubs, you know, where you join, you make friends there."

When discussing their own perceptions of themselves, three of the participants identified as extroverts, five identified as introverts, and five believed they were a little bit of both depending on the situation. Nevertheless, they offered mixed responses on whether or not they found it easy to meet new people.

The responses to the questions about whether or not it was easier to meet domestic or international students seemed to split along racial or ethnic lines. Four of the six respondents who identified as Hispanic/Latino claimed that it was easier for them to meet other international students. All four of these participants noted language as one of the main reasons that they felt more comfortable meeting other international students. One student explained that "if you hear someone speaking Spanish then you go and speak to them, like, oh, you speak Spanish." Another Hispanic participant explained that it had a lot to do with the way Americans communicate. He said,

> when I approach an American like to hang out or like making conversation...it's like an interrogatory, you are always like so what's your name, where do you live, and they say my name is, I live here, and they don't continue.

The only non-Hispanic participant to state that he had an easier time meeting international students believed it had more to do with interests and conversation topics. International students, he said, "know a little more about the outside world, and they are kind of interested to know, kind of meet people from other countries as well."

There were several different reasons provided as to why five of the participants believed it was easier to meet domestic students as opposed to international students. Two mentioned that they felt international students were less common than domestic students, which made it more likely to meet and interact with domestic students. The only participant who identified as Hispanic/Latina and also stated that it was easier to meet domestic students believed that the reason was due to the fact that many international students, especially Mexican students, only want to engage with locals so they tend to avoid interacting with other international students. Another student, who identified as White, expressed this same sentiment from her own viewpoint, she explained: "I came here to meet Americans and not to meet other Europeans or wherever they're from, so it's probably also what I am looking for."For seven of the thirteen participants their perception of their English-speaking abilities had at least some effect on their desire and ability to meet new people and develop friendships. Of these seven, five identified as Hispanic/Latino and two identified as Asian. One Hispanic student said,

> I am still working on it and it's still, it definitely affects friendships or just talking to people or even in class, I want to say something but I don't know how, so I am just not gonna say it.

The other six participants expressed complete confidence in their English-speaking skills. Of these six, only one identified as Hispanic/Latina and her confidence stemmed from the fact that she lived in New Zealand for several years prior to her arrival in the USA.

In regard to cultural differences influencing the participants' abilities to interact and develop friendships with domestic students, four of the six participants who identified as Hispanic/Latino mentioned that American culture seemed much more reserved than their home culture. One student explained, "In my culture people are very open and kind of like really friendly and stuff, you can just kind of be loud, and here I guess people are just a little more closed to themselves." For these four students, this difference often caused confusion about how to approach a domestic student for the first time or what is appropriate when greeting a friend or an acquaintance. Conversely, two of the participants that identified as White and came from Western European countries felt the exact opposite about domestic students. Both found Americans to be far less reserved than their home cultures.

The two participants who identified as Asian had very similar experiences in the cultural differences they faced. Both mentioned feeling unsure about what was considered polite or impolite. Participant 227 explained that her culture is much more indirect than American culture which would cause her to think American students were being rude when they asked her direct questions.

DISCUSSION

Utilizing both Schlossberg's Transition Theory and Goodman's 4 S's as theoretical frameworks, this study sought to understand the factors that affected an international student's social experience while attending ACC. A number of home countries and racial or ethnic groups were represented in the sample of student participants and it became clear that the students' perspectives and contexts varied and did have an effect on how they moved through the transition. For example, students coming from Latin American or Asian countries seemed to struggle more with cultural differences than students coming from Western European countries. Perceived language issues also had a greater influence on students from non-Western European countries. In terms of impact, all of the participants moved away from home leaving the majority of friends and family behind, yet eight of the thirteen interviewees choose to come to Austin because they had friends and family living in the area, meaning that they had at least a small social support network already in place. This fact lessened the intensity of the impact because they had someone who could assist them in settling into the community.

Goodman's 4 S's provided the theoretical framework through which to identify the factors that affected the students' ability to meet people and develop friendships. Many participants mentioned the fact that all students attending ACC commuted to and from campus negatively impacted their ability to develop friendships, especially close personal relationships. In addition, the lecture format of most classes did not provide any opportunity for the participants to connect with their classmates, and if the participants did have the chance to start conversations and begin to develop a relationship during class, once the semester ended, the likelihood that those students would attend another class with the participants was minimal. One student equated ACC to a workplace environment, saying "you go there to work, you go there to study, you go, study, get out."

Many of the participants attributed unwillingness to approach domestic students and start conversations as factors that affected their ability to develop friendships. For some, this was specifically a personality trait, such a shyness or introversion that kept them from making initial contact.

However, even the three students who identified as extroverts confessed to finding it difficult to approach new people. One student explained that this was due to the natural desire to surround oneself with similar people, such as people from the same region or who speak the same language.

For others, at least at the beginning of their stay in the USA, it was their fear that they would be unable to adequately express their thoughts in English that kept them from speaking to native English speakers. For others, it was cultural differences that caused them not to pursue friendships with domestic students. Cultural differences and language issues were more likely to create significant barriers for students coming from Latin American or Asian countries than the participants who identified as White and came from Western European countries. When asked if there were any major factors that affected their abilities to develop friendship with domestic students, both participants who identified as Asian and all but one who identified as Hispanic/Latino cited cultural differences and language issues as primary factors, yet the two students who identified as White and came from Western European countries stated that there were no factors, at all, that influenced their ability to meet American students.

Past research has shown that for international students attending community college frequently and meaningful interactions with faculty and advisors had a significant impact on the students' connection to and persistence in the college (Mamiseishvili 2012). However, none of the 13 participants in this study said that they visit their international student advisor or general admissions advisors for anything beyond paperwork, immigration status, or registering for classes. This suggests that, in contrast to Mamiseishvili's study, most international students at ACC do not view their advisors as an integral part of their social support network. The interactions with professors were even less meaningful, with only one participant mentioning that she had developed a friendship with her professors beyond that of faculty/student.

The participants employed a number of different strategies in order to manage the transition and build a social support network. Half of the participants reported joining a club or student organization in order to connect with other students, and one respondent joined a club not associated with ACC. However, five of the students mentioned that they either did not know the option to join clubs existed or that it was difficult to find information regarding clubs that were currently active on campus.

Karp et al. (2010/2011) posited that networks developed in the classroom created stronger ties than those developed by joining student clubs.

For many of the participants in this case study, developing friendships with classmates was difficult and they often attributed that fact to cultural differences (i.e. domestic students are more reserved and quiet) or to the commuter campus situation of ACC (i.e. students attend class and leave). Nevertheless, for 12 of the 13 participants in the interviews, having the chance to participate in group work during class allowed them to develop relationships, which helped mitigate some cultural stress, even though the relationships developed during group work were mostly acquaintance-style friendships.

CONCLUSION AND RECOMMENDATIONS

Each student faced a unique set of challenges and had a unique experience based on many factors, such as their country of origin, their age, their level of English, and whether or not they had a support network living in the Austin area. Nevertheless, there were specific factors that seemed to influence most of the participants' social experiences at ACC. Cultural differences, perceptions of English-speaking abilities, and willingness to engage with domestic students all emerged as common threads in the students' experiences.

Although every student faced different challenges, there is policy and programming changes that ACC could incorporate that might mitigate some of these challenges and assist international students in developing deeper social support networks. First, locating an international student advisor at every campus, which could assist international students through the entire process of arriving on campus, taking assessment tests, and registering for classes would be beneficial to the students.

Second, the international students' orientation could be redesigned to include time for engaging with other international students, beyond simply passing the microphone around for basic introductions. Also, seating students according to nationality or country of origin could provide them with an immediate connection to those around them. In addition, the students who speak better English could assist those who were struggling, so that all of the students would obtain the necessary information presented during the orientation. Student representatives for the various clubs on campus should be present at the orientation, so that international students who were interested in joining could meet with current members and learn about the different activities that the club hosts. This would also ensure that all international students were made aware of the possibility of joining clubs to connect with other students and make friends.

In the classroom, professors could assign group work more often, especially if they have a number of international students in their class. Not only would this provide opportunities for the international students and the domestic students to engage in cross-cultural interactions, but it would provide non-native English speakers a support system to turn to, if they needed assistance in their English only class.

Finally, ACC should develop a student-mentor program through which current domestic students could be paired with incoming international students. This would provide the international students with a peer who could help support them through the initial transition to ACC as well as introduce them to the social aspects of the Austin community.

There are numerous benefits to hosting international students at ACC, yet, it is imperative that steps be taken to assist them in developing the support networks necessary for managing cultural stress and having a successful sojourn. Providing international students with ways to connect with other individuals as soon as possible after their arrival into Austin is vital, because as one student said, "When you come here, the only thing is, you don't want to be alone."

References

American Association of Community Colleges. (2008). *2008–2009 International students' guide to U.S. community colleges.* http://www.aacc.nche.edu/Resources/aaccprograms/international/Documents/studentguide/0809sg.pdf

Anderson, Mary L., Goodman, Jane, & Schlossberg, Nancy K. (2012). *Counseling adults in transition: Linking Schlossberg's theory with practice in a diverse world.* New York, NY: Springer Publishing Company.

Austin Community College. (2014). *Student demographics.* http://www.austincc.edu/oiepub/pubs/factbook/2013-14/spring/fb13-14_student_demo_CB_spring.pdf

Evans, Nancy J., Forney, Deanna S., Guido, Florence M., Patton, Lori D., & Renn, Kristen A. (2010). *Student development in college: Theory, research, and practice* (2nd ed.). San Francisco, CA: Jossey-Bass.

Hagedorn, Linda S., & Lee, Mi-Chung (2005). *International community college students: The neglected minority? Online Submission.* ERIC. http://www.eric.ed.gov/PDFS/ED490516.pdf

Karp, Melinda M., Hughes, Katherine L., & O'Gara, Lauren (2010/2011). An exploration of Tinto's integration framework for community college students. *Journal of College Student Retention, 12*(1), 69–86. doi:10.2190/CS.12.1.e.

Mamiseishvili, Ketevan (2012). Academic and social integration and persistence of international students at U.S. two-year institutions. *Community College Journal of Research and Practice, 36*(1), 15–27. doi:10.1080/10668926.2012.619093.

Metropolitan Areas – Area and Population. (2008). Census.gov. http://www.census.gov/compendia/smadb/TableB-01.pdf

Community College International Internship Cultivation of Competence in Communication, Collaboration, and Critical Thinking

Marc Thomas

INTRODUCTION

By the nineteenth century and the onset of the industrial revolution, the power loom was replacing hand-weaving operations in the textile industry. Skilled weavers were trained to operate multiple machines at once to exponentially increase production. In the twenty-first century, advancements like the supersonic jet and the World Wide Web offer us virtually instantaneous transfer of people, goods, and knowledge. Not unlike the pursuit of manufacturing skills of a previous century, our contemporary quest for competence in the digital age has fueled a drive for state-of-the-art skills so employees can thrive in the new global economy. This chapter will explore the potential for education abroad at the community college as a vehicle for student global competence. This exploration will unfold first

M. Thomas (✉)
Consultant, New Orleans, LA, USA

© The Editor(s) (if applicable) and The Author(s) 2016
R.L. Raby, E.J. Valeau (eds.), *International Education at Community Colleges*, DOI 10.1057/978-1-137-53336-4_23

323

through a discussion of what global competence looks like. Then, through in-depth interviews and observations of community college students who participated in an international internship, four case studies will review the extent to which these students' competencies increased through participation in an internship abroad.

What Is Global Competence?

Educators and employers alike have chimed in about what it means to be globally competent. Morais and Ogden (2011) define global competence as "having an open mind while actively seeking to understand others' cultural norms and expectations and leveraging this knowledge to interact, communicate, and work effectively outside one's environment" (p. 448). Components of this definition include self-awareness, intercultural communication, and global knowledge. In short, the research on global competency has assigned emphasis in the following broad areas: critical thinking, communicating, and collaborating. A brief discussion of the skills associated with each competency category follows.

Critical Thinking. This competence begins with self-awareness gleaned abroad, evolving to becoming comfortable with the uncomfortable and problem-solving in unfamiliar situations. Morais and Ogden (2011) described the need for student recognition "of their own limitations and ability to engage successfully in an international encounter" (p. 448).

Communicating. Eaton and Kleshinski (2014) include foreign language fluency as an important part of communication competency, describing it as "critically important as a distinguishing characteristic for potential employees" (p. 51). US Silicon Valley CEO Pollock (2013) highlighted language fluency and cross-cultural understanding through interactions with people from other cultures as integral to global competency.

Collaborating. Pollock (2013) championed moving beyond insular teams of the past because "complex and dynamic teams are the norm. Success depends upon the ability to quickly pull extraordinary efforts out of a diverse team" (n.p.). Eaton and Kleshinski (2014) embraced the importance of making culturally sensitive decisions, "coupled with knowledge about foreign cultures and norms" (p. 51).

The case studies that follow explore the extent to which enhancements in student competencies in the key areas—critical thinking, communication, and collaboration—happened.

COMMUNITY COLLEGE STUDENT INTERN EXPERIENCES IN ASIA

Lansing Community College, positioned in Michigan's capital city, offered semester student internships in Japan beginning in 1982. The program's American architect was Dr. Tai Sung Kim, a South Korean native who as a boy lived under Japanese occupation. The Japanese steward was Megumi Shigematsu, president of the Biwako Kisen Steamship Company, Ltd., a tourism company operating a paddle wheel boat on Japan's largest fresh-water lake. Both Dr. Kim and President Shigematsu crafted the program with a clear vision of friendship and cultural exchange between the USA and Japan. By 2008, the struggling Japanese and American economies led the program to begin a three-year hiatus.

In 2011, the Japanese corporation and Lansing Community College launched a new program, designed to give American students practical cross-cultural experience while sharing the American experience with Japanese tourists. Under the smaller, renewed program, ten students enrolled in a four-credit community college semester internship course abroad. The international interns take food orders, serve American-style hot dogs and burgers, and practice English with tourists (including the frequent Japanese school groups that take the American-themed cruise). Students participate in a once-a-week internship class with an on-site faculty adviser, reflecting on their internship experiences and discussing workplace challenges and triumphs. In addition to the weekly internship reflection discussions among students and faculty leader, American students make a presentation to Japanese students who study intercultural communication at the University of Shiga Prefecture. Typically, presentation topics cover an area of cultural difference between the USA and Japan.

The program's primary intent is for students to improve their intercultural communication, language, and problem-solving skills through assignment as an intern with the Japanese company. The case studies that follow explore the extent to which student competencies in the key areas identified in the literature—critical thinking, communication, and collaboration—were improved.

ELLIOT, INTERNATIONAL INTERN: MAY TO AUGUST 2013

At age 19, Elliot approached the education-abroad program in Japan with a firm interest in economics, but unsure of where that path would lead. In a previous college history class, he analyzed the role of the railway in uniting early the American east and west coasts. In an honors writing class, with the role of mass transit in manifest destiny fresh in his mind, he wrote about the potential for a twenty-first-century American rail revival. He argued that Japan's experience designing trains operating at speeds of up to 320 kilometers an hour (200 miles per hour) to catapult its economy could be an important piece of the modern American economic infrastructure.

In Japan, his vision of economics—fused with mass transit—evolved. "I saw how mass transit affected economics and society as a whole." He witnessed firsthand the role of the train in getting "salary men" to work in Japan every day. He noticed there were dedicated tracks for freight, allowing the passenger trains to run on time. The discovery of how easy it was to take the train at a reasonably low cost, with trains arriving every few minutes—day and evening—inspired thought about the role of rail in his future. His own frequent train route in Japan, from the Shiga Prefecture to Kyoto Prefecture, cut through two ridges to carry people and freight hundreds of times each day through the city of Yamashina (which means roughly "mountain slope" in Japanese). He returned to America with a clear strategy to use his experiences and observations abroad as the building blocks of transfer to the University of Michigan and his long-term career plan to be part of shaping an American landscape with improved transportation infrastructure.

Competencies Reported from International Internship and Experiences

Communicating. Elliot reported significant on-the-job lessons in intercultural communication. "Whether it was figuring out how to communicate culture differences or adapting to a much stricter company and social hierarchy, different unanticipated challenges were always coming up." In particular, learning how to navigate communication between employees was a challenge 6000 miles removed from American workplace culture. For example, Japanese culture discourages initiating conversation outside one's social group. That reality, combined with the introversion displayed by many young children, motivated Elliot and the other American interns to employ different engagement strategies. "Often when we would approach the younger children—especially those age five or younger—for the English quiz during the summer we found that many of them were very shy - especially about speaking English." To inspire conversation, Elliot often spoke first in Japanese, and then switched to English. This approach often resulted in the younger kids having a short exchange in English. Elliot said his intercultural communication proficiency was enhanced through informal language discussions between American and Japanese co-workers, including discussions of how and when to use similar words (such as "onegai shimasu" and "kudasai"—different Japanese variations of "please").

Collaborating. Elliot savored the spirit of this workplace—Japanese and American workers teaming up for the common goal of providing an enjoyable experience for tourists. "Creating a working-relationship with people from different cultural backgrounds was challenging at first, but proved to be rewarding to learn about different perspectives and approaches to the working environment." For example, when temporary employees were brought in to help during especially busy times, the American college interns occasionally played a role in training the visiting employees, navigating Japanese business protocols of who reports to whom. Armed with some Japanese language training, Elliot and his colleagues chipped in to help these new workers, who often had minimal English language skills, find their place on the team. In summary, Elliot reported the greatest competence increases abroad in intercultural communication and making his career plan.

Competency reflection. Was there a competency Elliot wished he had improved more during the internship? His only regret was not making more professional connections to help advance his future career opportunities. Nearing completion of his bachelor's degree at this writing, Elliot is now actively plotting his future, which he hopes will include graduate school in urban planning and transportation management. "I want to make a difference in U.S. or international transportation policy," he reported. "High-speed rail has been proposed in the U.S. I want to be part of designing and implementing that."

ELIZABETH, INTERNATIONAL INTERN, AUGUST TO NOVEMBER 2013

A Japanese library card symbolized 19-year-old Elizabeth's immersion into the culture of the country. A first-generation college student of Mexican and Italian ancestry, she became a community college international relations major. Elizabeth had previously participated in brief high-school exchange program in Japan, with a strict daily schedule. In college, she had saved money for a car, but decided instead to use her savings to return to Japan for the international internship, knowing it would give her independence she had not before experienced in any country. "My favorite things to do were the things I could not do as a tourist, like getting a library card and running a 5K [kilometer] race." She jogged every morning, often spotting the same Japanese runners who shared in her exercise mission. She often earned a nod of approval from her Japanese running colleagues on their local running path along Lake Biwa. Her acceptance into Japanese society—symbolized by the library card and nods on the running trail—gave her confidence.

Competencies Reported from International Internship and Experiences

Collaborating. Elizabeth embarked on this journey hoping for more independence. Her new-found autonomy led to what she described as her most significant improvement during her internship abroad: improving her role as a team member through a new commitment to work ethic and personal responsibility. In America, prior to her education-abroad experience, she described her work attendance record as sporadic, occasionally being late to her service-industry job. Previously in America, she relied on the "comfort of home," often caught up in the flow of her family's operations, including occasional use of her mother's laundry services. Upon return to the USA, Elizabeth said she and her employer noted her spotless work attendance record. "In Japan, I had to figure out things for myself," Elizabeth said. In America, for example, when her Bluetooth speaker broke, she asked her dad to fix it, which he did. In Japan, she did her own laundry and navigated the complex three-tiered system of Japanese alphabets, even when she had not yet learned a particular word or character.

Critical Thinking. A meticulous planner, Elizabeth described one of the most important lessons learned was that a change of plans is ok, sometimes good. She described her internship abroad as honing her skills at better internal processing of managing change. Language miscues, busy schedules, and the complicated labyrinth of train and subway routes once in a while led to good intentions falling through. In America, she said, she'd be likely to abandon the plans after circumstances did not proceed as planned. In Japan, these kinds of unanticipated obstacles transformed into opportunities like salsa dancing with a Mexican karate team and meeting new friends by going solo to a live concert. She and others had plans to see the Korean pop band MBLAQ (Music Boys Live in Absolute Quality) perform in Osaka—more than an hour by train from her internship site. When work schedules prevented her friends from joining her, she went ahead anyway, a choice she probably would not have made previously. The education-abroad experience was the capstone of her community college experience in her hometown of Lansing, after which she transferred to Grand Valley State University. She began her university studies as an international relations major, but encouragement from her accounting professor led Elizabeth to change her major to accounting. This switch caused a delay in her planned graduation date. Before her education-abroad stint, Elizabeth said she would have focused more on keeping her graduation date on track. Accepting the ebbs and flows of life on another continent allowed her to accept this education, and ultimately career, change with ease. "When I graduated was less important, doing what I wanted to do was more important," she said. As she prepared for her planned spring 2016 graduation with a university accounting degree, she discovered that education abroad was helping her secure her future. She reported earning mock or formal interviews with the seven largest accounting firms. The mock interviews, arranged through her affiliation with an accounting organization on campus, allowed her to practice her interview skills with actual employers. One formal interview Elizabeth completed was with Deloitte, the global financial consultant, in Detroit—with strong ties to the auto industry in America and Japan—arranged specifically because of her experience in Japan.

Communicating. Being aware of her presence, particularly in her communications, was among the skills Elizabeth said she developed abroad. How she used her hands while talking, how quickly she talked, how often she said "um," and the extent of her eye contact with others came to the forefront during her intercultural communication transactions. Because of daily language barriers on her internship, she began speaking more slowly, in simple sentences, with minimal flowery language to ensure clarity. She rarely used sarcasm, a form of humor typically not used in Japan. She continued many of these communications characteristics after her return to America. In short, Elizabeth cited significant improvements in her comfort level in unfamiliar situations and adapting to change, as well as moderate improvement in her intercultural communication skills, including self-awareness in foreign language communication. Education abroad played a role in landing job interviews in her field. *Competency reflection.* Was there a competency Elizabeth wished she had improved more during the internship? In her words: "I wish I would have focused more on communication, specifically with relationship building. Not only with the language itself, but with meeting new people and getting out of my comfort zone. Looking back, I regret spending so much time skyping with the U.S., instead of building stronger relationships with the people with me in Japan." Elizabeth's future plans hold much promise: Becoming a Certified Public Accountant (CPA), being recruited into an international accounting firm in Michigan or California, and earning a Master of Business Administration (MBA) degree.

Michael-Vivienne, International Intern, August to November 2013

Michael was a 19-year-old white male when he attended the pre-departure orientation for his Japanese business internship. College international programming leaders typically strive for a life-changing experience for their students. Few experiences can compare to that of this student's Asian internship. As hoped, the student experienced advancements in collaboration and intercultural competency while abroad. However, unlike most student experiences abroad, this one coincided with a change in gender status. This student's self- and public identification as a woman happened in Japan. After returning from the education-abroad experience, the medical process from male to female was well underway. She now identifies herself as Vivienne and for clarity will be referred to as Vivienne throughout the chapter. Vivienne's motivations for applying for a position on the competitive Japanese tourism internship were not atypical: a commitment to Japanese language study, a fascination with Japanese animation, and a fascination with the country's literature and history. Her education-abroad goals were laudable: language practice (she felt confident in speaking, but desired more listening comprehension) and also visualizing and understanding the country she had seen only through the lens of Japanese media.

Upon her arrival in Japan and start of her corporate internship, Vivienne put emphasis on earning the respect of her Japanese co-workers and supervisors. She received accolades from her Japanese manager on her ability to communicate well in Japanese with tourists who rode the boat. Vivienne expressed gratitude for the support she received from her Japanese co-workers in improving her Japanese, including rehearsing business terminology generally not covered in her Japanese language classes, and practicing

Kanji, one of three Japanese alphabets, encouraging her to "write them three times each." She considered her education-abroad experience an important step in the gender identity change process. Because of her feminine appearance in high school, she described a "constant flow" of negative comments in her childhood, but no physical violence. She was nervous about embarking on her international internship. As any realistic education-abroad student might, she feared her Japanese language skills would not be good enough (although she had progressed through the intermediate college level). She also worried that customers would be offended by her appearance. In Japan, with co-workers, friends and faculty, she was called Vivienne, marking part of her early stage in the gender transition. She began her internship using her given name. On her internship shifts, her feminine appearance and male name tag sometimes generated curiosity, but she never sensed anger. Japanese business people who were customers on the boat, especially after drinking a Sapporo beer or two, were especially curious. "Is that your real name?," one businessman asked. Vivienne replied in Japanese, "Chotto," roughly translated as "Yes, a little," a polite way of answering yes, but acknowledging the unusual circumstances. The businessman, seemingly surprised but not judgmental, said, simply, "Wow."

She described the reaction of her Japanese co-workers as a mix of acceptance, indifference, and as occasionally slow to warm up to her. One co-worker in particular was curious, asking how she knew and when she knew her self-identity was not male. Vivienne's answer, in simple terms to facilitate understanding across language and culture, was that as a child she liked pink and had many more girl friends than boys. "I felt like a woman, like you feel like a man," she said. Her internship experience taught her that life as a transgender woman can be positive. "It didn't have to define me," Vivienne said. "It didn't have to have a negative effect on my job or personal life" And it was not all-encompassing. "Japan taught me it was a piece of me." Why did she choose Japan for her education-abroad destination? In addition to being drawn to its media and history, Vivienne thought it would complement her transition from male to female. The "beauty aspects" of Japan, including fabric and makeup, were among the relics that drew her there. She thought being in Japan might help with her feminine identity, to embrace her new persona. She had learned how to interact as a man in America. As the gender transition began in her homeland, her new "label" felt unreachable. In America, she felt her new gender identity was all on the outside, connected to her appearance. She shared that studying in Japan helped her learn how to interact as a woman.

"After Japan, it became me," Vivienne said. "Now, I wake up and I am a woman."

Competencies Reported from International Internship and Experiences

Critical Thinking. The vast majority of Vivienne's noted competency improvements fell into the category of critical thinking—particularly in self-awareness and adapting to the extraordinary. She described herself as an only child with strong guidance from her parents. In Japan, she had her own apartment, job schedule, and opportunities to travel. She described a coming of age and increased self-identity as an adult in Japan. If she can control her own destiny in Japan, "there's no reason I can't do that in America," she observed. She enjoyed and became proficient at navigating travel, including on the spiderweb Tokyo subway system. She reported a positive work experience that will lead her to find a job in America and "kick start her life." In the past, she often relied on parents for support and did not feel guilty about it. "Now, I take more responsibility as an adult." Her life-changing experience abroad included her gender transition. The experience helped her feel comfortable with her new identity. She went on a date in Japan with a man, which she described as an important step. Her time in Japan "helped me feel like I deserved a romantic life." And she realized there are good people in the world "who will treat me like a normal person." Later in her international internship, the Japanese company issued her a new name tag with the name, "Vivienne." In brief, Vivienne indicated dramatic advancement in the areas of self-awareness and feeling comfortable with unfamiliar settings, all in tandem with the gender transition from male to female. Vivienne did not report any missed competency opportunities.

FLOYD, INTERNATIONAL INTERN, MAY TO AUGUST 2014

Floyd was a self-described introvert. A quiet techie-type, he'd spent two decades in Midwest America, living in a handful of Michigan cities. "I wanted a fresh perspective," he said. Why Japan? Floyd, a 21-year-old African American male, had a longstanding interest in Japanese culture, including animation. And he saw a personal future that included a career in technology. A Lansing Community College computer networking and security major, Floyd considered Japan—a global leader in consumer electronics and robotics—as a key step on his path to a career in information technology.

Competencies Reported from International Internship and Experiences

Communicating. Floyd described his most significant gain during his education-abroad experience as interpersonal communications. Before the education-abroad program, he described himself as uncomfortable in many social and work situations, unsettled by conflict, and often reluctant to venture into unknown circumstances. During his first few weeks on the Japan internship, he worried about whether his work performance was living up to corporate and college expectations. He said this new experience—a different language, a culture steeped in formality and respect, and a starkly different business environment—combined with positive feedback from co-workers and supervisors, gradually led to a heightened comfort level in different social situations. The Japanese business culture is centered around teamwork, what their tradition calls wa, or group harmony. Japanese co-workers and supervisors took care to help Floyd and his American colleagues understand that working to achieve organizational gains was more important than getting ahead as an individual. He appreciated the interest his Japanese co-workers had in him, often shown in the form of frank questions and answers about cross-cultural differences. The discussions might touch on Japanese corporate culture and its nose-to-the-grindstone reputation. Or center on quitting smoking in a nation where cigarettes are omnipresent. The discussions might continue after work at karaoke, where his Japanese co-workers enjoyed listening to him sing "Let it Go" from the especially popular-in- Japan movie, "Frozen." In Japan, karaoke is more intimate than in America, sung in a booth or small room, only among friends. The shared word and song helped contribute to Floyd's sense of belonging, and his transformation to extroversion. His internship duties—taking drink orders in another language, serving food to customers, helping the band entertain the Japanese tourists by leading audience participation, working with school groups on their English skills—inspired movement from the introvert to extrovert role. Back in America, continuing his information technology studies and work at the college's IT help desk, he sees himself as more interested in meeting new people and having more significant interpersonal interactions.

Critical Thinking. Floyd believes the confidence he gained from feeling success as an international intern also led to improved academic competency. Interestingly, the experience may have led to improvement in his test-taking ability. In college courses before departing on his international internship, it was not uncommon for him to experience high anxiety during tests, including in subjects for which he was well prepared. Floyd reported this happening repeatedly in math. After returning from education abroad, he described much smoother sailing during exams, including top marks in college algebra. This personal transformation has led him to have the land of the rising sun as integral to his post-college plans. His life strategy includes application for the Japan Exchange and Teaching (JET) Programme, to teach English to school children in Japan, with a possible segue to a long-term information technology job there. "The concern of the group over the individual is the kind of life style I like," Floyd said of his desire to make Japan central to his professional life. "[Before study abroad], I was content with getting an IT degree and just moving where I would live comfortably, as my field is in high demand. After a while I realized that my personality, life style, and hobbies are compatible with Japan."

Communication. Floyd reported strong improvement in communication—in language and in increased comfort in participating in unfamiliar social situations. An unexpected competency—in improved confidence in test-taking ability—also appeared to occur.

Competency reflection. Was there a competency Floyd wished he had improved more during the internship? While Floyd is proud of the advancements he made in his interpersonal communications, he said he wished he could have developed even deeper understanding of the people, places, and customs around him during his education-abroad experience. He would have been happy to have this transcending knowledge occur in either English or Japanese. This quest for discernment has contributed to his interest in returning to his international internship country. "To me, understanding people there is just more than sight-seeing," Floyd said.

EDUCATION-ABROAD COMPETENCIES AMONG COMMUNITY COLLEGE STUDENTS: THE FUTURE

These case studies provide some evidence that education abroad can help community college students become competent global citizens. However, there is much more research, discussion and action that should happen to make collegiate education abroad more effective. As the quest for better results in helping students complete a credential or degree continues, education-abroad practitioners should strive to keep pace with this reality. It is no longer enough to parachute college students in-country and count on the immersion itself to land the students in global competence. Research by Williams (2005) helped document that "being abroad in and of itself is not enough—students must interact in the culture to receive the gain" (pp. 369–370). It could be this imperative—being purposeful in designing programming abroad—that inspires our students to improved global thinking, communicating, and collaborating.

REFERENCES

Eaton, Tim, & Kleshinski, Andrew (2014). Improving undergraduate learning for employability through international exposure. *American Journal of Business Education, 7*(1), 49–57.

Morais, Duarte, & Ogden, Anthony (2011). Initial development and validation of the global citizenship scale. *Journal of Studies in International Education, 15*(5), 445–466.

Pollock, Steve (2013, January 28). Cultivating 'global jinzai' critical to Japan's international success. *Nikkei Weekly.* http://www.turnstoneventures.com/cultivating_global_jinazi.html

Williams, Tracy Rundstrom (2005). Exploring the impact of study abroad on students' intercultural communication skills: Adaptability and sensitivity. *Journal of Studies in International Education, 9*(4), 356–371.

Conclusions: Focusing on the Future

Edward J. Valeau

This book clearly articulates the benefits of internationalization at US community colleges. The theories, research, and case studies assess prior advancements and skillfully offer solutions that have been proven and examined for their efficacy. US community colleges have the most diversified student body of any post-secondary institution and it is a foregone conclusion that educational offerings and services have an obligation to produce citizenry who have knowledge and skills that will both prepare them for a globally competitive workforce and that allow them to take their role in a culturally and pluralistically diverse world. It is this nexus between international education and student success that ultimately serves local communities and corporations, while allowing students to excel in the race to the top.

This raises the question of why internationalization at US community colleges is not widely established and institutionalized. The only longitudinal data comes from Institute for International Education *(IIE) Open Doors* which is answered by only 33 % of all US community colleges. Thus, although this book showcases pockets of excellence, there remain two-third of US community colleges that either have no internationalization or

E. J. Valeau (✉)
Hartnell Community College District, Salinas, California

ELS Group, Hayward, CA, USA

© The Editor(s) (if applicable) and The Author(s) 2016
R.L. Raby, E.J. Valeau (eds.), *International Education at Community Colleges*, DOI 10.1057/978-1-137-53336-4_24

337

whose extent to which they are internationalized remains unknown. Our failure to even know the extent to which innovative and creative pedagogies exist speaks to the continued periphery status of the field.

The need cannot be met if leadership and funding remains stuck in quicksand with no sustained will to get out. Since the 1980s, US ED Title VI grants and today, the 100,000 Strong in the Americas grants give priority to community college applications. Yet, national funding remains stagnant, the number of these awards is small, and there is no guarantee that future national funding requests will be supported in the amount needed to make a dent in all community colleges. State funding does not acknowledge the intersection of internationalization with the objectives of workforce development and transfer education. Moreover, there are no state initiatives designed to significantly counter this imbalance. Local funding sources, such as foundations, focus on tuition scholarships while capital campaigns and Bond Initiatives assist with renovation, construction, and replacement to build a physical environment conducive to the teaching learning process. Hindering internationalization are leaders whose ill-conceived reasoning is that dollars for international education distracts from the colleges' mission. Too many Boards still use the myth that support for internationalization is at the expense of resident students and represents a possible lost seat. CEOs, despite their personal feelings, are not aggressive champions because they are not likely to be evaluated on the success or existence of internationalization. Finally, traditional pipeline leadership training has ignored those working in international education and there is no staff development to help these individuals advance while allowing them to continue to support internationalization in new leadership positions. It should be understood by now that global is not in opposition to the local community college mission and such negative thinking and action contributes to keeping internationalization sidelined.

The authors in this book agree that leadership at the CEO level and organizational unit level help fuel the success of internalization. Raby and Valeau show how historic and current community college leaders redefine directions for internationalization as part of the community college mission. Rodriquez as well as Budd, Serban, VanHook, and Raby use leadership theories to define the importance of executive officers in charting reforms at community colleges. Using frames of organizational decision-making, Vargas shows how a president can transform programming level by institutionalizing international education and impact change. Valeau and Raby show that there is a professionalization for community college internationalization and that these individuals need to be part of the leadership transition pipeline.

International programming in the community college is not a solo act and relies heavily on faculty-driven efforts. Cierniak and Ruddy share how innovative pedagogies are governed by partnerships within and across institutions. When this occurs you get the results of planned and sustained programs akin to such things as a global learning certificate, e-portfolios, short-term study abroad, faculty-to-faculty mentorship, all coalescing to help student success. Leadership is also a sub-theme in faculty/staff development. Treat shows how mentoring of faculty and faculty-leaders signals a commitment to internalization. Bista examines faculty who are foreign-born, US-born with prior international experiences, and US-born who do not have prior international experiences to show how these profiles enhance campus internationalization. Finally, Bartzis, Kirkwood, and Mulvihill share how faculty-driven efforts at two community colleges impact overall college reform efforts.

Of course, the most important player in any and all of international education is the student and specific programs that are a catalyst for facilitating their success. Knowing who they are, what skills they lack, and what they are experiencing is tantamount to having a globally effective international program. Quezada and Cordeiro remind us of the importance of being mindful of the new and emerging demographics including students of color, women, and various racial and ethnic groups. Willis emphasizes the importance of being sensitive to all student experiences as a purposeful means to help intensify their learning outcomes. Hollis and Davis reveal how knowledge of Title IX regulations prohibiting sexual assault is needed and must be included in current student advising policies. Hagedorn, Pei, and Yan show how colleges can prepare more effectively to support student needs on the run up to their success. Zhang gives us insight in how to facilitate student success while acknowledging and respecting their voice and experience. Miller shows how international student advisors need to help international students manage cultural and social stress. Rhodes, Raby, Thomas, Codding, and Lynch reveal how education abroad influences student success. Charting the student experience allows faculty and the college to emphasize what works. Brenner provides examples of a college that is integrally involved in transformative learning based on lived student experiences. Zamani-Gallaher, Lang, and Leon share how the process of student self-authorship allows students to reflect that result in them being more career-ready. Thomas shares how education abroad can be a vehicle for building student global competencies that are attractive to future employers. Each of these authors intuitively understand that industry is in need of new talent that is internationally competent and that real-world experiences, when navigated through an internationalized program, not only help to grow these skills, but are also integral to serving the community college mission.

The ultimate focus needs to be on comprehensive internationalization that then has the ability to influence overall systemic change. Woodin shares how categorical metrics of leadership and policy, organizational resources, curricular, professional development, co-curricular activities, and international student services can track internationalization progress. Castro-Salazar, Perez, and Merriam bring to light how a single program can help establish new college procedures and routes of communication that results in a comprehensive college-wide planning. Sipe shows how environmental factors of setting student demographics in terms of ethnic diversity, and primary industry in the college's service area, can help to promote or discourage institutionalization.

This book provides a context that US community colleges must make international education the routine, rather than the exception and undeniably shows what can result from visionary thinking, committed leadership, relevant research, and reflection designed to make a difference. Common themes demonstrate a greater appreciation for what internationalization contributes to the local student in terms of building knowledge and skills for workforce training and for securing the building blocks of global citizenry for the good of society. These are undergirded by the need for discovery, planned change, bold executive leadership, innovative programming, and learning from the voices of students. We acknowledge that we surfaced just a few of the many changes taking place in US community colleges. However, this book provides theoretical foundations to help further guide new changes, research, and case studies upon which innovative programming can be adapted and replicated. As such, when compared to past publications, these definitive examples point to the fact that many of our colleges are, indeed, working to arrive at comprehensive change.

As editors, we are convinced that the authors have presented compelling reasons and hope for why massification of internalization in US community colleges is important, has a bright future, and is just over the horizon. We believe their work will contribute significantly to future efforts as the need and demand for internalization expands going forward into the second half of the second decade of the 2000 millennium.

ERRATUM TO: STUDY 3, 5 AND 12 OF INTERNATIONAL EDUCATION AT COMMUNITY COLLEGES

Rosalind Latiner Raby and Edward J. Valeau

Erratum to:
Study 3 in: *Juanita Gamez Vargas, The Texas/Czech Republic International Connection: A Reciprocal Exchange of Faculty and Students*, DOI 10.1057/978-1-137-53336-4_14
The affiliation of J.G. Vargas has been updated to "Jeanine Rainbolt College of Education, Department of Educational Leadership and Policy Studies, University of Oklahoma, Norman, OK, USA"

Erratum to:
Study 5 in: *Paloma Rodriguez, Global Certificates: Bringing Intentionality and Ownership to Comprehensive Internationalization*, DOI 10.1057/978-1-137-53336-4_16
The affiliation of P. Rodriguez has been updated to "International Education, Santa Fe College, Gainesville, FL, USA"

Erratum to:
Study 12 in: *Marc Thomas, Community College Education Abroad and Business Internship Programs Cultivation of Competency in Communicating, Collaborating, and Critical Thinking*, DOI 10.1057/978-1-137-53336-4_23
The chapter title was incorrect. The correct title is *Community College International Internship Cultivation of Competence in Communication, Collaboration, and Critical Thinking*

© The Editor(s) (if applicable) and The Author(s) 2016   E1
R.L. Raby, E.J. Valeau (eds.), *International Education at Community Colleges*, DOI 10.1057/978-1-137-53336-4

The affiliation of Marc Thomas has been updated to "Consultant, New Orleans, LA, USA"

Erratum to:
Notes on Contributors, DOI 10.1057/978-1-137-53336-4
On Page 343, the first line of Kelly J. Kirkwood's biography has been changed from "She earned her doctoral degree in Doctoral Candidate in Adult, Community, and Higher Education" to "She earned her doctoral degree in Adult, Community, and Higher Education"

On Page 345, the degree of Juanita Gamez Vargas has been changed from Ed.D to Ph.D.

On Page 345, the biography for Marc Thomas has been updated to "Marc Thomas, Ed.D. served as faculty leaders abroad and global education coordinator for Lansing Community College in Michigan for 10 years and was selected twice as Visiting Scholar at the Japan Center for Michigan Universities in Shiga Prefecture. At this writing, he is traveling and teaching."

The updated online versions of the original chapters can be found at
DOI 10.1057/978-1-137-53336-4
DOI 10.1057/978-1-137-53336-4_14
DOI 10.1057/978-1-137-53336-4_16
DOI 10.1057/978-1-137-53336-4_23

NOTES ON CONTRIBUTORS

Opal Leeman Bartzis, Ed.D., is the Vice-President of Academic Affairs at the Institute for Study Abroad, Butler University. She has chaired committees for NAFSA, AACRAO's and the Forum on Education Abroad.

Krishna Bista, Ph.D. Chase Endowed Professor of Education in the School of Education at the University of Louisiana at Monroe and has a specialist degree in Community College Teaching and Administration. He is the founding editor of *Journal of International Students in Higher Education* and is an associate editor of the *Journal of Interdisciplinary Studies in Education*.

Ashley Brenner, Ph.D. Teaches English as a Second Language at Community College of Philadelphia. She has led and participated in numerous international education programs in Asia, Africa, Europe, the Middle East, Latin America, and the Caribbean. Her research investigates the transformative potential of study abroad for community college students.

Deborah Budd, Ed.D., Chancellor, San Jose/Evergreen Community College District and former President of Berkeley City Community College with over 18 years of administrative experience. Her dissertation, "Institutional Effectiveness and the Relationship to African American and Latino Transfer Rates," highlights her extensive knowledge relating to the integration of planning and budgeting, accreditation, and suggestions for beginning to close the achievement gap.

© The Editor(s) (if applicable) and The Author(s) 2016   341
R.L. Raby, E.J. Valeau (eds.), *International Education at Community Colleges*, DOI 10.1057/978-1-137-53336-4

Ricardo Castro-Salazar, Ph.D. Acting Vice President for International Development at Pima County Community College District and Associate Researcher at the University of Arizona Center for Latin American Studies. Dr. Castro-Salazar was the External Advisor to the Mexican Government through the Institute for Mexicans Abroad (IME) of the Ministry of Foreign Relations.

Kelley Merriam-Castro, M.A., Faculty at Pima Community College (Arizona) where she teaches courses in Spanish as foreign language, US History, Latin American History, and Western Civilizations. She is also teaching in the Second Language Acquisition and Teaching Program at the University of Arizona in Tucson.

Katherine Cierniak, PhD candidate and Graduate Research Assistant at the Center for Evaluation and Education Policy (CEEP) at Indiana University's Education Policy Studies program, with a concentration in International and Comparative Education. She conducted her dissertation research on education for children in Dhaka, Bangladesh's slums with the support of a Fulbright Student Research grant.

Amparo G. Codding, M.A., M.S. Dean of Humanities and Professor of Spanish at Bergen Community College and serves as Academic Coordinator of the Department of World Languages and Cultures, Coordinator for the Faculty Development Program, Director for the Center for the Study of Intercultural Understanding, and is an International Student Counselor.

Paula A. Cordeiro, Ed.D., Professor and Dean of the School of Leadership and Education Sciences (SOLES) at the University of San Diego. She is a former teacher and school head for bilingual schools in Venezuela and Spain. Paula recently completed the 5th edition of her textbook *Educational Leadership: A Bridge to Improved Practice.*

Russell A. Davis, Ed.D. Instructor at Morgan State University. His teaching career has spanned 30 years at schools such as George Washington University, Howard University, Prince George's Community College, Frederick Community College, and Bowie State University. He also was president of Gloucester County Community College for five years.

Linda Serra Hagedorn, Ph.D. Associate Dean of the College of Human Sciences and Professor in the School of Education at Iowa State University. Previously, she directed the Institute of Higher Education at the University of Florida and was the Director of the Transfer and Retention of Urban Community College Students Project (TRUCCS).

Leah P. Hollis, Ed.D. An assistant professor in the Community College Leadership Program at Morgan State University. Her recent book, *Bully in the Ivory Tower: How Aggression and Incivility Erode American Higher Education* shows that workplace bullying occurs at higher rate in higher education than the general workforce.

Kelly J. Kirkwood, Ed.D. She earned her doctoral degree in Adult, Community, and Higher Education at Ball State University and is Assistant Director of Study Abroad at the Rinker Center for International Programs at Ball State University. Prior roles included Program Manager for The Study Abroad Foundation and Assistant Director of Study Abroad at North Carolina State University.

John Lang. Doctoral candidate, philosophy of education, in Education, Policy, Organization, and Leadership at the University of Illinois at Urbana-Champaign. He served as Managing Editor of Philosophy and Education and was a Harry & Dorothy Broudy Fellow in 2012.

Raul A. Leon, Ph.D. Associate Professor of Higher Education and Student Affairs at Eastern Michigan University. His work examines strategic diversity management, student success, and the internationalization of American higher education. In 2015, Dr. Leon received the UW-Madison Outstanding Alumni Award from the School of Education.

Yvonne A. Perez Lopez. Doctoral candidate at Syracuse University in Cultural Foundations of Education and is coordinator in International Development Department at Pima Community College District. Her research focuses on academic engagement, social inequality, and racism and colorism in Mexico.

Andrea Lynch, MBA. An Associate Professor of Business and Technology and Study Abroad Coordinator at Mercer County Community College. She has coordinated the Study Abroad program since its inception in 2009. She is an AAWCC Leaders Fellow and a Leadership Trenton Fellow.

Sharon Miller, M.A. Teaches at Austin Community College and helps to coordinate international student scholar services and education abroad. She studied abroad in Australia, lived and worked in England, and studied at SIT Graduate Institute.

Thalia M. Mulvihill, Ph.D. Professor of Social Foundations and Higher Education and an Affiliate Faculty member in the Women's & Gender Studies Program and the Honors College and serves as the Director of the Adult, Higher and Community Education Doctoral Program. She designed and taught the first graduate-level course in Comparative International Higher Education at Ball State University.

Shaohua Pei. Doctoral student at Iowa State University, specializing in International Higher Education. She taught for college English in China for nine years and has a master's degree in foreign linguistics. A passion for the enhancement and internationalization of the Chinese higher education motivated her to further her studies about international education in the USA.

Reyes L. Quezada, Ed.D. Professor at the University of San Diego in the School of Leadership and Education Sciences. He is a board member of the International Council for the Education of Teachers and Associate Editor for *Teacher Education Quarterly*. His research focus is on cultural proficiency, equity, family–school–community engagement, action research, and international education.

Rosalind Latiner Raby, Ph.D. Senior Lecturer at California State University, Northridge, in the Educational Leadership and Policy Studies Department of the College of Education and is affiliate faculty for the EdD Community College program. She also serves as the Director of California Colleges for International Education, a non-profit consortium of 89 California community colleges. She is also a lead faculty area chair of the College of Humanities and Sciences at the Southern California Campus of the University of Phoenix.

Gary M. Rhodes, Ph.D. Associate Dean, International Education and Senior International Officer California State University at Dominguez Hills & Director, Center for Global Education. He has taught courses at the graduate level at University of South California and University of California, Los Angeles, on administration of international programs in higher education, risk and crisis management, and has received Fulbright grants to India and South Africa.

Paloma Rodriguez, M.A. Coordinator of International Education at Santa Fe College. She serves as Project Manager for the Community Colleges for International Development (CCID) Global Certificate Learning Community and is a member of the Advisory Board for the Association of American Colleges and Universities Global Learning in College 2015 conference. She is completing a PhD in Classical Civilization at the University of Florida.

Anne-Maree Ruddy, Ph.D. Director for Education Policy and a Senior Research Associate at the Center for Evaluation and Education Policy (CEEP) at Indiana University. Dr. Ruddy did all of her higher education in Perth, Western Australia, and her experience in the USA and internationally has been in education systems with an emphasis on school environments and higher education using mixed-methods approaches.

Andreea Serban, Ph.D. Vice Chancellor of Educational Services and Technology at Coast Community College District and is the district chief academic, student services, and technology officer. Dr. Serban became the only current representative of a community college to be appointed to the US National Commission for UNESCO. Dr. Serban is the Board President of the statewide non-profit consortium California Colleges for International Education.

Deborah M. Sipe, Ph.D. Dean of Teaching and Learning at Chemeketa Community College. Previously, she was an administrator at Portland Community College, where she was active on the Internationalization Initiative Task Force and Asian Studies Committee. She works as a bilingual education teacher trainer and also works with The Asia Foundation on an international student program.

Janice M. Thomas, Ph.D. Director of the International Education Center at Brookdale Community College since August 2007. Her responsibilities include directing the college's internationalization efforts through promoting study abroad, international student services, and faculty development initiatives. Previously, she was the Director of the Office of International Students and Scholars at University of New Orleans.

Marc Thomas, Ed.D. served as faculty leaders abroad and global education coordinator for Lansing Community College in Michigan for 10 years and was selected twice as Visiting Scholar at the Japan Center for Michigan Universities in Shiga Prefecture. At this writing, he is traveling and teaching.

Tod Treat, Ed.D. Executive Vice President for Academic and Student Affairs at Tacoma Community College and is Assistant Professor in Education Policy, Organization, and Leadership at University of Illinois. He is co-author of Community Colleges for International Development's System and Framework for Comprehensive Internationalization, evaluated two CCID professional development programs, and coached the Strategic Partnership Accelerator.

Juanita Gamez Vargas, Ph.D. An Associate Professor at The University of Oklahoma, Jeanine Rainbolt College of Education, Department of Educational Leadership and Policy Studies, Adult and Higher Education program and in charge of the Community College Leadership (CCL) emphasis area. She has over 16 years of experience in community college administration.

Dianne G. Van Hook, Ph.D. Chancellor, Santa Clarita Community College District, where she has served for 25 years. To have a president for 25 years is atypical among community colleges and her focused, dedicated service has helped to expand instructional programs, secure significant increases in funding, launch a robust building program, and increase full-time staff by more than 300%.

Edward J. Valeau, Ed.D. Superintendent President Emeritus of Hartnell Community College, where he served for 12 years. He is also President Emeritus of California Colleges for International Education and is the founder and Senior Partner of the ELS Group, a national Chief Executive Search firm. He is an American Council on Education Fellow and Fulbright Scholar.

Tasha Y. Willis, Ed.D. Assistant Professor of Social Work at California State University, Los Angeles, and the Vice President of Social Work Abroad Program, a 501c3 organization providing international service learning opportunities to US-based social work students and faculty and partner communities.

Shawn Woodin, Ed.D. President/CEO of the Southern Scholarship Foundation. He was the former Executive Director/CEO of Community Colleges for International Development, Inc. He was a co-researcher of CCID's Framework for Comprehensive Internationalization.

Lu Yan. Doctoral student at Iowa State University, specializing in multicultural education. She taught English in both China and the USA. Her own experience as a Chinese international student prompts her interests in international college students' and she is doing her dissertation on the topic of critical thinking and Chinese international female college students.

Eboni M. Zamani-Gallaher, Ph.D. Professor of Higher Education/Community College Leadership in the Department of Education Policy, Organization, and Leadership at the University of Illinois at Urbana-Champaign (UIUC). She is Director of the Office for Community College Research and Leadership (OCCRL) at UIUC and is the past President of the Council for the Study of Community Colleges (CSCC) and is Director-Elect for Research and Publications for the American Association of Personnel Administrators.

Yi (Leaf) Zhang, Ph.D. Assistant professor in the Department of Educational Leadership and Policy Studies at the University of Texas at Arlington. Her research includes international student advisement, study abroad for community college students, and adaption of the community college model in other countries.

INDEX

© The Editor(s) (if applicable) and The Author(s) 2016
R.L. Raby, E.J. Valeau (eds.), *International Education at Community Colleges*, DOI 10.1057/978-1-137-53336-4

CPSIA information can be obtained
at www.ICGtesting.com
Printed in the USA
BVOW10*2029241117

501180BV00013B/443/P